HENRY MILLER

LETTERS TO ANAÏS NIN

Café nights! Room too
cold, fingers freeze. Halfway thru the last insertion
for I. of C. Got drunk on it.
To-night, reading Putnam's
"Rabelais," I see so many
points of correspondence —
amazing. His chapter on
François' first visit to Paris
interests me terribly — the
song of the streets again. And Putnam
anticipates me when he says: "But
Paris, despite the changes, always
remains the same." I have always
had a hankering to some day cover
the trajectory of a few great men
— like Hannibal, Alexander, Caesar,
Napoleon, Genghis Khan — and now
Rabelais' looks good to me. In fact,
at Dijon, I got the authentic flavor
of those cities from the students
— the very names of the cities are
familiar to me & mean things.
Just think — it was at 54 St.
André des Arts, Paris, that Rabelais
lived for a while" (the former Hotel
St. Denis). And it was only a stone's
throw away, on this very street.

P.P.S. Yes, I believe in that method of draining fever.
Track a thing down to the ultimates
and in the subsequent book —
make a fine style create a part of
Boone will mention in them. a little nauseous.

HENRY MILLER

LETTERS

TO ANAÏS NIN

Edited and with an introduction
by GUNTHER STUHLMANN

G. P. PUTNAM'S SONS, NEW YORK

Introduction

The letters of Henry Miller to Anaïs Nin collected in this volume span a period of fifteen years, from 1931 to 1946. These years were perhaps the most important in Miller's life, the most fruitful in his career as a writer, and the most decisive in his development as a man. In many ways, they were also the most difficult.

Anyone familiar with Miller's work, and its essentially autobiographical nature, will find much of the raw material of his art in these letters. He will also find the fresh components of a self-portrait of Miller the man and the writer, the very personal, unpremeditated reflection of a man whose image has often been overshadowed by certain aspects of his art. An incident related in one of these letters may be symptomatic of the all-too-common coupling which has linked man and work, from the very outset, in the popular imagination. Late in 1934, after the publication of his first book, Miller visited one of the two bookshops in Montparnasse most likely to order and stock copies of *Tropic of Cancer*. After some talk about the publicity attending the publication of the book, the woman in the store suddenly realized that she was talking to Miller, the author, himself, whereupon she exclaimed: "But you don't look so obscene."

Indeed, the controversial, sensational aspects surrounding Miller's work, the censorship battles, the clandestine traffic in his books, the legal hassles to get his most important work published in his own country—almost thirty years later—and Miller's own identification with the "I" of his books have tended to obscure not only the true nature of his enormous contribution to twentieth-century literature, but also the image of the man himself.

These selected letters to Anaïs Nin, his friend and confidante of many years, often scrawled or typed hastily on odd bits of paper, envelopes and the backs of old menus, without thought of publication

[v]

or posterity (Miller even jokes about this at some points), are perhaps the closest we will ever come to an unvarnished, unconscious "autobiographical" portrait of Henry Miller during these decisive years.

Here, without the filter of art, the conscious ordering and rearranging of incident, we are taken into the day-by-day confidence, the thoughts and, sometimes, contradictions of one of the important writers of our time, forever under economic pressures, hounded by the shadows of his past, possessed by a terrible need to express himself, and yet, somehow, always accepting, content, a "Chinaman" of his own making. "You say I am an idealist too," he writes to Anaïs Nin in July 1933. "Yes! With a vengeance. I have wanted so much, so much, that knowing my ambitions, my dreams, to be unrealizable, I can content myself with almost nothing."

Through these letters, we participate in the interplay of people and events, the stimulations and discoveries that gave birth to and shaped his major works: the first years in Paris which found their hymnic explosion in *Tropic of Cancer*; the encounter with the world of D. H. Lawrence ("It's not Lawrence—it's myself I'm making a place for!"); the genesis of his progressive self-discovery, and return to his American past, in *Black Spring* and *Tropic of Capricorn*; the experience of Greece in 1939 ("Only here have I understood the meaning of nature") captured in *The Colossus of Maroussi*; the stimulations which triggered the growing body of essays and character portraits (some included in *Max and the White Phagocytes*); the relentless record of his rediscovery of America in the early 1940s *(The Air-Conditioned Nightmare)*; and, finally, the beginnings of the *Rosy Crucifixion*.

We follow the long trail of his rebellion against a nightmare vision of America, symbol of a painful past, from the hard but joyous days of his self-exile in France to his flight from warring Europe ("I don't believe in sticking it out to the last minute") and the slow acceptance, the growth of a sense of "home" on the California coast in the 1940s ("I am more and more at peace with myself"). We also witness the gradual, painful process by which his work gains recognition, from the unpaid beginnings, the years of waiting and frustration ("I roll up failures and abortions and postponements"), of futile labor in Hollywood ("I'm surrounded by veils of miasma"), of mendicant letters and appeals to the world, to a point where a new generation, in Europe, in the wake of World War II, takes up his cause. "Don't bother to fight for my books," he writes to Anaïs Nin from Big Sur, in July

1946, "I don't believe any of these commercial American publishers have the guts or the power to do this. I can bide my time. I am being published in so many other countries, why worry about poor America?"

This singular record of a singular life—reflected here in a representative selection from a voluminous correspondence impossible to gather in one volume—was triggered by a friendship which began in Paris, in the fall of 1931, and has lasted for more than thirty years.

When Henry Miller met Anaïs Nin for the first time, he was approaching his fortieth birthday. He had been in Paris since March 1930, and he was going through what he in retrospect described as the "second ordeal" in his life. A penniless foreigner in depression-ridden and politically unstable France, jobless, without a working permit, and with only a smattering of the language, he had been living precariously for more than a year, homeless and sometimes hungry. But his breaking away from America, from the shackles of past and responsibility, had given him a sense of elation he had never experienced, apparently, in America. "To be a prisoner of the streets, as I was a long time," he later wrote in *Remember to Remember,* one of his many vivid recollections of these dark years in Paris, "was a perpetual recreation. I did not need an address as long as the streets were there free to be roamed."

After the bleak, stultifying years in America, although the circumstances of his existence in France were often worse than anything he had experienced in the United States, a deep sense of liberation, a new vitality, had taken hold of Miller. His first ordeal, life in pre- and post-World War I America, had been a continuous trauma, and the torments and frustrations of this period are woven into the fabric of his later work. He was haunted by the childhood on the provincial streets of pre-"metropolitan" Brooklyn ("Why do I detest the old neighborhood so—Decatur Street, near Evergreen Cemetery, where I lived from ten years of age until I was twenty-five?"); the youthful excursions on the "ovarian trolley" from the foot of the Brooklyn Bridge into lower-middle-class Manhattan; the days in his father's tailor shop at 5 West 31st Street; the stifling *gemütlichkeit* of the Germanic family in the sharply defined immigrant society on the banks of the East River; the first dull job, in 1909, at the age of eighteen, in the New York office of a cement company. From then, until 1920, a series of short-lived, unwanted jobs in New York and on the West

Coast succeeded each other, and were followed by four years—his longest steady employment—with the "Cosmodemonic Telegraph Company" in New York, which he quit in 1924, resolved "never again to work for any man but to be my own master absolute." An uneventful first marriage, in 1917, to his piano teacher (Miller had once contemplated a career in music), with a daughter, Barbara, born in 1918, resulted in divorce in 1924. In the same year he married June Edith Smith, a lively beauty whom he met working in a dance hall and who, for almost nine years, was the center of many emotional storms. ("If I were made to feel that I had to choose between her and what I call my art," Miller writes in April 1932, "I would choose her.") They endured years of poverty and hand-to-mouth living in Brooklyn, and a brief period when he was the proprietor of an ill-fated speak-easy in Greenwich Village. Underlying his almost anarchistic rebellion against the dull, bourgeois mold was the tormenting sense that "there was no tomorrow, only the endless prospect of a deadly gray sameness." He felt he was "the bull in the bull-ring, and the end was certain death." To escape from this vacuous, oppressive life became an essential need.

A sudden turn in their fortune, in 1928, enabled June and Henry Miller to spend almost a year traveling and bicycling (a sport he had enjoyed since his youth) through Europe. But while this first encounter with the "old world," apparently, failed to have a tremendous effect on Miller (perhaps because he traveled protected by the armor of being a "tourist"), he was determined to return.

"Desperately hungry not only for the physical and sensual, for human warmth and understanding, but also for inspiration and illumination," he had gone back to Europe in 1930. June had remained in New York and was to join him later. Miller's objective had been Spain —the sunshine land of his dreams—but forever impractical in matters of money, perpetually optimistic that somehow something would be coming forth, he soon found himself stranded in Paris. His hopeful forays to the offices of the American Express Company netted him little negotiable cash.

But true to his acquired motto—"Only get desperate enough and everything will turn out well"—Miller managed to survive. Alfred Perlès, whom Miller and June had first met in 1928, at the Hôtel des Écoles, in the rue Delambre, and who was working for the Paris edition of the Chicago *Tribune,* met Miller again and, realizing that he was "down and out," sneaked him into his own room at the Hôtel Central, in the rue du Maine. Richard Osborn, a young lawyer from Bridgeport, Connecticut, who worked for the Paris branch of the National City Bank by day and led a bohemian life at night, offered Miller shelter during the winter of 1930, in his spacious apartment at 2 rue Auguste-Bartholdi, near the Champ de Mars. Others came to Miller's rescue with a meal, a few discreetly passed-on francs (the franc was then down to about 4 cents), a suit, a pair of shoes, or sometimes a short-lived odd job (handyman, English teacher, publicist for a *maison publique,* ghost-writer for a businessman who published articles in Yiddish newspapers, etc.). In the early thirties, Paris was filled with refugees, displaced persons, who had begun to replace the once-affluent tourists. "A common need brought us together. Only the desperate ones can understand this sort of communion, evaluate it truly."

Nobody, in 1930, had heard of Henry Miller, the writer.

"Henry was more or less an unknown quantity for us when he first arrived in Montparnasse," Samuel Putman, one of the leading spirits among the American literary exiles of the period, later wrote in his memoirs (*Paris Was Our Mistress,* Viking, 1948). "Very few suspected that he was interested in writing, much less that he himself wrote." Yet Miller had been trying to write for almost twenty years. ("To become a writer," he later wrote, "was not easy for me.")

Miller's own recollection of the first manifestations of his desire, of his need to express himself in writing, go back to 1912, when he was twenty-one and working, temporarily, in his father's tailor shop. But whatever he jotted down during the next ten years (except for some free-lance newspaper work he did while working briefly in a government office in Washington in 1917), apparently never saw the light of print. In 1922, during a three-week vacation from his job as personnel manager of Western Union in New York, he dashed off a 75,000-word novel. But *Clipped Wings,* a story of the lives of twelve messenger boys, remained unpublished. (Miller subsequently dealt with this experience in *Tropic of Capricorn.*) When he quit Western Union in 1924, he took up writing as a profession. But, as he recalled, from the time "I began practicing the art, as they say, until the year 1934, nothing I wrote was ever published, excepting three or four short texts in magazines of no importance." According to the bibliography of the Henry Miller Society, a short piece, "Black and White," appeared in 1924 in the New York magazine *Crisis*. But it was published under a pseudonym, "Valentin Nieting," the name of Miller's German grandfather, born around 1850, who had emigrated from Hesse apparently to escape military service. Six years later a Philadelphia magazine, *U.S.A.*, published "Jazzazza," which is perhaps the first published piece bearing the by-line: H. (for Henry) V. (for Valentin) Miller.

While living at 91 Remsen Street in Brooklyn, Miller had also resorted to the ancient remedy of writers who cannot find commercial outlets for their work: he had some of his own writing printed. (Many of his friends, including Anaïs Nin, later followed this honorable literary practice.) On sheets of tinted cardboard, in editions of one hundred copies each, he produced a series of fifteen prose poems, "mezzotints" as he called them, most of them by-lined "June E. Mansfield," some under his own name, and June began to sell them from house to house, in cabarets and nightclubs. The first one was called "A Bowery Phoenix," and many of them—"Circe," "Dawn Travellers"— already showed the beginnings of Miller's later style.

Two other novels, both over 100,000 words in length—*Moloch,* and *This Gentile World*—also remained unpublished, "not because my work was larded with pornography," as Miller wrote in 1957, in his essay on "Obscenity in Literature," "but, as I am now convinced, because I had yet to discover my own identity."

When Miller arrived in Paris in 1930, he carried the manuscript of yet another novel, *Crazy Cock,* which he eventually cut down to three hundred pages and tried to have published in Paris. But, as he later admitted, the cutting ruined the book, the manuscript remained lost for a long time and, though recovered, was never published. Slowly, however, a few short pieces by Miller began to appear in print in Paris, under his own name and under various other by-lines. (Ironically, the English writer and critic Cyril Connolly spotted a piece by Miller published under Perlès' by-line, and congratulated the "wrong" author upon its originality.)

Elliot Paul, co-editor of Eugene Jolas' famous magazine, *Transition,* asked Miller to write a brief sketch about the "Cirque Medrano" for the paper Paul worked on, the Paris edition of the New York *Herald.* In 1931, the same paper published Miller's report on the "Six Day Bike Race." Samuel Putnam, who had started an English-language quarterly in Paris, *The New Review* (which boasted 73 sub-scribers), used in his Summer 1931 issue an essay Miller had written after seeing Luis Bunuel's surrealist film, "L'Âge d'Or." And in the third issue of the magazine he published Miller's first story, "Mademoiselle Claude," which since has found its way into many anthologies. "I liked it as a piece of prose," Putnam wrote in his memoirs, "but especially, I felt that it was a good expression of Mont-parnasse life in that era and of a prevalent type of expatriate—the Henry Miller type."

But if Miller ever was a "type," or typical of a new breed of expa-triate, he bore little resemblance to the relatively well-heeled American literary exiles of the 1920s. He had fled America out of a desperate personal necessity, not in search of colorful adventure, the gay "bohe-mian" life. "Can't bear the sight of the Dome or the Coupole any-more," he writes in the Mademoiselle Claude story. "These bastards sitting around on the terrasse looking so clean and healthy with their coats of tan, their starched shirts and their eau-de-cologne." And while he had many American friends and acquaintances in Paris, and often relied upon them for survival, in his search for "inspiration and illumination" he gravitated most strongly to what might be called the "European" element, those truly displaced, disinherited, and disen-chanted who, through choice or political necessity, had been divorced from their roots and now were at home in many cultures, the new "internationalists" without an Internationale. This inner circle included Austrian-born Alfred Perlès, who became his closest friend, Michael Fraenkel (who bore strong traits of his Russian heritage), Walter Lowenfels, Hilaire Hiler (both Americans with an "international" outlook), the Hungarian photographer Brassai, the German painter Hans Reichel, to name only a few. Miller also tried to transcend the inevitable ghetto aspects of expatriate life by his excursions into, and love for, the local life. He felt at home among the natives, the other underdogs, the blue-jacketed workmen, the prostitutes and the demi-monde. (He is delighted to be mistaken for a local worker when he goes to buy a pair of boots.) He approached French culture and literature voraciously. He began to study French with Perlès and later with a Frenchman from the Midi, M. Lantelme. He read French authors with the help of a dictionary, and France, as he later wrote, became to him "mother, mistress, home and muse. It was in Paris that I found myself, as a man and as an artist."

But Miller the writer, as the world was to know him, had not yet emerged. (And the man occasionally shed a furtive sentimental tear in a darkened movie house while watching a silent American film.) He had tried to resurrect *Crazy Cock,* as we have seen, but it had remained an abortive attempt. Yet it had carried him over into a new project, a savagely lyrical exploration of his life in Paris. "I grew so desperate that I finally decided to explode—and I did explode—I didn't write a piece of fiction: I wrote an autobiographical document, a human book."

"I wanted to reveal myself as openly, nakedly and unashamedly as possible," he wrote twenty years later in his essay on "Obscenity in Literature." "If I be asked why I should want to do this I can only answer—because my nature or my temperament compel me to do so. I am interested in life, all life, and every aspect of it. The one life I know best of all is my own. Examining my own life, describing it in detail, exposing it ruthlessly, I believe that I am rendering back life, enhanced and exalted, to those who read me. This seems to me a worthy task for a writer."

The book he had begun was *Tropic of Cancer.*

Miller met Anaïs Nin when he was working on the first draft of this book. Anaïs Nin then lived in Louveciennes, a quiet, cobblestoned village on a hill overlooking the Seine, from where, on clear nights, one could see Paris. Richard Osborn, who was engaged in some legal work for Miss Nin, had provided the introduction. The invitation had been casual and Miller, always ready to accept a free meal (indeed, he had worked out an ingenious card-filing system to keep himself supplied with invitations), had accepted gladly.

Anaïs Nin, at the time, was working on her first book, a sympathetic critical evaluation of D. H. Lawrence, who had died a year earlier, at the age of forty-five, and whose latest book, *Lady Chatterley's Lover* (1928), had aroused a storm of controversy by its alleged "obscenity" and had been banned in his native England. Hers was the first book by a woman which saw Lawrence as a great writer and sensitively explored his work. (In his introduction to a reissue of the book in 1964—Alan Swallow, Denver—Professor Harry T. Moore wrote: "The particular kind of intuition—emotional knowledge—for which we are so grateful in Miss Nin's own later fiction, she first applied to her explication of Lawrence. In making her first public appearance in print with this sensitive interpretation of Lawrence, she probably stepped across the distance from girlhood into young womanhood. And what she so wonderfully knew in youth, and could see in Lawrence's writings, is still very valuable, valuable to all of us.")

When Miller, the man of city streets, arrived in Louveciennes, he was apparently enchanted by the setting: the shuttered old house hidden behind a wall, with a creaky green iron gate, and an untamed garden in the back. The interior was colorful, exotic; the walls lined with books; and the house, to Miller, exuded a charmed atmosphere. Miller, apparently, was also enchanted with his hostess, a fragile-looking, delicate young woman who seemed to be the perfect embodiment of that cosmopolitan culture and open-minded, intellectual sensibility Miller had been searching for in Europe.

Born at the edge of Paris, in Neuilly, Anaïs Nin had spent part of her life in the United States. Her father was the Spanish pianist and composer Joacquin Nin, her mother the Danish singer, Rose Culmell, whom d'Annunzio had celebrated, and her family ties reached into France, New Orleans, and Cuba. Her parents had met in Cuba and, as a child, she had accompanied her adored father on the limelight trail of his concert tours throughout Europe. When her parents separated, her mother had taken her to New York, at the age of eleven. Brought up in the stern traditions of Spanish Catholicism and a male-oriented and dominated culture, she had suddenly found herself in exile, learning a new language, adjusting to a new way of life. But eventually she had returned to France with her mother and brothers.

While in the United States, Anaïs Nin had indulged her intellectual curiosity. An inveterate reader, she had begun, in teen-age enthusiasm, to devour the books of the world, alphabetically, in the New York Public Library. She had also begun to keep a diary, first in French, later in newly acquired English, which, faithfully kept over the years, has assumed the proportions of a major literary document. (Its publication is a recurring theme in these letters and Miller has called it "a monumental confession which when given to the world will take its place beside the revelations of St. Augustine, Petronius, Abelard, Rousseau, Proust, and others." He devoted to the Diary an essay, "Un Être Étoilique," first published in 1936, and incorporated in *The Cosmological Eye,* New Directions, 1939.) Initially a silent communication with the father who, she feels, has deserted her, the Diary slowly turned into the proving ground of an emerging writer, whose later novels derived their substance and their technique from it.

"It was while writing a Diary," Anaïs Nin recalled ("On Writing," The Alicat Bookshop, Yonkers, N. Y., 1947), "that I discovered how to capture the living moments. In the Diary I only wrote of what interested me genuinely, what I felt most strongly at the moment, and I found that this fervor, this enthusiasm produced a vividness which often withered in the formal work. Dealing always with the immediate present, the warm, the near, being written at white heat, developed a love of the living moment, of the immediate emotional reaction to experience, which revealed the power of recreation to lie in the sensibilities rather than in the memory or critical intellectual perception."

This sensibility, this immediate reaction, this readiness to embrace intuitively rather than intellectually, which was so apparent in her appreciation of D. H. Lawrence, must also have come into play in Anaïs Nin's spontaneous recognition of Miller's talent, though, at the time, he had as yet little to show as a writer.

At a first glance, Anaïs Nin and Henry Miller seemed to have little in common. Their temperaments, their way of life, their worlds, were utterly different. Here on the one hand was the vagrant, bespectacled, balding, middle-aged American "gangster author," as some of his friends jokingly called Miller, the former hobo, gravedigger, the "Chinaman" who had accepted and learned to live in a grimy world, who rolled with the punches and was to embark on a crusade for life draped in the battle flag of the four-letter word. And on the other hand was the sheltered European "child-woman" (to use Edmund Wilson's phrase) of-the-world who, in spite of hardships endured, had never given up her truly feminine desire to surround herself with a world that was harmonious, beautiful, colorful and richly textured (indeed, at times she had been accused of being precious).

As artists, too, they seemed to have little in common. While Anaïs Nin, as a writer and as a woman, was involved in what Oliver Evans, in a perceptive evaluation of her later work (*Prairie Schooner*, Fall 1962), called the "discovery of inner space," Miller pursued an autobiographical explosion. He gorged himself with the world around him, the world of dirty streets and dirty people, and spat it out again— transformed, vitalized, reborn in a twentieth-century manner no writer before him had achieved. Like Picasso, who transformed an old bicycle handle into the head of a suffering animal, Miller drew upon the wastes of the world—the stock quotations he proofread, the casual encounter, the street sign, the snatch of conversation overheard, the ideas ripped from a book—and tossed them back into his work, the luminous, idealistic, sentimental "garbage can." While Anaïs Nin sought to probe for the reality behind the surface, the reality of dream and the endless facets of character, Miller amalgamated, synthesized, caricatured, juxtaposed in his discovery of a new world—a "dadaist," a "surrealist" of his own making.

Yet behind the surface disparities there were deeper affinities. Self-educated (Miller quit City College after a short stint, Anaïs Nin learned outside the groves of academe), voraciously curious, dissatisfied with the conventional means of expression, both writers were searching for new forms, adequate to encompass the new reality of the twentieth century. Both were involved in discoveries of the self, in autobiographical journeys, only their directions and methods differed. Both refused to become engaged in the surface ideologies, politics, causes. This was a major literary crime in the days of the proletarian novel, the Spanish Civil War, Hitler and Stalin, and unforgivable to the "socially conscious" critics. (See George Orwell's essay, "Inside the Whale," 1940, the first general evaluation of Miller's work.) Both writers proceeded individually, without a school or literary movement to back them. (Indeed, the acceptance of their work, not easily pigeon-holed, suffered for years from this—aside from censorship in Miller's case—and even today very little valid criticism of their work has appeared.) And both writers, by conventional standards, remained "un-commercial" to most publishers for many years.

Another aspect, probably, also entered into Anaïs Nin's evaluation of Henry Miller. Just as she must have seemed to Miller the embodiment of everything "European," Miller in turn must have held to her, as to any European, the promise of those positive traits of "America" which a worn-out, intellectualized, satiated Europe most cherished: energy, enthusiasm, the somewhat naïve but refreshing Gargantuan hunger to absorb, ingest, the entire universe of culture, which, at worst, exhausted itself in shipping castles to California and, at best, was a driving motive behind a phenomenon like Henry Miller.

At first, Miller hesitated to show Anaïs Nin parts of his new book, or even the manuscript of *Crazy Cock,* for fear that it might offend the young woman. ("I have trepidations. It is a crude thing.") Yet Anaïs Nin reacted very positively. "In a world grown paralyzed with introspection and constipated by delicate mental meals this brutal exposure of the substantial body comes as a vitalizing current of blood," as she later wrote in her introduction to the book. As in D. H. Lawrence, whose work she championed against the currents of criticism, she recognized in Miller a vital new quality. Indeed, behind the subtlety of her own work, behind the glittering, polished prose, behind the surface of a mythical personality, there was, and always has been, a down-to-earth cognizance of the real world, a solid, strong awareness, hidden in the folds of her red-lined velvet cape. And Miller, undoubtedly, realized this very quickly.

"To say (as has sometimes been said) that Anaïs Nin does not write about life is absurd," Oliver Evans wrote in 1962, "she does, but she writes about it on a level to which very few novelists aspire: in her work, the motivation and characterizations are enormously complicated, for what interests her is the ultimate motive behind the apparent ones, the genuine self beneath the many false ones." And a young West Coast critic, Deena P. Metzger, writing about Miss Nin's most recent book, *Collages* (Alan Swallow, Denver, 1964), extended the point: "There are some who believe the work of Anaïs Nin is dream-like, that her subjects and images are from the dream life. They say this because they are afraid of her language. She is too sensual for them and she tells too many truths. If her stories are not real, then nothing is."

When June, Miller's wife, arrived in Paris in the fall of 1931, she and Anaïs Nin, mutually fascinated by the polarity of their personalities, became friends (and June, eventually, also appears as a character in Anaïs Nin's fiction). But June, tired of sharing Miller's wretched circumstances for long (the grimy hotels, the suspicious concierges, his "crazy" friends), unable to appreciate the work he has embarked upon, eager to return to her New York habitat, soon departs; and Anaïs Nin, in Louveciennes, becomes the recipient of a vast outflow of letters from Miller, the inveterate letter writer.

In January 1932, Miller had left for Dijon, in the hope of improving his economic circumstances, to work as a *répétiteur d'anglais,* an English instructor, at the Lycée Carnot. But the flight from misery in Paris only opened up another nightmare: a frustrating job, without pay, in a dismal boarding school, an episode later incorporated in the final section of *Tropic of Cancer.* Miller, after the first shock had been absorbed, was determined not to let down his friends who got him the job. But when Alfred Perlès wangled a job for him as "assistant finance editor" of the Paris edition of the Chicago *Tribune*, Miller escaped from Dijon, "happy as a convict getting his release."

While the new job turned out to be little more than that of a glorified proofreader, it paid a monthly wage of 1,200 francs (about $45). Now "affluent," Miller, after a short stay at the Hôtel Central, decided to share an apartment with Alfred Perlès in the working-class district of Clichy, at 4 rue Anatole France, which reminded Miller of the barren reaches of upper Park Avenue in New York. The apartment had a kitchen, bathroom, hall, and two separate rooms. For the first time since coming to Paris, Miller had a permanent address, a place of his own. Since he and Perlès worked at night, they had the days to themselves. In the mornings Perlès worked on his novel, in the afternoons he liked to go bicycling. Miller, finally equipped with a typewriter and mountains of books supplied by Anaïs Nin and the American Library in Paris, embarked on what was perhaps his most fruitful period as an artist. "I can't remember any period in my life when the time flew more quickly than it did at Clichy." His letters attest to his feverish activity: "God, it is maddening to think that even one day must pass without writing. I shall never, never catch up. It is why, no doubt, I write with such vehemence, such distortion." And: "I feel that I am somebody, a force, a necessity."

Aside from the new, explosive novel (he had finally abandoned *Crazy Cock*, after some further efforts to salvage the book with Anaïs Nin's help), he had also begun to write a "brochure" about D. H. Lawrence. (Anaïs Nin's *D. H. Lawrence: An Unprofessional Study* had appeared in the spring of 1932, in an edition of 500 copies, under Edward Titus' imprint of the "Black Manikin" press, which operated out of his bookstore in the rue Delambre.) He was accumulating notes on various subjects, particularly the cinema, which played an important part in his life at the time, and he worked on his watercolors (see his essay, "The Angel Is My Watermark"). But above all, he was locked in never-ending battle with his American past and his relationship with June (which had reached a critical stage and eventually ended in divorce in 1934). He was finding his way through "the palace of entrails" in a gigantic effort to liberate himself from his former self. "Wherever I have made my bed," a line in *Black Spring* reads, "I have fought like a maniac to drive out the past."

His job with the Chicago *Tribune* lasted only a short while and

Miller's circumstances remained extremely precarious. Anaïs Nin was able to brighten his day with small gifts: a lamp, a bicycle, a record player, books. And always she was there to watch the growth of his work, to stimulate. The kitchen in Clichy became a battleground of ideas, the "black lace" laboratory, a communal workshop and a place of laughter and fun. "Perhaps our ebullience was due to the fact that for the first time in many years we were enjoying what might be called a relative security. For the first time in ages I had a permanent address."

After Miller had finished the first draft of *Tropic of Cancer,* then still untitled, he handed the manuscript to an American of his acquaintance, William Bradley, who had become a literary agent in Paris. Bradley, in turn, passed it on to Jack Kahane, with his "cautious and non-committal blessing," as Kahane later recalled. An Englishman who had set up a small publishing firm, the Obelisk Press, in Paris in the 1920s, Kahane had published a number of somewhat controversial, somewhat salacious books in English, mostly for the tourist trade. One weekend, he took the manuscript of Miller's book to his country home, Le Fond de Forêts, and, as he wrote six years later in his reminiscences (*Memoirs of a Booklegger,* Michael Joseph, 1939): "I began it after luncheon in the shadow of the great copper beech tree . . . and the twilight was deepening into night when I finished it. 'At last!' I murmured to myself. I had read the most terrible, the most sordid, the most magnificent manuscript that had ever fallen into my hands; nothing I had yet received was comparable to it for the splendor of its writing, the fathomless depth of its despair, the savour of its portraiture, the boisterousness of its humour. Walking into the house I was exalted by the triumphant sensation of all explorers who have at last fallen upon the object of their years of search. I had in my hands a work of genius and it had been offered to me for publication."

Yet for all the enthusiasm Jack Kahane here described in retrospect, a frustrating two years went by before the book was published. Though he had signed a contract with Henry Miller, Kahane hesitated to bring out the book. His reasons were partially economic (the fluctuating currencies, the lack of buyers), but partly, no doubt, he was worried about possible repercussions if the book should run afoul of French censorship. While Kahane had successfully published Frank Harris' *My Life and Loves,* and other "risqué" books written by himself under the pseudonym Cecil Barr, a book he had turned down, D. H.

Lawrence's *Lady Chatterley's Lover,* had provoked a scandal when published by Edward Titus, and only the intervention of some French intellectuals had secured the release of the book by French authorities. But who would intercede on behalf of the unknown Henry Miller? Undoubtedly, the memory of that recent *cause célèbre* remained a factor.

By May 1934, both Miller and Anaïs Nin had grown tired of Kahane's vacillations. Wrote Miller: "If this isn't soon published it will never be. It will be outdated. There's a time for everything—and this is the time." So, Anaïs Nin decided to back the publication of the book herself, ensuring Kahane against any possible financial risks. In a preface to the book which, though a scant three printed pages, is still perhaps one of the most perceptive evaluations of Miller's first book (it was reprinted in the U. S. edition almost thirty years later), as well as of the tenor of Miller's future work, Anaïs Nin wrote:

> Here is a book which, if such a thing were possible, might re-store our appetite for fundamental realities. The predominant note will seem one of bitterness, and bitterness there is, to the full. But there is also a wild extravagance, a mad gaiety, a verve, a gusto, at times almost a delirium. A continual oscillation be-tween extremes, with bare stretches that taste like brass and leave the full flavor of emptiness. It is beyond optimism or pessimism. The author has given us the last *frisson.* Pain has no more secret recesses.
>
> It is no false primitivism which gives rise to this savage lyri-cism. It is not a retrogressive tendency, but a swing forward into unbeaten areas. To regard a naked book such as this with the same critical eye that is turned upon even such diverse types as Lawrence, Breton, Joyce and Céline is a mistake. Rather let us try to look at it with the eye of the Patagonian for whom all that is sacred and taboo in our world is meaningless. For the adven-ture which has brought the author to the spiritual ends of the earth is the history of every artist who, in order to express him-self, must traverse the intangible gridirons of his imaginary world. The air pockets, the alkali wastes, the crumbling monuments, the putrescent cadavers, the crazy jig and maggot dance, all this forms a grand fresco of our epoch, done with shattering phrases and loud, strident, hammer strokes.

Between the time a contract was drawn late in 1932 and the publication of *Tropic of Cancer,* in September 1934, Miller had revised the manuscript three times. He had also continued his obsessive labors on the "World of D. H. Lawrence," the "brochure" which had grown into a wildly monumental manuscript, a "slaughterhouse of ideas." Miller had designed wall charts, on big sheets of paper, to outline the themes of the project. He had taken on the "diary habit," and gathered ideas, quotations, excerpts and sketches in a number of "notebooks" which provided the raw material of his future work. He had also begun another project, a "self-portrait," as he first called it. Once more, he battled with the memory of his childhood in Brooklyn ("The Fourteenth Ward") and family life ("The Tailor Shop"). He pinned down in exuberant caricature his Paris friends ("Jabberwhorl Cronstadt") and synthezised his vision of life ("Walking Up and Down in China"): "I am not a traveller, not an adventurer. Afternoons, sitting at La Fourche, I ask myself calmly: 'Where do we go from here?' Here at the crossroads I sit and dream back through all my separate and immortal egos." Gathered together in the volume *Black Spring,* dedicated to Anaïs Nin, the "self-portrait" became Miller's second book, published by the Obelisk Press in June 1936. To Miller, *Black Spring* was a book "which came nearer to being myself, I believe, than any book I have written before or since." (*The Books in My Life,* 1952.)

Anaïs Nin, during this great period of productivity, had introduced Miller to many of her friends, including Antonin Artaud, the surrealist poet and man of the theater, and the two well-known psychiatrists, Dr. René Allendy and Dr. Otto Rank, with whom she studied and worked. In April 1934, Anaïs Nin had gone to London to visit Rebecca West, an admirer of her work, carrying with her the manuscripts of Miller's *Black Spring* and the *World of Lawrence.* But the English literary establishment was not yet ready to embrace Henry Miller's work. There was a polite silence. *The World of Lawrence,* as a matter of fact, was never published as a complete work, though sizable fragments appeared in Miller's later books *(The Cosmological Eye, Wisdom of the Heart* and *Sunday After the War).* With her return from London, Anaïs Nin moved to Paris and the volume of correspondence diminished to a trickle for the next four years, except when she was away from Paris, in New York and on a trip through North Africa (in 1936), and little of this correspondence, apparently, has survived.

When *Tropic of Cancer* was published in September 1934, "the general opinion was confused," as Jack Kahane wrote in his memoirs. "Some thought it great, some thought it vile; some thought it mortally dull, others wildly exciting. It took nearer three years than two to sell the first thousand copies."

Yet Miller's first publication in book form marked a decided change in his life. After years of frustration, after ten years of seriously "practicing the art," he had been published and other writers—Ezra Pound, Katherine Anne Porter, T. S. Eliot—began to acknowledge his existence. Miller wrote hundreds of letters to "all and sundry" to get the book read and reviewed. While the reception of the book was mixed, and his financial situation had not improved, he felt "the lean and fighting spirit is on me." In December 1934, he writes: "I certainly feel like one in action. I'm fairly sizzling with excitement and nervousness, with interviews, with letters."

Simultaneously with the publication of *Tropic of Cancer,* Miller had moved into a new environment (after giving up the Clichy apartment, he had lived again, for a while, in various hotels and apartments), where he was to live until May 1939, the longest period of continuous residence in Paris. "When I moved to the Villa Seurat a whole new atmosphere was created." The Villa Seurat was a short, dead-end street, crowded with workshops and artists' studios, in the 14th Arrondissement, near the Métro station Alésia. For a brief time, Miller had already lived in No. 18, as a guest on Michael Fraenkel's couch, but this time he moved in as a bona fide tenant. Nearby, in the Impasse du Rouet, his friends David Edgar and the painter Hans Reichel were located, and Alfred Perlès, after having tried a dozen different quarters, also made his home there. A local bistro, the Café Zeyer (later the Boléro), became one of their meeting places.

The first signs of a public recognition of his talent reached Miller at the Villa Seurat, and one of the first Frenchman to pay him a visit was Blaise Cendrars. This visit by the one-armed French writer, who had lived a life of adventure himself, had a profound effect on Miller and he became an ardent admirer of Cendrars' work.

In November 1934, Anaïs Nin had left for a visit to New York and Miller, too, returned to the States for a few months early in 1935, only to hasten back to Paris. *Tropic of Cancer* had been tagged "obscene" by the keepers of our morals, the Treasury Department, and the book —as subsequently *Black Spring* and *Tropic of Capricorn*—could not be brought into the States legally. For many years it also remained banned in England, though a clandestine traffic of Miller's books (including pirated editions) trickled into both countries.

Back in France, Miller resumed his work at a furious pace. An addenda he had written as a joke to include in *Black Spring* became the preface to Michael Fraenkel's *Bastard Death*. After reading the first hundred pages of Alfred Perlès' novel, *Le Quatuor en Ré Majeur,* Miller sat down, in September 1935, and wrote an "open letter"— "What Are You Going to Do About Alf?"—suggesting that since Alf was "always looking for a comfortable room in which to write," his friends should raise some money by subscription to send him to the Balearic Islands to Ibiza, so he could finish his novel. (Perlès had lost his job with the Chicago *Tribune* when the Paris edition folded in 1934.) But this—like other half-jesting schemes concocted by Miller and his friends—produced no results. On November 2, 1935, Miller began the so-called "Hamlet" correspondence with Michael Fraenkel, conceived and initiated at the Café Zeyer, which picked up a discussion begun in 1930 and continued for the next three years, while Fraenkel was traveling in Europe and North America. Out of an exposition of Miller's ideas on art and a variety of subjects, very few of them related to "Hamlet," it grew into an ideological feud with Fraenkel. (Collected in two volumes, this correspondence was eventually privately published by Fraenkel, in Puerto Rico and Mexico.) Throughout the year, Miller had been expecting the publication of *Black Spring,* but time and again the book was postponed. Once more, Miller experienced a frustrating wait.

In January 1936, Miller made a second trip to the United States but by April he was back in Paris. America had not been able to reclaim him. Anaïs Nin had gone on a trip through North Africa and a few letters were exchanged before she returned to Paris and rejoined the "Villa Seurat" circle. Miller pursued his "Hamlet" correspondence and worked on *Tropic of Capricorn* and a series of stories, essays and portraits which were eventually gathered in the collection *Max and the White Phagocytes.* By August, Miller had made plans to leave Paris and travel about in Europe. He had cleaned house and thrown away many of the notes he had laboriously made on Proust and other subjects. But by the end of the year he was still in Paris. The prospect of travel, somehow, held little appeal for him. "My mind always remains at home when I travel," he had written in 1933. "I don't know why. I make my best voyages at the desk." In January 1937, he finished the story of his abortive trip to England, "Via Dieppe-New-haven," and by May the manuscript of *Max and the White Phagocytes* was ready. The publication of *Tropic of Capricorn* seemed definitely set for June 1938. Jack Kahane had wanted to follow *Black Spring* with *Tropic of Capricorn,* but after much back-and-forth, *Max* was published in 1938, and *Tropic of Capricorn* postponed to the following year.

Alfred Perlès, in July 1937, had become editor of *The Booster,* a magazine originally published on behalf of the American Country Club in Paris. With great gusto, he turned it into a "house organ" of the Villa Seurat circle, with Miller, Anaïs Nin, William Saroyan, Hilaire Hiler, Lawrence Durrell, Abe Rattner, et al., among its contributors. But after three lively issues, difficulties arose, and the magazine was renamed *Delta.* And three issues later (in 1939), it folded, like so many of the short-lived "little magazines." While it lasted, Miller and his friends had fun.

In September 1937, Lawrence Durrell had followed Miller's invitation and arrived in Paris and soon the idea for a joint publishing program, the "Villa Seurat Library," was born. Miller was to contribute his *Max and the White Phagocytes,* Durrell his *Black Book,* and Anaïs Nin her *Winter of Artifice.* (Anaïs Nin's first book of fiction, the prose poem *House of Incest,* had been published in 1936, and inspired by the book, Miller had written a "scenario" for a film with sound, which was later included in his collection, *The Cosmological Eye.*) Between May and October 1938, Miller had worked on the final revisions of *Tropic of Capricorn,* and in January 1939 the proofs of the book were ready. But publication was again postponed, from April to May 10. The Munich crisis of 1938 had shown that the world situation was progressively deteriorating and war was in the air. Miller was determined to get away. At the end of May, he bade his final farewell to the Villa Seurat. His few possessions were dispersed, some of his papers put in storage, and after a short journey through Southern France he embarked from Marseille, on July 14, 1939, to visit the Durrells in Corfu and to spend the rest of the year in Greece. His European exile was coming to an end; Miller was approaching his fiftieth birthday.

Already in February 1939, a new mood, a new cognition, had begun to take hold of him: "When I say, as I often do, that my life since twenty-one up until recently was but a detour I mean that a large part of my efforts were wasted in an unacknowledged struggle to adapt myself to the world, the final adaptation masking itself as an effort to conquer or seduce the world through my creative powers as a writer. I should have been adapting myself to myself. I should have been trying to bring about that identification of the two vital centers, as in the example of the horse I told you about. Unconsciously I was, no doubt. With endless groping one finally becomes aware—the random shots in the dark are too striking to be ignored. Every deep realization of this sort is a real advance, a real consolidation in the hitherto blind grasp at the truth. Suddenly you perceive that, if you listen properly, the truth is always speaking in you. And then you become terribly quiet and contained. You cease trying to do more than you can do. You also never do less than you are able to do. But you work and act from a new level which is like an inexhaustible reserve of strength and inspiration."

The end of Miller's ten years in Europe also marked the end of his most productive, most ebullient period. *Tropic of Cancer,* the eloquent tribute to his "liberation" from America, summarized the experiences of his first two years in France and captured in caricature and barely disguised some of his friends, the "desperate ones" (Fillmore, Carl Van Norden, Boris, Peckover, Cronstadt). *Black Spring,* the "self-portrait," already indicated a return to his preoccupation with the past, and *Tropic of Capricorn,* which ends with his meeting of "Mara" in 1923, brings him back, fully, to the "first ordeal," America, even though there is a hint of Paris in some sections. And after his return to the United States, he revived—first in 1944, and again five years later—the multivolume project of the "Rosy Crucifixion," which had been dormant since he left for France in 1930. ("The truth is that I wrote this dread book in my head when jotting down—in the space of about 18 continuous hours—the complete outline or notes covering the subject matter of the work.") But by going back to his sources, Miller found a way into the future.

Of the 197 letters in this collection, selected from a larger body of correspondence for their relevance and literary interest, more than half were written in Europe, most of them during the years 1931 and 1934, and between 1938 and 1939, periods when Anaïs Nin and Henry Miller lived in different places. Little correspondence seems to have been preserved for the years 1935–1938, when both writers were mostly in Paris. (This period in Miller's life is covered to some extent in the correspondence between Henry Miller and Lawrence Durrell, published in 1962.) Over the years, a few letters by Henry Miller to other individuals (Emil Schnellock, Herbert F. West, Walter Lowenfels, et al.) have appeared in pamphlets and magazines.

Most of the letters in this collection have been reproduced in full, but in some cases small deletions have been made of irrelevant details (which would have been meaningless without an extensive explanatory framework), and a few repetitions and asides have been cut. A few errors in transcription have been corrected and the spelling made consistent. A substantial portion of the letters was in handwriting, and some written on café or hotel stationery Miller had a habit of collecting. While these stationery headings were colorful and evoked places mentioned in Miller's work (Café Wetzler, La Fourche, the Dome, La Coupole), they often were misleading as to where the letter had actually been written, and thus have been eliminated. A major problem was the dating of the letters. (The majority bore no further identification than the day or the hour of the writing, and of the 107 letters written in Europe, only 23 were dated.) Here, the editor is grateful to Henry Miller's own recollection, which established the broad outline of chronology, and to Anaïs Nin, who made her Diary available, which was of invaluable help. Wherever supplied by the editor, the dates are given in square brackets, and any possible mistakes are the editor's. Of the 90 letters in the U.S.A. section, 37 were dated on the originals, and accurate dating of the letters written during Henry Miller's American journey, in 1940 and 1941, was made possible by notes Mr. Miller kept which are preserved in the facsimile edition of his "Red Notebook." The originals of some of the letters included here are now in the manuscript collection of the library of Southern Illinois University. The rest are in the voluminous collection of Miss Nin.

The question may very well be asked why none of Miss Nin's letters to Henry Miller have been included in this volume, at least to the extent they have been preserved. The answer, essentially, is simple. Technically, it would have brought the size of the present volume to unmanageable proportions or caused the elimination of valuable material. But more important, Henry Miller's letters, as any reader of this volume will soon realize, simply do not call for a reply; they stand very well on their own. Essentially this collection is a monologue,

Miller's own story of these fifteen decisive years in his life. It is "auto-biography," in the best and truest sense of the word. Anaïs Nin's letters to Henry Miller would have added little to this story. They are a part of her own autobiography which has found its most eloquent crystallization in her Diary. And the Diary, hopefully, will become available in the near future.

In a letter from Anderson Creek, Big Sur, of May 17, 1946, Miller wrote to Anaïs Nin: "You are the only one I ever knew who used silence effectively. It was really devastating sometimes—but I don't think you were aware of it. But people get more answers, and effective ones, from you than they ever did from me, with all my shouting and ranting, or cajoling and persuading."

Perhaps Miss Nin's silence in this volume only helps to bring to the fore a new, a fresh, an exciting "self-portrait" of the writer and artist, Henry Miller.

GUNTHER STUHLMANN

New York, December 1964

Part One : Europe

Café de la Liberté

DEAR ANAÏS NIN:

If my wise and goodhearted friend [Richard Galen] Osborn *
sees fit you will receive in advance of my coming a few pages of the
book I am now engaged on [*Tropic of Cancer*]. The novel I am withholding for a while because on reviewing it the other day, I felt it
needed such severe, radical alterations that to show it to you in its
present state would only prejudice you against me.

As a matter of fact, so may these few pages of the work in progress,
but then I don't care much whether it pleases or displeases since (for
the time being) it gives me some joy or satisfaction.

But I have trepidations. It is a crude thing. And I have not begun
altering it—not a word has yet been changed. That will come later,
much later, when I have run dry.

Actually, there has been an interruption of three weeks, dating from
my wife's arrival.** Everything has stopped since she has come. I
have not been able to find myself. I have lost something.

In any case, I shall probably bring the remaining pages and some
diary notes and letters along, if that will interest you. I want you to be
interested. I feel very warmly the hospitality, the sympathy and friend-
liness you have shown toward me. At the same time I feel very sensitive—a fear of being misunderstood, or something perhaps less
definitive and crude than that but akin. I don't want to be thought of
as having a dirty mind. On the other hand I don't wish to palliate the
writing, to make a defense, etc. I want it to stand (or fall) on its own
merits. I know that it will reveal a great deal about me and to all that
I have no answer. People will always know me better than I know
myself.

---

* See Biographical Notes.
** June Edith Smith, Miller's second wife, remained in the United States
when Miller left for France in 1930, but visited him in 1931 and again during the winter of 1932. See also Biographical Notes.

It is out of delicacy, then, that I take this step of asking Osborn to read it first. I have very poor judgment. I know very little about discretion, diplomacy and such things. I hate all that. In my enthusiasm for people I am apt to blunder. Well, then, I had rather not blunder. I had rather remain your friend than hurt you by any coarse language. Perhaps I am making a mountain out of a molehill. I will not say any more.

I shall be very very glad to see you again on Saturday, to see the little maid too, and the sparkling glasses and the shelves filled with books. It gave me such a splendid feeling of peace and security when I stepped into your home. Here people are really living, was what I thought. Do go on living that way. Don't fear the compromises. One is always obliged to compromise either in one way or another. But your lives seem beautiful to me—*your life,* I should say. It is just that—the unity, the harmony. Believe me, I am deeply touched.

Sincerely,

HENRY V. MILLER

Dijon, le 29 Janvier, 1932

DEAR ANAÏS NIN:

The Lycée Carnot, as the establishment is called, so far as I am concerned seems just about a peg above a penitentiary. To call it a Spartan regime, as Dr. Krans put it, conveys nothing.* Perhaps the weather also contributes toward making the picture a morbid one. Certainly, except for London (which even in February was milder than this) I have never experienced anything like it. The town seems to be shrouded in a thick blanket of icy fog, the trees are white with frost, and everybody looks raw and chapped. No, this is quite a different Dijon from the one I knew in the summertime.

I was received cordially enough and everyone acts graciously but— the buildings are like refrigerators, sinister withal, in disrepair, mouldy,

---

* To solve Miller's economic situation, a friend had introduced him to Dr. Krans, an administrator of the French school system, who had found a job for him in Dijon as a *répétiteur d'anglais,* an instructor in English.

what not. I find myself surrounded by a dozen monitors, called *surveillants,* all poor devils struggling to get degrees, and putting up a bold front despite the poor food, the cold, the general unattractiveness of life here.

Frankly, my first impulse was to beat it this morning. A frightfully cold room, no running water, on the top floor of a dormitory that gives you the pleasant sensation of entering a morgue. Listen, I don't want to lay it on thick. I am writing this to you privately. After a week or so I shall probably not notice the discomfits. But the first few hours— horrors! No place to send a white man. That's entre nous.

To add to this picture of cheer let me say that this morning I was informed that there is no compensation attached to the job—just board and room, such as it is. Upon my soul, had I suspected anything like this (despite the word "spartan") I would have remained in Paris under no matter what circumstances. As it is, I feel obliged to give it a fair trial. (The teaching is not difficult at all and there is only 9 hours a week.)

I am not writing Dr. Krans yet. He said expressly, I remember, "not to go by first impressions," but had I been morally free I would have turned back at once. In any case, should you be seeing him soon again, just mention please that I was somewhat disappointed in not getting a stipend. Both he and Desclos (of the Office National) stated definitely that there would be. As for the rest, hold off on that for the present. Perhaps I will be able to adjust myself, and I am especially eager to since I was so ready to take anything. I don't wish to appear ungrateful or a weakling either. Nevertheless, the previous two teachers, one an American and the other an Englishman, couldn't stick it out either. The Englishman, I was told, beat it the second day under cover of night without saying a word.

I dislike writing you this, except that I feel I can speak freely to you. Naturally, I'm going to stick it out as long as I can. In fact, I have no other recourse. I've now burned all my bridges behind me. Certainly I would request you not to make any fuss about it. It is, what I imagine, a typical French situation, and there is nothing to be done about it. And no matter what you or I said, we would be considered as crazy Americans, who have been spoiled by too many physical comforts. When I think now of the Hotel Princesse, which June found so difficult to tolerate, it seems lovely.

I'll just give you one picture—of the "refectory." Here is where we eat, the surveillants and myself. It is like a cheap Jewish clinic, marble-top tables cold as ice. The food is brought in all at once— soup, meat, vegetable, dessert. Mornings you get a bowl of weak coffee, already sugared and diluted with milk. The rest—bread, without butter or confiture or anything. That's at 7:30 A.M. By noon you're famished, what with the cold etc. Next meal seven o'clock. No coffee with big meals. To make up for it, to put a face on it, the guys sing and wrestle and argue politics. Jesus, I feel sorry for them. They're good sports. Hard by is the infirmary where the pupils are treated when they are ill. The dormitory where they sleep is cold as all hell. The staircase reminds you of a setting for Edgar Allan Poe—or a sort of Grand Guignol tragedy.

But hell—enuf of this. Perhaps I can write more interestingly the next time.

Sincerely,

HENRY

[January, 1932]
Lycée Carnot
Boulevard Thiers
Dijon, Côte d'Or

DEAR ANAÏS NIN:

Here I am at the lycée and all my bright hopes dashed. The dinner hour is over and as there is nothing I can possibly do but go to bed I will regale you with a meager account of the life as I find it here.*

INTERRUPTION

The most astonishing thing has just occurred. A bee has suddenly come to life and is buzzing furiously about the room. How and where it has managed to keep alive is beyond me because, as you will soon learn, one only keeps alive here by dint of supreme struggle. It is not only winter here but death, misery, ennui, above all "le brouillard."

---

* The final section of *Tropic of Cancer* gives a detailed, slightly fictionalized account of Miller's experience at the Lycée Carnot.

This last is something that defies description. It is like being gassed and having no helmet. It penetrates through the keyholes and the toes of your feet. It leaves you gasping and spluttering. Though I seldom feel uneasy in a strange town this place gives me the creeps. I feel lost, frightened, a little mad, walking about the streets. This afternoon, coming out of a shop (I was buying a mirror in order to shave) a prostitute nudged me. I talked to her a few minutes in a desperate effort to get at something real. It was a human being and not fog, not a silly curriculum, not an abstract consecration to a dead ideal. You know, I never had a taste for universities. This joint makes me physically ill. It is revolting.

Let me go back a bit. The time I had leaving Paris! A last-minute scramble for funds. Once you get to Dijon, I kept telling myself, everything will straighten itself out. I saw myself paying off the small debts I had accumulated, and in the back of my mind all the while was that final picture of Majorca.

I can't possibly tell you how bad I feel now. Perhaps things are not really half as bad as I make them out, but that doesn't alter anything. It's all very real and very terrible to me. I was thinking this afternoon, in my distress, of Unamuno—that story of his in the *New Review*. I feel very much now the exile, the outcast. The young men with whom I am obliged to associate (les surveillants) annoy me with their forced gaiety. They are under illusions. They are living on the future. They are terribly young and terribly romantic, or at least enthusiastic. They sing a great deal at the table, and normally that would delight me, only I realize that they are singing in order not to weep.

This morning I sat in a classroom, listening to the head professor of English teach. The man is a perfect sadist. I felt at times like getting up and punching him. And what nonsense! Imagine making French boys of twelve to fourteen read a thing like "John Gilpin's Ride." When they fail to answer properly he pinches and pushes them, calls them imbeciles and what not. The whole thing disgusted me. A sort of Chinese education, absolutely without rhyme or reason. He said to me, on the way out, "It is good to give them difficult things; it keeps them on the alert."

The introduction was funny. M. le Proviseur was away. I was conducted by a half-wit to the office of M. le Censeur. A typical functionary, with a wig, wearing a frock coat, a greasy one. No blood in his veins. Immediately discusses the problem of my work, conducts

me to the office of M. l'Économe and takes leave. Then a dwarf takes
me in tow—the chef des garçons. When you read *Mysteries* of Knut
Hamsun you will get a picture of this guy. Finally I am passed on to
the garçon himself who has a wooden leg and together we go to the
station with a pushcart and fetch the luggage. Then I am shown how to
light the stove and warned not to use too much wood. Everything is
doled out on a strict basis, from wood to learning. Of course the stove
went out in the middle of the night and when I got up I was frozen.
No running water, a washbasin with filthy rings around it—my
predecessor's dirt, no doubt, etc. I lay awake most of the night wondering what to do. Also in fear of missing breakfast at 7:30 A.M. as
I have no alarm clock and am isolated from the others. The breakfast was a joke. A bowl of blue coffee, very slightly sweetened, and
bread without butter. The meals are poor. And to make matters worse
the food is slung at you all at once. You eat as fast as possible so as
not to have the dishes grow cold. Tonight, for example, I ate the
soup last because it looked the hottest. The whole atmosphere of the
place is like a reformatory. If you go out at night you take a chance
of standing in the cold for an hour while the night watchman makes
his rounds. No keys are handed out because they are afraid women
may be sneaked in. It's all stupid, dismal, thwarting.

If things do not look brighter to me in a week or so I will get back
to Paris somehow. Should it come to the worst I can probably share
Fred's [Alfred Perlès'] * bed or go back to my old schedule of wandering from place to place, work up a new list of places to eat. Paris, at
any rate, has a warm human throb. This is death and stagnation. But
my pride is touched somehow. Whether it is that I am unduly sensitive
or not, I have a feeling that everyone was immensely relieved to see
me off. I feel that I have been a problem. And that hurts a lot. Poor
[Walter] Lowenfels,* for example, will not get his hundred francs.

INTERRUPTION

The bell is striking ten. It sounds like the knell of a cemetery bell
when the hearse passes thru the gate. I used to hear it regularly when
I lived on the rue Froideveaux opposite Cemetery Montparnasse. Add
to this that I am thirsty and have no glass, and the water in the lava-

---

* See Biographical Notes.

tory where we shiver and shave I fear is non-potable. All these little impediments are so silly. France is bursting with gold. . . .

Somehow I feel as Dostoevski felt when he wrote *The House of the Dead*. One gets to feel like a beast. And it's all going on in the name of civilization, culture, education etc.

Pardon me for raving this way. If I were back in Louveciennes * I would be smiling when I say this. God, your lovely place seems so far away, so unreal. Walking thru the town here one feels that everybody is living this sordid, mean life. Churches and monuments everywhere—relics of a glorious past. But sinister now in this twentieth-century atmosphere, in this civilization which has not even secured to man the freedom from physical worries.

A volume of Proust lies before me on the table. I have not the heart to open it. One of June's stockings that I brought away with me is on the dresser. I shine my shoes with it. But I can't believe that June's leg was once in it, or hardly that there was a June. It's as tho' I had been away from Paris a year or more. And June? God, I don't dare to think of her. If I did I think I would yell. I sit facing a bleak window that opens on the street. The impulse is to open it and jump. One cold solid smack and it's all over. But even that I haven't got the courage for at the present. No, I will probably crawl in bed soon and pray that I don't miss breakfast. It's the hideous, futile waste that gets me. Forever being thwarted. Terrible. Lousy. I hope you understand.

I am addressing this to Switzerland. I wonder how you are faring, and if you at least are making some headway. The book was so beautiful. ** I have great, great faith in your ability. It was astonishing to me the distance you have covered in so short a time. And I sincerely hope that I did not confuse you by my extemporaneous criticism.

Saturday eve.

The surveillants have been here in my room and we have had a heart-to-heart talk. Also more song. I explained to them, in my poor French, their characters one by one. Then I gave them a few glimpses

---

* Anaïs Nin lived in Louveciennes, near Paris, in a country house which once belonged to the estate of Madame du Barry.

** Anaïs Nin's first novel, untitled, unpublished. The manuscript is now in the library of Northwestern University, Evanston, Illinois.

into my life in Paris. What they appreciated most was my taste for wine. It seems that my predecessor was somewhat of an aristocrat. I suppose he was a snob. He did not associate with them at all, and hardly spoke, even at meals. Well, I have been talking to them constantly, and there are three or four who already show that they desire my friendship very much. They seem to be touched by my open manners and not a little amused by my speech, patting me on the back whenever I say something witty (in French).

They urge me to stick it out. In another month, they say, will come the good weather, le beau soleil, and there is talk of wine and women and dancing and good food. Today I was escorted by two of them thru the town in search of a typewriter. They were going to get me one without paying in advance. But alas, we learned conclusively that there are no machines for rent in Dijon which have American keyboards. And I find the others impossible, as I type quite rapidly, practically by the touch system. I regret now that I did not avail myself of your offer to borrow your machine—or perhaps yours is a French clavier too? So what to do? On all sides obstacles. I simply can't write by hand. I don't think that way.

In any case I am improving my French, but that is a luxury. Today the sun was out and the town looked considerably more attractive. Thursdays, I am told, one can take a shower bath—but only in the morning. Voila! Today I found the rue Émile Zola. The plaque read: "E.Z.—romancier des idées matérialistes." Today too I was made acquainted with the nicknames of all the surveillants. One of them, a dour sort, they call "Le Pénible." Rather good. Rather. He is against war. They are all against war. But they dispute hotly as to whether France should arm to the teeth or disarm completely. I think what they like is that I speak to them quite openly. I tell them what I am for and what against. They are surprised and very gratified to observe that I have not much regard for America. And above all, they are pleased with my descriptions of Paris, with la vie bohème, as it is called. It really does seem bohemian now.

Hearing me mention vin d'Anjou so often they have decided tonight to take me to a café and buy some for me. And very soon, as is the tradition here, they promise to escort me to the bordellos. Just to look—they say. They have already warned me that there is a great deal of disease in Dijon. It is supposed to be the second worst town in France in that respect.

Well, I think this is probably enough gossip. Please do let me hear from you. If I should bolt suddenly I will leave a forwarding address. I hope your stay in Switzerland will be conducive to work.

Sincerely,

HENRY

[February 4, 1932]
Lycée Carnot, Dijon
Thursday

I don't know where to begin! My mind is flooded, saturated with material. Alors, I got your letter, the telegram. First of all, bravo! I am immensely elated by the interest you take—and that is quite enough to sustain me. It will not be necessary to return to Paris, or Louveciennes, tho' certainly I deeply appreciate your hospitality. Let us reserve the occasion—there may come a worse day. For the present I feel sufficiently fortified to stick it out. I think the volume of this letter will testify to my rising spirits. The physical handicaps I am learning to surmount. The typewriter is all I lack, and today I am going to make an effort to induce one of the firms here in Dijon to send to Paris for a machine. Should I fail I will write you, enclose the necessary money and ask you to try to arrange it from the other end. (The rental is usually 60 frs. a month.) Today also I go "for a walk" with the head professor of English, and I am going to ask him if he can aid me in getting private pupils. They tell me he is a good scout, despite his severity, his sadistic turns in the classroom.

Perhaps I sounded like a crybaby. What a yawp I set up! Damn it, I wasn't supposed to fall into a bed of roses. So, if in the future, I rave or rant, just set it down to literary ebullience. Everything has its compensations. . . . Now that I have cleared the deck with these practical explanations (and hell how I detest them) let me make other apologies—and then to more interesting matter. First, excuse the paper. I have good typewriter paper which I am holding in reserve, and if you do not mind the lack of formality why O.K. Maybe the random notes on the reverse side will titillate you. They are of no use to me any more. Secondly, excuse the absence of salutation. I haven't yet learned to call you by your first name, and Miss Nin sounds so stiff, like an invitation to tea. I should like to say simply Anaïs, but it takes time. (Osborn, for instance, is still Osborn.)

How Germanic this is. Well, that's me. At any rate, I assume you are now in Switzerland—here goes. I am enclosing various things— an article of mine on the "Cirque Medrano" * (which I would ask you to return as I want to write about the Medrano in my book), some notes on Proust, excerpts from *La Nouvelle Revue Française,* etc. This last, if it interests you sufficiently, I will make typewritten copies of, so send it back. It sounds well to me—so well stated, the difference between France and the rest of the world. And it is a German who writes it. I found it in the December 1931 issue, together with a short story called "Le Cirque" by C. F. Ramuz, and which I enjoyed very much. Perhaps the more because I am in Dijon and "from 7 to 9 P.M. there is the walk for a little air—*et c'est tout.*" You will understand better if you should happen to read the story. Sometimes I think I am a little askew on the subject of French literature. It sounds so beautiful to me because there is still an element of mystery, of vagueness, which my imagination fills in somewhat ecstatically. The language of Curtius, however, I enjoy for its precision and clarity. "Le Cirque" is quite another matter.

As for Proust—I have been reading him betweenwhiles. Last night a big dose at the Café Miroir, a huge, lugubrious place with orchestra. All those concert numbers which give one melancholia: the "Bohemian Girl," "Mignon," "Élégie" of Massenet, Rudolph's Narrative, etc.; the way the French sit around and pretend to enjoy this music is simply fantastic. Either they have no taste, or they are aesthetically starved. They sit and sit—it drives you mad! But the style of Proust! Now, reading it in the French (and, by the way, I am marking it up with your permission) how orthodox it sounds to my ears. Whatever caused the stir? Aside from the excrescence of language, there was nothing here to frighten anyone. It seems absolutely conventional, almost classic. But oh what a treat. That perpetual sundering of veils, those terrible glimpses into reality, into a fate more cruel because it is so entirely different. Seldom is there what one might call profundity. No, it is again thoroughly French—seeing with the

---

* New York *Herald,* Paris, 1931.

naked eye, accepting, subjugating by reason and intellect. And always
(what Curtius points out so well) the form! Ah, that! That I would
love to capture.

For instance, today I miss my friend, M. [Jean] Renaud, who is
gone to Beaune to visit his family. M. Renaud is barely twenty-one.
He is going to become professor of German. Well, last night I went
out alone to the town. On my way home, saturated with Albertine, I
passed by the Church St. Michel on the Place Edgard Quinet. One
leaves the Place by way of a little alley called rue de la Monnaie—a
wonderful old alley. I recalled passing by her for the first time with
M. Renaud, stopping and taking a last glance at the cathedral. M.
Renaud's words—believe me, as marvelous as Proust's very own description of the spires of Martinville, or of Elstir's seascapes, or of
the still lifes in the hotel at Balbec. M. Renaud is one of those born
literary men (tho' he does not yet suspect it). Language exerts over
him the power of magic. He describes—at first simply. Then he returns, weaves, fabricates, colors, plays with the subject, pursuing all the
nuances and fleeting ideas that it evokes. And, after the concrete, the
plastic, commences of necessity the generalization, metaphysical, logic,
form, value. There are no men of 21 like that in America. He is wise,
sage. His tolerance, judgment, discernment, simply extraordinary. It
is such as he I think of when I referred earlier to "compensations."
I have much to learn from him. In him there is crystallized the beauty,
the wisdom of France. Hats off to M. Renaud!

Since I shall not be back to engage in long discussions (except perhaps during Easter, or will you be going away then?) why let's thrash
things out by letter. The notes I send you, after you read them, please
hold them. As I said, so much was left out of the novel.* I want to
return to it, supplement it by incorporating some of my material in
this present book. Naturally you have divined how precious this
"Albertine" must be for me. Is not June very similar—perhaps much
more complicated, orchestrated, as it were? How many more enigmas
are there for me to solve than was presented by Albertine? How much
more I know, have lived, have endured, suspected, discovered—and
yet, how vast the unknowable! That is why reading Proust is a form
of ecstatic suffering. And then beyond June—the whole area of my
private experiences . . . God, it is maddening to think that even one

---

* *Crazy Cock,* an unpublished novel H. M. wrote in 1930.

day must pass without writing. I shall never, never catch up. It is why, no doubt, I write with such vehemence, such distortion. It is despair. . . . And with it grows a certain hard selfishness—or self-interest. I don't know whether I am becoming a solipsist or a narcissist. Certainly, more and more the world revolves around me, in me. This Krans idea of "studying provincial life, or French, or University ways"—how pale, remote, silly it seems. What have I to do with all this? God, I feel that I am somebody, a force, a necessity— and by some delicious irony I am planted in a desert, on an absolutely futile, ridiculous errand.

Yes, I do hope, Anaïs, that you will write. There is lots I have to say which does not fit into books. And I want to know what you think. I come back again to your book, to my first, vivid impressions. Certain passages in it of inestimable beauty. Above all, a sureness, a grasp, a mature dexterity which I, alas, will never attain. The very composition of your blood, your inheritance, has without your knowing it, perhaps saved you from problems and pains which most writers are obliged to suffer. You are essentially the artist, whether you choose a small or a big canvas. You have a power, through sheer feeling, that will captivate your readers. Only, beware of your reason, your intelligence. Do not attempt to resolve. Rather, if you will pardon the advice, seek to posit problems, questions, difficulties. Cultivate the madness. Do not run from it. In madness there is wisdom for the artist. Let everything go to the head and let it boil there. You have the form, the mastery over your medium. *Don't preach!* No moral conclusions. There are none, anyway. No, I remember the passage (I can never forget it)—up in the prow singing. How did the words go exactly? Oh, that was magnificent. And not there only, but elsewhere, now and again. Yes, take it from me—you are made. I congratulate you. Don't hesitate. Write! Keep on, even if you go from Switzerland to Timbuctoo, though why Louveciennes shouldn't suffice is an enigma to me.

For myself, I have learned to write most anywhere. What was bad about Dijon I have already converted to good. I will write here, you will see. It is good that I have no contacts. For the present I am reading a great deal and tranquilizing, as it were. I still hear the blood hammering in my ears. Sometimes it frightens me. But I am laying up for tomorrow when the machine comes. I will actually assault it. A barrage of finger work. I love the very sound of it when I go at it con furioso. Later, as I have the time, I will make a transscript of my notes on June for the novel. In the meantime, should it give you no great inconvenience, mail me what you like of your notes on her. The pages on "The Mansfield Woman" * I have here, but they look sick to me and I am withholding them, for a while at least. It seems ages ago that June was with me in Paris. Can you imagine her walking the streets of Dijon? What a fatality it would have been to bring her here. We would both be insane by now.

I am making notes on the life hereabouts, and when I get the typewriter you will get a better close-up. I am a long way from being dead. Things happen just the same. Not so exciting, but nourishing. I have set myself the task of translating [Duhamel's] *Salavin—The Journal.* It is a bigger task than I thought.

Incidentally, the American author most popular here is Jack London. I get it from all sides. And then, too, *Babbitt* of Sinclair Lewis. (Today at the refectory I found that "The Rime of the Ancient Mariner" was also highly regarded.) What anomalies. Already I have infected the "surveillants" with the virus of Spengler. Amazing what one can do with a foreign tongue when one is obliged to. Fancy me explaining Spengler in French. Or, for that matter (as I did the first day) *The Physiology of Love* by de Gourmont. The boys fairly ate that up. Especially when I got down to a description of the elephant in love. Some of them stay beyond their time—apparently quite interested in the English course. I treat them nonchalantly, joke etc., and stand beside the stove smoking. One of the boys has promised to initiate me into the mysteries of Spanish.

Hold on. Miracle of miracles! The other night at a mass meeting on Russia, who was the chief orator but the Latin-Greek professor of the Lycée. It was a marvelous affair. I got easily nine-tenths of it. The professor was a red-hot Communist. His colleagues were there in the audience with their wives. Toward the end a fracas—because of some nasty language directed against M. le Curé. The crowd quite Rabelaisian—or better, Burgundian. I enjoyed it immensely. And regret now that when in Paris I wasted so much time among Americans.

In the refectory "Little Paul" (a surveillant, a dandy, a reactionary) has written on the blackboard: "à partir de jeudi je ne parlerai plus de femmes!" To appreciate this you would have to know little Paul. He

---

* June Smith, Miller's second wife, occasionally used the name "June Mansfield." See also Biographical Notes.

is a meridional. There are more from the Midi—they are the best. Lusty, healthy, carefree guys. Warm blood. Fiery in dispute. Careless with the bottle. Coarse. . . . Well, the professor is expecting me. We go for a walk. Until further notice I will hold the fort. Today we had goose bones for lunch. The menu is looking up.

Sincerely,

HENRY

POSTSCRIPT

The professor and I have been all over town and no concern is willing to demand a machine from Paris. May I impose on you still further and ask you to inquire of some agency in Paris if they would be willing to send me one. I am beginning to grow very dubious about it. Perhaps I will have to come to Paris myself and fetch it. I hope not.

The professor has just left me. He wanted at first to take me to the park ("nature is always beautiful" he said) but I easily induced him to change his mind. We had quite a good talk about literature, and hit it off all right. As for getting pupils here he doesn't sound encouraging. But I imagine something will turn up. Something usually does. The professor has given me a lot of beer and there's nothing to do with it. It's Thursday but it seems like Sunday. The orchestra has just played "If the flowers only had eyes" by Massenet. Execrable!

Did I tell you that at the table the surveillants belch freely? Oh yes! It's a sort of free-for-all competition. Only M. le Prince does not belch. He is an athlete. He keeps in perfect trim. Doesn't even drink wine— or très peu.

Well, after a couple of hours with the professor here are his likes and dislikes:

For	Against
O'Henry	Proust
Norman Douglas	Wm. James
Sinclair Lewis	Huxley
Anatole France	André Gide
James Joyce	Dostoevski
Le Mercure	Paul Valéry
H. L. Mencken	La Nouvelle Revue Française
Dickens	The Soviets

For	*Against*
Duhamel	Jack London
Dos Passos	Theo. Dreiser
Remy de Gourmont	H. G. Wells
Nietzsche	Bernard Shaw
Ruskin	Ibsen
Robinson Jeffers	Strindberg
Walt Whitman	Carlyle
	McFee
	Emerson

Blanks

Élie Faure, Spengler, Henri Fabre, Jean Cocteau, W. H. Hudson, Thoreau, Gertrude Stein.

Unanimous:

We are both against America. We are against war. We are for: Wine, Woman, Song, Good Food, Comfortable Seats, Ventilated cinemas, the summertime, return to the status quo ante.

All in all, you see that we have enough in common to get along. I'll leave something for the next letter.

HVM

Sunday, Feb. 7, 1932
Lycée Carnot

Proust is going to my head. I am nearing the end of the first volume and have deliberately stopped reading because I want to ration my enjoyment and my suffering. I have put it down at the point where a letter from Aimé describes what went on between Albertine and the little blanchisseuse. ("Tu me mets aux anges"—do you recall the passage?) It seems that the more I penetrate this work the more frequent become my interlineations, my marginal rhapsodies. Truly, this symphonic treatment of jealousy is so immense, so thoroly annotated and documented, that it exhausts the subject. The only thing one can

think of, by way of comparison, is the complete domination of a
form which Bach accomplished in music.

What happens to me after reading *Albertine* is that I am on fire.
It is all I can do not to mark every line. The man seems to take the
words out of my mouth, to rob me of my very own experiences, sensations, reflections, introspections, suspicions, sadness, torture, etc. etc.
etc.

I ask myself—am I unique in feeling this, or is this the general feeling of those who swallow Proust avidly? In this book, mind you, I am
less aware—much less—of the beauty of his language, his nuances
etc. It is the content which grips me, and the feeling. I can't help repeating it—it is as though he wrote it for me privately. And therefore
I wonder very sincerely what it is that others derive from it—those
who have not tasted this peculiar experience. Instead of being fed up
by the excessive massing of detail, by the repetitions with variations
which he employs so skillfully, I am fascinated and dread the inevitable end. There is no end, truly, to such a treatment as he uses. It is
as limitless as the universe itself.

This afternoon I was reading him in the Café Miroir (the lugubrious
salle I mentioned previously). The place was crammed full and between the spasms of the orchestra applause and talk. And, tho' I am
obliged to read with the utmost concentration (because of the French)
I held to it excitedly, neither the music nor the applause disturbing
me in the least. From time to time I looked up and allowed my eyes
to rest on the string of café crèmes that ran from one end of the hall
to the other. Certain types here interest me, too, and I would commence dreaming about them. I mean particularly the women—the
sort whom Flaubert would have chosen to write about. Some of them
show signs of suffering—a certain haunted fear between the eyes—
fear of not getting a man, fear of remaining all their lives in this dull
place. There was one especially (I had seen her before in the "caveau"
downstairs). She was so much the lady, the woman of intellect, of
sensitivity. She walks entirely different than the other inhabitants here.
A carriage that a queen might envy. And withal a splendid figure.
Unfortunately, she is not beautiful—nor is she ugly (as most of the
women here are). No, she is just a little âpre, a thin trace of cruelty
or meanness about the mouth, a certain way of sniffing the air dis-
dainfully which will become too painful later as she withers away. She
could almost be saved now—but where is the man?

I almost summoned the courage to go over to her and talk. But the moment she heard my French she would be suspicious—she would not believe that I chose merely to talk.

Another digression, if you will permit it. Last night the fellows took me from one Bal to another. At one of the places I saw a girl (they tell me she is a whore) whom I fell for at once. Many congratulations and pats on the shoulder for my choice! But what they did not perceive was that I fell hard. You know, they take these things so delightfully easy. Their approbation would have been no different had I ordered a very choice wine, for example. Well, I did not dance with the young lady. I sat and watched her dance with the others. I deliberately tortured myself by observing how familiarly the others handled her. I permitted myself to imagine how nonchalantly she gave herself to the first bidder. And I, yes, I would be willing to get down on my knees to her. When she looked my way (and she looked right thru one without being either coarse or bold) I actually began to tremble. I am reconciled to regarding her as unattainable. I want her to be, in fact. I want to feel that, as I walk the streets, I may sometime encounter her, and without her knowing it, follow her from a distance. Only a week here and voilà, une femme! Always seeking for something to worship. Always choosing those who may be had for the asking. What a spectacle!

On the way home, a peculiar little incident. Two young women ahead of me. Rather good-looking. Suddenly, the one drops her bag and all her possessions spill out on the street. Instinctively I bend down and begin collecting the objects (making mental note at the same time of their character). The woman bends over too and our hands touch. And then as she rises—"C'est *trop* aimable. Merci bien, monsieur." All I do is tip my hat. I forgot completely how to say "don't mention it" in French. I was hypnotized by her voice, the emphasis she laid on the words. And then she had said "trop aimable" and my brain worked feverishly to ascertain whether this was an added touch of graciousness or just a variation of the usual thing. And not only that, but the liaison between the "p" and the "a." It was the second time that I had caught it—and foolishly or not, I adore it. "Trop heureux," "trop aimable." Yes, and her hand had touched mine, whether by accident or intentionally, I could not say. Perhaps she had dropped the bag purposely. No, but then why did they giggle when I stepped on, after doffing my hat?

This recalled to my mind the necessity of reading *Buvard et Pécuchet* by Flaubert. M. Renaud characterizes it as a work dealing with two idiots. "Idiots?" I ask. "Are you sure?" "Oui, idiots," he answers. And when I remark enthusiastically that, if it is truly about two idiots I must read it immediately, M. Renaud says: "Vraiment, vous êtes amusant."

M. Renaud and I have been in hot dispute about a short story in *La Nouvelle Revue Française* (Dec. 1931) called "Le Cirque." He finds the language idiotic. There are not sufficient "verbs" in it. The thought is good, but what wouldn't a Flaubert have done with it? And I maintain stoutly that Flaubert could have added nothing—in fact he would have spoiled it. We revolve continually about the subject of form—the classic form. M. Passeleau, on the other hand, excites me by his admiration for Rabelais, Villon, Ronsard. He calls Verlaine the greatest of French poets and recites verses to me (impairs toujours,* he insists). "Impair" to me has this significance only—that at the Métro station d'Iéna, I believe, and perhaps too "Marbeuf" it says "Numéros Impairs" with an arrow. It took me ages to dope out that that meant "odd numbers this side of the street." You see what curious things go on in my mind as I listen to the French language. While M. Passeleau is raving about *La Colline Inspirée* I am asking myself if Maurice Barrès could have been an illegitimate child of Sarah Bernhardt. When he says François Ier I think of: the crazy staircase at Fontainebleau and Henry the Eighth on the field of the cloth of gold—and not a damned thing beyond these. I become furiously impatient to study seriously the entire history of France—from the very earliest times.

At dinner table tonight M. Renaud returns the book on New York which you loaned me. The best thing in the book, he says, is this: "L'écrivain américain a beaucoup à dire, mais il ne sait pas encore s'exprimer. Tandis que vous, en Europe, vous avez maté l'expression, mais vous n'avez plus rien à dire."

Just above this I notice that Waldo Frank is quoted:

"L'Amérique est un géant inquiet, mais encore sans parole."

And now to return to Proust. As soon as I finish the first volume I will send it to you (unless you have already read it). I want you to go

---

* "Always uneven" or "odd" can refer either to the poetic meter or the apparent unintelligibility of many of the poems of the symbolist school to which Verlaine belonged.

over the passages I have marked and sort of cogitate over them. If I can talk it out with you when I get back to Paris, excellent. To write about these passages would require immense patience, though meanwhile, when you have the time and are in the mood, I would welcome a few lines about them. What vitally interests me is the reaction of a feminine mind.

There is one big question in my mind—and that is regarding Albertine's sex. Is it true that the prototype for Albertine was a man, a homo? There are rumors, as you probably know, that Albertine is still alive and may be seen frequently at the Trois Colonnes in the rue de Lappe. I went there once and tried to inquire but got absolutely nowhere. Personally, it is very difficult for me to believe this. I have tried rereading certain passages bearing in mind that Albertine was a fairy and not a lesbian. Some say—what difference does it make, it comes to the same thing? But I am sure you will agree it is not at all the same thing. We know, for example, that Proust married (into Bergson's family, wasn't it?). Wilde, too, was married, and had children, I believe. But Wilde was a satiated individual. Proust I cannot think of in this way—and if he were an invert I can't imagine him marrying. For what reason? Further, his horror of knowing that Albertine was perverse—horror of the thing itself, so far as I make out. And then, all those cruel descriptions of inverts and perverts. (Could this be a manner of turning on oneself, rending oneself?) I doubt, I doubt. And yet, June, for example, showed my novel to a man who is in love with her, and he accepted it as hers, saying at the same time that the woman (knowing it to be June) was a son-of-a-bitch, vile etc. Did he really believe she could write this way about herself? He is supposed to be *quite* intelligent. I don't know him. If I ever ran across him, what a treat it would be to sound him out. The fairy, for example, believed she was the author of it, and he is acutely intelligent—*péniblement*. It was the fairy, too, who insisted that Proust was a homo —"a grand invert"—and regarded me rather contemptuously when I accepted it skeptically. He as much as said that my obtuseness was typically masculine. He pointed out that Proust's excessive ornamentation, his sensuous qualities, his gossip and maliciousness as regards certain characters, were all only too clearly manifestations of the homosexual strain.

Yet, with all this in the back of my head, I cannot feel the truth of it. If for Gilberte, the Duchesse de Guermantes, Odette, etc. etc. I ought to substitute Mr. So-and-So, well then he is a magnificent acrobat. In any case he remains magnificent. In any case we get a full and impartial account of the homosexual field. It seems exhaustive. You remember, he was originally going to call the whole work *Sodom and Gomorrah*. Does the true invert, I ask you, think of his heaven as Sodom and Gomorrah?

Frankly, I am puzzled. If you can marshal any authentic information on the subject, I would be elated.

Tell me a little about *Buvard et Pécuchet* and *La Colline Inspirée*.

I find that the bawdyhouses are grouped right near the lycée. The street bears the delightful name of "Philibert Papillon, Bibliographe." I have not yet been inside one, but the outsides are pleasant. One of them has a beautiful little outhouse attached to it, whence comes the odor of fried chicken, pommes frites, garlic etc. If my sailor friend were here he would by this time have made the acquaintance of the Madame and be inviting his friends to dinner on the rue Philibert Papillon. My own inclinations lean that way. I am sure they eat better and more enjoyably then we do here.

Incidentally, the conversation at table is of an order beyond description, as are the manners. It is absolutely Rabelaisian. No pruriency, but a great gusto, an insatiable lust. Everything is tied up with the sexual organs and the process of evacuation. Betweenwhiles a great belching on all sides together with dogfights for the last morsel of meat, the last piece of cake. The only thing that remains is the wine— and that is where I display my swinishness. Sometimes, for the love of the spectacle, I refuse to eat my allotted share. The scramble that ensues is hilarious. They go at it like a pack of hyenas. The conversation at table is damned near incomprehensible to me. It is explained to me later. And, to be sure, the same chaps who were spilling this jargon a moment before are the very ones who delight me with the purity of their speech. It is now or never that I am going to become acquainted with the poetry of Rimbaud and Verlaine.

In closing, I give you a little excerpt of Proust that jolted me:

> "Je me disais, 'Elle aime peut-être les femmes,' comme on dit 'Je peux mourir ce soir'; on se le dit, mais on ne le croit pas, on fait des projets pour le lendemain."

Sincerely,

HENRY V. MILLER

[February 12, 1932]
Dijon, Lycée Carnot, Friday

ANAÏS—

At midnight last night my table was so littered with notes that, unable to digest it all and frame a coherent letter, I gave up in despair and went to bed. The room has become infinitely more habitable since (after two weeks) I discovered that the light could be manipulated. I must tell you that the big coal box in my room is an object which I look at with a deal of affection. It is the best object in the room.

It is freezing now (as I suppose it is in Paris, too) and all the plumbing is out of order, frozen. That means that the Lycée is deranged. That means a sort of existence which you got vividly in *The House of the Dead* [Dostoevski]. In addition, consider that owing to the bad diet in the last few days every one is constipated or showing up with "buttons"—and so, just at the moment when the plumbing fails every one is taking laxatives. My fear of going to the trenches has been based largely on a horror of vermin, on lack of sanitary conveniences—not fear of bullets. This is just a step beyond trench life.

So, all your talk of Dostoevski hit me hard. I was full of him last night. It seems that everything you said against him you retracted magnificently as you went on. I thought the line "is guessing at something so fantastic that he writes like a medium" very good; swell. Of course "he could not coordinate the vast chaos." But the attempt! And what does it matter about *wallowing* in it? It is a bath in the richest effluvia we have ever had. And when you said "he did not grasp psychology with his two hands" why I said to myself "fortunately no!" Psychology is the attempt to give name to the nameless. You know that every few years will see the terminology change and with it the theories, interpretations, etc.

It is a pity that we shall never have the opportunity to read again or see a man placed at the very core of mystery, and by his flashes not merely illuminating things for us, but showing us the depth, the immensity of the darkness. You yourself, as you reread Gide, caught this—but then there is a phrase "perhaps not with just enough mind to be fully aware of all the secrets." The mind doesn't help, don't you see? Gide has mind, Dostoevski has the other thing, and it is what Dostoevski has that really matters—whatever it be called. I recall my discussions with June who worships Dostoevski, and how I picked flaws in him, pointed out his bad artistry, all those things which annoy you so much. I did that when confronted with a June. But when I confront you I defend him arduously. As Nietzsche said somewhere— "you have to first learn to love before you destroy," or something to that effect. He was referring to those anti-Christians who had not yet learned the wisdom of Christianity. Do I make myself clear? Or am I perhaps unfair in citing this? Yes, I agree with you, Gide's explanation aroused in me the same admiration. There were passages that almost baffled me . . . it is three or four years since I read it so I cannot speak more specifically. But then, as I once told you there is a Scandinavian who has done even better than Gide in a book of the same proportions. I think his name is Janko Lavrin, and perhaps he is Hungarian and not Swedish.*

Regarding the *Idiot* and those two years of Stavrogin's in Moscow we get so ineffectively, do you know that this part was eliminated from the book (I think it was censored). Anyway today there is a book giving you passages and notes on all this which was merely hinted at. And remember above all, that Dostoevski had neither time nor money. He was writing for money which he always used up in advance. His life was terrible, terrible. No chance to fashion things out artistically, to digest the problems in his mind. He had to write against starvation, sickness and what not. All in all, it is nothing short of a miracle that he accomplished.

There is another man who has understood him well—John Cowper Powys. I had the pleasure of hearing him lecture and later read his books. There is one—a criticism of modern authors—I forget the title. Look it up; you will find it absorbing. And you will begin to appreciate Conrad too, whom I suspect you feel tepidly about. Finally, I feel about Dostoevski now that anything he did was all right. I not only forgive, I applaud, I admire. (Only, no reverence!) I leave that for June.

As for Goethe—that is another story entirely. He is one whom, like Dante, I always felt I *should* admire, and never could. The other night I attended a celebration of his anniversary at the University. I feel more than ever that I am right about him. I am *against* him, against his placid, serene, super-bourgeois attitude, his healthy pantheistic

---

* Janko Lavrin, born in 1887 in Croatia, wrote *Dostoevski and His Creation, A Psycho-Critical Study,* London, Collins, 1920, and his book, *Studies in European Literature,* London, Constable, 1929, contains a chapter on Dostoevski and Proust.

embrace of the universe, his imitative reverence for Nature, etc. etc.; Nietzsche and Goethe? How do they reconcile them? These things baffle me. I am sure that *Faust* is tedious, and if it's Gothic, then it bears no resemblance to these marvelous cathedrals that I adore. No, these Germans who stood up solemnly and recited Goethe in their barbarous tongue left me cold, and slightly melancholy. I put Rabelais over and against Goethe. Even Cervantes or Swift. I enclose the program notes to convince you. Read what Goethe said about the German cities. Fatuous!

Oddly enough, I picked up last night an article on "Sénèque le Tragique." Remark the following:

"Par cette intelligence, rival de Sophocle, Sénèque est pourtant plus près de nous encore: car tous les sentiments que nous croyons avoir inventés, il les connaissait. Le gout maladif de la pitié, presque sadique, ce ne sont pas les romans russes qui l'ont mis à la mode pour la première fois. Sénèque en 1900 eut-il aimé Dostoevski?"

Then this which I question. . . . ". . . Sénèque le Tragique était un très grand poète et que, comme Eschyle, Shakespeare ou Baudelaire, il était joint au monde par des liens mystérieux . . ." (Why Baudelaire?)

This I like very much:

> "De celui qui a touché les lacs des serments divins
> Il ne reste rien, nulle part! . . .
> Il n'y a rien après la Mort, et la Mort elle-même n'est rien,

> "C'est la borne suprême d'un stade vertigineux . . .
> Où seras-tu, veux-tu le dire, après la Mort?
> Où sont les êtres avant de naître."

Put beside it this of Max Jacob: "Musique Mécanique Dans un Bistro. Le corbeau d'Edgar Poe a une auréole qu'il éteint parfois." Or—
"Le pauvre examine le manteau de Saint Martin et dit: 'Pas de poches?' "

O.K. Max. A good attempt. You have listened to the music of Picasso's guitars. (Apologies to Cocteau)

I sent a second letter to Switzerland, did you get it? And did I enclose the book list I had promised? Don't be terrified by the avalanche of mail. It is a bad habit of mine, and as I can do no work with the pen it is just a way of letting off steam. You almost make me weep with your flattering words. No, I am far from being the artist you imagine. Maybe there are in me possibilities—they have not yet come to fruition. But your friendship, your wonderful sympathy, is everything.

Have just come from class after a fine session. It is astounding the progress these boys are making. What a multitude of subjects we cover in a short time, and as the news goes around that I am a good egg the class increases in size, a number of them returning day after day because it's warm and entertaining in my class. It seems that my predecessors used to hand out newspapers and ask them to read, which bored them stiff. Again and again we come back to the subject of woman. Today in search of beauty we went all round the globe, with pleasant stop-offs in Japan, Tahiti, Martinique, Bali, Polynesia. And they admitted that the French woman is rarely beautiful (I find we don't talk about America so very much; in fact, I am letting them educate me; my questions are inexhaustible). As for the profs they never notice me. In the hierarchy that exists here I fall somewhere between the repetiteur and the veilleur de nuit. The latter is marvelous, perfect, as a type. He is stiff like an automaton, from cold and rheumatism. Has big red cheeks, close-cropped hair, a magnificent paunch, and speaks slowly, caressing the words gently as a dog; when he comes in for his two glasses of wine in the evening it is a treat. I wish I could paint him!!! Van Gogh would have adored him. And if everyone spoke French like him how easy it would be for me. He liquefies everything; when he opens his mouth I feel that I am in Capri or Naples, warm Mediterranean sunshine, Pompeiian ruins, olive groves, succulent oranges, the whole earth in flower. *He is really the only human being here!* (Underlined for posterity; my indictment of French educational system.) And for this he is given a lantern, a bunch of keys, rheumatism and two glasses of vin ordinaire gratuit. It is Monsieur l'Économe who should be given the night watchman's job. I would change all this. When he opens the door for me he inquires so solicitously if I am cold, if I were waiting long, etc. And then suddenly I see beyond him a constellation hanging brilliantly over the chapel and I have a feeling of envy for him. It is wonderful on a mild night, to stand in the courtyard in that silence which makes your temples hammer and look up at the brilliant sky. Then too he has his little cubbyhole in the loge where he cooks and reads and snoozes, no doubt.

Every hour or so he picks up the lantern and the keys and makes the rounds—through the frozen halls, the paint peeling off, the stairs clammy, the windowpanes frosted. It's the most eerie sight, entering the dormitory; I'll never forget it. How much more wonderful is his life (for the poet) than that of M. le Proviseur. Does M. le Proviseur ever look at the stars? Does M. l'Économe ever take a swig from the bottle or pronounce his vowels? There was one grand night recently when I had such a sense of well-being that I could scarcely support—what? I don't know. Everything affected me to an unusual degree. I was waiting a half hour or so for the door to open. I had a chance to take in everything leisurely—the dead tree in front of the school, with branches that looked like rope, the houses across the way which had taken on different colors in the night, the sound of the train rolling through the night . . . then from somewhere two lovers suddenly appeared and I watched them. Every few yards they stopped and embraced, and when I couldn't see them any more, I could hear the footsteps, the sudden cessation and then once again their steps as they slowly meandered along. And then I thought of June—was she wandering around alone, leading a solitary life? Not likely. And if I could know at that moment where she was, what she was doing, what then? The horrible thing is, not that we care so much, but that we want to know. And when we know the facts that doesn't satisfy either. We want to know her thoughts, her attitudes, her real longings and desires. We want to know what even she herself does not fully know. In your letter there are two or three paragraphs which torture me. Albertine = June . . . "this world, etc. you are not meant to enter." True, but I will never cease to bang my head against the doors. If I don't get a glimpse of that world I shall go mad. No, I do not want it symbolically. You are making it too difficult. It is already obscure enough and now you want to tack on a long vestibule through which I must grope painfully. Already in these lines you mystify me. You are talking a language that is beyond me. And the elusiveness of it enrages me. What good is my intellect? What new organs must I grow? A sentence, for instance, like—"It is a matter of language"—baffles me. It *must* be a matter of language, else why wouldn't I understand it, seize it? I mean this in many ways. I mean, for example, that it is so paralyzingly baffling to know when a woman says one thing that she means another, many things, yes and no at once. Proust points out numerous examples, *but* . . . how do we know that he knows what he is talking about? It is splendidly convincing because there is no real, tangible Albertine, or Andrée, or Duchesse de Guermantes to jump up and contradict him. It has the verisimilitude of art, and that is all I can concede. Of course, his frequent reiteration that "we are absolutely alone, isolate, incomprehensible and mysterious" is the admission of his ineffectuality. But we need to say it over to ourselves again and again, day after day.

I read *Vol de Nuit* [by Saint-Exupéry] recently and found it splendid. All the surveillants are reading it (it is in good condition). And the opinion is unanimous, that it is of high merit. Those passages above the earth, especially that final flight—simply superb. If an American wrote with such tempo he would lose everything. Gide's preface adds nothing to the book. He might better have kept his mouth shut. And Rivière, the boss, have you noticed what a Jack London superman he is? Yet, of course, his ruminations were infinitely better than the Sea Wolf's. He had digested his Nietzsche better, and the distance in time added softness to the rugged contours of the philosophy. But I imagine such a type as Rivière is rare in French literature. He comes with the machine. M. Renaud finds the style eminently satisfactory— the classic and the modern are united harmoniously. It is not idiocy, as in "Le Cirque." Alors, qu'est-ce que c'est l'idiotie? On ne sait pas ici.

One little echo of Proust—an arc instead of a rainbow:

"Pour cette femme aussi la mort de Fabien commencerait demain à peine, dans chaque acte désormais vain, dans chaque object. Fabien quitterai lentement sa maison."

Many, many beautiful tender bits. I can't refrain from citing this one, toward the end:

"Fabien erre sur la splendeur d'une mer de nuages, la nuit, mais, plus bas, c'est l'éternité. Il est perdu parmi les constellations qu'il habite seul. Il tient encore le monde dans les mains et contre sa poitrine le balance. Il serre dans son volant le poids de la richesse humaine, et promène, désesperé, d'une toile à l'autre, l'inutile trésor, qu'il faudra bien rendre. . . ."

Put that into the Queen's own English and it will never approach the beauty which the French gives it. You don't know how grateful I am for the loan of these French books. When I return at Easter I will bring them all with me and ask you for a few more if I may. Your home reminds me of that line from the Bible—"in my father's house there are many mansions" . . . only I am not sure now—is it *house?* House sounds wrong. But it's the mansions I'm thinking of.

Incidentally do you know the Book of Ecclesiastes? That, you know, is my favorite, when it comes to Biblical gems. That language of the Bible—if you can swim in that you've got the English language. It remains the very best that ever was written in our tongue.

I could gallop on like this all day. It reminds me of Fred. What letters he wrote! In French, German, English, now and then Italian and Latin. Now and then illustrations. Now and then slipping in a page of mine (written to someone else). Fred's friend swallowed them like oysters on the half shell. More, more! she cried, and Fred would beg me for carbon copies, for old newspaper articles. What a hungry maw she had. Simply insatiable. And if the letter dwindled to nine or ten pages she would commence to whine.

Which reminds me—before leaving Paris I wrote X. asking if I might borrow some of my letters in order to copy out certain passages. I received the more or less stereotyped reply that she had destroyed them "on the day when my actions no longer corresponded to my words." I think that's the exact phrase. That tells you precisely what she was like. And since I never *did* anything, except to ignore her, it becomes almost comical. But I can tell you, I dropped a few beads of sweat when I read that the letters were destroyed. (Frankly, I don't believe it!) It wasn't X. I was writing to. She was just a pretext. She used to write me the most inane replies and I would take them, work over them, blow them up to monstrous and hallucinating proportions. Half the time I was writing for Fred's benefit. And if there was anything incomprehensible, anything inapropos, mysterious, off-key in my letters she never observed it; they were always "beautiful, touching, marvelous," etc. Once I gave her a dose from "Le Poisson Soluble" *—she thought that was touching, fine, etc. too. But I must admit I loved her . . . for a while. I suppose I'll go on loving, one after the other, this way, but June always holding me, negating them all, proving to me how insignificant are the others. God, if she only realized how tremendous is my passion for her. She would never then be the least jealous. It infuriates me to see her jealous. It's like being hanged for a wolf instead of a sheep, or a rabbit.

---

* André Breton's Surrealist manifesto, 1924.

Do you think of writing June sometime? I am curious to see if she will answer you. Have you an address for her? That story about the man whose love she killed for me—I was wrong when I said she lied. No, I was confused. I know now whom she means. I was thinking at the time of another man, a recent one, and I thought she meant that it was from him she had run away. I wish I could open up a section of my brain and show you just my thoughts about that episode. How the devil one can manage to lock all the doors that lead to the madhouse is beyond me. I only need to put the door on a crack, just one door, and there is enough to provide a night's rich meditation. A night! A euphemism!

Haven't heard anything yet about the salary. Wrote Krans a letter last night. Have you heard anything?

Sincerely,

HENRY

[Dijon, February 13, 1932]
Saturday

ANAÏS:

Just received your two letters and realize that you did get the second letter sent to Switzerland. If the typewriter has a standard American keyboard I certainly will be able to use it, and even if it is somewhat different I can no doubt get adjusted. My desire for the regular keyboard is because I type very fast and if I have to think where the keys are I get lost. The first letter says you are sending it and the second one asks—can you use it? I dispatched a long letter last night.

That you found the old novel [Crazy Cock] good in parts and that you think it could be doctored and made publishable is well. Sure I would be delighted if you would go over it and prune it. Even if only a hundred pages remain and they are good, why O.K. Perhaps I could reciprocate some time by doing the same for you. Go ahead and make a stab at it. Nothing but good can result. I can always trim down to French proportions. I think too I would agree with you on whatever you wanted to cut. And after you get through with it I be-

lieve I would have sufficient enthusiasm to make further revisions myself. I remember the dream passage—I know I could improve that
too. You get me excited about it.

I think you are dead right about the hyper-sexuality, the effect of so
many women, etc. Strange that the Cora episode came off so feebly.
Cora was the most important influence in my early life; I think she
maimed me. (I saw her later after she was married and had a child—
and what a wet rag she turned out to be. But when I dream about her
as I sometimes do, she is magnificent. I'll touch on all that in the
book.)

Jesus—about the typewriter! No, damn it, I may be a rogue but I
wouldn't do that.* I have done that sort of thing in the past. You make
me laugh when I read your words. How well you know the artist's
irresponsibility. But I seem incapable of that now—I think I should
regret it, don't you?

You also make me laugh talking about Casanova. You don't know
yet what men are like, pardon. I am fairly normal. It is true I swim
in a perpetual sea of sex but the actual excursions are fairly limited.
I think it's more like this—that I'm always ready to love, always
hungry to love. I'm talking about love, not just sex. And I don't mind
at all saturating my work with it—*sex* I mean—because I'm not afraid
of it and I almost want to stand up and preach about it, like that nut
in [Robinson Jeffers'] *The Women at Point Sur*. He was cracked and
people forgive that, but I am quite sane, too sane almost, madly sane.
No, I'll stop explaining myself. I'll let you explain me to myself—that
sounds intelligent and fantastic. Don't worry about offending me—
that's quite impossible.

You did jolt me anent Proust. Then I was quite wrong. Then he
was a homo after all. All right, I accept your dictum—probably you
know. But what a jackass I am! No, it still mystifies me. Agreed, that
Albertine is unsatisfactory—incomplete. But, I can show you dozens
of examples in literature where the women are incomplete—and they
were men who wrote the books. What I am overlooking perhaps is
that Albertine or no Albertine, *or just Albert,* it makes no difference.
What we are enthralled by is the vast panorama of deceit, treachery,
lying, jealousy. It's the phenomenon and not the creature who pro-
vokes it. Cézanne took artificial flowers and fruit, other men's

---

* Anaïs Nin had jokingly suggested that Miller might hock or sell the typewriter she was trying to get for him.

chromos, and behold! Van Gogh looked at a field of corn, a blazing sun, and my God, does one see corn or sun any more?

About your book [*House of Incest*]—it is hard for me to deal with it specifically without having it before me. I have only the flavor of it now. As a rule, I have a very bad memory for plot. I could not tell you the story of even my favorite books. I don't care much about that element. In your case I was so interested in the way you went at it that the story was almost effaced. It was only when I was brought up with a start at that one point that I was obliged to become aware of the story. My best recollection of that swift reading was that I was living a dream, and that's what I think makes it a beautiful book. If I could help you concretely believe me I would be only too glad to. You see, I read to appreciate, and not to criticize. If, for example, you are retyping it, and you would want to send me a carbon as you go along I would sit down and give you criticism and suggestions. Maybe it is too late for all that. My impression is so favorable that I doubt whether you actually need help.

The folder of B.F.P. is impressive.* What is very curious is to find you in company with Mark Twain and Djuna Barnes. Do you know her? I once interviewed her with Wambly Bald.** She was cool as a cucumber, quick-witted and very tastefully dressed. We asked her if she had ever heard of June Mansfield? † She said no. As for that Mark Twain thing, I remember reading it years ago, but I am damned if I saw anything Rabelaisian about it. Anyway there you are—"between the boards" as they say. Congratulations! How does it look to be in print?

As for names. In Paris, I can't think of anybody who has money to buy, except [Michael] Fraenkel.†† I give you these names, in case you are also able to send books to America. And if I think of others in the future I will send them on. I think June ought to be able to interest a number of people. Send her a few circulars. . . .

I have been wondering if I might not be capable of translating a modern French book for sale. I started on *Salavin* but I am afraid,

---

* *Books from Paris,* a mail order service, announced Anaïs Nin's Lawrence study.
** See Biographical Notes.
† "June Mansfield" was the pseudonym under which Henry Miller and his second wife, June Smith, sold privately printed copies of Miller's prose poems during the days they lived on Remsen Street in Brooklyn.
†† See Biographical Notes.

owing to Duhamel's present popularity, that the rights for translation have all been arranged for. This seems to me the only method of earning a little money. I have spoken to the Proviseur here and the English professor and they don't seem very optimistic about my getting pupils at this time of the year. Pupils too can be out of season.

HENRY

P. S. I must seem pretty nonchalant in the way I pass over your gifts and aid. I appreciate very deeply your lending me your own machine. Does it mean, however, that you won't have one yourself? Or can you rent or borrow one in Paris? Because I have just received a letter from my former pupil in Neuilly—the businessman. He offers to rent one for me through his firm at a moderate price and says that I will not need to put down a guaranty. Please state frankly, therefore, how you are situated. It hurts me to know that you are pinching and scraping to aid me. I think sometimes I'm nothing but a big bum. Damn it, if I could find a way to earn a living I'd sell myself for the remainder of my life. That's honest!

HVM

[Dijon, February 21, 1932]
Sunday

Encore une et c'est fini, la grande correspondance.

I'm quitting—happy as a convict getting his release.

I received a telegram and letter from my friend Fred saying that the editor offered me a permanent job on the *Tribune* as assistant finance editor. Salary to start 1200 frs. [about $45] a month (pas beaucoup!) but a chance for an increase soon. The hours are 8:30 P.M. to 1:00 A.M. (my hours) and the work easy.

What could I do but accept? It means a sort of independence, *Paris,* and *life.* I will be able to write as the day is mine. And I get a day off a week.

Do you blame me for accepting? I hope not. I think it was prudent and wise. Believe me, if they send another American down here he better be a Chink or an Eskimo.

Incidentally, the machine did not arrive yet. I do *not leave until Tuesday noon*—reporting for work that night. I think the machine ought to arrive before then. But if not, I will leave explicit instructions with one of my trusted friends here.

I had no dough to return with and could not be sure that Fred would raise it—he is always in a hell of a mess. Hence the telegram. I asked for a little more because of taxi, my laundry and shoes which I have not been able to take out. You see, the other money went largely for supplementary meals. Everybody eats on the side here—impossible to go along on their grub.

My address temporarily will be % Chicago Tribune, 5 rue Lamartine, Paris. Excuse haste—mailing this in a hurry.

HENRY

[Paris, February 27, 1932]
2:00 A.M. Saturday

Any paper but ordinary white paper! I have been making the rounds of humble and obscure restaurants of late. I found a good one —for rotten food and droll types.* It is alongside the stage entrance of the Folies Bergères where I used to deliver insecticide with my Russian friend, Prince ——, whose father was admiral on the battleship *Potemkin*. Cité Saulnier is one of my favorite streets after dark.

The answer which I had commenced to your letter I destroyed. I am answering it piecemeal. I am thinking of so many things now that I am a little crazy. You see I have begun to think again—to think in terms of writing. I am falling back into myself. Monday a typewriter arrives, and soon a batch of mail from June, according to a little note appended to the letter of a friend which she sent me today. Big doings afoot, she says. She speaks optimistically again. There is something in the wind.

And as for me, things are looking up. I am elated. I wake up now after five or six hours sleep and am thinking of the next line for my book. At the same time I am thinking in terms of color. I want time too to make a few water colors, at least one or two every day. I want to read all the French books I can get hold of. I want to do everything.

---

* The café Au Rendez-vous des Machinistes in the rue Saulnier.

I am alive again and my fingers fly over the paper. Bon! Yes, and
Rilke is good in spots. Very much like Duhamel in *Salavin* at times. I
will show you what I mean later. I am marking several passages. I
join up with them, with Salavin and Laurids Malte Brigge. I am a sort
of a quelconque quiconque also. A saint. I am thinking in every direction . . . the new explosivism.

The article was a little enigmatic to me. Some times my French
breaks down—especially when I am fatigued. I am going to tackle it
some morning when I am shaving and whistling. Yes, I have begun to
whistle and sing mornings. Oranges first, and then porridge at the
Coupole. Dinner at Fred's [Alfred Perlès'] room, where we fry pork
chops and potatoes over an alcohol lamp and look at our old water
colors sort of hypnotized. Yes, I mentioned Stefan Zweig's book * to
you—and so did June. She was impressed by it. I was keenly disappointed, especially since the French critics had praised it highly. We
had a big battle over it one night in the Rotonde and I vanquished all
my adversaries together. Zweig is old-fashioned in this. Belongs to
the Buddenbrooks school of writing . . . too much antimacassar. (I
sorely need some new words; my vocabulary is rusty of late!) But
read that story of 24 hours in a woman's life—I want to tell you what
is wrong with it psychologically. There is another story which is better.

HENRY

[Hotel Central, 1 bis Rue du Maine, Paris 14
March 6, 1932]
Sunday, 1:30 A.M.

ANAÏS:

The most grueling pace tonight. Have just been to the Trois
Portes for a couple of beers. Trembling as I swallow them, from the

---

* Born in Vienna, in 1881, Zweig belonged to the neo-romantic School of
German-language writers. Known as a poet, essayist and dramatist, Zweig also
published a few volumes of novella collections, among them *Amok, The
Necklace,* and *Conflicts (Three Tales,* including "24 Hours in a Woman's Life,"
translated by Eden and Cedar Paul, New York, The Viking Press, 1927), to
which Miller refers. Zweig committed suicide in Brazil in 1942.

pace at which I worked. Absolutely dizzy with figures . . . dizzy, dizzy, I tell you. And the strange thing is I don't mind it. I get keyed up.

And today, bundled up in bathrobe, an overcoat, a muffler and hat, I sat down and wrote ten more pages for the book [*Tropic of Cancer*]. After writing ten pages Fred drags me to a restaurant on the rue St. Anne to show me a princess whom he discovered the other night. I didn't want to meet any princess, and fortunately she wasn't there. But there was a priest opposite us and a giant, and they talked Spanish all during the meal.

I am being constantly interrupted. I will try to continue at home.

Have been to see Leo Stein [brother of Gertrude]. A rare Sunday afternoon in the presence of a man with a mind. The word human never entered our conversation—we dwelled for three hours in the realm of pure ideas. And though I shall have lots to say and write about him, this bores through everything he said and penetrates me: "The word *real* should not be used as an adjective; we should say only *really*" . . . *really what?* At sixty he is just learning to conquer his inhibitions. I thought I should be intimidated but I found I could play with him. I was kind to him—I scarcely opened my mouth.

I learn from Fred that we have to traverse a dangerous district on our way to Clichy—that is the short distance from the Porte to the house. Feel good about it. Planning to get back the heavy Mexican cane that I brought from America, a cane I gave to the son of Admiral Potemkin. Fred wants to carry a knife. Fine. I can see in advance the state of the office upon hearing the news of our death. Jules, the editor, will say— "Fellows, stop a minute. Miller and Perlès have just been killed. Will somebody write a little notice?" And then, Egan, the sports writer, will start a collection for flowers. And at the Trois Portes they will drink a little heavier during the break in order to brace themselves. And all I would wish is that I might have eyes to see their faces on the way to the cemetery. Lee Dickson, from Tin Pan Alley, wiping his eyes and saying "my buddies." The compositors chalking up the collection on the sheet next to the telephone—ah, les Américains, mon Dieu!

Off for Street Scene . . .

HENRY

[Clichy, April, 1932]
Sunday

Have just left the cinema after seeing *City Lights* with the profound conviction that Chaplin is great. For years I have been railing against him, but now, after those last two minutes of the film, I believe in him. He will give us something powerful in the years to come. This picture marks a turning point. It has almost a Shakespearean quality.

I looked around me when I left to see if anyone else had wet eyes. There was a dead silence at the close—it was impressive. But I did not see any one weeping. Why was I weeping then? I tell you, I wept bitterly. That moment when he turned and confronted her in the window—that very moment I let out a sob. I couldn't stifle it. He had prepared it well. There was a splendid somberness in his movements as he wandered forlornly through the streets. Certain gestures in front of shop windows, gestures of futility, of hiding away, began to register on me with terrific force. I know precisely what it is to feel hunted, to stalk aimlessly up and down a street, staring idly at things, being shoved and pushed around and yet so blunted or stunned by an inner pain as to welcome it, as though each contact with an elbow or shoulder helped to restore you to physical awareness. I know exactly how one stands with hand in pocket and coat collar turned up—a sort of glorious feeling of disreputability. Did you know that I have actually panhandled—*in New York?* Yes, once I even trailed another guy and cornered him, threatened to shake him down if he didn't come across. That was at Times Square during the theatre rush. It's a marvelous story and sometime I'll tell it to you.

It is hard for me to get down to what I wish to say. I was intending to go to the *Tribune* to type but I felt I would lose everything before I got there. I went up to my room, but it was so cold I came right down again. Then I dashed to the Select, and in my excitement I ordered food that I didn't need. I changed my place because of the draft and then gave the chasseur a big tip for changing my pen. In this mood I am crazy enough to spend a hundred francs for a pen point, but as I never carry a hundred francs with me it's all right.

It all starts from the time I got up. I woke up bursting to write. Had made a date with [Wambly] Bald to call for him soon as I got up, have breakfast with him and help him write his column. Well, I ducked him, thinking it more important to do my own work. But as luck would have it Osborn sees me and I am obliged to sit and listen to his nonsense about Spengler for an hour and a half. Finally, just as I am breaking away, I stumble into Bald. "Jesus, I've been looking all over for you," he says, beaming with joy. "Yeah, I've been looking for you, too," I say, lying gracefully. "Joe," he says, "you don't know what a service you're doing me. There's an English lord in town who thinks I'm hot. He may give me a job on his paper. We gotta write a good column. It means everything to me."

When I hear that I melt. So we go to his room and he gives me an idea of what he wants—only it's terribly vague. "Do you need a bottle, Joe?" he asks. "No, Joe, I'm O.K. only beat it. Let me get to it." "But do you know what you're going to write?" "No, but I will soon."

But before he goes he tells me a story about some woman whom he had in his room recently. The story robs me of my wits completely. I shut the door on him and look at my money. The temptation is to bust right out of the room and go somewhere. I pace up and down feverishly. Then I get angry with myself, sit down and begin to punch the keys. When I have written a page he returns with a bottle of Cointreau and a woman. The woman throws herself on the bed and Joe falls on top of her. In desperation I tackle the bottle. Now I am completely unnerved, but it has become a point of pride— to finish the column under any circumstance. So while he mauls her I write about thermometers and mental climate. I don't know what I am writing but I keep draining the bottle. Every once in a while he opens the window to let out the smoke and then the girl puts her dresses down. It takes me a couple of hours to finish page three. Finally Joe asks for the key to my room and goes off with the girl. When I stagger out of the room I am completely drunk. After dinner I sober up a bit and look at the papers to see what cinema to go to. It is my night off, and since I can't write I decide to entertain myself. I feel it's coming to me. What I wanted to do was to go to Studio 28 but it is too far and I am dead on my feet. So I go to the Rue de la Gaieté prepared in advance to be disappointed.

The first picture I see, Bebe Daniels and Ben Lyons, softens me up. Jimmie and Gertie are a couple of crooks. They try to go straight and it's a hard job. That gives you an idea what it's about, but it doesn't explain my reactions. It is a silent picture, you see, and when I find I can read their lips I experience a strange elation. For one thing I suddenly get homesick. All my Americanism asserts itself, and it astonishes me. For instance, when at a crucial point, Bebe says to him mutely: "Do you mean that, Jimmie" (which is not translated on the screen) I live for a moment so tensely that I am afraid my temples will burst. I see all over again how immature our women are and at the same time I see its charm, and I know that nobody in the audience is getting what I am getting—this blood secret. At the end I turn to my neighbor, a young Frenchman, and ask him how he found the picture —I must get somebody's reaction. "Pas mal, monsieur," he says. "Pas de tout." And that pleases me too—his putting it negatively. It is so civilized. Of course we use the same expression, but the French seem to employ it more intelligently. My ears were still ringing with a drunken speech of Osborn's and this was refreshing by contrast. I liked Bebe Daniels in spite of her oyster eyes and cruel mouth. I know she's an ass, I know the play was poor, but I was reliving certain scenes in America. One thing particularly—it was suggested by the detective. You see, once June and I had a strange experience with a detective. We were eating in an Italian restaurant in Brooklyn Heights, where they served red wine. We were known there and always well received. One night whilst eating we had a discussion about the police. I had received a visit one day from the lieutenant of the precinct because of an article which I wrote about the brutality shown by a cop to a Negro. The article, which was printed on cardboard, fell into the hands of the police. We were living then in a gorgeous place on Remsen Street—an old mansion. The lieutenant was rather amazed when he saw the joint, and I think, at the same time, rather suspicious. June was there fortunately. I say fortunately because I became so insolent, during the course of the conversation, that I am sure he would have made trouble for me. June, however, extricated me and the lieutenant left in good fettle. However, at the restaurant we got talking about the subject. There was a young woman at the table, rather good-looking. She was enjoying it. At the next table sat a detective, taking it all in. Finally he came over and asked permission to sit down. I was annoyed. I sized him up immediately and again became very insulting. Instead of resenting this, he became more and more friendly, and ordered wine and then cordials. Finally he invited us to go with him to a cabaret. This was a droll scene. June and I were completely out of place. We stood at the door, hesitating to go further. And then suddenly, just as it happens in a Dostoevski novel, this dull oaf jerked out a crucifix and kissing it first himself, begged us to kiss it in turn and swear eternal friendship. Can you see us going through that farce? Can you picture me on the morrow, writing with a clear head, a letter begging him for the rent money? Reminding him of our eternal vows? I don't know whether you understand this. We did not need the money. I did it in order to outrage him—a protest against that stupid scene in the cabaret. Naturally, he never answered the letter. That irritated me too. So I sent him a telegram. Nothing availed. The incident was closed.

All right, I'm getting closer to the Chaplin film. At the Coupole this afternoon I ran into the fairy. He told me he was going back to the States in two weeks. Now, despite the fact that I know how he has stuck his money away—in ten-franc notes and dollar bills—I have a hunch that June sent him money to return. It's a mad idea, but I have a hunch. You know, June wrote about three lines—a postscript to the letter of a friend—saying that things were good and that big mail was following on the S.S. *France* which isn't even listed yet. Believe me, there will be no such mail on that boat. Wait and see. Anyway, she is well and apparently in good spirits, and that buoys me up considerably.

I am going to bring the notes tomorrow that I promised to show you. Perhaps a few other things. Not having been to the office today I don't know if there is mail—that is, if you have canceled the meeting at the Rotonde for Monday. But I shall be there nevertheless. You don't know what you have done to encourage me to write.

So I come to Chaplin—to his grandeur. How I trembled for him as the final scene approached. That humiliation, which was very cruel, at the hands of the newsboys, that augured well. (I wondered fleetingly how much he owed to Jannings—the "Blue Angel" scene.) But then he went on to something more profound. It was perfect, the acting at this point. When he said "You see now?" and she replied "Yes, I see . . ." that was splendid. We've had it from time immemorial in legends and fables and fairy tales, but it was new again. When we open our eyes we suffer. How true that is! Heretofore he has not had the courage to conclude at this point. He has always done some silly things to divert us. But now, as he grows older, he learns. What he has been hinting at for so long may yet be realized. One day we may get from Chaplin a tragedy of the highest order. It is in his blood. There is so much I want to put in the book. I made notes in Dijon

which now, when I look at them, I am almost afraid to transliterate.
June will never, never appreciate this. It's like sealing my own death
warrant to write these things, yet I must. I have an impersonal feeling
about it, despite the immense amount of ego sticking out everywhere.
Really, I can't consider myself an egotist, or egoist (June loves to
dwell on the difference between these two). No, I feel merely like
a force which must express itself, at any cost. I keep on writing preliminary things out of fear that I will scorch and sear. You encourage me in this. Listen, with your clear, bright head, are you sure I
am not crazy? I mean, is all this personal narration justifiable? You
see me weak for once. It is mostly a question of art. No, that's untrue.
I really don't give a damn about art. But I sense already the storm
of antagonism which this book will provoke. People are going to say
that I am a monster, a moral imbecile, that I belong in the asylum. I
know I am sane as the devil. Almost too sane. Do you know what I
mean by that—how, when you are too too sane you come close to
madness, to criminality?

And I must confess that if I had to battle this out with June I would
surrender. In a way, it is fortunate that she is gone. Because if I were
made to feel that I had to choose between her and what I call *my art,*
I would choose her. I am a coward where she is concerned. No other
woman could do that to me—I swear it! What then am I doing when
I write these things? You don't know all that I mean to say. I begin to
think even you will balk. But I have said to myself "there must be
no limits." I must be the one person in the world to risk everything,
tell everything. I am positively fanatical about it. So, too, I don't
care much if the writing gets sloppy or awkward now and then, though
before I am through with it I *will* make certain revisions, and perhaps
do some healthy pruning.

When you asked if I thought my writing might be interpreted as
erotic I must say yes, but that isn't enough—just yes. I don't think of
it as being defined by this or that, as representing this or that. I am
trying to be a man, to speak as a man speaks, and not to leave out
anything because of principles, art, or whatever it may be that has
constrained men heretofore. And I write in the first person in order
to get closer to verisimilitude—not for the sake of realism. Certain
things in Joyce, who went so far, offend me because they are artificial,
secondhand. I never wholly concede to the fiction which an author
builds up in creating his characters. It is difficult enough to reveal

one's own thoughts and sensations. I know full well that fiction creeps into my most sincere endeavors. But then, where I fail in that direction, I succeed inadvertently in another. In other words, if you read properly, even the false paths, the blind spots, tell you something significant about the author. I lie occasionally—why not? My lying is in keeping with giving the truth about myself. It is not a machine that is registering this record of a soul, but a human being, and I am putting myself forward first and foremost *as a human being*. (It is not deceit, for example, to be aware as I write this that these remarks would serve excellently for a preface. I am aware, aware, always aware. Often, when I have gone with a woman, that same awareness has made me laugh at the wrong moment. And a woman is absolutely right in hating, detesting the man who can be guilty of such a *misdemeanor*. It is a real piece of sacrilege. I recognize that.)

I must stop. I want to read a little of Rilke before going to bed.

HENRY

[Clichy, April, 1932]
4:15 A.M.

Instead of a letter I am sending you a carbon of today's output. It is an experiment. Began it in Bald's room this afternoon and finished it early this morning after work, after an extra session of work in which I read every goddamned stock from A to Izzit, highs, lows, opening and closing prices, dividends, etc. Perhaps my thirteen pages show the cost.

At any rate, I will respond to your big letter in due time. At this point I am completely fagged out. There is a poker game going on at my left and the noise is driving me out. Enough for today.

HENRY

P. S. The first sentence of the Rilke book augurs well: "C'est donc ici que les gens viennent pour vivre?"

There are some books which you throw aside after reading the first line.

[Clichy, April, 1932]
Saturday Night

It's just midnight, and I've broken all records for getting the work out. I've been out for a couple of beers already with Louis the Atlas, who just advanced me twenty francs on the stories I wrote for the Jewish syndicate. I learn, oddly, that my articles appeared in Jewish papers in Ireland, Scotland and New Orleans, and that the one on the mathematician (who laid Einstein low—this I took in French, mind you!) was considered masterly. In fact, I'm a little drunk with Louis' praise. He says I have the stuff . . . why don't I prostitute myself a little more and write for the Sunday supplements in America? Little love stories of 3,000 words for the tabloids—$25 apiece, or articles about Paris with photographs. . . . Yes, I would like to prostitute myself, but I'm no whore. I fall just a little short of the mark.

But I'll tell you what—if I write these two articles on Montparnasse and on Lawrence I'll send them out. As for the Lawrence thing, I am almost afraid to embark on it. I want to say so much that I am afraid it will be too long to fit any magazine or newspaper.

Tonight I bought on credit two tickets for the Sweepstakes in June. Maybe I'll pick a winner. That would clear up a lot of difficulties.

HENRY

[Clichy, April, 1932]

ANAÏS:

I want to talk about the Lawrence book.* It excites me immoderately. Such a big, full portrait—I like the book for that, but the woman—she is an abomination! On every page I feel like disemboweling her. And you know, Lawrence too diminishes in my estimation—with every fresh story I read about him. I think he was intolerable—a little runt, a nasty devil, a dry, thoroughly English type. I despise his workingman's (no, it was bourgeois) attitude about things—scrubbing floors, cooking, laundering, etc. And his being alone crap! Not sensitiveness, but timidity, lack of guts, lack of

---

* *Lorenzo in Taos* by Mabel Dodge Luhan, 1932.

humanity. Oh well, more of this when I begin my annotations. Every page is pregnant for me—points of similarity and dissimilarity.

Do you know what I find astonishingly good—almost magnificent? His advice to the young man about to be married. "Be alone always. Be gentle with her when she is gentle, but if she tries to impose her will on you, beat her!" You don't know how swell that sounds to me. Wisdom . . . essence of wisdom in man-to-woman matters. I feel if I had known that before I might have averted so much trouble . . . useless trouble. And by God, according to accounts, he did beat the fat German woman up. She appeared with bloody nose and eyes black and blue. I do hope that's not literature!

More coming. I'm rushing off now.

HENRY

[Clichy, April 22, 1932]
ANAÏS—

Started to write you last night at office but was ill—bellyache —too much home-fried cooking—or is it vin rouge?

Nevertheless am bringing over with me an article to be written on Lawrence—or, on that goddamned book you lent me, by the monster, Mabel. I want to expand—make it any old length—and then *sell* it. Yes! And if it won't sell, then bango! Into my book—the garbage can!

And maybe I want your help. I don't know. I understand now why you were raving. But this book is so extravagant—such a burlesque —that I feel Knopf put it out as a joke on the public. I can't see it any other way. So I'm going to start in—and if I get stuck I'll call on you for help. This person has to be scotched. And personally, for a job like this, I want money. Blood money. I'm savage about it, do you understand? Seeing my name over the article won't do. I want to be paid handsomely for it—for the privilege of spitting on her, on her Taos, her Tony, her California, her Jung, her Gurdjieff, her esoteric twaddle. Oh, I'm raving—and I still haven't finished the book. The idea of saying—"you know Jeffers"—on every other page. What sort of man is [Robinson] Jeffers to permit this?

Did you remark the sickly letters Lawrence wrote? How could he have allowed himself to fall into the clutches of such a woman? There was something feeble about him—despite his glorious language. I tell you, I have committed crimes and foolishness, but that sort of thing—impossible! I despise him for that—and for his $2,000 that he held onto—for paying his way so decently—for his silly "aloneness."

But I'll tell you—it was moving when at the banquet [John Middleton] Murry and the others tendered him, he put his head on the table and wept. I appreciate that to the very limit.

Got news last night that I commence the other job immediately I'm finished upstairs. I think that made me sick. I hate the idea now of slaving away in futile labor. I am surcharged, and my output has been restricted. I could cry about it. It's all spoiling inside me.

I wrote Fraenkel today about what you said. Guess he'll communicate with you. The *European Caravan* * hasn't arrived yet. Impatient. Impatient. That I don't want to die. It is important, what I have to say. Very very grateful for all these books—you raise me to ecstasies. I want to ask more of you—yes, I am avaricious, devouring. I want you to get me someday a good-sized notebook that opens flat, and stays flat, with paper on which I can write and paint water colors. I'd like a permanent place for all my notes—my drunken dreams, my lecherous drawings, my wishes, requests, book lists, street names, etc. etc. When I croak maybe that would sell and net someone a little profit —and I owe so many people. (I'd like my kid to be taken care of, and my unfortunate sister.) You know, Fred and I talked of a strange thing the other night. Rare, rare, I talk this way. I thought of my daughter—she must be somewhere between 11 and 13 yrs. old.** I can't figure it out exactly. I want to see her before she becomes a young woman. Oh, we talked crazily. We talked of getting her here to Paris. Impossible—for many reasons—of course. But there you are. If I ever see her again I don't know what will happen to me. I loved her so terribly—and I was cruel. I wonder if she would forgive me ever? She belongs to me—I feel that. She is my little girl, more than my wife's. And I want her someday. I want to explain things to her.

Is this sentimental? Hell, I don't care. It is so seldom I indulge myself this way.

---

* An anthology of contemporary writing from France, Spain, England and Ireland, edited by Samuel Putnam, Maida Castelhun Darnton, George Reavey and J. Bronowsky. Brewer, Warren & Putnam, New York, 1931.

** His first child, Barbara, was born in 1918, when Miller was married to Beatrice Sylvas Wickens.

I have just written Renaud a fine letter—and requested again news of the machine. Hold everything!

I figure humbly that certainly I am not a god. Maybe I'm just an exaggerated foetus—one of those goldfishes that swim night and day in a bowl on the rue des Martyrs.

I'm nuts today because I can't use the machine. Fred is still knocking out Port Editions—on oil and gloves—peanuts next, I suppose. And when it's all done—do you know what happens? They send out a few to subscribers and the vast bulk of them is destroyed. I pass them every night in the hallway—tons and tons of them. Foul, I tell you. This world is crazy. Makes my hair stand on end. Damn it all—nothing can be too violent. All this must be destroyed someday.

Yours in a fury—

HENRY

P. S. Do you like "Bubu"? * How did you like syphilis standing at the door—kind of swell, don't you think?

[Clichy, May, 1932]
Sunday

ANAÏS:

Your wire says to call mardi, but I am calling Monday. Rushing off to meet Fraenkel—tomorrow Osborn and [Walter] Freeman.** Am bursting to write. A month off will not be any too much. Ideas, ideas, ideas. . . .

Meanwhile, here are some copies I promised you, and intervening pages of my Ms. which I forgot to mail you. When you come—a few suggestions:

Bring the Ms. of the first novel and whatever letters from Dijon you thought fit to incorporate in the book. Also that *Nouvelle Revue Française* containing the "Circus" story—I want to recapture a mood

---

* Bubu de Montparnasse, the hero of Charles Louis Philippe's (1874–1909) novel of the same title (Paris, E. Fasquelle, 1927), was a popular legendary figure of the period. An English translation of the book by Lawrence Vail, with a preface by T. S. Eliot, appeared in 1932 (Paris, Crosby Continental Editions).

** See Biographical Notes.

and also write something in that vein. It belongs to Dijon recollections (and you can have it back again). Have you, among my looseleaf notes, pages giving names of streets and actresses and painters? Not forgetting Bubu of Montparnasse and the Spanish grammar. And alors, one thing else (I'm voracious)—Gide's *Dostoievsky*—but only if you own it . . . don't go out and buy it. And then, whenever you have leisure for it, make me a copy or two copies while you're at it, of those excerpts from Hardy. It's the Biblical lines I want more than anything. I am going to the library soon and look up the Book of Apocrypha—it sounds swell. [Eugene] Jolas' * address in Paris, I am told, is 40 rue de Sévigné. I am writing Brassai ** about that photograph of June's. The clipping from the *Daily News* might interest you —and June! As for *Digit of the Moon*—no, I haven't read it. It was recommended to me once when I was playing pool in a hospital in the Bronx. The young man was in love with June and I played pool with him to hear what he had to say about June. Hence *Digit of the Moon*. But more important to me now is: what is *Le Grand Meaulnes*? I see this everywhere and the title means absolutely nothing to me. But I have a feeling it is important. (Just as I did when I first saw *A Man Cut in Slices.*†)

You see, most of the things for which you want answers you will find sooner or later in my manuscript. I am sending you the carbons as I go along. Tonight I will not write as I have several important long letters to write.

I should like to know from whom you borrowed that line in your letter commencing "pouvoir, au milieu de la folie, etc." †† I like that immensely.

About Goethe, we are soon going to hear something important from Fred. He knows Goethe inside out. We have had some interesting talks already on the subject, and now he is still unsatisfied and promises me a long letter, which I will relay to you in due course. But about

---

* See Biographical Notes.

** The Hungarian photographer (Halasz). See Biographical Notes.

† In *Tropic of Cancer* Miller describes how he saw in a Paris bookstore window a display featuring the life of a man as seen through the eyes of his family, through the eyes of his mistress, etc. Every day the window trimmer turned the pages.—Alain Fournier's *Le Grand Meaulnes* was translated into English as *The Wanderer*.

†† A quote from an observation in Anaïs Nin's Diary: "Pouvoir, au milieu de la folie, redevenir humaine."

Nietzsche—no, you are absolutely wrong, unjustified. You must change your mind here. Nietzsche is of the very great and his language, far from being fatuous, is superb, magnificent. Read first *The Anti-Christ,* then *Human All Too Human* or *Beyond Good and Evil.* No, I adore Nietzsche. He knew how to write, and he is so different from the Germans.

About saying that I was carrying a corpse around—yes, it has been imputed to me, and it is possible I may have said so, but I do not remember any longer. Many things were imputed to me which I did not recognize. Everything was quite distorted.

HENRY

[Clichy, May 26, 1932]
Thursday

ANAÏS:

When I got home I found a big crate here filled with excelsior —and there was the lamp, a beauty, a dazzling beauty, and I'm crazy about it. In order to show you how much I appreciate it I overhauled my room thoroughly, rearranged my papers, scrubbed the floors and the bathtub, cleaned the kitchen, and taking a big piece of wrapping paper made an inventory of all the things I intend to do and tacked it on the wall. I'm just getting set to go on with the book. If I have time I will enclose in this some more dreams, which I found in a "dream book" I began several years ago. One or two of them are magnificent. I also enclose a copy of the letter to [Pascal] Covici *— am holding the original until you O.K. it. Now I know where the missing Ms. of the novel is—[Samuel] *Putnam * has it!* You were right, you did give it to me. . . . If you go to see [Edward] Titus,* don't forget to ask him for a copy of the "Surrealist" number.**

The lamp is not working yet as I have to have a prise put in, but I guess it will be done before Saturday when I hope you can come. Reading the first few pages of the diary † you gave me I see how

---

* See Biographical Notes.
** The spring 1932 issue of *This Quarter,* the magazine edited by Edward Titus, was devoted to the Surrealist movement.
† Written when Anaïs Nin was sixteen years old.

extravagant you felt once when you spent 25 cents on a book. (And now?) That little bit about looking in the windows of the dress shops on 5th Avenue and waiting to be handed Cuca's cast-off gowns— rather touching. And you were *revolted* by "modern" literature. That modern you mention—I never heard of him. But I see you were reading Mark Twain and Thoreau and Emerson. (We must find out the meaning psychologically of [Sherwood] Anderson's *Many Marriages*.) You're wonderful.

HENRY

[Clichy, June 1932]
Paris, Monday

ANAÏS:

    La cerveza no es buena aquí.

Jesus! A new language to learn! Awful! I'm scared. But it says: "The infinitive of *every* Spanish verb ends in *ar, er,* or *ir.* O.K. No hablo Espagñol. It sounds crippled. This elimination of the pronoun, as in Russian too, I believe, always strikes me as very primitive—or is it a sign that the self is not so important?

God, so many new words to learn—new cases, new conjugations, new rules. I'm almost afraid to think of going to Spain alone. I must know at least a hundred convenient phrases. I'm up to page 15 and it seems as though I'm chewing hay. Ch-ch-ch- th-th-th. . . . Say sixteen in Spanish! It looks formidable. But I notice many of the words bear great resemblances to the French, and to Italian. *Usted* is, I think, adorable. It's a discovery. The language that created *Usted* has genius behind it. "No got had, *Usted?*" "No, no got!"

Listen, this needs deep concentration. I hate grammars—and vocabularies. You teach me, señorita? When I see "estar" *and* "ser" I get heart failure. "No es inglés" *but* "el Banco de Inglaterra està en Londres." That's complicating things unnecessarily. Patience! I'll tell you better what I think of my chances in a few days. Now I see nothing but verbs, pronouns, adjectives, genders, etc. Estoy ocupado.

Hurriedly,

HENRY

P. S. There were no tickets to be had for L'Argentina.

[Clichy, June, 1932]

A little later coming home in the train I looked at the booklet on Chirico. Just what I wanted. All I have been thinking of in connection with Halasz's [Brassai's] photographs this man Roger Vitrac has said about Chirico.* Usually one feels frustrated on finding his thoughts already printed by another. This time no. I am simply happy to find another mind playing with the same ideas in the same fashion. It's too bad you hadn't read it first. All I have felt about Surrealism I believe is quite right. I give you one or two passages to show you what I mean. . . .

"Il est certain que sur ses toiles tout se pose. Nulle recherche de conventionelle harmonie, du sens de l'équilibre ou des proportions. Chaque élément prend sa place aveuglément et tout jouit d'une égale intensité. Tout s'ordonne dans le chaos, tout s'exéante avec ignorance, toute émotion se guérit de son inquiétude." **

This, I felt, was what you were approaching in your original *House of Incest*. You will notice that the condition he describes is very much like what we are so frequently ascribing to the *Spanish* character.

I hope I am not reading too much into this paragraph. It seems to contain a great deal—and the expressions he employs match the thought admirably.

Here is another—

"Vôtre récent séjour à Paris m'apparaît comme une fête. Rien ne laissait insensible. Les enseignes lumineuses, le bébé Cadum, l'Américaine Palmolive, les *manèges* (?), les affiches de cinema, les chantiers de démolition, vous parliez de tout cela comme d'illustrations d'une nouvelle légende et vous y voyiez un 'Départ des Argonauts' où les hommes mêlés aux femmes s'endormiraient devant une gare dont les trains trahis par leur seule fumée s'enfonceraient dans la mer ou dans le ciel." †

---

* *Georges de Chirico*, Paris, Gallimard, 1927. 63 pp. 59 plates.

** "It is certain that on the canvases everything is stated. No search for conventional harmony, for a sense of balance or proportions. Every element takes its place blindly and everything exerts the same intensity. Everything arranges itself in the chaos, everything works out quite unself-consciously, every emotion cures itself of anxiety."

† "Your recent stay in Paris seems to me like a special occasion. You responded to everything. The glowing advertising signs, *Cadum* for babies, the American Palmolive, the manèges, the movie posters, the wreckage yards, you spoke of all this as the illustrations of a new legend and you saw a 'Depar-

Finally these words by Chirico himself:

"Ce qu'il faut surtout, c'est débarrasser l'art de tout ce qu'il contient de connu jusqu'à présent, tout sujet, toute idée, toute pensée, toute symbole doivent être mis de côté. . . .

"Il faut que la pensée se détache tellement de tout ce qu'on appelle la logique et le sens, qu'elle s'éloigne tellement de toutes les entraves humaines, que les choses lui apparaissent sous un aspect nouveau comme illuminées par une constellation apparue pour la première fois." *

Soit!

HENRY

P. S. I know now that the ride home always seems so rich because I am loaded always with your gifts.

[Clichy, June 17, 1932]
Friday

ANAÏS—

When I got home last night I found a woman there—a Mlle. Paulette, dix-neuf ans, une amie de Fred. No more housecleaning for us. Paulette will do everything. You ought to have seen her dry the salad in a towel—marvelous! She's going to economize for us. Had a dispute with her father and so she won't go home any more. She's quite adorable. Fred's already worried that he won't write any more. She can do anything. Dix-neuf ans! Maybe we'll have dinner together Monday. Paulette must change her hours—she is used to getting up at 7:30 A.M. She makes me very happy to watch her—just like a child. Alors, lundi chez Fraenkel. Tout va bien?

HENRY

ture of the Argonauts' in the mingled mass of men and women who had fallen asleep at a railroad station where the trains, betrayed by their single columns of smoke, dug their way to the sea or into the sky."

* "Above all, what we have to do is to rid art of everything it has known until the present, every subject, every idea, every thought, every symbol has to be tossed aside. . . .

"Only when our thinking has been cleared of all that we call logic and sense, when it has removed all its human shackles, will things appear to us in a new light as though illuminated by a constellation that has appeared for the first time."

[Clichy, July 26, 1932]
Tuesday

ANAÏS:

Just got Dr. Krans' pneumatique today and immediately wrote the famous Paul Morand * that I would be glad to see him. I surmised it must have come via you. How funny that will seem, translating the successful author's speeches for his American tour! Do you know why I accepted primarily—the money he offers isn't much (500 francs for twenty-five pages—each speech 25 pages . . . so it seems). I want to meet him and see if I can *break him down,* make a friend of him, invite him to Clichy, take the lead with him, and get him to introduce me to a publisher. I don't suppose I can, he must be pretty hard-boiled by now—and then he owns a Bugatti and he talks with a stopwatch in his hand (so I'm told). But that's all the jollier. I don't believe I can do a good translation, but Fred has promised to help me and I will split the profits with him.

You will notice from the enclosed that I was just writing to Caresse Crosby ** myself (and I was intending to send you the letter before mailing it). I don't think you will approve of it, so don't send it without seeing me first. Today I answered the Captain's letter—it's a joke, please understand. I don't mean a word of what I wrote. It's just to make the Captain nibble and write me some more preposterous letters. When I get a file of them I'll be able to invent something equally preposterous.

No more stomach-aches—just a sort of low rumbling like those lava beds that you look down into from the mouth of a crater. Paulette seems to grow younger-looking every day. We are asking each other if she is more than twelve. At dinner this evening Fred describes to me, in front of her, how undeveloped she looks and when she says "Tu dis?" he says—"Monsieur Henri, he is saying that you have a faraway look in your eyes," and Paulette says "Est-ce vrai?"

The work is progressing fine. Let it grow hotter. I'm thriving under it. Tonight I must go to my bureau in Montparnasse and see if there is any business on foot.

---

* Born in 1888, Paul Morand had published 40 books by the end of 1931. See also Biographical Notes.
** See Biographical Notes.

You say Friday? No, I will have a stomach-ache before that. I think Paul Morand will give me a stomach-ache.

Hastily,

HENRY

[July 30, 1932]
Saturday, Clichy

More carbons! Here is an attempt to rewrite the Bunuel article.* I give you the original draft of it along with this present effort to make a comparison. I don't know whether I have improved it or not. The mind is entering into it now, and that unsettles me. Besides, it is not just my own mind—you will discover traces of Fraenkel and yourself, perhaps spots of Lawrence. I don't know whether I have knitted it together solidly enough. Does it make sense? That is, are the ideas connected intelligibly? I hope I am not disturbing you in your work with all this miscellany I have been showering upon you the last few days. I am rushing this off to you because I am in hopes of receiving word any day from Caresse Crosby, and I would like to present this Foreword along with the book. I cut down on the sex stuff which permeated the first writing, but stuck it back in another way at the tail end. I rather like the ending— Do you understand clearly the different ways I have used "fuck" here? When I say "Because now you're fucked!" I mean it in the way the French mean it when they use the verb, whose parts I don't know yet, in that expression "je m'en fous." I explain all this to you because I don't know for certain, when it comes to these strong expressions, how much of it you get. *My idea* (in collaborating with myself) was to use the nasty words in their strongest form, and not to make people lascivious. Give me all the criticism you can, because I am not entirely satisfied with it

* Luis Bunuel, whose films *Un Chien Andalou* (1928) and *L'Âge d'Or* (1930) established him as one of the great directors of his time, was greatly admired by Miller, who published his first essay abroad about Bunuel's *The Golden Age* (screenplay by Salvador Dali) in Samuel Putnam's *The New Review* ("Bunuel or Thus Cometh to an End Everywhere the Golden Age," Paris, May–June–July, 1931). Miller later rewrote his study about this masterpiece of the surrealist cinema which he described as "an exposé of society's refusal to come to terms—or even admit—the real nature of love."

myself. I have gone from ecstasy to cold writing, which is against my preaching. At the same time I want to prove, if I can, that I am capable of thinking, and thinking hard and straight. Have I shown it? I'm afraid I'm a bit of a muddlehead. (Why *afraid*—No!)

You don't know how much I enjoyed those wild, extravagant statements of Tristan Tzara * which I gave you in the excerpts. See how much of that relates to our present ideas, to Bunuel, to Fraenkel, to your Lawrence study. But how much stronger they are in this vagabond, quixotic style! His humor is really dynamite. He is saying something all the time, and the idiots imagine he is just a naughty boy putting his thumb to his nose.

Between you and me I am sure that Bunuel does not understand his film as we do. My remembrance of the talk with him at the Select is quite good. I remember certain direct questions I put to him and his candid admissions. But he understood instinctively, that goes without saying. And that sort of understanding, coupled with his sincerity, I like. It is more like what I have myself. (Why I like it!) Moreover, part of the barbs I put in (and maybe I stressed it too much) was done to rescue him from the danger of being considered a mere Communist. I think of him now as a sort of mad, passionate, violent Spaniard (antitheses and conceptualism) who is drawn this way and that by conflicting forces, who is not quite sure where he stands, but where he stands for the moment he fights with all his strength. No, I don't put his intellect too high. He's not that kind of Spaniard. (He was bitterly contemptuous of Unamuno!)—I'm all for Unamuno. What a poison he distills!

HVM

P. S. The best thing in Dada was—"God can afford to make mistakes. So can Dada!" (That's a very old idea of mine.)

---

* French poet, born in Rumania, who was the founder of the Dadaist Movement in Zurich in 1916. He published the "Manifeste Dada" ("We have a great task of destruction ahead of us") in 1918, moved to Paris in 1919, and became the forerunner of the Surrealists, from whom he dissociated himself in the late 1920's. His major work is *L'Homme Approximatif* (1931).

[Clichy, August, 1932]
Wednesday

Have written four more pages in addition to the enclosed, but I don't want to give it to you in the middle of a part. This is all a result of meeting Eduardo * in the library yesterday. He looks good in the library, as though he were born to it.

You understood why I didn't show you the pages on Bunuel? You were supposed to have read them already. Why I got a headache? I don't know. The film made me drowsy. It wasn't as good as I had · expected it to be—I was straining to appreciate it all the time.

About [Dr. René] Allendy **—notice how I wrote about Bunchek †—just before getting your pneumatique. (You can't notice because they are among the succeeding pages which I am withholding.) I'll bring whatever I have tomorrow when I meet you. I got the mandat too. I ran off the other night without thinking of the money in my pocket.

In my cable to June I told her to bring all my manuscripts. This reads like a telegraphic message—it's because I'm hurrying to go out. Don't sniff the air, don't paw the turf! I'll be seeing [William] Bradley †† at noon.

I'll be waiting at the café corner rue Mozart, wherever this is.

HENRY

P. S. You must read *The Dance Over Fire and Water* by Élie Faure. I am rereading it at library—that and the travel diary.

[August, 1932]
Friday, Clichy

ANAÏS:

Am sending you the enclosed letter and excerpts, with copy of open letter to Bunuel, all to be forwarded to my friend, Emil Schnel-

---

*Eduardo Sanchez, a cousin of Anaïs Nin.
** See Biographical Notes.
† Bunchek, the cutter, appears in the chapter "The Tailor Shop," in *Black Spring.*
†† See Biographical Notes.

lock,* to whom I have addressed an envelope enclosed. It is not just the lack of stamps (that is a trifle I could easily solve), but I thought you would enjoy reading the letter. Emil is my best friend back there in America.

Tell me if you think the Bunuel letter weak. I don't know where I stand these days. I am forcing myself to write.

I expect a *long* letter from you. I am temporarily exhausted. Just the same I squeezed out a few good drops in the letter to Emil. If you squeeze hard enough there is always a drop or two left. But I don't want to squeeze drops.

HENRY

[Clichy, September 28, 1932]
Wednesday

I'm giving you the fragments of a dream last night; it seems slight to me and uninteresting, but perhaps you and [Dr.] Allendy can prove it otherwise. How this man can interpret my dreams without knowing me I don't understand.

What I recall, then, of the dream is this: that I was being escorted by a stranger, a young man, to a restaurant; I was intensely delighted to find myself in a section which I had been to once before but had never been able to find again by myself; it seemed to me that I was in the lower end of Brooklyn—I recognized the scene as from a previous dream—it was very vivid, a very picturesque neighborhood, in which the old dominated. Why I was explaining to the young man the reason for my being here, or searching for a restaurant, I don't remember—but I do recall distinctly, as if it were quite important, that I told him I had just come from an old tailor, a very American tailor in the lower end of Brooklyn, who had been established for over a century—and my impression is that I was telling him a lie, in order to impress him—though why he would be impressed by a century-old establishment, going by a very American name, I don't understand; I believe I had the feeling even in the dream that it was a little silly. The strange thing is that when we got outside the restaurant—which was more like a French restaurant, with a terrasse and an awning,

---

* See Biographical Notes.

and a bar inside—he suddenly stopped and began to remove something from a post, like a tall hitching post, saying that it was time these things were removed, that he would give them to the proprietress of the restaurant; when I saw what he was doing I was astonished to see two silver coins attached to the post, one smooth and plain, the other a little larger and the edges serrated. It struck me as very absurd. When we went inside I noticed to my disappointment that the place was divisioned off like a market, with areas denominated 6 frs., 6.50, 7.00 frs. etc. and that I couldn't bear the idea of having to eat in that fashion, and that it was too perplexing to choose. The interior seemed more like an old English tavern, the bar was attractive, and in the dim background stood a waitress with a towel on her arm waiting for me to decide; she was dressed in black and had on a white apron. She tried to persuade me at first and then she behaved toward me as if I were a foreigner and didn't know any better. Going out I again was pleased that I had found myself in this neighborhood and tried to read the name of the street on the wall across the street, but was unable to decipher it.

The other fragment, and I can't find the relation between these two, is as follows: I am toying with a word. I don't know the full word, but it seems to end in opolis and when I detach opolis it makes *crime;* I awake but am so intrigued with this game and want so much to know the word that I immediately relapse into sleep and dream again; I realize that the word has to do with a corner of Southern Russia and that now Heliopolis comes to mind but is at once rejected as being a forced solution. Sebastopol seems more like the word but that doesn't make sense—it doesn't make crime, and besides I am not sure but that I have supplied this when I am awake. I don't know whether I am awake or dreaming any more. I am tremendously annoyed not to wrestle the thing out. It is this that makes me determined to record the dream and to practice remembering my dreams each morning upon awaking.

For the benefit of whoever interprets this dream I supply gratuitously the following (to me) pertinent antecedents, the stuff of my reverie and also my conscious mind prior to sleeping. Was quite annoyed that I could not have finished what I wanted to read from Lewisohn's * book, because I had found a great deal that was interesting, that you would even have found admirable. The stuff on Puri-

---

* Ludwig Lewisohn, *Expression in America,* New York, Harper, 1932.

tanism, which I had swallowed in a large dose, against the grain
(because I did not want to miss the drift of his thesis), remained in
my mind with this peculiar flair—that I wanted to defend it! I think
I only wanted to do so because he was a Jew and it disturbed me that
a Jew could so keenly and rightly put his finger on the source of
American puerility, sterility and paralysis. I was formulating an attack
that was indefensible, even to myself, and I was annoyed again that I
could not justly, logically defend the issue. I kept saying over and over
again to myself, like a refrain, "But perhaps another man, a real
American, would find a wholly different answer to this question of
Puritanism." Further about Lewisohn—I was thinking that Anaïs
could dismiss the book so peremptorily only because she was a Latin,
and that these were never her problems, but that they were very warm
and vital to me, however stale and well-known to me, because I
sprang from that soil, I had to fight against it, I had to apologize everywhere for myself and my countrymen. I wanted to raise Waldo Emerson to the skies, just to prove to the world that once there had been
a great American—but more than that, because I once had been
greatly influenced by him, he was bound up with a whole side of me
that I consider my better side, and that I was reawakening, consciously, directly, purposively, through Keyserling. And with all this
about Anaïs' hidden or unexpressed view there came a deep start
when I read some lines quoted from Santayana, who despised the
whole Germanic culture, was proving it childish, brutal, and ignorant.
This linked up with the humiliation I felt when Anaïs pounced on me
anent the subject of Nudism; when I dropped the subject, apparently
vanquished, I was in truth anything but vanquished—I felt that my
point had gained in strength and was proposing to myself to write about
it more expansively and more fierily—and add to this that I thought
it's a typical woman's response, a Latin woman's response, a decadent
woman's response . . . this is where the Germans are right, in their
fanaticism . . . it is this kind of barbarism with which they are destined
to regenerate mankind. And I thought Santayana's Latin solution to
life a too easy, indolent way out—and was amazed that a Jew like
Lewisohn should have warmed to it. Further amazed that he should
have extolled Henry James so much, and yet dismissed Lawrence with
the one word "pornography." But most of all amazed that he should
have written his best and his fullest on Emerson . . . trying to explain
that to myself on this ground—that Emerson, like the Biblical Jews,

was a fiery prophet, an evangel, an iconoclast. But that Lewisohn didn't really "get" Emerson—he converted him into a prophet in order to understand and appreciate him. (All this I admit to myself, at the same time, is indefensible—he is just as intelligent as I am, and has just as much right to like Emerson as I have.) I am agreeing with him all the time and yet the more he exercises his powers of persuasion the more I rebel against him. But I will not rebel for the reasons that Anaïs does—that seems too ignoble, too unjust, too blind.

Going home in the train, I had a tremendous surge of ideas, caused by seeing the houses lit up in early evening; their bleak barren ugly qualities impressed me, and yet the soft light, often in a red-papered room, with people quietly sitting at the table, and coming in such quick succession—window after window—like souls exposed (where were the curtains . . . why hadn't the French used curtains?), affected me strongly, affected me with the sense of drama, universes of drama in a short stretch between train stops. Got to thinking of the complications in people's lives, of how mysterious and baffling it was to them and how easily solved by strangers, by psychologists, for instance, and then to the thought that the poor psychologist was too easily satisfied, too quickly impressed, his answers too ready-made, everything in the nature of a problem viewed from the angle of how to put it in a pattern (of his own making!); from this to the fact that a writer could completely baffle a psychologist; not only that, but that he was more of a psychologist than the other since he ramified the mysteries, extended them, developed them, and left the answers to go hang, because the answers weren't important, it was the drama, the mystery, the undecipherable pattern that was vital. And by a quick flight, as again with the Lewisohn problem, to a realization that the psychologists were more right than I was—that it was ineluctable—the fact of there being but a few fundamental patterns to the whole groundwork of human behavior. That life's problems were too limited, that it was a pity, that the function of an artist was to increase these problems, to cause upheavals in the brain, to make people wild and free so that there would be more drama to their lives, more windows to look into, more of that red glow in riding a train. That the only excuse I had for writing was to write something so disturbing, so volcanic, that America or Europe would not be the same after it—and then how to do that . . . was I doing enough . . . could I make them hate me sufficiently? (Fear, no doubt, behind the thought, that my first book would not create a stir, that it might be considered *entertaining* or merely *risqué*.) Remembrance of Krans' words (not uplifting for mankind) and being unduly incensed about it—not because of those words, or their implication, but that it did not rock him the least little bit. And all my objections to Lewisohn also revolving around a strong and constantly repressed desire to wound this man Krans by my criticism of his idol, Lewisohn. (Remember on greeting him that day how I detested his cold, steely greeting, so matter of fact, so pragmatic, so utterly indifferent in a real human way. Thinking to myself that my first impression was right, that I always make a mistake when I retract my first judgment, when I modify it through deeper contact—because what they reveal to me at first glance contains nothing that I have loaned them—afterwards, I am looking at my own reflections in people . . . I have given them a little warmth, a little spark of enthusiasm and they come to me constantly to have me fan it, blow on it.)

And this man Krans being a perfect American type—deploring his bad French over the telephone (why did he expect me to use good French when he was sending me to Dijon—what has he learned from his wife, his relations here, etc. etc.?). Noticing his stiff white collar, his primness, his brittleness, his voice rasping over phone, a lynx-like smile—not of cordiality but of lulling one to sleep in order to pounce on one. Detest his Yankee traits, don't understand how he fits in the picture here. And this man daring to offer me this book, in a spirit of opening my eyes, culturizing me, broadening me, etc. Remember my opening words to him, how I prepared the words a second before, in order to throw him off the track. "He does not expect politeness of me—feed him it in big doses!" And he is so susceptible to flattery.

All this tied up with the mist still left over from writing about the "old neighborhood" where I was raised, which I pictured as so American, so representative of another period in our life when things were better, or more leisurely, more wholesome and European. Only beginning, as I wrote this section (and I hated to make it so brief—it was a compromise again!) to understand why this period of my life (from 5–10) was so meaningful to me. For instance, why should I always tell a stranger, when it gets around to the subject of where you hail from, that I hail from the 14th Ward? Only nine years there, at a very tender age, but that I call the place where I was raised. Why do I detest the other neighborhood so—Decatur Street, near Evergreen Cemetery, where I lived from 10 years of age until I was married (25)? * I was always running away from this neighborhood; I had no particular sorrows there, I had a happy boy's life, but it was here that I had my first love affair, and then my unhappy affair with Pauline. And my first love hailed from the old neighborhood—a little distance away from where I was raised, but still more autochthonous, as it were. This neighborhood, Williamsburg, bordering on Greenpoint, seemed to me always as representatively American—and yet outwardly, physically, it is the nearest approach to the dirty sections of Paris which I love, it is more European, in other words, than any section of Brooklyn or New York I can imagine. It is here one finds "shanties" (chaumières)—I was much impressed when I first saw the chaumières of Paris; I love old ramshackle buildings, dilapidated buildings, buildings that are good to draw or paint, that have atmosphere about them and tragedies inside them, or misery, or starvation, or just bleak nothingness. Buildings, at any rate, that permit one to dream—that are like dreams themselves, in a way—because they seem pointless, often absurd, always mysterious, frequently awesome. My life, a good part that I remember, in that old neighborhood is spent running loose at night, playing wild games in which we ran through crazy, tangled streets, broke into shanties, climbed fences, got lost, had wild adventures, were lawless, were lacking in respect, etc. etc. Great remembrances of *chases*—for miles, flopping down exhausted finally, fears of meeting a rival gang and being soundly licked. Running games, hiding games, cruel games—the taste of this is still in my mouth.

My mind surcharged on the train coming into Paris. Wanted to get home more quickly than I knew it possible, in order to write. Thought of Fred waiting for me—in order to get his meal—and not wanting to cook his meal. But he would not eat if I didn't go straight home. Knew if I didn't go straight home I wouldn't write, and the thought "maybe you would like to get out of writing, that's why you're getting hungry now and must go to a restaurant." Knowing that the mere act of getting off the train, the very stop of the train, the change of position, would burst the bubble. Fearing that greatly. Always the fear

---

* In 1917, H. M. married pianist Beatrice Sylvas Wickens; the marriage ended in divorce in 1924.

that one is not doing enough, that one is too indulgent with oneself, that the best thoughts are never written because they occur always when one cannot have access to the typewriter—and the question in my mind, is that so, or is that a weak man's defense? (Lewisohn again—the great writers were strong men . . . Shakespeare settling down on his great estate etc. Also the line I read to you—"the rounded classical works are those in which a complete catharsis occurs," etc. I want to combat this idea—that's the truth, no doubt, and I am not a classic individual, and so why should it disturb me . . . why am I not serene about it—there we are—two types in the world —I'm the other type! But no, worrying about it, like a dog over a bone. . . . Weakness . . . weakness. Detest this weakness.) Going over the problem of Fred's need—have no compunctions about dishing him—it's good for him to starve a little . . . his stomach is out of order . . . besides he needn't starve . . . there is King when he gets to the office . . . "Use your noodle, Fred." But I know that Fred will greet me with an air of one who has been ill-used—"You thought only of your own pleasure." But he is wrong, it wasn't my pleasure that detained me . . . it was my work. That's a lie. You're making a big issue of this in order to wear yourself out and at last succumb to the pleasant idea of going to the theatre or elsewhere. You really hate to work. At bottom you're nothing but a pimp, a bloodsucker. You'd take the pennies off a dead man's eyes. Etc. ad nauseam. But I go home nevertheless—after first debating whether to ask the tobacconist where there is a good, cheap restaurant in the neighborhood. But knowing that it is useless, the French bastard doesn't give a damn about helping me, and I will find the place expensive and be all riled up about it. No, I go home (I take a bus which costs a few centimes more—let the first one go by, because I am conscience-stricken about the few centimes). When I arrive Fred is not there. I begin to curse —the goddamned bastard making me hotfoot it here when I wanted to go to a restaurant. And why did he clean up the joint so thoroughly? To show me that *he did his part* even though I didn't do mine. That's his way of trying to get back at me. The hell with him— I won't go to the office as I intended, in order to lend him a few francs for dinner . . . he can find his own way out of the difficulty.

There is lots more I can think of, but this is getting too long and perhaps too tedious? Who gives a damn about my divagations? I could write a book, going on at this rate, about a few hours' events—interior events. I'm telling you that I have merely skimmed over it and that some things I am leaving unsaid—because they're too delicate! I should perhaps have added one more item in the carpet: that there was a fear, during the train ride, that June might have come and would be sitting there in Clichy reading my manuscript, perhaps tearing it to pieces. I didn't intend to expatiate so much—but I got started and it sounded interesting to me—more interesting than the dream.

HENRY

P. S. I made no copy of this—please hold it for me—I might want to refer to it. There is a germ of an idea for my book in it.

[Clichy, October, 1932]
Wednesday

ANAÏS—

I am giving you this through June to remind you of several things I wish you would bring tomorrow night when you come to Clichy. As June will explain, the book is definitely accepted *—I am to sign the contract in a few days. June will give you the situation in its worst light and I will present its best aspects. As things stand now, I am to get 10% and no advance of any sort. Bradley seems to think it a fair and reasonable offer, and I am trusting his good judgment and his own selfish interests. The price of the book is to be 50 frs. However, the details later.

I would like to get the copy of the book which you have, as I may make still more changes of a minor nature. [Jack] Kahane ** was impressed with the revisions I made and seems enthusiastic about it. Both he and Bradley feel there is money to be made thru it, if the police do not get after them.

In addition to the Ms. would you be good enough to lend me the

---

* William Bradley, the literary agent, showed the manuscript of *Tropic of Cancer* to the publisher of the Obelisk Press in Paris, Jack Kahane, who decided to publish the book.

** See Biographical Notes.

following books: [Edmund Wilson's] *Axel's Castle,* [D. H. Law-rence's] *Fantasia of the Unconscious* and [Hermann Count] Keyser-ling's *Creative Understanding?* I don't suppose you have any of Jung's books that I once spoke of?

I am also reminding you that you wanted to see Brassai, the photog-rapher, and now that June is here she could have you meet him, as she wants to see him also.

Strange thing Kahane asked me was if I could write a brochure of 50 or 60 pages for him on Lawrence or Joyce by way of advance pub-licity. I told him I didn't think I could, cold-bloodedly, but should I get a desire to I may do so. I am wondering if I could say anything now (about Lawrence) which you left unsaid—that is why I wanted to glance again at *Fantasia of the Unconscious.* What I would really like to do is write a brochure on "Nudism and the Revolution." I feel rebellious already however to be asked to do things for a "stunt."

HENRY

[Clichy, October, 1932]
Monday afternoon

You want to know all the details. I'm afraid I can't give them all in a letter. Lots happened. Have just left Kahane's office—he is waiting for the contract to be drawn up, which we discussed all three the other day at Bradley's office. I agreed to the option on the next two books; Kahane seemed quite fair and his courage improves as he goes along. I don't remember the exact terms any more (too many figures!) but in substance I am to get 12½% up to 5000 and 15% over 5000 copies on the next 2 books, plus an advance of ½ the amount represented by the sales on the preceding books at time of ac-ceptance. Is that clear? Also a clause about how much Kahane is to get on my American rights (½ *if there is any sale*—I think ⅓ on the 3rd book—I don't know, bewildering!—and ⅓ on foreign rights). He and Bradley are quite sure about a French translation and will find a good man for it. Kahane said just now that, if he does not give the French book to the N.R.F. [Nouvelle Revue Française] to publish it will be because he might publish it himself in the French. Hachette, it seems, owns the N.R.F. and whoever this guy is, he is the man who has just returned my Ms. to Kahane, saying that *they would not dare* to handle it yet—*but!*

Says Kahane (quoting the man in French)—We had a 20-minute conversation about the book. He says it's magnificent, overwhelming (épouvantable *etc. etc. etc.*) beside which *Lady Chatterley* and *Ulysses* is *lemonade.* He says I'm a powerful, formidable writer—and he has never seen a book like it. (I think they're all going mildly crazy—losing their perspective, etc.) He says that just as soon as they see there is no danger they will handle it and be damned eager to do so—they have been eating themselves up ever since they made the mistake of refusing to distribute *Lady Chatterley.* They advised Kahane, for the sake of precaution, to first bring out a small edition labeled "Privately Printed" (as Lawrence did) with the name of the printer (Obelisk Press) in tiny letters at the bottom of the next to the last page, etc. etc. Kahane asked my opinion and I bowed to his more practical judgment. What the hell do I care about these matters? He thinks too it may be wise, more effective, to launch it after Christmas (about end of February) because it would "hardly make a good Xmas gift." He said very forcibly he wants to put it over with a bang —he wants no errors, no fumbling etc. Said Joyce and Lawrence were sort of "sneaked over," but that now the time had come to do it boldly, etc. (There seems to be an inconsistency here, but it is only on the surface. He is being wary at the opening only to entrench himself more solidly.)

Alors, reports to me a conversation with Grasset (and with his subaltern, Henry Müller, who refused my first book). Told them he had the "book of the century" in his hands and had them goggle-eyed with horror and amazement. Then he sells them someone else's book and gets a 50,000 frs. advance for the author. (That bastard ought to split with me!)

He gives me such earnest attention now (and Bradley too) that I have to laugh. It seems that in the interim between my visits they get swell reports about the book and that bolsters them up and they imagine that they themselves have these ideas. They're like thermometers. They're rubbing their hands, like a couple of Jews, in anticipation of the dough that's going to roll in. O.K. Let them rub their hands. And let them cough up, too!

However—more details! At the tripartite meeting I was won over to write the brochure. They gave me carte blanche, conceded every point—and I left them with a promise to think it over. On arriving home I got furious (for no good reason) and said to myself "Yes, I'll write it, to take it out of Kahane" and I sat down (no, that was 2 days later, after making voluminous notes) and wrote the first three pages attacking Kahane. I can cut them now—they served to warm me up merely. I also tried to get you on the phone to ask for any dope you had on Lawrence (the Luhan book) etc. but no answer. I now have twenty pages or so written and may go on to write a small book, such as yours (*D. H. Lawrence*). At any rate, I am excited about it (and forgetting Kahane entirely) and just as soon as you get back I want to see you and discuss it with you. I need your help, your criticism. I am taking Joyce and Lawrence *both* as my theme, but of course I have a lot to say beyond or around all that. I have loads of ideas—so many that I have been almost ill, too choked up etc. Kahane today said at first it might not be necessary to put out the brochure (if the first edition was to be "private") but when I told him I had got started and was slamming him to begin with and that I would go on with it in any case (because now it was *my* affair!) he got excited and begged me to show him what I have already done.

So it may turn out to be more important than a brochure. If you can come to Clichy so much the better. Come prepared to roll up your sleeves.

Furthermore—I got a swell idea, during my fever, for an additional chapter to *Tropic of Cancer*—a gratuitous one, born of my antagonism to Kahane's suggestion. I have done a few pages and can let it rest for a while as it's firm in my head. It will rival, or excel, the last chapter of *Ulysses,* without being "imitative." At least, that's how I regard it. And it has that violence of *Tropic of Cancer* which makes it highly suitable. However, I'm blowing off steam. I'll call you Wednesday morning.

HVM

P. S. Do think about the Lawrence material. I want to say everything you omitted and wished to say. I want to exhaust my ideas on these two men, and have done with them for all time. I don't care how much I write!

P. P. S. You *overlooked* something magnificent in Proust in the last volume. The best he has written. I feel sorry for you. Wait—wait!

Final *P. S.* 5 Star Edition: This is one of those letters that will be worth money to the holder if I should croak day after my book comes out. Put a red ribbon on it.

[Clichy, October, 1932]
Monday

ANAÏS:

You will see from the enclosed how I am progressing. I have been up to the neck in it these last few days.* Principally enlarging the scope of my notes, adding more, reading more, pondering on the organization of the material and searching for the clue on which to hang the whole business. Tentatively I have drawn up this scheme of FOUR PARTS, with a large Introduction, as you see. I have only begun today to rewrite the notes, following this broad scheme. I had first to go over my notes and book references to classify them. Now, with these four divisions, five counting introduction, I can write largely and loosely, as I said, and put them in their respective folders and let them germinate. If you have any ideas or criticism now to make—of the general arrangement—let me have them, as I need them. There may be overlapping in these rough divisions. But I think it will iron itself out as I go along. I couldn't go on writing straight, as I had for the first twenty pages, because the thing has grown too big and required more knowledge of what I was attempting, more direction.

I made a big speech to June last night, after working my way out of the forest; in explaining the broad outlines of the scheme to her I cleared up many problems in my own mind. There are plenty more left unsolved, but I have made a good start I think. The thing is growing enormous in conception—as I said, I want to rid myself once and for all of this incubus—of all the influences, gods, books, great names, etc. which throttled me before. I want to free myself by one herculean effort, and in doing so I give the finest counterpart to my creative books. Let them jeer, if they will, at the emotionalism or the lack of form, etc. in the novels. This will offer them a piece of solid meat to bite into—and I hope I give them lockjaw.

---

* Miller set out to write a small book, a brochure, about D. H. Lawrence which grew into an enormous manuscript, *The World of Lawrence,* and was never finished. Various parts of the work were later incorporated in magazine articles and in some of his books.

June has been in a much better mood, as a result of a talk in which I let her talk herself out. Treated her as if I were a psychoanalyst. Result is, she is content.

Which is all I ask just now. To work, to work. I see months of labor ahead of me—and I need strength and courage, to say nothing of vision, of understanding.

I have made oodles of fresh notes, and will go on doing so. One whole batch on the cinema (for future use), if you ever get round to collaborating with me. Am thinking out in all directions at once— which is a good sign. Everything seems to connect. That means I'm centipetalized, or something.

I never mentioned your letters. Yes, I enjoyed everything you said; all true. And I was stirred. Only I haven't time to seem to be interested in anything except what's under my nose. Do you understand?

HVM

P. S. I would like Osborn's letter back sometime.

[Clichy, October, 1932]
Thursday

ANAÏS—

Just a brief note—am up to my ears in the Brochure, a veritable slaughterhouse of notes, etc. Need very much the Jung book— 2 *Analytical Essays* because I have notes from it which are not clear and which I need to read again for my Surrealist pages. And how about *Lady Chatterley*—have you a copy of it? Does he give a preface explaining his use of obscenity? At any rate, what I want to get clear is—which are the chapters dealing with sociologic matters, conversations in drawing rooms, etc.—"the impedimenta." I want to see if he had a good, justifiable reason for these—Putnam wrote that the *2nd* chapter was the only one worth anything—and I think that's my idea of his worst!

The Brochure keeps expanding—I am drawing up a new plan—a sort of outline with 10 major divisions. Getting a tremendous grip on it and it's deepening.

Listen— I don't miss anything important by not glancing at the

[John Middleton] Murry book on Lawrence [*Son of Woman*], do I? You ought be able to judge.

And *South Wind* by Douglas. I wanted to say something apropos of it in connection with "false primitivism," "false Hellenism," etc.— but it has faded pretty well. You read it not so long ago. Do you recall the flavor and substance of Keith's speeches—where he gives his views on life? That is why it was important—as an attitude—*not* so much as literature.

You are going to step into a slaughterhouse. All these pages of notes are like pages of the brain. I could go mad. But I am sane as all hell. I feel like a seer. And a prophet. A scourge.

"Big Macrocosmic Connections!"

HENRY

P. S. "L'Oracle," I have decided, ought to cover one entire wall.* A fresco of Past and Present. But I lack one thing—I am no painter!

P. P. S. Reread the Dandieu book **—and with such ease and clarity! Found it simply marvelous. It makes me drunk. How do you account for such things? One day a blank—the next day an apocalypse!

P. P. P. S. Does your English dictionary give definitions of these: "ecumenic," "caducity," "incunabula," "vascular."

[Clichy, October, 1932]
Thursday Night

ANAÏS:

Voici a few more pages—cut short in the middle of my panegyric. Feel I'm going good now—and loads to come. The notes pile up around me like weeds. I know I'm repeating myself a great deal, but I can't recall any more what I say and I'm afraid of losing a thought. There are a few things I must investigate quietly when I get relief from this surge of ideas. I must, for example, have a look at the introduction to *Lady Chatterley,* the first volume of Spengler (for the Renaissance), Unamuno's *Tragic Sense of Life,* introductory

---

* Miller drew up, on big sheets of paper, outlines of his projects.
** Arnaud Dandieu, *Marcel Proust, Sa Révélation Psychologique,* Paris, Firmin-Didot, 1930.

pages of *Sodom et Gomorrhe* on homosexuality, Jung on the Unconscious, Faure on India, Keyserling's chapter on Jesus ("Figures Sym-
boliques"), last chapter of *Ulysses*. I mention these because you
probably have some of them and can help me; there are lots more
things to probe, but you may not be able to help me there. If you do
come across anything relating to these subjects tell me:

House of Atreus—in Greek mythology and drama.
Orphic myth (*Birth of Tragedy* gives it better than anything).
Rabelais and his times.
Shakespeare and his times.
Introduction to *Memoirs of Foreign Legion*.
Lawrence's letters.
Attitude of Greeks toward homosexuality and deepest psychologic
understanding of problem today.

Did you read Wilhelm's book—is there anything in it for me?
I am trying to get Janko Lavrin on *Dostoevski*.
And how about the Surrealist number of *This Quarter?* Is it worth-
while? Studio 28 * has marvelous collection of documents and bro-
chures on film and Surrealism too.

                                                    HVM

P. S. For my horoscope—was born on a Saturday *noon*—between
12:30 and 12:45—December 26, 1891—New York City—East 85th
Street. *Manhattan,* near the East River!
      Everything can wait! If I never see these very important things I
will still be able to finish the book!

                                              [January 1, 1933]
                                                    Sunday
ANAÏS:
      I'm writing you from 4 Ave. Anatole France, to my great sur-
prise and your own no doubt. I never got to London at all. Was held
up by the immigration authorities at Newhaven, the English side, sub-

---

* This later became the Cinémathèque Français; equivalent, perhaps, to the
Film Library of the Museum of Modern Art in New York.

jected to a grueling cross-examination as a suspect, locked up overnight and sent back the next morning. It's a long story and I want the
pleasure of recounting it to you in detail. The excuse given me was
that I had not sufficient money to justify my trip—I had only 187
francs, you see, though 300 or 800 wouldn't have made any difference either. In fact, when I asked them how much ought I have they
refused to say, refused to commit themselves to any definite sums. It
was a very humiliating experience: they treated me as a cross between
a criminal and a demented person. I'm thinking now that perhaps they
suspected me of being a Communist. At any rate, after passing the
night with the constable, under lock and key, I had great qualms as to
whether I would get back in France all right. They handed me over
to the French authorities as if I were a thief. But there I was received
very humanly; my French visa had run out and I was obliged to pay
for a renewal, and that was all. They treated me again like a human
being—no grilling, no suspicions. I was almost in tears and overjoyed
to think I was safely on my way to Paris. My great fear was that I
would be shuffled around from one country to another, from one jail
to another, as a vagabond. And the greatest fear was that I might be
deported back to America. When I thought of that my heart sank.
That is the last place I should want to go to.

I feel good to be back in Clichy, good to be sitting at the typewriter
again. My only thought now is to stay here in peace and work. I feel
as though I had been through an ordeal. The thought of packing my
bags again makes me sick.

You don't know what a sweat I was in, thinking of my baggage
which had been shipped on to London. Again all my manuscripts were
out of reach, and I feared that the English would go through my bags
and confiscate things. Fortunately I recovered everything. I'd like to
finish up things before I make another move—it frightens me to think
of having my papers stolen or confiscated. Anaïs, it's a long story and
you will enjoy it—it was an adventure, but I tell you I went through
some agony.*

HENRY

---

* For a full account see the story, "Via Dieppe-Newhaven," which was published in *Max and the White Phagocytes*, the Obelisk Press, Paris, 1938, and
subsequently in *The Cosmological Eye*, New Directions, Norfolk, Conn., 1939.

[January 17, 1933, Clichy]
Tuesday

I was on the point of going out to Louveciennes today, after calling up, and then I feared you might be coming here by accident.

Do you want any help in the work you're doing? * I'm ready to come if you can use me.

Have been working successfully ever since you left—ought to be cleaned up with the *Tropic of Cancer* by the end of the week. My brain is functioning again and I'm all there in every respect. Could I drop out some afternoon for the wheel ** just the same? You let me know if it's all right, and when.

Just when your pneumatique arrived I was figuring out how to get hold of you and take you to the Club du Faubourg this evening. I went—because it was about "inter-sexuality." It was all right as a French lesson, but not too "advanced." Diluted for the public, no doubt.

If you are coming into Paris daily and have an hour to spare I'll meet you any time, any place. Things are just tranquil here, which is excellent, and may give me just that continuous moody obsession with work to finish everything in time.

When you mention the kilo. of notes, I see another book evolving out of the air, as it were. He works while I sleep. *Formidable!* I only hope it isn't literature.

I'm well pleased with the metamorphosis of my novel which is now sandwiched into *Tropic of Cancer*. Such a fraud—and yet it fits marvelously. Certain things I had credited to myself, as author, I credit now to June—and that goes too. I think it's the best part of the book, tho' it wasn't written for it. Other scenes have gone in well too. I'm plowing thru! Fred and I are going to give you a surprise. We're going to search for material for a dress. You need more clothes! The green dress and that belt—swell! I like it more and more. I'll give you a good line from the typewriter. This is just a scratch. I'm growing absorbed.

HENRY

---

* Anaïs Nin was engaged in research for Dr. Allendy.
** Miller's way of referring to his bicycle.

P. S. I've been wondering what you really need—what would constitute a genuine surprise. It's difficult.

P. P. S. Haven't written [Dr. Otto] Rank * yet. Would you believe it, I can't seem to frame a letter that would not sound foolish or else too important. I'm thinking, too, of the expense. I wish I could help you with that work you're doing!

P. P. P. S. Having some strange homosexual dreams—will record them for you. Women with *leeks* growing out of their organs. Is that bad?

[Clichy, January 22, 1933]
Sunday

Café nights! Room too cold, fingers freeze. Halfway thru the last insertion for *Tropic of Cancer.* Got drunk on it. Tonight, reading [Samuel] Putnam's *Rabelais,* I see so many points of correspondence —amazing. His chapter on François' first visit to Paris interests me terribly—the song of the streets again. And Putnam anticipates me when he says: "But Paris, despite the changes, always remains the same." I have always had a hankering to someday cover the trajectory of a few great men—like Hannibal, Alexander, Caesar, Napoleon, Genghis Khan—and now Rabelais' looks good to me. In fact, at Dijon, I got the authentic flavor of those cities from the students— the very names of the cities are familiar to me and mean things. Just think—it was at 54 St. André des Arts, Paris, that Rabelais lived for a while (the former Hotel St. Denis). And it was only a stone's throw away, on this very street, that I sold my clothes for a song to a Jewish merchant. Great street. And at La Rochelle, where Osborn went with Jeanne, Rabelais sojourned and was fascinated by the sights—it was then second to Lyons in size, a great commercial port. *Also*—Rabelais has strong words to say about the institutions of learning, their physical aspect, the rotten eggs they served and the lice in the rooms. (Dijon!) It was at Avignon he had a fling with a woman—then a loose city. And, did I ever say how fascinated I was by this city, when I stopped there—that little square opposite the Palais du Pape—and the monastery outside the city where once the monks made Chartreuse. And, back in Paris, Rabelais even knew the *Vanves* district!

---

* See Biographical Notes.

Interesting is the difference 2 centuries made in Paris—between Villon's time and Rabelais'. Does this interest you?

And then Étienne Dolet, his friend and betrayer, the man who printed his *Pantagruel* and was executed for using Rabelais' own words. (I think of the woes that are going to descend on my poor publisher.) And I think of that statue to Étienne Dolet on the Blvd. St. Germain, which I used to look at wonderingly every time I went to the woman dentist. Interesting neighborhood when you ascend the hill—Mont St. Geneviève. And Rabelais placed great emphasis on Sport—Athletics. Gave it great prominence in his educational plans. Loved it so much he almost forgot his learning! Do you see why I am interested? That he was an encyclopedia of learning, there is no doubt. He drank in everything—was insatiable—so that that cry of the baby Gargantua, or is it Pantagruel, "A drink! A drink!" becomes a fine symbol.

Meanwhile that shadow of a Rabelais, Osborn, has sent me some more hefty letters and a copy of his story "Janine"—"An Impressionistic History of Prostitution in 4 Parts." You must read it to appreciate it. Words fail me. (Albeit I wrote him a 12-page letter of criticism. Nobody but myself, I suppose, would waste that much time on it. But, damn it, there is a volcano speaking, a chastened celibate who says "he is thru with all that.") His letters touch me. Fred says I am paying him back full measure by my letters, by reading his junk, etc. but I say he is an interesting human being in torment and distress—and who knows but what he may be some day a real writer? He is simply 50 years behind in style and ideology. But all that can be overcome. He waits dotingly for [H. L.] Mencken to say something. Pathetic, that! I know too what that once meant—waiting for a kindly word of criticism. So do you!

He is going to send me shortly his second story "#2 Auguste-Bartholdi" in which he says I figure big—along with my genius friend John Nichols and that Russian woman, Irene.* I am curious to see it. (His picture of Les Halles was truly fine—it harks back to Rabelais' picture.) Now and then I recognize phrases, ideas, overtones of my own writings—but I think he was unconscious of it. Oddly, there is

---

* Miller had spent the winter of 1930 in Osborn's apartment, 2 rue Auguste-Bartholdi, which looked out on the Place Dupleix, not far from the Champ de Mars and the Eiffel Tower. Irene, at the time, had been Osborn's girlfriend and Nichols was a young American painter whose work Miller admired.

next to no prostitution in the narrative—and, it is scarcely a narrative. Mr. Niagara Falls! That's what he is.

Incidentally I took the wrong portfolio the other day. Brought back *Tropic of Capricorn*—so those pages I took out *do* belong herein. If you come to Clichy in a day or two, will you bring the other along?

More dreams. Falling behind on the records.

Everything is well. I see that 2nd book [*Black Spring*] falling quickly into line. I'm going to fall on it and assassinate it. Wasted too much time on it already. Dostoevski weather, eh? We bought a marmite and made a wonderful pot-au-feu which lasted two days. *Fills you marvelously.* I love it. We'll make it for you someday.

At rue St. Honoré I saw a picture in window one night (store closed) that I am going to look at again. Has an astrological aspect. If you are in that region, notice it. I have you in mind—it was pretty dark and I couldn't well make it out.

Will be having my corduroy coat tomorrow—altered as per suggestion. I love it. Jesus, when I put on my glad rags now I don't recognize myself any more. Everywhere I look I see a me that you have made. You inhabit the walls. Bought 2 fine big sheets of white paper and pinned them to wall. Watch them burgeon! Anything may develop therefrom. I realize more and more that I am leading an *interior* life. Nothing outside excites me very much any more. I walk along with thoughts, always a little "en retard."

Your letter—yes, that was precisely it. But don't *overelaborate!* Nevertheless, raise the roof. Keep writing—write when people are around—it lends a hectic quality. Wrote Rank and await his reply. When do I see you?

HENRY

P. S. Where Fred is a genius is in the bedbug ideas he gets. He describes the evolution of his narrative—"all the hotels with a certain kind of wallpaper—I'm not finished with them yet—30 pp. of it!"

P. P. S. Yes, I believe in that method of pursuing germs. Track a thing down to the ultimate—and in the subsequent book make a fine, edible croûte au pot of it! Bones with marrow in them. A little marrow on *bread!!*

P. P. P. S. If you let the meat boil too long it gets tough. Fine maxillary bones that make gravy. What was once a sentient spinal column!

[Clichy, January 29, 1933]
Sunday

ANAÏS:

Am sending herewith two envelopes, one containing Osborn's last two letters, the other containing his story "Janine." Don't skim over them—read them carefully. They're pathetic, and I prize them as human documents. The last is especially sad, as you will see. When it came to Putnam and Bald—their faces *chalked*—I gasped. And the rue *Dupin!* Truly, he's gone. . . . Can you imagine now what that "Auguste-Bartholdi" story will be like? A riot I suppose. And what on earth can be the "hotcha" drawings of my friend Nichols?

Incidentally I have worked like a Trojan since seeing you. Must have retyped another 30 pages, with interesting changes—particularly on "Eugene," * which I finish off with a dream, and the Olga Tchekova episode, vastly improved (Venus in all 12 houses). And I have shuffled the parts around, given a better order. Yes, big good changes. The thought of handing it to Rank spurred me on.

HENRY

"Folle à la messe—molle à la fesse!"

Paris, 2/7/33

ANAÏS—

When you come to Rabelais you are going to open your wide eyes a little wider. Note the chapter on "How to Rebuild the Walls of Paris!" That's all. Not a word more. That, my dear woman, hasn't been surpassed since, before or— There was a guy! An age! Courage! And these bastards today asking me to lop off a little here and a little there—for fear it may have an excitatory character! (Read Rabelais —and then read Petronius. You have missed something.)

Passed the store with the astrologico—cosmico—macro-micro— dingus in the window. Went in. 200 frs. Too much! But it's a hand

---

* Eugene, the Russian refugee, who leads an impoverished life in Paris, and sings in the pit of an empty movie theatre "as if he had for audience all the crowned heads of Europe," appears briefly in *Tropic of Cancer*.

engraving in color. Very fine—*but*. Make Popper Allendy buy it—it's up his street. Very astrol—d'you know!

Fred says if you intend going to French library more than once for research work you need a card—first get a letter from your Embassy (go to Geneva and see League of Nations!).

I'm feeling swell, bully. Passed the crisis. Saturn must have cast a cusp of melancholy over me. Taking wing again with Mercury and by Jupiter I'll have my fling.

American Library has no copy of *Revue Psychanalyse,* so if you can grab it off do so. I'm getting you another *This Quarter*. Hope you had a fine goofy half-hour with Messrs. [René] Crevel, [Paul] Eluard and Cie.* Always stand near gentlemen who are swallowing themselves.

HENRY

P. S. When you're having a Porto with Hermeneutic ** ask him nonchalantly what he knows about the "House of Atreus" or any other fine involutional maisons publiques.

[Clichy, February, 1933]
Sunday Night

Enclosing all the recent dreams and a copy of my notes on the "world-ash" Ygdrasil, which I promised you long ago. Freeman has been here and we had an amazing talk on things "macrocosmic." According to his "numerology" bunkum this year is to be a splendid one for me artistically, involving some travel and around October a complete change of activity, the beginning of a new cycle and the end of my last 9-year cycle.

With the typing of these dreams and various other notes I have

_____

* Crevel and Eluard belonged to the inner circle of the Surrealists, grouped around André Breton, who was the prime mover of the circle and its chief propagandist. Crevel, in 1932, published one of the best surrealist works, *La Clavecin de Diderot*. He committed suicide in 1933. Eluard, during the 1920's, published *La Vie Immediate, Le Livre Ouvert,* and *Donner à Voir* but returned to the Communist party (from which all three had been expelled in 1933) and a "natural" style.

** Hermeneutic—"the explainer"—is a joking reference to Dr. Allendy.

cleaned up my affairs. The notebook has grown tremendously and is
more exciting than ever. You will see from the last dream what a kick
I got out of the last pages of *This Quarter*. (Incidentally, have you a
copy yourself? If not, I am going to get you one. It is important.)

After coming away from Louveciennes I had some tremendous
ideas. Remind me to show you *This Quarter*—in connection with
Dali, Crevel, Bunuel, Eluard, etc. Strange how when I lay a thing
aside it is only to pick it up again at precisely the right moment.

All that you told me about the horoscope and the "theatre" sunk
deep—I may not have shown it. Things are moving along cosmically.
I look forward confidentially now to a successful issue with Rank.
An eventful issue. My instincts are warning me in advance.

The only thing is, I mustn't die. There is a possibility of death, according to Freeman—but since I weathered the other great cyclical
changes there is a good chance that I will weather this one. I am entering upon a period of lowered vitality, he says, prior to a big change.

As I read the symbols, this death business, transliterated physiog-
nomically, can mean a rebirth. I think that is what is happening. At
any rate, I may run out to the American Hospital just the same. I
found a soft lead pencil—good for wall notes.

HENRY

[Clichy, February, 1933]
Paris, Monday, 1933

Just a hurried note to say—"go to see *L'Extase* immediately.
It's splendid. And the audience is baffled. Hissing and cheering afterwards. Cries of *Encore!*

But—most important of all is, I am sure it's a D. H. Lawrence
theme—must be taken from one of his short books which I don't
know. Perhaps *The Woman Who Rode Away*. Anyway, even if I
had had no suspicions I would have said it was Lawrence immediately.
(Not a word concerning the authorship—this is very suspicious.)

I want you to see it and tell me which story it is. I shall probably
write about it tonight, taking it for granted that it's Lawrence's. I'd
like to have my version of it posted on those billboards outside. The
French critics seem to appreciate [Gustav] *Machaty's* work—its film

qualities—but have not a word to say about the *ideas* expressed—all over their head, I'm afraid.

This is exciting. Something must be done about it. Maybe you'll sign your name to my criticism (it's foreign enough—A.N.).

The film is great in a new way, which derives from Germaine Dulac. I don't credit Machaty with exceptional ability or originality. But he caught *one* great Lawrence idea—*slow motion*—and he's capitalized on it.

HENRY

P. S. Forego answering your letters now—later—am excited. Wrote some swell pages last night—but want to add more. It's all going great.
P. P. S. Ordering a Welsh Rarebit because you say I should eat.
Rien. Rien. Everything's *swell*—I'm telling you.

[Clichy, March 5, 1933]
Sunday

Stay neuralgic so that I can send you more to read! Here is a fresh batch from the black lace laboratory—ten pages of excerpts from Rank (which you probably don't need), ten pages of expanded outline for section "Universe of Death," and six pages of balderdash on Spring which the walled-up soul of the Late-City man is sensing through his pores.* (Fred says he read the last twice—no comment! I think he's disappointed now, which is good. He will be glad to see that I have lost the faculty of writing "literature." No, this is not a fine flowerpot. I have lost the faculty. Hurrah! I wrote it only as a concession to my blood. It stinks, and I know it. My blood has gone entirely to my head, as Ruskin went to Proust's head.)

When I read those two-month-old notes I did not notice that they were about me. I was thinking who is that guy, I ought to know him! You crucify me with praise, if this be praise. Nobody could live up to such a peroration. (But this probably accounts for the ten pages which I just knocked off on the "Universe of Death," which ran away from me, became a little more than outline.) Today, when I awoke and saw that clear, bright sky, looked at my hands and saw that they

---

* See "Third and Fourth Day of Spring" chapter in *Black Spring*.

glowed, I wanted to be in Spain where it is always sunshine—I cursed Paris! And when I saw the headlines in the newspapers—complete close-down of all banks, moratorium, disaster, etc. in America, I shouted Hurrah! Maybe I will have to live out the Unconscious in Spain, with flowers and sunshine; maybe it is there that Eros will be enthroned again.

Am going to Lowenfels' for dinner this evening—says he has a message for me from Fraenkel. And tomorrow (Monday) at five-thirty I have an appointment with Rank. But if you have the time and can get away come here early. Or, if I get up early, maybe I will telephone you and come out to Louveciennes for lunch! I hope so. I can't believe you are ill—especially with neuralgia. I believe it is only the periodic procrastination brought on by biologic necessities (a metaphor in periphrasis for a common complaint).

I am going to Rank in full panoply, with questions and with indictments. Still breathing mountain air, dizzy from the heights, but closing in on the problem more and more, getting supersaturated so that when the discharge comes it will be a cloudburst. I want it to rain blood.

About Marie Bonaparte, did I not forsee something like it? Did I not say what a queer name for a psychologist? People can't have names like that and do serious work. Tomb psychology. I detest the very name, Edgar Allan Poe. It is a raven's croak.

If all the banks crack will your life be happier? Will you accept a vice-presidency in the empire of neurosis? Or the republic of schizophrenia? After all this is out of my system I want to write a burlesque on it. Only in the realm of ideas is life serious; otherwise it is merry and tragic. More merry perhaps than tragic. Spring is here, and even if Sacré Coeur is more or less than I say, it is Spring nevertheless. Even the rust spots proclaim it.

HVM

[Clichy] March 7th, 1933

ANAÏS:

I know what your impatience must be like and that even this brief interval is too long. Consider above all that I did not leave Rank's office in a state of drunkenness (as I did Kahane's that day), but in a state more like that which must have been Napoleon's when he came away from the signing of the great treaty—a mere affixing of the signature to something long ago inspired, envisaged and destined—the seal of conviction, as it were. And for all that it was not less portentous than the Kahane affair, rather more. The whole interview, lasting over an hour, passed off with the rapidity of a nightmare, and if I use the word nightmare unconsciously it is because there is significance to it; for, in a sense, there was in that quick, brilliant challenge of minds, a tremendous and fathomless exultation going on in the depths of me, a trampling down of many lives in me, of many failures, of many misgivings. Coming away, for example, I had a most intense appreciation of the powers of an analyst—in this sense, that quick to divine the situation, quick to evolve all the material of our discussion into the highest possible synthesis (an effort which I made with him, and perhaps even more than he!), what had been achieved was no less than a brilliant, an artistic cure. I mean, that by dint of my own long preparation, my receptivity, my thirst, I was able, through the swift contact with the very core of the man, to emerge "cured"—cured as one can possibly be. Cured. Of what? I almost deplore the use of such a word. Certainly it was not as a sick man that I went to that office, and certainly I was not *cured* in the sense in which that word is employed, even in psychologic parlance. Cured I was of certain terrible timidities, which we discussed only a few minutes before my going there. What I needed was the high challenge, the acid test, and I got it. And where Rank stands after thirty years of struggle, diligence, research, exploration, etc. etc. there I stood, equally firm, firmer I'm telling you, despite all the temperamental diffidences and all the questions and obscurities and contradictions in my soul. The triumph lay in the feel of the whole situation—there was no duel to vanquish, rather it was like some preliminary passage of arms where you test out each other's strength. And, if I may continue with that metaphor, I may say that I felt my wrist stronger, firmer, my aim more accurate, a deadly aim. Yes, this is a dramatization, but that is all I can do for the moment—dramatize it, poetize it. Perhaps I exaggerated when I said over the phone that he employed the word "amazing." Perhaps that is my representation of it; but it was there, whether he used the word or not; it shone in his eyes, it revealed itself even more by his temporary bewilderments. Read into this all you want of ego, make the necessary subtractions—it remains a fact that I conquered, and not the least important fact that I consider the conquest a victory over myself, my Romantic self, if you will.

That, in discussing his views, his book—his macrocosmic picture, what?—I should have seized on the most salient things, should have penetrated right up to the hilt, I do not give myself too much credit for. That he admitted to me that what I admired were precisely the things he himself was pleased with, was something; but that he (and here lies his excellence) should have unequivocally admitted the weaknesses, that speaks worlds. And by what was he convinced? By the fact that I put my finger on his "optimism," the illusory, lying, self-deceptive things, the Germanic striving, the dynamic, aggressive, hopeful, wishful thing which always leads the German mind, in the end, into the bogs of hopeless mysticism. That I had to remind him, and receive his wholehearted agreement, of the fact that he had not advanced a step beyond Nietzsche, that in fact, he had really lost his grip on that high view temporarily. That the parallelism between his soul-theories and development of soul to the Spenglerian one was only a parallelism, a description of the trajectory of the individual soul from its earliest beginnings to now, whereas Spengler's was a description of the seismographic course of the soul which lives in the Cultures. That these two views were equally valid, not antithetical—that they were points of view. That, rooted as he was in the psychological ambiance, he was more suspect in his views, that his own hopefulness was a shutting of the eyes to destiny. He tried to make clear what he meant by that last chapter, "Renunciation," and the possibility of a higher development of the personality. In the end he had to restate it —he put it in the form of a concession to me, an admission of temporary doubt, etc. That there was no possibility of achieving anything in art any longer so long as we believed there was, but that of course the creative instinct was imperishable and would always reveal itself; that only when we had given up, recognized the end, as it were (died, I might almost say), could we hope for a resurrection, in what form or manner no one could say. That the old ideologies had been exhausted, used up. That before the creation of a new one, a new art, a new expression of the soul, there had to be that employment of the creative faculty upon oneself (remember always his theses: the conflict lies in the dual aspect of the artists's creativity—creative impulse seeking to express itself in life *and* in art). Here we arrived at the very

gist of things by a sudden mutual agreement of the vast importance
of that chapter "Macrocosmic-Microcosmic." (This chapter and the
one on "Language," he agreed were his *real* contributions to the subject.) You know how much I got out of them both, how I raved about
them. Here he was quite amazed that I should have been prepared for
him, and that, as I hastily sketched in the outline of the brochure,
where it touched upon his theories, that I had already embodied so
much of his thought. Here we went over the ground of "death," its
importance, and here he made great revelatory flashes. Because precisely here lies the crux of the whole problem, or point of view. As he
said, that chapter "Macrocosm" is really the point of departure—you
can look backwards toward the beginning of the book and forwards
toward the end from there. Here we both agreed, Lawrence had an
intuitive perception and he was quite splendid in his admiration for
the passionate, poetic expression that Lawrence gave to the idea, ad-
mitting of course that intellectually Lawrence was inadequate to it.
(But, he added significantly, who was prepared then to do it justice?)
All this went on, with the question of "Sexuality" in the offing, an
undertone that had been sounded several times, a continuous probing
on my part to get to the root of it. (Here again he agreed that
Lawrence was weak and vague, that he lacked the larger framework
in which to insert his sexual mysticism, as it were.) Most vital to understand, Anaïs, is this: that long before man was aware that there
was any relation between the sex act and reproduction, fecundity, he
had begun the macrocosmization of the world—that is, the elaborated
picture of life, first magically stated, later metaphysically put, whereby
he explained his existence; a projection, in other words, of his self-
study, his body feeling and knowledge, into the universe. The great
irrational fear (he was mighty proud that I had caught the purport
and value of that phenomenon) one might say crystallized in this
primitive man into the more concrete and tangible one of "fear of
death." The conception of the soul takes its stance here in the idea of
that something which was part of the body, very real, visible, etc. that
lived on perpetually and contained in itself the seed of future rebirths,
reincarnations, etc. And here art takes its rise, art being nothing more
originally than the endeavor to make concrete that abstract idea of
a soul; and that concretization proceeds by means, naturally, of plastic
representation. This, then, in its crude way, in its staggeringly real,
corporeal aspect, is his view of the genesis of art. Now then, much

much later (when, cannot be defined precisely) primitive man does learn of the vital relation between the sex act and birth. *But*—and this is simply marvelous, on the surface incredible, and yet, as you will understand later, perfectly natural and comprehensible—but even when he does perceive that relationship he rejects it! The idea is thoroughly inimical *because* it disproves his theory of death, or rather of immortality which the soul achieves as a triumph over bodily death. But since it is a fact which he cannot deny, this reality of the sexual act, this birth and dying of the individual, he incorporates it into his cosmological scheme, his metaphysics, if you like, and gives it an exaggerated emphasis, a sacred character, a symbolic import, etc. etc. Do you follow me?

This then is what Rank means (and he has explained it elaborately in an untranslated German book) by the "era of sexuality," that era, coming quite late in art development, when art receives its sexual cast. But all primitive art, wholly contrary to the general and vulgar belief, is devoid of sex emphasis; sex appears only incidentally, as it appears in actual life, and even less than that because it is allied to the hostile forces of life, it is inimical to man's projected macrocosmic picture. How important this is you appreciate. Here lies the root of all that *evil* and *destructive* aspect of woman which man has created through his varying culture patterns—persistent, ubiquitous, and ineradicable quality of his thought processes, directed not against woman per se but against that generative symbol which she expresses and which negates his cosmical view of life and birth, of creation and death. Marvelously clear to me. And what did I say now and then about the recurrence of the "Woman Question" in connection with great eras of discovery? Why was it that during the Renaissance, the discussion was waged for over a hundred years—discussion that to us seems so futile, so naïve, so malicious and unintelligent? Because, as I see it, with that revival of soul-stirring, soul-birth, man was looking for a *higher* explanation. And remember about the Renaissance that it was exceptional in its spawn of great individuals, men *and* women (probably never were there such high types of women as then!); remember that these men of eminence were discussing that very problem (perhaps not understood as herein) with those very women whom they admired. Remember all I have been trying to say about the masculine aspect of the civilizing process, that all culture is built up on an evasion (that's how I was putting it to myself, perhaps not so neatly as Rank) of that sex problem—that *dilemma* really. For when you consider woman, in her role of generator, of begetter, when you consider how analagous she appears, to man's mind, to the role of Nature, Nature which spawns ceaselessly and carelessly and destroys at the same time, how natural, inevitable it is that this artificial, this abstract, this thoroughly *mental* image of life which his Culture is should be opposed to the female view, the female principle. Woman is, man becomes—I think that was one of Spengler's phrases. The becoming! That is pure ideology, an invention, an illusion that nourishes man. And so, when man comes to macrocosmize his world, that tiny inner world of his, that microcosm which baffles him eternally, man tries (and indeed he has succeeded, if the existence of civilization is any proof) to establish a creational view of things, not by sex, but by fission, by parturition. Here again Rank makes a great contribution. Man, says he (I am not quoting literally), in his creative life finds himself obliged to spew out, as it were, that huge riddle, that macrocosm which he has ingested (for if he has created it he is also consumed, swallowed by it); he must disembody it (*se débarrasser*—his words), and since he cannot, as I pointed out earlier, resort to sexual symbolism he resorts to a still earlier one, birth as parturition, the body splitting into two or three or four, but a fission, a simple division, a world produced from a world as a planet is produced from a sun. So that later (and here I am building up not from our talk, but from conclusion of previous reading), when he accepts the rationale, as it were of sex, he falls back again most naturally upon the incest idea—why? to discredit the father-mother relationship. Precisely this way, as I see it—that in performing the murder of the father and the unnatural violation of the mother he performs a dual role: he accepts the element of sex, along with its fatality (and you see how the undertone of the myth gets its tragic impress), while still clinging to the older and the more potent conception—parturition, self-creation. He makes of his necessity an act of freedom again. He persists, in other words, in restoring the magic, the deeply religious quality to his creative faculties. His incestuous longing then is a sacred characteristic; it is this perhaps that Nietzsche meant when he spoke of the necessity of man to commit the unpardonable sin, to commit the crime against nature, against instinct. Man *is* the crime against nature—or that is, his representation of Life is such a crime. It is something he can only adhere to by a violation. Here, and am I happy to state it, lies what there must be of Orphic mystery! This incest route, traversing as it does all the ramifications of the sexual anomalies (the mating of man with mother, with sister, with animal, with goddess), this route leads man perpetually back to the fulcrum on which his universe rests—"the irrational phenomenon of fear," says Rank, "world-fear and dread," says Spengler, the tragic springs of life, from the Nietzschean point of view. Anyway, life reduced to its fundamental terrors, its horrors, its awfulness, its absurdity, its sublimity. But *Life*—even though the way be through Death. And therefore, Q.E.D. and reply to all the optimists or pessimists, to all the jugglers of thought and the archangels of logic, the right way to look through the telescope is from Life. Death is a point of departure, a crossroads whence there are infinite possibilities. But all the possibilities must be lived out in Life.

And if this contains anything of revelation, of wisdom, of real vision, take it as a gift which only you have made possible for me to offer. You have been the teacher—not Rank, nor even Nietzsche, nor Spengler. All these, unfortunately, receive the acknowledgment, but in them lies the dead skeleton of the idea. In you was the vivification, the living example, the guide who conducted me through the labyrinth of self to unravel the riddle of myself, to come to the mysteries.

Often, when you deplored your ability to act as analyst I had glimpses of what I now perceive clearly. If one goes the whole way with you, if one *can* go the whole way, indeed, one is rewarded by a different product entirely, something quite unpragmatic, something, and I am glad to say it, *unreal*. One is privileged in the end to drink of wisdom. I say this very, very romantically! It is sheer romanticism in this day and age to speak of the value of wisdom, for it is a value that is no longer wanted. It has no efficacy in this world of reality which has been created, because this world of reality is a world of death. It is the bitter unreality, the world that lies outside of the psychologist's ken, the world to which we *should* never become wholly adapted, that you have led me.

HENRY

P. S. I think that was the last word with Rank, as I left him—wisdom!

[Clichy] Mar. 8th, 1933

ANAÏS:

It was by mistake that I kept your Nietzsche volume, and a very good mistake, as I had the opportunity to glance over "Ecce Homo," which I last read in the kitchen of Pauline's flat [in Brooklyn] just about eighteen years ago. And the flavor of it was very familiar to me. Sandwiched in between a mass of drivel you will find some startlingly penetrative utterances—all based on an examination of the self which here takes on an aroma of luxury. Fundamentally he is sound; superficially he is a jackass, a clown, a megalomaniac. But where he dwells on the creative aspects of himself he is amazingly instructive. Certain phrases of his have sunk deep in me. And this obliges me to recognize to myself something which I may perhaps have said before in different fashion—that once you have recognized the deep truth of a statement you are permanently altered. The man I was at twenty-three, who felt Nietzsche so powerfully, was indelibly influenced by his thought. It is that which sustained me, without my knowing it, perhaps, all these years. And I think it was Nietzche's withering skepticism which preserved me from the meshes of catching abstractions, even though I appeared to be foundering now and then.

At any rate, this evening, whilst lying on the couch, I made a discovery, or at least reaffirmed a discovery which had been dormant. It is this: that while one tackles a job, writes a book, one must write several books concurrently. Not write them, as it is usually imagined, but let them grow. For it is when you are in the throes of a creation that you create multilaterally, as it were. He who finds himself obstructed during creation, finds himself invaded by extraneous ideas, should welcome these irruptions, and not seek to deflect or suppress them. (And that is the universal sin among artists.) Therefore, as I already informed you, I am giving ear and voice to these intrusions; I am going to let grow the various books that have already taken root in me; and as time goes on, while I am finishing the allotted task these notes and hasty expressions, these unbidden ecstasies, will accumulate in their separate folders and one day I shall look at them and behold, there will be the books that I was going to write! What are these books? Principally, the saga of June (*Tropic of Capricorn*), the Cinema (about films and the art of the cinema), the Scenario (*Palace of Entrails*), the Dream Book. Since it has been made so clear to us, through Gide's words on Dostoevski, that each book contains the germ of the next, let us take advantage consciously of this condition of creation. The author is like a tree in the midst of his creations; his creations are the atmosphere in which he bathes; as he grows he sends down roots and it is from the roots that the future trees grow, not from the blossoms and the acorns. Or, think of a snake: a snake does not shed the old skin until he has grown a new one. The book you write is the old skin that you are shedding. The important book, the new skin, is always the one that is unborn, or, if not unborn, unseen. The life in the womb, the embryo. And just as each child born is only the miraculous resultant of chance, the one out of the infinite possibilities, so the book which comes to light is only one of the many forms of expression; the great author is like a monster who produces not a single prodigy, but a whole litter!

HVM

[Clichy, March, 1933]
Thursday

ANAÏS—

Got your letter shortly after telephoning. The 100 frs. came in damned handy. I was walking around in Fred's patent leather shoes which didn't fit me and caught a fresh cold changing from his shoes to my thin sandals. Anyway, I just bought a stout pair of workingmen's shoes here in Clichy. They asked me if I worked in the quarter. I said yes. Nice to be taken for an ouvrier instead of a rich American.

I had a rendezvous with Halasz (*Brassai*) at the Colisée in the late afternoon—he had asked me to accompany him while taking some photographs. We missed each other and I sat there an hour and a half waiting and watching. What a world! It interested me—*for an hour and a half!* Beyond that I think I should get up, and shout. But what's amazing, Jenny darling, is the airs they wear! As tho' there were no crises, no war impending, no Hitler, no Soviet Russia—nothing but prosperity à la française. Like ingrown toenails. Fatuously unsuspecting and indifferent. Reminded me of what life was like in Vienna, say, before the war. Curious Thursday afternoon atmosphere—with delicate children, blue-veined, white-skinned, sipping expensive ices, etc. A crime! against the children.

What do you mean quoting the numbers of those pages? I will look them up. Looks mysterious. I just glanced over a volume of Edgar Allan Poe's *Weird Tales*. Remind me to show it to you—how putrid, tame, feeble. Why did Baudelaire pick him out? I read all the stories named after women first. Came upon that "Ligeia" with the larger than usual eyes which Lawrence objected to. No wonder. Terribly archaic language. *Really infantile.*

Got seven new poems from Osborn, including one on myself—accusing me of treachery. And one on Freeman whom he calls "Peeping Tom, the Flute-player"—rather funny.

I'm curious about the [Blaise] Cendrars * book. If you happen to see the Marc Chagall book, bring it along, will you? I'm drinking hot grogs.

HENRY

P. S. I'm telling you that both the original *House of Incest* and this new one will come out O.K. And you'll sell them! I feel sure of it.

[Clichy, March, 1933]
Tuesday

Enclosing more pages done last night. Have just read *all* the references to Nietzsche in Spengler's book—and what a revelation! With this I start on a new tack. This crystallizes my whole conception of the brochure. Wherever Nietzsche's name appears you put your finger on a vital spot.

Also including Wambly Bald's column—see mention of "Ygdrasil" —I had nothing to do with it.

HENRY

P. S. (*Hidalgo* means son of *some*body.)
P. P. S. I saw my name in Spengler opposite Alexander and Napoleon—"*paroxysms.*"

---

* The French writer (1887–1961) who, with Guillaume Apollinaire and Max Jacob, was one of the precursors of the "new poetry" and a man whose life of adventure and travel made a deep impression on Miller. Before coming to France, Miller had read Cendrars' *African Anthology* and *Sutter's Gold*. (See also page 143.)

[Clichy, March 29, 1933]
Wednesday

Not eight A.M. yet and I'm up, fresh as a daisy and full of ideas that have been stewing all night. Am going to the bank on my wheel and will try to find some of these red envelopes for you. That fatigue of last night has disappeared. I want more and more about Lawrence—the Murry book and Colin's book * and even the Mabel Dodge Luhan one, if you still have it. I'm going to tackle him, while I'm at it, from *every* possible angle—want *all* the facts and interpretations possible. I may never refer to him again in my life. Must wash myself clean of him.

Friday! Why not come here if possible? See my daytime self. It's wonderful to get up at this hour—for a change. The world looks sternly impressive.

HENRY

[Clichy, May 7, 1933]
Sunday

You don't know what you handed me when you loaned me *Death of a Porcupine*. The essay called "The Crown"—about a hundred pages long—is far and away the best thing Lawrence ever wrote. In one way I am sorry I did not see it earlier—it might have saved me a lot of work. On the other hand it was terribly good to win through to this and to find the answer to all the enigmas he presents most wonderfully treated. It was written in 1915, same year as *The Rainbow*. It is prophetic and a judgment upon mankind. The language is matchless—reminiscent of the best in the Bible. The thought is superior to any of Jesus' sayings, in my opinion. It is like a new Revelation. It is based on Spengler, even tho' Lawrence may not then have known him. And it goes beyond Spengler—the true artist's conception of the process of life. It is difficult sometimes but never unclear. It should have *rocked* the world—but alas, who ever has heard of "The Crown" outside the elect few? The seed of all Lawrence's writing is

---

* Saul C. Colin, *Naturalisme et Mysticisme Chez D. H. Lawrence*, Paris, Lipschutz, 1932.

here—and more than just seed. It is the mystic at his most mystical. I am in love with it. *Don't*, for God's sake, sell this book! It's your great Lawrence treasure.

I have a lot to show you, but I am waiting, withholding yet a few days. You are going to be distracted, occupied. I want you to read this coming stuff with the clearest head—absolutely free at mind. Otherwise it is ruined, lost. There is a time for everything.

All this sounds pretty mild and contained. But I have been in 7th heaven—considering myself one of the luckiest of mortals.

I also gave myself the treat of rereading a certain section or two of *The Magic Mountain*—and before I return it to the library I hope to write you about it. My instincts were right. There is a character whom Mann apotheosizes toward the end of the book—he stands for life— he stutters—he is grandiose—chaotic—a force like a cataract—something quite magnificent. It will remind you somewhat of the things you wrote about me. This is another great symbolic work. You must own it.

But to return a moment to Lawrence. It is criminal that everyone ignores this "Crown" essay. It has as much importance as Luther's manifesto. I am amazed that it was written at such an early age—30 years! It is profound, moving, beautiful. It is like a Testament for a coming age.

I feel I have said unkind, unjust things about Lawrence. He is far greater than I ever dreamt.

I think I shall annotate the excerpts I have made—it is worth doing. I have copied out just about one fourth of it because I didn't want to mar the beautiful book. I have a copy for you.

And my notes have expanded. It will make a fine gift for you. It was right that I gave so much time to this work. I don't know anything more important.

Now I can agree with you—that Lawrence will not be understood for a hundred years to come. Maybe longer. We are headed in the opposite direction. He knew it. But he was not deterred. He stands out like a rock. He bides his time. I was practically ignorant of Lawrence when I began this study. Now I appreciate him deeply.

But all this probably sounds incomprehensible. Wait! You are going to see. You are going to get God and religion and all the things you never wanted—and you're going to like it—cry for more.

Anyway, we came awfully close to understanding him. But no one can truly say he *knows* Lawrence unless he has absorbed the meaning of "The Crown." This is the last word. The Revelation!

And it will last a long, long time! I feel humble and chastened. But I am more now than I ever was before.

HENRY

[Clichy, May, 1933]
Sunday

ANAÏS:

A few more pages of "Self-Portrait," * for which I begin to see the germ of an idea. Maybe you'll think it utter rot—I am dubious about its quality. But I like enormously the idea, if I can succeed with my purpose—of putting down that large irrational area, of grappling with the unseizable. Anyway, I'll let it take its course; it's a carrying out of that idea I broached a few days ago of proceeding mutilaterally in all directions. As experiment alone it may provide interesting material. (The letter about Lowenfels, for example, really belongs here too—or parts of it; and so do certain expunged passages from the old *Tropic of Cancer,* and certain extravagant, incomprehensible (emotionally or artistically) scenes from *Tropic of Capricorn,* such as that scene on the terrasse between the rich man, the whore and the beggar—there was inner violence, warping, etc. in it. That's what I'm ferreting out, as a book in itself.)

You observe, of course, that Lowenfels is exciting me. He's good for me, very stimulating, and in a way that I appreciate. Don't worry about idolatry—I am aware of everything, but I am utilizing a certain deformity of vision that he has bequeathed me. As I say this, it must seem harsh. Your own writing expresses a thousandfold better this thing I am talking about—but I can't get stimulated to do anything for myself when I read you; you floor me because you have put it all down—there isn't a remnant, a crumb, for me to pick up and start with. Do you see? Lowenfels on the other hand is like a man who is always talking off key, always sounding false notes, always tangential to my thought. That produces in me an irritation and it is the irrita-

---

* This grew into *Black Spring,* first published in June, 1936, by Obelisk Press, Paris.

tion of the mucous membrane that makes the pearl in the oyster, as you know. At the same time I have a very strong growing appreciation of his value—I had really grossly underestimated him, misjudged him, both as man and as artist. This enthusiasm, therefore, is simply the effort I am making to rectify the image. (I wish I didn't know all this so clearly!)

I am shelving and shelving your book [*Winter of Artifice*], because I can't quite make the effort to knuckle into it thoroughly, as I want to do. I am beset with more problems than ever, but not any feeling of inadequacy. Very very shortly you will see how I am tackling the Brochure—a twofold attack which ought to yield the utmost in results. I must explain it to you—but not here. Anyway I'm wheeling along grotesquely: the gas cocks are open. Funny thing is, now that you broach Poe, Poe is in the air; people are talking to me about him and about Baudelaire. Things are too quickly communicated. Let's put him under a glass bell. (*And,* please mail me, or bring me next time that poem of Lowenfels—if you have any criticism to make, let me have that too, as I am vitally interested in getting your reaction.)

HENRY

[Clichy, May 27, 1933]
Sunday

Sitting up in bed and writing this. Not ill. Just tired. Came home with intention of writing and found I had left my key at home —had to go to *Tribune* and borrow Fred's. Got home and lost my appetite. Tomorrow I start on *Lady Chatterley*.

But this is to tell you what a great joy it is to have the victrola— you couldn't have made me a better gift. It's something I have long wanted. Have had a growing need for music! You may expect some interesting remarks on music—in the "Self-Portrait" or in my letters. I have been listening to the Beethoven Quartet with keenest relish— and also very critically. Beethoven, like Shakespeare and Goethe, is one of my constant objects of attack. And I know why now, much much better than before. This chamber music is the nearest thing to perfection in musical composition—and it is therefore also the supreme test of a musician. I hear all the "clichés," the repetition, the windiness, the mock-heroics, the ranting—as well as the divine organ quality of it. I see Beethoven springing right out of Mozart and the 18th century—a divided man, again—belonging to the future more than to his epoch. I can understand the antagonism between him and Goethe—it is like Lawrence's detestation for Conrad and Hardy.

Anyway, Beethoven is the beginning of the modern malady in music —he starts the self-conscious ego business. All the dark, tortured, introspective notes are there—and the windiness, the verbosity which is the spreading out thin as the forms give way. In these superb quartets (they *are* great, you know), you feel his Mozartian influences. You feel that fine cultured culmination of things which was the 18th century. But there was Napoleon—and they had their feet in the 19th century too. They were bent on smashing the old order. Both fierce democrats. Fanatics. Idealists. They were also heroic. Beethoven once admired Napoleon—dedicated his *Eroica* symphony to him, then changed his mind. Beethoven, too, was searching for a MAN. He found none. He was himself the great man of that epoch. Vastly more important a figure, in my humble belief, than was Goethe. In a way, Beethoven is the German Shakespeare. The German soul expressed itself best, most completely, in music. Bach is a Milton or a Dante— the great *formal* genius, the rigorous, disciplined soul, sure of itself, master, eloquent, inexhaustible. Beethoven, like Shakespeare, is filled with doubts, premonitions, forebodings. Disease speaks. Great neurotic tempests. Prophets of doom!

I was thinking today how infatuated I once was with music, how I sometimes paid five, six, even seven and a half dollars for a single record, when I was only earning a boy's salary in the cement company.

The first gift I made my wife was a $250.00 victrola—true, I never paid for it in full and finally I had to sell it—but there you are. Music! I used to go to bed so often with the *Egmont* overture. I was hungry for it then. If my wife had been a genius of a composer, instead of a virtuoso, God knows what might have been my lot.

I listen now to the old pieces, the old composers, with a fine appreciation. Get so much more out of it than before when I had only a great hunger. Now I really hear! I can relate these themes and motifs and big canvases and little to all things. It isn't music alone— it's all life, all history. And it has a great lulling and provocative effect, *both*. It drives you deep inward and permeates the tone of your feeling, your thought. Music purifies, no doubt of that. Especially, the highly organic, the great formal compositions. They seem to light up the soul with a hard, gemlike flame.

Oh yes, I'm going to unload some things—you'll see.

I feel surcharged anyway, what with the enforced layoff. I enjoyed my cold immensely.

I'm like a miser now surrounded with his hoard. But a happy one, for a change.

HENRY

[Clichy, June, 1933]
Thursday

Sending these pages anyway, tho' there is more to follow. Wrote some of the best ones after you left—I think you will spot them. When I get to the subject of music I feel I am on the brink of something profound. Are you *sure* you get all that on music which Nietzsche gives? I have some questions to ask you.

We must devote a big afternoon to Nietzsche, another to Dandieu —to Surrealism (*This Quarter*) and to Rank. I have already ordered the Dandieu for you. When you read Joyce it doesn't matter if you skip around. After you read that last chapter read the next to the last (if I remember right)—the question and answer business. I like that immensely.

And listen—what does "prise de conscience" mean precisely? I am just about getting to my notes on Jung and Breton—where I left off when I was in Louveciennes weeks ago.

I shall buy some gouache tubes now and make a few illustrations in the Notebook for the 1st Volume.

HENRY

[Clichy, June 2, 1933]
Friday

Enclosing some more pages of notes which I did this morning and which should interest you now in your reading of Nietzsche. If you perceive anything valuable I am overlooking say so—there are yet a few more pages to come on Nietzsche. You see how I am trying to allocate these sections of his book—and the relationships his words evoke.

I am asking myself now—just what it is that marks Spengler's advance beyond Nietzsche. I want to have this thoroughly in my grasp. There is a danger, in my enthusiasm for N., that I may overlook wherein he is out-of-date, wherein he has been proved wanting.

What I think is vastly exciting is the similarity now and then between such opposites as Proust and Nietzsche. That is one thing I hope to do in the Brochure—reveal unsuspected affinities.

Apropos Proust—I discovered some very pregnant notes in my early American notes on him—most of them taken from *Sodom et Gomorrhe*—most of them a mere indication of my thought—the passages left unfinished. Inasmuch as Dandieu so often refers to that volume also, may I ask you (I hate always asking you to bring things) to bring it along next time? Has it a preface, or rather a large introduction on the "Invert"? I am looking for that. The line in my notes that sets me off is something like this—"he saw in the invert the symbolic victim of society." That means meat for my section on loss of polarity, homosexuality. How true this remark is I don't believe Proust himself knew.

Last night, adding a few lines to my "Palace of Entrails," I saw a possibility. Why should I not join up my film notes, the wall plan for Entrails, my dream book and my surrealistic sections in novel and *Tropic of Cancer* in one grand *Scenario?* Tell the story, with all the psychologic, aesthetic and metaphysical adumbrations—and leave it as a book from which the scenarists can plunder all they want. But my eye, what things I have to give them. That's why all this laboratory work I have been doing is good and will bear fruit. You may have thought it a silly expenditure of time to recopy notes just to allocate them in my folders—*but* there are no *waste* motions. This stuff is the very sinew of more books to come—it is my museum.

Another thing—I am looking for problems, discordances, contradictions—I want to outline them sharply to myself as I go on with the Brochure. Not how to make everything fit into a scheme, but to also leave big blocks of irreducible enigma.

Do you get this straight—difference between schizoid and schizophrenic? The former being the neurotic tendency, the latter the actual fruit of the pathologic condition—an insanity? Is that O.K.? You understand, when I read French I read with intuition often. It is hard to struggle with both language *and* ideas at the same time. And what, for instance, would *"l'action sacrée"* be in English? I think I am quite clear as to his ultimate meaning always—but the *subtleties*—God, if I knew French well I imagine I would unearth a great deal more in that book.

The program you sent is interesting—particularly because of that reiteration of "pensée primitive." Does she know her onions, Mme. Bonaparte? What a name for a psychologist!! The Brochure is like an accordion—you can open and shut it—it makes music. You don't need to be blind to play the accordion.

HENRY

P. S. Sitting here [Le Café d'Harcourt] so as not to interfere with the femme de ménage. Une vie ménagère!

[June, 1933]
Thursday, Luxembourg

DEAR ANAÏS—
Everything dumb, beautiful, clean, tranquil, healthy—just the place for a man of the late-city period! Were terribly disappointed until we reached the border (no customs or any examination).* East France is like a vacant lot, dismal, depopulated, cold, frozen, heather-ish—a blank—where things are grown, I suppose. But immediately we changed cars at the frontier we had a rise in spirits. Fine half-wits in the train speaking a horrible and ridiculous patois, teeth missing, hair parted in middle, darning, very clean—beautiful toy train, like in a surrealist dream. Very picturesque country in middle of city— the valley of the monks. Will describe it for you later. Things are quite a little cheaper here than in Paris. A place for your old age, regardless of what language you speak. German predominates—the type is thoroughly German. At night it is as quiet as Louveciennes. It has all the elements of caricature, down to the ducal palace built in *Spanish*

---

* Alfred Perlès and Henry Miller went on a vacation tour together.

Renaissance style. Music everywhere—but *schrecklich!* They are living a vegetable life here. Nothing happens and nothing will ever happen—only erosion. The place is only interesting geologically—the valley is enchanting and otherworldly. No insane asylums, no neurotics. Beer and Moselle wine. Everything liquid controlled by one, Henry Funck whose brother was an authority on the Middle Ages. Everybody gives wrong directions—but graciously. The intelligence is wanting, that's all.

In all neutral countries you will notice "space." And sentry-boxes to protect the sentries from inclement weather. (A beautiful street called *"The Holy Ghost."*) The Synagogue is Moorish, or Byzantine, in design.

Am very glad we chose Luxembourg. I perhaps will never revisit it, but I shouldn't have wanted to miss it. Nobody will ever want to annex it—it would be like inheriting some useless trinket of your great-grandfather's. There is one traffic cop and he is perfect. He *creates* traffic! We go back and watch him whenever we are at a loss what to do. Fine cigarettes, 25 to a pack, for 1.50 frs. (Belgian francs, which are 1.80 to the French franc).

The meals are stupefying, the sun shines brightly, the air is invigorating, the music makes you sleepy, the cafés are filled with cigar smoke, the entertainers are feeble-minded, the prices are absurd, the banks are cathedrals, the doors have no keys, the whores look like duchesses and the duchess raises children.

Altogether opéra-bouffe, baroque, polyglot, brittle, tinselly—the German spirit *in extremis*—Germany as it might have been under the house of Nassau. Age comes, but the body does not wither. Snow comes, but the pigeons are still cheerful.

Everything immaculate. But now one understands why the French turned their backs on cleanliness. Cafés "free of Jews," as the card indicates. Imagine a principality of 250,000 hectars devoting itself to that age-old problem of Anti-Semitism. Is there a crisis? Luxembourg will know in 1950. "On August 2nd, 1914, the Germans invaded Luxembourg, as they did Belgium, but they regarded the Luxembourgeois as *neutral* and the Belgians as *enemies.*" To be neutral is to be dead. I am against *neutral* countries: Monaco, Andorra, Switzerland, Finland, Estonia, Luxembourg etc. War—more war! You will find that Nietzsche is always right.

HENRY

P. S. A good Havana cigar—1 *Belgian* franc! Fred is studying the patois—*"Gukuk."* (a kind of cuckoo.) Here there could not possibly be a *Pension Orfila.**

[Clichy, June, 1933]
Thursday

About ten pages done of very hot stuff. Still at it and don't want to spoil it by sending it in installments. I'm enclosing your telegram to show you how it sounds to the French ear. If I didn't know where you were the telegram wouldn't help much. I sent you a letter yesterday—Poste Restante—before getting your telegram.

Am in the café now where I wrote you from when I returned from the bicycle trip. It's like the monkey house. If only they behaved this way on the Champs-Élysées—what a sight it would be. Negroes sitting with white women and squeezing their breasts like lemons, grinning all the time. And such a noise! Laughter from the bar, like shrieks from the madhouse. I don't know of any café in Paris where there is such a diversity of types. It's foul—but exhilarating. And you can get a casse-croûte at all hours.

"Chez Boudon!"

There's only one thing left to do—and that's to install beds. That would be a swell touch. There's nothing more wonderful than to see a Negro handling a white woman carelessly. It thrills me. If only they were American women—Southerners! I'd pay money to see it. And for all their carelessness these Negro boys are a lot more gentle than our chivalrous white Southern men.

Right now—there's a crazy man outside directing imaginary traffic. He's eating a pear at the same time. His gestures are marvelous. And nobody pays the least attention. That's still more marvelous. Now he's raving—cursing at the top of his lungs. He might as well be praying—it makes no difference.

Be sure to let me know when you are leaving. I hope to be able to send you the pages tomorrow.

Love,

HENRY

---

* The Paris hotel where Strindberg wrote his *Inferno* (1887).

[Clichy, June, 1933]
Thursday

Promised to write yesterday, but here it is today, and only by
an effort of will that I sit down and write. Tired, tired. Exhausted.
Sleep for hours on end, like a ground mole or a weasel. The weather
has something to do with it now, but I can't lay it to the weather altogether.

Fred writes me letters every day telling of the wonders of Poitou
and of Anjou. Tells me it's a Paradise. Paradise always a few kilometers distant.

I'm occupying myself with little things, such as getting my room
properly installed. You'll see some changes when you get back. Yesterday I sent you two books: the Nerval I bought at the victrola shop
on the recommendation of my friend Paul Villain. He says it is the
most well-known one. I haven't read it yet, so you tell me what you
think of it. The Chagall book interested me considerably—maybe because I was always fond of his paintings. It's a very human book. (The
word "human" is cropping out all the time now in my criticisms.
What's the meaning of that?) I must be sick of literature, I guess. For
the summer, at least.

And though I can't write a line, I am thinking nevertheless that
some of my tour de France will crop out in the "Summer" book which
I have yet to write. China no doubt, and Mexico. I am waiting impatiently to know what you think of the Élie Faure book—China and
Mexico especially.

Last night I met "Max." He stopped me on the Grands Boulevards,
as I was searching for a cinema. Said I looked like an American and
he wanted to talk to someone. He was hungry. So I bought him a
sandwich and a beer and sat and talked to him until one in the morning. Then he walked me home. Max is an ex-tailor from London and
New York. He gave me such a pathetic and humorous account of his
life in the sweatshops that I was between laughter and tears all night.
For instance, in New York—there was an overseer who watched him,
timed him, whenever he went to the toilet. One day he said to Max,
"You take too long." Max was angry. "Then I'm a slave?" he said.
"You're getting paid three dollars an hour," said the boss. "If you paid
me ten dollars an hour," answered Max, "I would still have to go to

the toilet. How long does it take you?" The result of the colloquy was that Max was fired.

He wanted very much to make friends with me, to pay me a visit, etc. But somehow or other, while Max is excellent material, I avoided coming to close grips. So Max said to me with tears in his eyes: "What should a guy do? I want to go straight. I want to earn a living, settle down somewhere. But where can I go? America won't have me, England drove me out. France won't support me. The world is too small. There aren't enough countries for me." When he said that I felt terrible. It's so horribly true. Not only for Max, but for millions of men today. At forty Max said to me: "I'm getting old. I've got to think about the future." And then he looks at me helplessly. And I can offer no suggestions. I say, "Yes, it's so. It's like that. There's nothing you can do. If it gets too bad, jump in the Seine. That's the best thing."

Five years ago I would have brought the Maxes home to live with me. There would have been some solution, if only for a year or two. Now I say to myself, there is no solution. This is how the world is today. Millions must go to the wall. Millions must suffer, and die. No man can do anything. These are the lean catastrophic years. No Joseph to lead men out of the wilderness. Seven lean years, after the years of plenty. Lawrence can do these men no good. Nor Mussolini, nor Lenin. Nor Jesus Christ. Nor Jung, nor Salvador Dali. There are such bad, such evil times now and then that not even God Almighty can raise a finger to help men. So it is. Men must not only suffer for their own sins and omissions, but for the sins of others, for the sins of the past, for the mistakes of history. Because a Caesar or a Napoleon had ambition, a surcharge of vitality, these present ones must suffer.

When I was looking over the album of discs yesterday I saw so many records that I once owned or that my friends owned. I heard the music over again, lived over again all those wonderful hours in twilight which I had passed alone or with a few friends. And I felt that music blots out so much. Music blots literature out completely. Life too. Music is a sedative. It makes one contemplative. It makes one dream. And I have gotten the habit now of turning on the machine when I cook or when I wash, or when I do this or that. And I grow more and more thoughtful, more and more sad, morose, melancholy. Beautifully so. As tho' I had taken a drug. And since the windows are all wide open now I often wonder, as the music plays, what goes on in the minds of the neighbors who listen to my records. "Here Lies

Love," is one of them—by America's most famous crooner. It makes one weep sentimental, idiotic tears. Not the words, but the lilt, the soft slush, the romance, the bedazzlement and bedevilment. America! With her men of iron, her skyscrapers and bridges, her two-fisted guys, her thugs, her Roman senators and crooks and what not. And yet, "Here Lies Love" sums it all up. You can wring the whole passion of the people out like a dirty dishrag.

At the famous bar I pointed out in my first letter on returning to Paris, I remarked that there were many Negroes. Heard one striking conversation between two minstrels. He was explaining, the big buck, that he felt tired out. And he says, "Yah, das how ah feels. And Joe Boyd, he broke jes like dat too. In fifteen days he broke. Couldn't recognize him no more. Old man. He broke, jes like dat." Mentally I felt myself all over. Was I breaking like Joe Boyd? What was it that got into men that made them break suddenly? As the big buck said to his friends—"The doctor he tells me I'm too high-strung, too nervous. Says I'm like a tight string and I'll just break like that if I don't be keerful."

Well, I'm neither high-strung, nor nervous. Nor quite broke yet. The miseries of the world are lying in my belly like stones. I'm suffering for others. Foolish. In the afternoons I go to Neuilly and sit by the bedside of my uncle's present wife. She has just had an operation. They are two beautifully ignorant people. Know absolutely nothing. I sit there and listen to them and all the words drown inside me like a lake. They say they are glad to see me. I don't know why they should be. I have nothing to offer them. I sit by the bedside and count the flies as she nonchalantly brushes them away with her hands.

My Uncle likes Paris because it reminds him of New York forty years ago. That's all. He hasn't the slightest conception of what it is all about. He says they are way behind the times. That's the most he can say about Paris. Tells me by way of news that another blood relative, my father's sister, died of cancer. That makes three in the family who died of cancer. Voilà, *Tropic of Cancer.*

So when you write about sun baths, smiling whores, gambling casinos, lakes, castles and all that, I stare at it with mouth open and uncomprehending. Everything seems far away. The typewriter doesn't make the same noise it used to. Far away noises. Fred asks if the electricity is repaired here. But there never was anything wrong with the electricity. He must be dreaming too.

I've got to see Uncle Dave again now, to bring him an English book to read.

HENRY

[Clichy, July, 1933]
Tuesday

What I meant by "writing again" was, not letters, but "literature." I meant that I felt I could begin again. "Listless" is perhaps just the word for my beginning. I am doing this damned article * over again because I always wanted it to mean something. It meant a lot to me, that Cinema Vanves experience. But, as you pointed out apropos Élie Faure's writings, I did not carry my vision along with me. I not only write on the flat sometimes, but I stencil it. But I'm going to tell you something—I never in my life have voyaged with any feeling of being a writer! I never remember being inspired to write on a trip, no matter how glorious the trip. In fact, the more wonderful the places, the less desire I have to record my impressions. Because, I imagine, the impressions are too many, and too chopped up, and too overwhelming, and too impersonal, etc. etc. My mind always remains at home when I travel. I don't know why. I make my best voyages at the desk. Or in bed. As every one does, I suppose. When I travel streets, intimate streets, that is different. My desk is with me somehow. I can't explain it. Perhaps it is because I know I can run to it at a moment's notice. But en route there is no desk to run to. I think a lot would change for me if I carried a machine with me, and if I stopped long enough in a place to know it intimately. I feel, after my trip, just like a tourist, and an *American* tourist, to boot. That is, empty, unappreciative. In Chambord we had dinner just opposite the château. An elderly, loquacious, and much-traveled Frenchman asked permission to sit with us, Fred and me. We assented cordially. In a moment he was chattering away, not uninterestingly (to me) telling us what there was to be seen here and there, in France . . . an apse of this epoch, a finger of the Madonna, a Roman porch, a 12th-century

---

* On Gustav Machaty's film, *Extase,* which became "Reflections on 'Ecstasy,' " included in *Max and the White Phagocytes,* Paris, Obelisk Press, 1938, and later in *The Cosmological Eye,* Norfolk, Conn., New Directions, 1939.

tapestry, etc. I stopped him rudely, in the midst of his discourse, and I said, just like an American: "I don't really give a damn about seeing these things." He looked at me in astonishment. I amplified. "I must find these things in some kind of living atmosphere," I added. "There must be people, scenery, life, houses around these things which are interesting in themselves, in their 'eternal present,' as it were. I will not move a yard to see a ruin, or a relic. I want to stumble on these things casually, accidentally, not seek them out. They are not all important to me. Voilà."

Fred was gulping his food nervously, because I had made a terrible faux pas. But oddly enough, the man warmed up to me, he swallowed it all, and agreed with me quite sincerely.

I never cut loose once on my vacation. I stopped and weighed every move along the way. Disastrous, that. I remember as a high spot Tarascon. Ville morte. Beautifully dead. That afternoon, in a tropical heat, sitting on that wind-swept highroad of the main street, the terraces deserted, the whole town dozing off behind the iron shutters. But I saw Tarascon in retrospect, as the native village of Alphonse Daudet, author of *Tartarin de Tarascon,* which I only came to read in my 35th year, upon the earnest recommendation of my friend Stanley Borowski, poet of the kitchen sink. I read *Tartarin* in that beautiful apartment on Remsen Street, where we lived for a year and were ejected finally, where I refused to clutter the place with furniture, where I moved the bed or divan into the middle of the big open room and thought I was in Japan all the time, everything so clean, so polished, so decorative, so bare. A sort of splendid poverty about us then. I read Daudet there and dreamed at night of seeing Tarascon someday. And of course I pictured it all quite differently. And then a day came when we were on our bicycles, June and I, and June was too tired to stop off and see my wonderful Tarascon. We saw the towers of the château de Beaucaire from the highway, going in to Arles. In Nice, or Monte Carlo, outside the marvelous gardens of the gambling casino, I was thinking again of Tarascon.

Five years later, alone and full of bittersweet memories, I plug along into Tarascon on the wheel. And the first thing greets me, at the entrance to the village, is a sign reading—"Nomads not allowed to stop in this town." I got off under the sign and sat down on a stone bench. I thought of my friend Stanley. I would have liked Stanley to be with me. We who were such ragamuffins on that dismal Driggs

Avenue, Williamsburg. What would Stanley have thought? While I am
sitting there, pondering the past, a peasant comes along the road,
furiously whipping three animals: a horse, a jackass, and a little burro.
He is demented. He talks to them volubly, and while he whips them
with one hand, to make them trot faster, he checks them with his other
hand. Jesus, if that wasn't just what one might expect of Tarascon!
That seemed to me expressly made for my benefit. A *Tartarin* setting.

A little later I am sitting on the main street, opposite the Hotel de
Louvre et de Poste, and a village girl passes. And upon my word of
honor, she is one of the most beautiful women I have seen in France.
Saucy, impudent, her hips swaying, her skirt, loose, full, blowing like
a sail. She is for me what Bizet, in his music, has tried to incarnate—
L'Arlésienne. And that reminds me somewhat sadly of my old friend,
George Schneider, a concert singer who would invite me Sundays to
his home, where I would meet another concert singer, a Japanese
tenor, Tomajiro. . . . All this passes in review in Tarascon—and lots
more.

I think that the moment one begins to travel one is really wretched.
One becomes stupefied by the succession of petty, annoying, perplexing trivialities encountered. "Abruti"? Is that the word? A word I like,
whether it means stupefied, or not. One travels to form associations,
comparisons, to live back. I hate that. One is always detached, uprooted. One doesn't think consecutively. One thinks fragmentarily. Or
I do, at least. When I return to the hotel at night I feel like a prisoner
returning to his cell. A place to pass the night. Not a place to live in,
think, or plan. What tip will I leave the chambermaid? Is the tooth-
brush packed away? Do you change trains? And most of all I wonder
if at the last moment there is going to be some unexpected and staggering sum added to my bill which I shan't be able to pay. It is a
torture to go to the desk and ask for the bill. I am almost afraid to look
at it. I always think—if you only knew how little money I have in my
pocket you would not be so polite to me. You would treat me like
a criminal. And I leave, skulkingly, as if I really were a criminal.

That's traveling for me. I'm cured. Never again, until I can do it
with a free conscience. I am so afraid of being cut off from my base,
Paris. Of getting to some distant point and being told "you can't go
back . . . vamoose!" Why? Because, when I look back on it, all my
traveling has been done under great anxiety. I shall never forget my
terrible mortification one day in North Carolina, when we were hitch-

hiking. We started out, as we always did, without a cent in our pockets, intending to get a hitch for a couple of hundred miles and return to Asheville, where we were living, by nightfall. Everything goes well. We go a tremendous distance, in fine cars. Always hailed only the fast cars. On the return, we somehow are picked up by a Ford car. The man is a convalescent. Had been working on the telephone poles and was permanently injured by an electric shock which threw him off the pole some forty feet away. He tells us all the way back about his life in the hospital. Finally he deposits us on the road near our joint. I get out and shake hands with him, thanking him for his courtesy. Suddenly he sits bolt upright and stares at me uncomprehendingly. What! Aren't you going to pay me? I explain that I never paid for a lift before, that we've been doing that all the time. . . . "But I'm a poor man," he says. "You could at least pay me something for the gas it cost me." I tell him I haven't a cent in my pocket. He swears. He thinks we have a hell of a nerve. I feel so conscience-stricken that I could get down on my knees and apologize to him. But June is herself, and very impudent. She walks off courageously. I stand there and babble with the guy. I don't know whether you know what an ignorant Southerner is like, a mountaineer who lives that desolate life which only people in Tennessee and West Virginia and such places understand. Anyway, I walk off too, finally, leaving him to curse and shout after me. But that experience takes the heart out of me.

Before that, I had tackled all sorts of people on the highway. I had had my pockets searched before entering the car, to see if I carried a gun, I had been made to sit in front with the driver and watched like a hawk, and I had been feted and wined, so to speak, too. I had even run off with a murderer who was escaping the sheriff. But after that terrific bawling out on the North Carolina highway my stomach turned. I can't stand that somehow. I can't stand being humiliated.

So, like Salavin, I must avow that in some matters, I am the greatest coward that ever lived. It comes pretty close to Lawrence's fear of dealing with people. It is somewhat different in this, only, that when it comes to a showdown I will abase myself voluntarily. But as long as I can avoid it I will steer clear of injury. When it comes time to take the licking I can stand it, because, I suppose, I figure that the other person is within his rights. But it hurts like blazes. I never get over it.

The smallness of people is always a discovery for me. I never habituate myself to it.

Whew!

HENRY

[Clichy, July, 1933]
Saturday

Meant to write you a long letter by machine, but after typing these pages the weather turned sour, hot, sultry, makes you stick to your seat. I sent you the telegram in great jubilation, like a man who has suddenly recovered the use of his limbs.

These pages are the beginning of a complete rewriting of the old article which I am almost ashamed to show you. I am making a very free transcription, practically a new thing. Don't know whether it will impress you or not. It doesn't matter, if it isn't so hot, because it is the means for me to get started again. You can't imagine my perplexity and despair on returning to Paris and finding myself incapable. And when the desire to write fails, everything fails. It all goes at once. There is no separating life from art, or art from love, etc.

Today no letter from you. Watched under the door every hour, hoping to find an envelope there. My letters must have discouraged you.

You say you are gambling! *Tiens!* (!) Well, and how does it go? I expect you to be broke, broke. I don't believe you are a gambler at all. I think you would be frightened if you won 10,000 francs all at once. You would be afraid of the consequences. Did you ever stop to think what you would do if you won a fortune overnight—*a real pile?*

My hope, in rewriting this "Cinema Vanves" article, has been to sell it to an American magazine. I even thought of *Liberty*—that 5¢ review! They pay well. A decent check might pay for the printing press * and keep me going a month or two besides. Do you suppose I shall

---

* Anaïs Nin and Miller had discussed the possibilities of setting up their own printing press and publishing their own works in defiance of the hesitations and problems of "commercial" publishers. While these plans did not bear fruit in Paris, Anaïs Nin eventually set up her own press in New York, more than ten years later. (See also page 198.)

ever sell anything to a magazine? I might ask, Do you believe in miracles? I suppose.

You ask about Rank. I have been thinking of him lately. I believe I shall get up courage to see him. Anyway, I shall certainly see Bunuel.

Began to read that long article on "Napoleon" in the *Psychoanalytic Review* you got me once. Do you know, it sounds absurd to me. Like a chess puzzle. On the other hand there were some very, very interesting observations. Concerning N.'s attitude toward women particularly. I wonder if you read the article? Otherwise, it is difficult to explain—it is terribly drawn out. And so damned German! Such thoroughgoing minutiae—foolish ponderosity. It reminds me of an athlete lifting dumbbells. The most interesting thing to me about the whole discussion is that it raises a question I never knew of. Why, at a certain age, did Napoleon suddenly turn against his idol, Paoli, and from a bitter enemy of the French, become their supporter? How he detested the French! That was new to me. And apparently no one knows the reason for his sudden change of front. But psychoanalysis is going to explain it. *Yeah!!!!* Psychoanalysis will explain everything in time. The new state religion. Sic hoc semper aeternitus—or some such crap.

I think the most absurd thing about human endeavor is this infernal looking backward, digging and grubbing among the ruins and skeletons. You say I am an idealist too. Yes! With a vengeance. I would, if I had the power, forbid $\frac{9}{10}$ of human activity today—as useless, as retrogressive. I would abolish every school, museum, library. I would wipe history off the slate. Begin afresh, absolutely afresh, whether for good or bad. But as men, not as earthworms, not as grubs.

One little thought stuck with me on reading of Napoleon. My incommensurable desires! I have wanted so much, so much, that knowing my ambitions, my dreams, to be unrealizable, I can content myself with almost nothing. The intermediate is only an insult to my exorbitant fancy. For some reason I was born a fanatic, an extremist. That is why I can accept French balance and wisdom. It is the end of the tether. And only an arrant egotist can be truly humble. Any man who is humble, without being in his heart a swollen Caesar, a mad, vaulting fool, is a liar. They say Napoleon loved his mother secretly—or rather, unconsciously—and because his father had tacitly allowed his friend to betray him, Napoleon arrogated unto himself the place of father, from father to emperor, to god, to insanity. Q.E.D.

Well, what do I remember most about my coming of age? That I showed no signs of responsibility—toward my parents at least, and later toward my own family. I hated my mother. I hated my wife. What does that prove, if anything?

One day I saw a whore sitting in this café. I had noticed her often, because she sat always in the same spot by the window, and she sat apart and aloof, and seemed not to bother attracting anyone's attention. She had a regal air. The other night, passing the café I observe her there again—same posture, same disinterestedness. She has a certain beauty too, I must tell you. Well, all of a sudden, as I rounded the corner, leaving her out of sight, suddenly it occurred to me how this woman resembled three women—a composite. And who were they, do you think? June, my first wife, and my mother. A hell of a lot of my mother in her. When I got to thinking about my first wife and about June, I was amazed to discover how much there was of my mother in them also. What should I say was the chief ingredient of this composite? *Scorn.* They all three had it, in generous measure. *Scorn.* I see the three of them by their nostrils, that telltale dilation, that instinctive flair for bad odors in people, events, situations.

There you are! A discovery. A single thread of aristocracy in the family shuttle. I have large nostrils, like my father. He, too, could be beautifully contemptuous and scornful.

Enough. I am reading with interest, in *Paris Soir,* the memoirs of the Kronprinz. What he thinks of Greta Garbo, of the machine age, of Caruso, of this and that.

When do you plan to return?

HENRY

Postscriptum.

Listen, the *Firebird* was great—*is* great! I am going to write again about it—pretty much like I wrote about it some six or seven years ago. I wish I had that now, just to compare. But I must calm down. I can't write about everything at once.

First Beethoven—then Stravinski.

Oh, so much to say now! I think I get these savage moods because I see it is hopeless to believe I can ever put down a tenth of what I want to. I have no enemies but myself—my own lack of strength or will. I want to say *everything!*

HENRY

P. S. I have to go to the store where you bought it. They sent a *wrong* record by mistake. I'm not going "to give them hell"—just rectify the little error.

P. P. S. Last night (after "Napoleon") had a very strange dream— of seeing my sister on the rear platform of a train, naked, and covered from head to foot with tomato-red vomit. I awoke sorely puzzled. May write it out in detail.

P. P. P. S. Brushed into "Max" accidentally. He was out searching for me. But I am immune. No Max can lure me from my appointed rounds.

P. P. P. P. S. No day passes without music. It's as if I had discovered an old and neglected friend—like Anatole!

[Clichy, July 28, 1933]
Friday

DEAR ANAÏS:

No, I have not been myself, but I am getting to be. I tell you, and you may believe it or not, that one of the great troubles with me is, when traveling, that my imagination is too great. Everything fails to fit into my preconceived image of things. And just to prove this, in a silly but awfully truthful way, I must confess to you that this morning, upon receiving another installment of Osborn's major opus I was carried away, exalted, by his descriptions of the Loire, the châteaux, Venice, Capri, etc. He visited all these places, they burned deep into him, and he retained his image of them successfully until the moment he sat down to record them. I have never been able to do that. I confessed to myself that I have never gained anything imperishable from my travels. The letters I wrote to my friends, on these occasions, are banal, trivial, petulant, impersonal, lacking in vision, in tenderness, in sympathy, in everything. I see it all as a grand waste, relieved by momentary, episodic patches of whimsical and highly personal values. These nobody is interested in, unless the man who writes them is already an accepted figure, and consequently everything happening to him is important. They will not tell the reader much about Venice, Carcassonne etc., but they will reveal something about the author's state of mind, his soul condition. But all these revelations come afterwards, with me. They come involuntarily.

In thrashing about I have hinted at a certain chagrin—that you and Lawrence could write so continuously, so personally, so wisely, so uninterruptedly, during your changes of time and place. Perhaps you give the clue in your last letter—you carry your vision, your philosophy of life with you, it is something solid, real, tangible, and vital all the time. I don't. I am amorphous, spiritually speaking. I suffer from my colorative adaptability, to use a Darwinian image. I take on the dullness of the landscape, the torpid heat of the day, the barren vista of rocks, the anonymous stream of humanity that sluices back and forth through city after city endlessly. I am protean, to the point of disease.

But I forgot to conclude what I had begun previously. Reading Osborn's passages about the great cities of Europe—excellently done, by the way . . . truly!—I realized that for me it is only and always the "literary" appeal that people and places make. The reality is void of interest. Flat. Osborn's descriptions of Chambord and of Amboise have life for me. The actual châteaux had none. Spengler's great panoramic view of the past is again full of life and meaning for me. The actual events always left me cold.

I like what you said about your own absorption of the past. You stated it beautifully. And it also disturbs me a little, how you can dispatch things so beautifully. How you can know so definitely, so cleanly, so intelligently, when a thing is finished for you and when it is not. You have no grand blurs, in this respect. You are fortunate.

I must end this in order to mail it in time.

HENRY

[Clichy, August 1933]
Tuesday

ANAÏS—

Bradley left me, as you see, a batch of printed proofs of a coming book by Brett, *Lawrence and Brett*.* Rather interesting in a human way. I'll hand them to you soon.

Have written Bradley to come here and have dinner with me soon,

---

* The Hon. Dorothy Brett, *Lawrence and Brett, A Friendship*, 1933.

as I had long promised. Maybe the night he comes you could get off
and come too?

It was rather nice of him coming here with his "proofs"—tho' I was
not here. You see from his letter that he is still hipped about you—
and *your writing*.

You make quick converts to your cause.

HENRY

P. S. Hope to start a section today on "Lawrence, *the Man*."

[Clichy, August 8, 1933]

ANAÏS—

I have the two volumes of *The Magic Mountain* for you from
the library. Should I decide to take a ride on my wheel, I will drop
them off at the house before seeing you.

I noticed that your book is in the library—it was *out!* Someone
reading it! Gave me quite a thrill to see that.

I have drawn up a tremendous outline of *ideas* (over 15 pages not
finished yet) for the *Man* Lawrence. These notes contain some of my
best synthesis. You'll see, as I begin typing. I'm going to save these
pages for you, along with the other outline pages I showed you. I almost hate to. I see now what a hellish grip I have got on him. Everything falls into whack, and with a vengeful click. (Funny thing about
L. is his fervid description of boyhood—"running wild at night"—just
as I described my own life.)

Spoke to Kahane over telephone. He says everything is okay—
never loses enthusiasm, never changes his mind. Just crowded with
non-literary (money-earning, I suppose) jobs for his press. Right now
—the "Congress of Vienna." *What* Congress? Imagine such idiocy!
Anyway, I'll have my turn soon, he says. He sounded sincere enough.
I suppose I ought to believe these bastards. Somehow I don't. But I
asked him point-blank if he wanted to renege. He protested quite
positively. He says, "We'll both go to jail together." Am still pepped
up from the "vacation." How are you?

HENRY

"Immortality is a question of character." That was a pregnant line of Lawrence's, eh?

Excuse paper—writing from my little restaurant in some heat. The night has a soft bloom.

[Clichy]
Thursday 8/10/33
*Dated by request!**

I'm not enclosing the pages after all. Because I think it spoils the effect to read in driblets. I know your impatience, but just now I don't like to be chopped up too fine. I want to be able to live up to that encomium of yours about "most eternal pages." You know, the adjective "eternal" never takes "most" before it. A thing is or is not eternal! No gradations.

The change in the room is so great! I sit in a corner facing the wall —crucifixion of Christ, Africa, and a wall fragment of a sacred cave. You can sit on the divan without facing the light. More space. I had an unusually sound sleep last night for the first time in ages—because I lie below the level of the windowsill and see no sky. Subtle differences. And my trunk is shut and makes a stand for the victrola, lying on its side. A wonderful suggestion you made. Tomorrow evening I expect the bookcase. I heard him scraping it in the court during my concert intime. Oh yes! You came a day too early. I have another set of records—marvelous things. A whole symphony of César Franck, two organ records of Bach and Franck, part of a Beethoven quartet and one part of a quintet. The purest music imaginable. I can think of nothing beyond this. This is the frozen absolute of perfection.

How different my mood now from my return! It's like the needle running off its groove when I get melancholy and despairing. It spoils the record too! I feel so solidly entrenched that only a war could rout me. When I say, "Bring a water color or two" it's merely to remind myself of others I want to do. I want to do everything again.

The book must be good now because *I am good*. Serene, serene because I am left with only my *inner* violence. At this stage music is not distracting, nor is it a sedative either. When Lawrence created

* Anaïs Nin had asked Miller to date his letters, but Miller never quite acquired the habit.

himself a *flautist* (and Salavin was one too—not so remarkable, the coincidence!) it was for a very good reason. I used to ask you if Lawrence ever mentioned music. I said it was a strange omission. Well now—and behold!—music enters in *Aaron's Rod*. It has to be a very *pure* music, too—not literary, not program, not plastic. The choice of flute is very very wise—excellent taste. You have only to think a minute, to realize how cheap, how vulgar it would have been to introduce a pianist, or a violinist, or an orchestra conductor. He has the Marchesa (being more intelligent, more cultured, more withered than himself) say her say, or *his* say, about the "noisy" symphonies, etc. Very good taste, but thin too. No power of imagination, *no great love* of music, as he has no great love of art in any form. The English blood simply will not yield a passionate aesthetic. No, Proust is an ocean, by comparison. Proust dealt with the very act of creating, in music. He is talking always about *creators*—Vinteuil, Elstir, etc. Lawrence tries to narrow his aestheticism into a religious frame. Art has to suffer. But the flautist—Aaron, Salavin—the flautist is a genuine lover of music. He plays alone, in the dark. He improvises. It is the instrument of meditation—the solitary man's delight. I should not be surprised if Nietzsche played the flute!

Anyway—remind me of this when you come. I hope to make some red-hot notes on *Aaron's Rod* before it is too late. The flute—music —very important. (So much here I can't dwell on it. But—think of it: the spirit of tragedy and the double theme. Schizophrenia. Narcissism. Flute. Masturbation the great sin! Toccata and fugue on the self. Aaron's letter has a terrific meaning then.)

Remind me of Huxley too. I want to rewrite it, if possible, with more implications.

And bring *Mon Périple* if you will.

I am going back to write more.

The gas cocks were open where I left off.

In the restaurant the proprietor was closing up as I was finishing the meal. Suddenly I look up and there is a big papier-mâché chef standing beside me. If this had occurred in a movie you would claim it as a masterful touch of Surrealism. These things happen, every day, everywhere—*when I'm alone*. I don't imagine them either.

HENRY

[Clichy, September 1, 1933]
Friday

ANAÏS—

Rushing this off to you because I think it's extra hot. You will recognize a lot of things—but the schemata! Do you like it? Jesus, I'm hoping you'll find time to read all I've sent you. I'm waiting to know whether it's good or bad. I'm in a torment.

Your letter came this morning. I'll write you more later in the day most likely. I've got to get out and walk now. My pants are burning off.

Regards to Paderewski. Ask about Beethoven deaf. And about the quartet in A Minor that Huxley used at the end of his book when Spandrell commits suicide. Ask him about the stars and the moon and what side your horoscope is buttered on. Is he horoscopically minded? And how does he eat his snails? He likes *just* the movies. That means nothing else, eh? O.K. Just the movies. Ask him without what flavor.

And as for the Padre *—no, no! I don't like *padre*. Sounds as if you were talking about a priest all the time. Why not dad? Hello Dad —Sweet Caporal cigarettes. A soubrette in every package or the Cuban flag, if you like.

I am rereading that article in the *Psychoanalytic Review* by [T. F.] Wittman—on the Modern Artist. It's all just too marvelous. According to this I ought not to be ashamed of myself—not ever. I'm a modern artist. That means a léger tendency toward schizophrenia. Just *léger*. Otherwise we suffer from the same ills as the rest of the world. No, but in God's truth, it's a fine article. I would like to tear it out and put it in my vest pocket—consult it in dreary moments. Signing off. More later.

HVM

---

* Anaïs Nin referred to her father with the Spanish word "padre."

[Clichy, September, 1933]
Tuesday

ANAÏS—

After writing the little note, made more notes on *Aaron's Rod* and they seemed so interesting to me I thought you ought to see them —and further, tell me if you think I am *putting too much* into L.'s book. This is how I see it now. Along with "Crown" and *Fantasia* I see it as one of the very *important* books he wrote. I haven't finished the notes, by any means. Doing them leisurely in odd moments. But am rather anxious to know what you think. If you haven't a copy of *Aaron's Rod* I will lend you my Lowenfels copy (library copy is stolen).

Hated to fold the pages but have no larger envelopes. Return them when you see me as I need to look back sometimes in order not to repeat myself.

HENRY

P. S. And I had also intended to show you my notes in the bound volume marked "Novel." You see, I am getting the Diary habit— from you. I notice that with the pen in hand it's a question of *"ideas."*

[Clichy, September 6, 1933]
Wednesday

Now I'm writing a small book of notes [on Lawrence] for you to bind with the outline. Up to p. *26. Point no. 86.* Like a treaty of Versailles. My head's bursting. Never made so many connections, synapses, syncopes, ellisions and syntheses in my life. And the end not yet! And, despite the note form, quite lucid, final, in statement. I have just worn down to a flame in the last two days. I can't go much further than this. It's like I reached the point of saturation—exhaustion of present potentialities. I'm amazed by it all myself. And now I see that I can really *complete* something. I started in the fullest way —something I have never heretofore done. Previously everything has been aborted by this or that—by *myself,* I suppose. Now—not even an earthquake could keep me from carrying out my plans.

Murry has put me to a supreme test. The others don't count at all
—just fuel. I'm impatient to start typing, so you can see what it's all
about, but I won't this time until I write out *all* the points. *86* so far!
That's something. Eh? It began by thinking of the *man,* Lawrence.
How he *embraced* everything. And the only way to do justice to a
man like that, who gave so much, is to give *another* creation. Not
explain him—but prove by writing about him that one has caught the
flame he tried to pass on. It's nothing less than heroic, what I'm
doing—and it will put Lawrence high and dry above the sniveling
corpse-diggers who are writing about him. If I have buried him, I at
least have buried him *alive.* I like awfully what he wrote to [Richard]
Aldington whose little brochure I just read. I want to put it in the
beginning—as frontispiece:

> "You say I am wrong.
> Who are you, or anybody else, to tell me I am wrong?
> I am not wrong!"
>
> D.H.L.

I find that *quite quite* perfect!!!

Today I got *Studies in Classical American Literature* from library.
Tomorrow, weather permitting and work not interfering, I may ride
out to Louveciennes and deliver the Thomas Mann and the "Brett-
Lawrence" proofs. Maybe.

I got three of my notebooks from the binder. The big one, like the
first, has to be torn apart. It was set up completely out of order—
ludicrously so. Otherwise damned good work—and less expensive
than your binder. I'm marvelously delighted with them. *Treasures.*
Even where there are blank pages. I'll fill in all the holes left everywhere before I'm thru.

I don't feel vain, or too important, but a force.

I *know it now.*

And to reach the realizations of today and yesterday is to verge on
madness. I am not only "not wrong." *I am right!*

HENRY

P. S. I had a clipping on the "Theatre Fontaine" but forgot to bring
it with me. Anybody would know it once you stand near the "Fétiche."
P. P. S. Epoch-making days, I tell you! It's not Lawrence—it's myself
I'm making a place for!

[Clichy, September, 1933]
Thursday

Didn't write any more this afternoon, but will go at it again this evening. Head was bursting. Here are pages of Ms. (and perhaps not so hot?) with pages of *notes* which is now my preoccupation. Must clear the decks while the spirit moves me. It's a crime to let this go to waste. And heavy dreams. Sent you a few of the *rough* notes, as I wrote them—more to follow. I know you like to keep them.

Am planning several "wall charts"—this time with very precise and purposive intent. Something on a big scale and fairly permanent which I can refer to as I work. The great need I have, with the terrific mass of data in my head, and in my notebooks, is to *see* it before my eyes, to *see it in some order*. Therefore, it may be wise to spend time on such a task—in my spare hours, of course. One idea I have is with reference to the principal characters who figured in my life. Show them and their relationship as in an astrologic chart.

I think, for example, I must have some such chart, clearly referring to my notes, on June for the *Tropic of Capricorn*.

I feel that these notes I send you today, marked "Tailor Shop," contain fine things—some that could stand almost as written *despite* or *because* of their crudities, and of the swift tempo.*

I don't want to be *Dreiserian* now—that is why I am spilling it out in notes. When I get thru perhaps I will discover how it fits into my scheme. *My China.*

But you see what a mess—glorious mess—I am in. Don't count on tomorrow. If I don't phone by one o'clock you'll know I'm busy.

HENRY

P. S. When I get ready for these "wall charts" would you *lend* me the one you have—on the plan of Novel?

---

* See chapter with the same title in *Black Spring*.

[Clichy, September, 1933]
Tuesday

Now 3 A.M. and I'm trying to decide whether I'll go out and mail this to you instantly. This is what the "city" theme is getting to. Still unfinished. May be some awkward spots in it, but I feel it has some power. Or don't you? You see the themes—music, death, labyrinth, womb, insanity, destiny etc. Some rag carpet! The key word—this is important, as technique!—is "disoriented." Maybe it's too subtle, but with that in the back of my head I am trying to weave the carpet design. There's so much good stuff in the navel = labyrinth idea—wonder if I get it over? *

I'm trying to contribute my share toward the marriage dot. The last five minutes must yield the "most eternal" pages. Because there isn't anything beyond this. As Fraenkel said, the artist then earns the right to his own madness. (Did you notice that I put lightning in the membrane of the self-portrait, to give it structure?)

HVM

P. S. Don't work your fingers off for me—just take the pages out into the street and let them explode. *You* stand still. Let *him* talk! Colossius 3. (You never asked me if it is Colos*sius* or Colos*sians*.)

[Clichy, September 21, 1933]
Friday

Had a big day yesterday at the library looking up all the odds and ends I had accumulated—the Firebird Legend, Tamerlane, Genghis Khan, fairy tales, etc. Got out Kay Boyle's *Year Before Last* —not bad, not good—rather interesting on the whole. And also that article of Fenollosa's on "The Chinese Ideograph" which is all I had expected. Will hold it for you to see!! (I'm intuitively very accurate about China!) Then I sat in the children's room, on a little chair at a little table, and I waded thru many of my old favorites—Robinson Crusoe especially. (I will take this out later to show you some quite astonishing things in it which you have probably forgotten. Remind

---

* See the chapter, "Walking Up and Down in China," in *Black Spring.*

me to show you my notes from the "Preface to the Original Edition"!)
And finally I walked out with a neat little volume of *Through the
Looking Glass* which is now my own private property. *Elated.*

A day of reading largely—and note-making. *Notes on Cronstadt.*
Expect to start typing tonight after dinner. If I have the right mood.
Have fantastic ideas for it.*

Enclosing you some pages of transcriptions from my notes on
"Urinals." Oh yes! I also got the two books which were bound for
me. They are beauties! The Lawrence one is yours! You'll like it. I
feel crowded. What a congestion! *A plethora.*

Got your note, *etc.* Is everything O.K.?

More later. Rushing out to eat.

HENRY

[Clichy, September 25, 1933]
Monday

Terribly tired. Maybe not so many pages, but I'm doing a lot
of work on it. The best is to follow. You'll see.

Discovered some strange things going along. For instance, that the
cat (*Jocaste*—not Jocatha) was the *mother and wife* of Oedipus!
That *Muller*—man who mulls wine—comes from Icelandic, I believe.
Derivation like this—*molde-ale* = funeral banquet: *molde* = grave
earth and *ale* = feast. Hence Heinrich Muller! And writing on both
sides of page, as Lowenfels does, is called *"opisthographic."*

Oölogy is the science or study of birds' eggs.

Onager = the wild ass of Central Asia.

Eventration = the act of opening the belly.

Melasma = skin disease, producing dark spots.

Listen—I've put in long hours. I haven't yet got to reading your
pages. Don't want to in a fatigued condition—might get blurred impression. I'll do a good job of it when I pick it up—and soon. Forgive
me.

What about Wednesday? I'm tired, tired. But no discouragement.
Mull a little wine.

HENRY

---

* See chapter "Jabberwhorl Cronstadt" in *Black Spring.*

[Clichy, October 3, 1933]
Tuesday

ANAÏS—

Got a flood of mail this morning, but everything's ad hoc and and post rem for the time being. Got the following letter from Bradley —copy that Kahane sent him for my benefit:

"Dear Bradley—with regard to Miller's *Tropic of Cancer* circumstances have been such, as I informed you the other day, that I have been unable to get out this book within the contracted time. I have every intention to publish it and would like to if you could obtain from the author at once the time limit in the contract to be extended for six months by which time I agree to have the book out."

And Bradley writes that he advises me to accept, as Kahane evidently means to publish it.

My first impulse was to say NO, give it back to me. But what is the wisest thing to do? I've waited a year—will another six months matter so much—from the standpoint of Herr Lowenfels' statistical I-ness? He just sent me a copy of his revised version of the "Suicide" poem today. And in the same mail comes clipping from my father, a marvelous news item out of an American paper, describing the new fortifications France is building on the German border. I want you to read it. It's terribly impressive. They have built deep down into the earth and several kilometers back a concrete volcano loaded with guns, ammunition, high explosives, all the black magic conceivable. The whole border is a sunken fortress, more impregnable than was the China wall under Kublai Khan. It is so vast and luxurious that there are railroad trains underground which convey you at rapid speed from point to point. It terrifies me. It's so secure that it just invites destruction. And believe me, the Germans are not going to walk across this yawning mouth of hell. They are going to find another way of destroying their enemy.

And Lowenfels will publish his "Suicide" in nice white kid from Belgium no doubt. Another poem from "Some Deaths." He creates an anthology as he goes along. And I roll up failures and abortions and postponements. I feel flattened out this morning.

BUT NO DISCOURAGEMENT, as Monsieur Datz says. You say you are wild, feverish, mad. Good. Write your blooming head off. I am going to pick up your book tonight and read it with an acrid eye.

Hereafter, sling it into me hot off the griddle. Don't let it accumulate. The time is now—not when I get ready. Get out the *House of Incest,* dust it up and send it round to someone else. Don't wait for a rainy day. Don't be discouraged. *This is war.*

Much as I hate these delays, much as I am disgusted with this off-hand, roundabout way of doing things, I think soberly, wisely, looking at it from every angle, that the best thing to do under the circumstances is to let Kahane have his six months extension.

I am doing everything I can, Anaïs, to get this book finished. I read it all through the other day, in a hurry, and it looks quite satisfactory on the whole. Also skimmed through the materials to be inserted—everything fits. It's just mechanical labor. I don't want another bit of material or inspiration. This Cronstadt installment will be the last fresh item—the rest is in my notes.

And tonight I settle down to devour your book.*

HENRY

[Clichy, October 17, 1933]
Wednesday Midnight

A most beautiful end to a most wonderful day was Sylvia Sidney's performance of Cho-Cho-San—*Madame Butterfly.* I was thrilled. More than that, deeply moved. Having seen the celebrated films by the Japanese players some time ago (Ancient, Medieval, and Modern Japan) I had some basis of comparison whereby to judge her interpretation. All that an Occidental could bring to the role I felt she had brought. It is one of the most restrained, most artistic films America has produced. A pure film with the operatic melodies well subdued and never intruding. The dignity of the theme worthy to make you weep.

I beg you to go see it at the earliest opportunity. It is in French fortunately, a language more suited to the noble etiquette of the Samurai. The American, Pinkerton, plays his part very well—better than you would ever suppose. The drama is kept rigidly within the framework

* Manuscript version of *Winter of Artifice.*

of the problem and the problem is a beautiful one. Don't think that it is the first time I have ever seen *Madame Butterfly*. It was the first opera I ever heard—and with Geraldine Farrar! I used to have the records. "Some day he'll come"—I remember that so well.

Whether it's because I am becoming so definitely Oriental or what, I don't know, but I am stirred all over again. I would like to write a letter to Studio 28 and request them to include in their coming program those three Japanese films I mentioned above, or the beautiful Chinese film written by Clemenceau's son, one of the few rare films I saw when in America. These two on the one program would make a wonderful cinematic program. With *Of What Are the Young Films Dreaming* as an entr'acte! Do you know this last?

The heat is turned on and it's delicious here. I come back to my room and it looks bare, austere, glowing. It's the most beautiful room in France. Has it not an Oriental character? The blue and black of the rug, the severe wood bookcase, the prints on the wall, the maps, the plain chest of drawers, the svelte divan, the blue pillow, the trunk, the green lamp? Can you see me sitting here in a Chinese mandarin's jacket with a faraway look and my opium ranged in sedate order on the bookshelves? The floor clean and polished. Dead silence. Harmony. A philosophic calm and wisdom.

I feel excellent. I am still thinking about that dismal urinal by the cemetery. Tomorrow I will write about it. Perhaps a little of the Orient will creep into it—into Levallois-Perret with its black logic and its cold justice.

One of the last things you mentioned was the books that we want to read. I give you a list of the chiefest—not to do anything rash about, but to keep before you as a guide. . . .

Jung's *Three Essays*
The Tristan Tzara book
Wilhelm on China (yes, after all—I *must* read it!)
The Giles book on China (to read again and note this time)
The book on symbols
Artaud—*La Mort et l'Amour*
Tales of Old Japan—Lafcadio Hearn (in English)
Spirit of the Forms—Elie Faure
Les Chevaux de Diomedes—de Gourmont

Histoires Magiques—de Gourmont
Jung's Introduction to *The Golden Flower*

Go to see *Madame Butterfly* when you are in a fine mood—not otherwise.

HENRY

[Clichy, November 7, 1933]
Tuesday—later

Got the pneumatique—I could tell already from the three fat
envelopes in the morning that you must be in fine fettle. As I said, I
don't know yet whether I'll get out to Louveciennes or not before
Friday—feel snowed under with all I want to do. About Friday—
about my meeting you out there—more later. Better not let me see
too many new books—just now! Enjoying the [Joseph] Delteil book
—reading only little snatches of it in the subway.

You did really go to see Rank? Dying to hear what happened.
When I tried seeing [Hilaire] Hiler * Sunday he was not home—so I
stopped in to Lowenfels' across the street and found him all keyed up
and almost insane about Rank's book. Did nothing but talk about it
—but all at cross purposes. He thinks it's great. Also has strong criticisms to make of it.

I read all your pages of *House of Incest* and the impression left by
the whole is again good—warm and vital.

I forgot to say, in sending you the earlier ones, that my criticism
may seem oversharp at times. It is because I constantly lose sight of
the fact that you intend revising and expanding it yourself. However,
when I write *weak* in the margin, it may act as a caution when you
come to the final draft. Usually what is *very* good strikes one as *very*
good right from the first writing. Isn't that so?

I enclose the dope on K. A. Porter with my carbon reply for your
amusement. Lowenfels says she's a pretty good and fairly well-known
writer, poet I believe.

I do hope maybe tomorrow to send you some pages on the

---

* See Biographical Notes.

Scenario *—but don't think I've lost heart if I don't. I'm engrossed in pushing the book to completion—in resynthesizing it. *China*.

HENRY

P. S. My seemingly *futile* discussions with W. L. always result in my growing more clear as to my own ideas, own attitude. I have to fight him tooth and nail. There is a terrific non-understanding between us. What is the *9th* house precisely? Never mind—I'll consult *your* horoscope!
P. P. S. I like and dislike Maryse Choisy somehow. She understands everything. She's nonchalant, too, with her fine understanding. Quite masculine, in one sense of the word. Again, very feminine—with her too-clear, too-ready syntheses. *Aber, wo ist der Mensch?* It's like a game to her. But she does say striking things! It's so funny—that was one of the books I used to look at in the shop windows hungrily when I first arrived in Paris.

[Clichy, November 27, 1933]
Monday
Am enclosing the *full* [Hilaire] Hiler letter **—notice the last pages which I added on coming home Friday. And from that to the color business was a natural progression. I don't know how this latter will strike you—it may not hold water, but it was very useful to me as idea. You can't imagine what satisfaction it was to strike a solution, through another picture, of the fundamental snag which I have been wrestling with. I mean that by seeing the whole business as color I

---

* Inspired by Anaïs Nin's *House of Incest,* Miller began to write a scenario for a film with sound, which was eventually completed and published in a limited edition of 200 copies, with a frontispiece by Abraham Ratttner, by the Obelisk Press, Paris, in 1937, and later included in *The Cosmological Eye,* the first book by Miller to be published in the United States (New Directions, Norfolk, Conn., 1939). The *Scenario* was broadcast in 1952 over the French radio with an introduction by Blaise Cendrars.

** By writing to his friends—here to the painter Hilaire Hiler—Miller often laid the groundwork for future articles and essays, like his "Open Letter to Surrealists Everywhere" (published in French in *Volontés,* Paris, February 20, 1938, and included in his book *Max and the White Phagocytes,* Paris, Obelisk Press, Sept. 1938), which is forshadowed in his letter to Hiler.

think I made more true relationships between the ideas than by the use of language symbols. It's arbitrary, and it may be weak too in spots, but it did something for me. It took the rigidity out of certain conceptions I had. It gave a more flexible equation for the death nonsense. I think this—that I managed to throw a bridge over the impasse between Spengler's ideas of cultural births and deaths and Lowenfels' ideas on form and structure, preserving what was best in Lawrence's vital picture of things. I wonder does it make any sense to you. Some of it is farfetched I guess, but in the main there's a thought, a tenable one.

Any way, what I mean is, I have dissolved the hard lines between birth and death, between an age of thought and age of soul-feeling, etc. etc. I have tried to show how all the fundamental factors—say the three primaries, the three vital aspects of life—are always there, and how in emphasizing one of them above another at different epochs we get a whole new system of thought, of form, etc. It's getting around the always dubious language of actual birth and actual death—which never happens—as there is always only this rearrangement, this new setup.

If I don't add it now, I may later add a little more about the function of the Surrealists—their way of going yellow, their use of nascent forms, of fragments of old forms as dynamite and ridicule, their exploitation of the substrata, the common Id possession, etc. Not that their vision of yellow is the lasting one, or the whole or the best, but that it is altogether in the key of yellow, and for that reason valid and valuable.

I worked hard—there are things on the walls to show you when you come. I feel that I cleared the shoals and can go about calmly writing out what needs to be written—as literature. I just had to do all this first—some inner necessity. And I think I struck a very good note in what I said of "significance." That is what prepossesses me —the significance, however tiny it may be.

I will call you in the morning—anxious to know what all has happened since and what you are going to do this week.

HENRY

[Clichy] November 28, 1933
Tuesday

Am I going dippy? This is positively the last word—for a good while—on Form and Significance. This probably belongs, as the pages of yesterday, with other stuff I wrote for "Scheme and Significance"—all smells like material for the Brochure—section, the *Artist*.

I notice that I seem to revolve like that—from life, or experience, to expression or art, and then run into the dry banks of thought, which I am calling significance—but which is surely = explanation, self-analysis.

I feel I am coming out again into art. I think the ideas now take the place of experience in giving me stimulus for expression.

Is it awfully bad? That's what I wonder. Expecting you tomorrow.

Had a letter from Lillian Lowenfels inviting us to Thanksgiving dinner Thursday—between five and six. I am telling her that you may be there. At any rate, Hiler and his girl will be there for dinner too. I think you may enjoy it.

HENRY

[Clichy, February, 1934]
Saturday

With the arrival of your note I've thrown everything on the floor. What I once thought was the material of a book lies about me, not in fragments, but in shreds. It would take a wizard to put it together—*and I am that wizard!* I've discovered in myself what I've been shouting about in the theory of annihilation, via Nietzsche, Jung, Father Orpheus, Mother Incest, etc. etc. I've smashed the fucking thing into a million pieces in order that I may ingest it piecemeal and throw it out again in a macrocosmic poem. I am learning method, structure, order—teaching it to myself, the highest kind of order, of form and structure, the poem in itself, as it were. I use this word "poem" in a new sense, please notice. I borrow it from my friend Walter Lowenfels—*my friend!* Note! Yes, I feel proud of it—as if it were an achievement. It was a creation, if you like. Last night the great conjunction, the breaking down of all asymptotical relations by the creation of new orbits. Is it Lowenfels I see truly now, or myself? Same thing. I see that in him which was blind in me, or vice versa. I went down with him last night into some kind of a chthonian underworld of the mind where the supreme point of identification is reached. I come home and order my book: Part 1.—Genetics of Idea; Part 2.—Poem and Exegesis. Important to note is "Poem." New meaning—*for me*. Here I have been complaining all along that I know no one in Paris with whom I can communicate, no man of sufficient stature. And by the most roundabout route I have come to exactly the man I wanted to meet. Did I create him, or did he create me? He is my counterpart, the other half of me which has been wandering through the underworld in search of Eurydice.

Something snapped in me last night. I saw the drunken poet, the goat in the man, the veils sundering, the cosmic pulse shaking his leg, illustrating his technique, exorcising his abstractions. I saw what Dostoevski permits us to see when he dives into that plasmic soul stuff in which only the divine is recognizable. I saw all the poets of creation and I wanted to shout out: Mother, mother, my heart's on fire! I saw the pictures of Picasso chanting the doxology of reason, saw the steel frame of our world sagging, the whole gaseous vertebrate of life reeling in dissolution. I see Lowenfels as probably *the* poet of the age, a fine relaxed image of a man with his Janus-faced door greeting all and sundry, his hearth full of cigarettes, his gizzards whiting with Pernod, his lust for life animating all the biological processes, down to the amoeba. Saw life in its scission and fission, saw life glab, glairy and glabrous, and *healthy and wealthy* and gladrous. Saw myself writing poems over the walls, over my frescoes, over my palaces of entrails, saw my pineal eye winking and blinking, throwing off the cover of the middle brain; I saw the personification of all poetry, the *man* rooted in earth and blood, the dumdum bullets of his brain splashing against the ceiling of the sky, encrusting the oysters with pearls, sewing the cosmos with gem-studded ideas dripping flesh and gore; I heard the weasels of his poems running through all the cellars of music, the scratching of their paws on mica eyes, the screech of his voice in isolation, the wild hysteria of his longing. He opened the accordion of his mind and it collapsed with a bang. He ran a dagger through his heart and it burned away. He opened his blood vessels and music poured from his veins. He is the man I have been looking for and I found him with my pineal eye. He is the man I have created in my loneliness and his image is heartening.

Today I get a letter from America, a letter long awaited, but it does me no good. Too late, these letters from America. Too late, O lost and by the wind blown down. Letter says "I am rereading your wonderful passages about Gauguin." Fuck Gauguin. Gauguin is literature to me, literature from the reign of Mayor Hylan, Brooklyn, Italian restaurant, dago red wine, macaroni, world of illusion, dead adolescence, idolatry, altar-smoke. Fuck Gauguin. I have no need for Gauguin. I *am* Gauguin. I am all the Gauguins that ever were, even if I never stir from my chair. I have made the farthest voyages, have circled the globe; I have gone beyond the globe, into Ultima Thule.

Today, by an act of heroism, I shattered the work of months. I am setting up a new cosmos. I have shed the brochure in order to write *the* book of the century. I have transferred the this to the that and back again. Everything lies on the floor. The shreds must be reintegrated. The shreds must make membrane, tissue, epidermis. But the Idea is glowing inside, incarnate, a world shedding its skin. The idea has two parts—its soul and its exegesis. The idea is welded by Death. Everything that cannot be integrated forms the "Soul of Death." The Soul of Death is the introduction, the Holy Ghost of the corpus. I am living in the Holy Ghost, it is Death that inspires me. Death is ecstasy. Death is not the ultimate, but the now, the immanent, ever-present. Death has been misunderstood. It is *dying* that is important about death. The switchboard of the light-world is the diorama of death. I am not interested in the switchboard any longer; I am interested in what makes the switchboard possible.

Today I could cry, if I were not so happy, because of the many deaths on the floor. Today I know what must have been God's despair when he created the universe. It is the infinite possibilities which kills God. When you say universe you think of a particular universe, and you stick God's name on it; but God is the possibility lying behind the actual. God does not exist. God is a creation because the actual is not enough. Glab, glairy and glabrous.

Salute to the Cosmos! The gas cocks are open and the form of the world is wavering. Behind the cement guitars and the word written in vellum, behind the yawp and the gibberish, the green bottle and the anodyne of *ismus,* behind all the form and actuality lies the dying, a navel nostalgia that lends to art its ether. Either ether or either, the green bottle and its broken guitars, the glabrous pang and the foot sliding off. . . .

Food! Says Fred: food! Nice wine, no cunts, no death with the meal.

Signing off. The epileptoid genesis of *ismus*. Signing off. Patina of the brain. Down through all the geologic strata of the "I." No death with the dinner. Cunts flying on angels' wings. Detachable. Gas cocks open. World wavering in formlessness. The guitar strings snapping. Picasso. Embedded in the idea of cement. Embedded morphologically. Structure. The world-as-poem. Philosophy of——sign here!

HVM

[Paris, March, 1934]
Saturday

I went to Kahane all right but the place was closed—*as usual.* However I am writing him now for an appointment.

I got *Mysteries* by Hamsun from the library for you. *Wanderers* was out, but I have put in a reserve for it. Happened to see [John Erskine's novel] *Unfinished Business* on the shelf and picked it up—*but,* despite all my curiosity about the content I could not go on reading it. It was simply terrible—*terrible.* On the other hand, I also reserved *Sanctuary* by Faulkner. I have a feeling that he is the only possible rival I have today in America. I am very curious to read him. Even the librarian, in taking my reserve card, could not refrain from remarking that it was an extraordinary book. I was wondering what he'd say if he read *Tropic of Cancer.* . . .

Also took out another very very interesting book—*Folkways* by Sumner—for that chapter on "Cannibalism." It will fascinate you, I am sure, even tho' it is written by a sober sociologist.

Have cleaned up all the original pages now, of dreams, and gotten a good lead into the final bit on Decatur Street and the snow fight. Burned right up writing an imaginary throwback to Glen Island—the couple walking in the snow water etc. Don't send it now because I don't want to spoil the *total* effect for you.

Also got two fine pairs of socks! Progress. Progress. Feel that when I next see you I shall have written the final pages of the dream and with splendor. Feel it sure now.

Somehow all you said about your father affected me deeply. Never so thoroughly realized *what* a fight you are having. But also never was happier to notice how really *nobly* you are playing your part. Was very deeply touched—bewildered, in fact. And more than sad. I'll call up Monday.

HENRY

[Paris, March 26, 1934]
Monday

I saw Kahane, after the third attempt, and finally had a good chat with him. Nothing is wrong, except that the world is out of joint —his buying public has temporarily vanished, he is not publishing a thing until something definite is done about the pound, the franc, the dollar. He was very reasonable, sympathetic, and sincere, so I thought. Wants to publish but says it's just ruining both our chances at this critical period. We understood each other quite well. My belief in his integrity and good intentions is improved. He's intelligent, alert and direct. No need on either side for equivocation. I told him of my plans—and all the details of our conversation and the net result I'll tell you more fully when I see you. For the present, the crisis stops everything! (I'll give you *figures* and illustrations.)

The pages are not many but I think good, and consider that I am just arriving at the birth of reality and it's not so easy, tho' my head is full of images. (Have had some bad interruptions.) Going back now to continue.

Meanwhile, riding the subway, I reread *Mysteries* which I am holding for you. It swept me off my feet again. And what resemblances there are between Hamsun and myself! *His* dreams, his crazy stories, his buffoonishness! It's a *deceptive* book! If you were to pick it up all by yourself and *skim* thru it, you would probably say it was *trash*. But, believe me, it isn't. And you *can't*, or *mustn't* skim it through. He *was* and still remains one of my idols. I wanted to get *Wanderers* for you but this is equally representative—if not quite so poetic. But all his force, his passion, his whimsicality, are here. You ought to adore it.

They are closing up here. Must close.

HENRY

[Paris, May 3, 1934]
Thursday

ANAÏS—

This is just a whiff, in between the time I await your letter * and the Madame telephones the propriétaire to start the heat going, to let you know that I saw Sylvia Beach—who is a *little* "subglacial," abstract, retrousée, etc.—and that it's all right, but between ourselves I don't think it's necessary to invite her—just a politeness. She's got snow in her veins.

I bought [D. H. Lawrence's] *The Man Who Died* (in a Tauchnitz edition, with the Ladybird etc.). Fine, fine stuff! Swallowed it in one gulp! Everything I anticipated, however. *Resurrection in the flesh!* (The title originally was *The Escaped Cock.*)

Am writing from a café because the cold drives me out of the room. Am going over the *Tropic of Cancer* with a fine comb. A little dull, here and there, but on the whole good. If anybody had written a preface for it, they might have explained that the book was written on the wing, as it were, between my 25 addresses. It gives that sensation of constant change of address, environment, etc. Like a bad dream. And for that it is good. Hectic. Kaleidoscopic. Here and there a bit sentimental—sententious even. But I'll try to weed this out.

Your infallible taste, of course, is right. It is *not* on the level of *Black Spring.* But, if this isn't soon published it will never be! It will be outdated. There's a time for everything—and this is the time!

Now the sun is shining. In a minute it will be black again. Foul, miserable weather. I do hope London looks more cheerful to you. Dying to get your first impressions.

By the way, I think Cab Calloway is now in London. Heard him Tuesday night. Fine! He's a bit *daft!* Wiggles his ass at the audience.

---

* Anaïs Nin went to London to visit Rebecca West and other literary figures to interest them in Miller's work.

Brays like a jackass. But he knows how to make 'em play! If you go, watch the pianist! He should give a solo. Stupendous technique. Altogether original. The audience here enjoyed it immensely. It was a *release* for them! Hear the "St. James Infirmary Blues!"

Also, got straightened out at Prefecture on my carte d'identité— to my untold relief. Am good till July!

Fred tells me that your hotel is not so hot—rather a "commercial" hotel, run by the Lyons Coffee House people. But you'll doubtless fend for yourself quickly. And forget the statistical tables for the taximeter in pounds, shillings and pence. Try the Métro! It's great! See Russell Square.

As I say, there is nothing much to convey for the moment. I saw the Utrillo exhibition also—but his life (*by Carco*) is far more interesting to me than his work. He is certainly *not great!* Interesting, yes. But beyond that . . . ? No portraits, no still lifes! *Only street scenes!* With grotesque marionettes for his human figures. That too is strange. *N'est-ce pas?* as Cab Calloway says.

Yes—if you get the opportunity, please go to a *Variety Show*—of the popular order—and tell me about it. I have always imagined them to have a special flavor.

So long for the present. Going to Lantelme now. And good luck! And don't think of gifts—*but enjoy* yourself. Remember—Fitzroy Tavern, Soho!—The *Bohemians!*

HENRY

[Paris, May 5, 1934]
Saturday Afternoon

I went to bed laughing over your letters—the first two, which arrived simultaneously last night. Nothing since. Waiting impatiently —not for a cable, I don't expect that! but for any crumb of real news —a reaction of some sort, good or bad.* Yes, I laughed over your letter. How would I ever have fit into that dinner you describe? What would I have to say to those stuffed shirts? My God, if the *Well of Loneliness* is still banned, what then?

---

* Anaïs Nin had taken with her the manuscript of *Black Spring* and a version of *The World of Lawrence*, but neither elicited much response.

I didn't get your reference to Lawrence's friends—you put an O
after it—you mean they are all regarded as zero? And that [John Mid-
dleton] Murry is still a kingpin, still telling them things? Well, I'll wait.
The next letter will undoubtedly tell me more. Of course I don't
expect anybody to read the Mss. in a hurry. Neither must you. I had
to laugh to think how you rushed them. Like a football player. Now
you're a princess, but before you leave they may eye you askance.
They may think you had a hell of a nerve thrusting my stuff on them
like that. They may . . .

I won't anticipate, however. . . .

Right now, since you left, in fact, I have been reading and rereading the *Tropic of Cancer*—making *big* alterations now. Principally
eliminations. Cutting out all the extraneous stuff, which smelled of
other days, other moods, other powers, etc. And am going to rewrite
certain parts which are a little feeble perhaps, but which still belong.
The book is much faster now, more action, pace, story, etc.
Which is what it badly needed. After all—and how I hate to admit it!
—both Bradley and Kahane were right in their criticism. It was this
they objected to most—not the smut. Even some of the smut I have
canceled—not because of it being smut, but because it was often just
"dragged" in. (All of which you have told me before. But now I see!)
Even the Cinema Vanves comes out—with good old Dr. Cassius looking into the old woman's womb, etc. It smells like something that
came out of the icebox. Warmed-up steak.

At the same time—if only the sun would shine a little harder, a little
brighter and warmer, I would rewrite certain parts—I intend to do it!
—put a little more glow and fever into them. After all, after all the
sacrifices you are making, this book has to be good! I won't turn out
a sloppy job. No siree. So this interval you are away is just right for
me. I had hoped to finish for you, as a surprise, the remaining pages
of that *House of Incest* film, but it is more urgent now to finish the
book, don't you agree? If you are to have it done by June it must be
handed in soon after you return. I believe it takes about two months
to set up a book.

Aside from the book, and my preoccupations with it, there is nothing much to tell you in the way of news. You're on the news end. I'm
all ears for the present. The bookcase arrived, to my surprise—I

thought you had decided to keep it. Anyway, the room looks good now, with my trunk out and the Ingres sofa resting at the foot of the bed. A strange décor—but I like it! If a letter arrives tonight with news, I'll write you posthaste. Just now I am inbetween-like—waiting, waiting. And yet not impatient. I don't look for miracles, you know. I sent a letter to the first address—did you get it?

HENRY

P. S. Still cold here—but a little sunnier. Are you *warm?*

[Villa Seurat] Dec. 4th, 1934

I'm going like a steam engine. Retyped and revised somewhat the two sections of *Black Spring* enclosed. More to follow soon. I'm sending you these in the hope that they may be sold to some magazine over there,* through an agent. Or if you see any more direct way to go about it, do so. I have a hope now that some of my things will sell.

I sent the duplicate copies to [Frank] Dobo to see what he could do for me in England—they can be published in both countries simultaneously, you know. And now I am going to write a letter to Kay Boyle, enclosing the triplicates, and ask her what she can suggest. I have an idea that I may make the grade with *Story* magazine, or again with *Esquire,* in Chicago.** Besides these blocs from the novel, which seem complete in themselves, I am going to write a couple of fresh ones also. And maybe an article on Surrealism—based on some old material I have.

I have had two strange postcards from Ezra Pound, who read the book [*Tropic of Cancer*]. Notice what he says about *Esquire*—which is supposed to be "a magazine for men" (but more of a fashion plate, I think). Here's his cryptogrammic language, as is:

1st card: "Very able/ have just writ 2 post cards to 2 edtrs/ to see

---

* In September, 1934, at the time the Obelisk Press published Miller's first book, *Tropic of Cancer,* he had moved into an apartment at 18 Villa Seurat, a small private street in the 14th Arondissement, near the Métro station Alesia and the Parc de Mountsouris, where he lived for the next four years. Anaïs Nin had left for a short trip to New York in November.

** Neither of these magazines printed anything of Henry Miller's during the 1930's.

if they will rise to my offer to review it/ useful (I mean to the seeree-
yus critic) as means of allocating Joyce's kinks, and W. Lewis' ill
humor. *That,* I take it is the last thing you are going to worry about/
why not look oh hell, for a reason/ I see you, looking up the rain
spout for the monetary system/ which does however make RAIN/ It
makes the why it AINT at the Am Express/ and WHY the double
harness/ and the WHY noo Yok is that g/d/ vacuous, vitreous, useless //// Do I recognise mr Lewisholme at a certain point ? well;
well/ book really impersonal and that is a point up. Thanks for the
vollum."

2nd card: "Great deal more to the book than I thought when I
wrote you yester/ after reading about 40 pages. NEVERTHELESS,
though you realize the force of money AS destiny, the one question
you haven't asked yourself is:

What IS money ?

who makes it/ how does it get that way ? /// *

A. Gingrich, by the way, 919 No. Michigan Ave., Chicago, runs a
magazine called ESQUIRE and *pays,* believe he wd/ like yr/ stuff,
and will use, if not full stink, at any rate things that wd/ have been
impossible a few years ago. Ezra Pound"

I'm going to see Kahane tomorrow, as I have a lot of things to take
up with him. Will handle him gently. Primo, I've got to see what can
be done about mailing copies to you.

Tonight I am seeing a guy named Malkine, friend of Hiler's. Hiler
had recommended him to me as a possible translator—for the French.
Seems he is a personal friend of [the publishers] Denoël and Steele.
I see him on the slight chance that he may reopen the subject with
them. When I see Kahane tomorrow I shall broach the name of the
owner of the Surrealist bookshop, rue de Clichy. He has printed a lot
of daring books—mostly, of course, for that gang. But maybe I'm a
Surrealist too. These last few days I certainly feel like one in action.
I'm fairly sizzling with excitement and nervousness, with interviews,
with letters.

I have 30 pages done on the "Tailor Shop" **—still unfinished.

---

* In September, 1938, Miller published a 64-page pamphlet, "Money and
How It Gets That Way," which is a spoof on the same question.

** Miller's reminiscences of his father's business on West 31st Street, off
Fifth Avenue, in Manhattan, which later became a chapter in *Black Spring*
under the same title.

But what's done is good, and you'll like it. I think I will send you the original, to do with as these other sections I just retyped. That is, if it is not too far off base. Now the lean and fighting spirit is on me and I am tapering down for ring weight. Every day I drink champagne *nature* with my meal. Got the idea from Melville. Listen to this:

"Feed all things with food convenient for them—that is, if the food be procurable. The food of thy soul is light and space; feed it then on light and space. But the food of the body is champagne and oysters; feed it then on champagne and oysters; and so shall it merit a joyful resurrection, if there is any to be." (From *Pierre*) Not that I read the book—no, too dull for me!—but glancing through it my eye hit that passage, and I like it, and I believe in it.

Listen, this is terrible—all these notes. But that's how I am—feverish, excited, hustling, crazy with anxiety and with desire to do something. Rent coming. Know its gonna be hard. However, in no way desperate or gloomy. Au contraire. "What *is* money? How does it get that way?" Marvelous, eh? What a line!

I haven't yet received a letter from you—still too soon, but expect one this week. Know you can't say much—must have just arrived. But what was that first look like? And how is it now, dear old New York? Keen to know if you met Emil.*

Saw Marcel Duchamp the other night and gave him a game of chess. He is really a very nice chap. Gave me the name of his printer in the provinces, who does very reasonable and very excellent work—in any language.

Again I am rushing to make the boat mail. Forgive the business character of the letter. I hope soon to sit down quietly, all by myself, in some café and write you in pen and ink. I can't get quiet, and can't sleep either. But it's good for me. I hope I can go quite crazy and write like a madman.

HENRY

---

* Miller's school friend, Emil Schnellock, who had staked him to ten dollars when he went to Paris in 1930—the only capital Miller then possessed. (See also Biographical Notes.)

[Villa Seurat, December, 1934]
Midnight, same day

When I got back to the place this morning I shaved and sat down to the machine immediately and wrote the enclosed for Kay Boyle's *Anthology of 1934 Stories*. It doesn't matter whether it's good or bad—the thing is, I felt like doing things and I did it, and it rolled off just as is, without a pause. Then having to go to town, I stopped off to see Mr. Davis again, at Brentano's, and had a good chat with him. He reassured me of his desire to do everything possible for me—said things were very slow, but that he was selling one or two copies every day, which I don't think at all bad. I came back and put the place in order and wrote the letter to Kahane—a good, tactful letter. And then 20 copies of the book arrived, which I had asked for a few days ago.

What I discover all over again is that the will reasserts itself when the soul is intact. Whatever was the matter with me I don't know, but I know I couldn't force myself, by sheer will, to finish the *Black Spring,* as I did with *Tropic of Cancer*. I didn't want to commit another violation, for that's how it seems to me.

I opened the Jung book toward the closing chapters, intrigued by the heading "the spiritual problem of modern man." After saying that the modern man is he who is aware of the immediate present, he goes on to say this: "He is rather the man who stands upon a peak, or at the very edge of the world, the abyss of the future before him, above him the heavens, and below him the whole of mankind with a history that disappears in primeval mists. . . . The man whom we can with justice call 'modern' is solitary. . . . Thus he has become 'unhistorical' in the deepest sense and has estranged himself from the mass of men who live entirely within the bounds of tradition. . . . An honest profession of modernity means voluntarily declaring bankruptcy, taking the vows of poverty and chastity in a new sense, and—what is still more painful—renouncing the halo which history bestows as a mark of its sanction. To be 'unhistorical' is the Promethean sin, and in this sense modern man lives in sin. . . . He must be proficient in the highest degree, for unless he can atone by creative ability for his break with tradition, he is merely disloyal to the past."

This "being proficient in the highest degree" means a great deal to me. At one stroke it clears up that whole business of the "past," of my warfare with the past, of my "mere disloyalty to the past." At the same time I discover that I had most unerringly seized the truth when, in the Lawrence pages, I emphasized "the psychological reality," which is situated between the false cultural reality of the past and the reality of nature—the thing you were always a bit dubious about. It's this reality the artist is always dealing with—it's his own private atmosphere, and the sign of his real continuity with tradition, which people are always suspicious of because they see no liaison. I wonder do you get me?

Anyway, this evening I bumped into the man who had said to Halasz of my book "sheer porno"—you remember? Tonight he reversed himself and said I had penetrated to the very core of truth, said he was recommending the book to his friends in England and thought I ought to have a big sale there. You can imagine that I was quite pleased. The more so in that, left to themselves, people have converted themselves to the right way of thinking. I have no fight on my hands.

HENRY

[Villa Seurat, December, 1934]
Tuesday

So many things have happened, Anaïs, that it doesn't seem like a week since you left. It's only the last two and a half days that I have settled down to serious writing, and it's going good after all the postponements. I'll be sending you very soon the finished section of the "Tailor Shop." Am going to finish each and every part that I originally planned. Then if any seem out of place, out of joint, I'll weed them out. But I'm writing to finish now!

Meanwhile, I wrote Bradley about the option business, as Kahane had enclosed an option for me to sign, giving all the terms I had requested. His letter happened to cross mine in which I said that I wanted no definite terms. The same day I received a money order from a guy in Philadelphia whom I don't know and whose address wasn't stated. The next day I met by accident Jacques Baron, the poet (Surrealist) and [Raymond] Queneau. The latter was very friendly and

wanted to know why I never sent him the Lawrence book.* So I
finally sent him it, together with a copy of my book. It was at an exhibition of reliures that I met them. And there I bumped into Mary
Reynolds and Marcel Duchamp. The latter led me aside mysteriously
and asked me in a low tone if I would like to have a little notice of my
book put in a revue called *Orbes* which appears every three months.
I said yes naturally. And then later I went to have a look at this
Orbes in Corti's bookshop. I don't know what to make of it. But the
way Marcel Duchamp grabbed hold of me made me feel that he was
doing me a real favor.**

And then, the same evening, walking with Benno † down the rue
Bonaparte we stopped in at the Galerie Zborowski. Z. is a friend of
his. Benno started talking about my book and Zborowski immediately
wanted to read it and, as he was due to go back to N.Y. soon, suggested that I get him a few copies. So we took a taxi back here and
I dedicated a copy to him and he fell in love with the place and like a
real Pole became quite sentimental over me and said he would call for
me soon and take me out.

The next evening, strolling along the Boulevard Montparnasse I
stopped in to see Tschann, the bookseller, the man I once introduced
you to. While talking to him I noticed two of your Lawrence books
stuck away on the shelves. Immediately I conceived the idea of swap-
ping two of mine for these, and sending you them, which I have done.
I thought you might be very glad to have these extra copies in case you
meet any publisher or editor. If I discover any more I will send them
to you. The funny thing about this incident was that Tschann tore
the slips off the book (reading "ne doit pas étre exposé, etc.") and
stuck the books on the shelf in the front window. The only place in
Paris so far that they are visible! And then I went to the other Montparnasse bookshop and I deposited a few circulars with them; they
are considering whether they will order the book or not. Wanted to
know if it had a lot of good publicity (sic). And when they finally

---

* Queneau, who had published two books of his own by 1934—*Le Chiendent*
and *Gueule de Pierre*—had connections with various publishing houses. He became an editor at Gallimard in 1936, when he was thirty-three.

** The first review of *Tropic of Cancer*, written by Blaise Cendrars, appeared
in *Orbes*.

† For Miller's portrait of Benno, "the wild man from Borneo," see the essay of the same title in *The Wisdom of the Heart* (Norfolk, Conn., New Directions, 1941), which first appeared in *The Booster* (Paris, September, 1937).

comprehended that it was *my* book the woman exclaimed: "But you don't look so obscene!"

Have had a lot of mail and have written a hell of a lot of letters. Feel I'm quite through now. I've done all I can, for the time being at least. Kay Boyle wrote, accepting the short story I sent you with pleasure—saying it would make just the right contrast to the others they had received. Wanted to know if I could send more—"but not too symbolical!"

I was busier than a hornet the first few days. Had postcards from Huxley and Ezra Pound saying they would like to receive copies of the book. And then a short note from Katherine Anne Porter, apologizing for not responding sooner, saying they had just moved. Adding this: "There is a great deal I want to say about your book; just at this minute I can only say thank you enormously for sending it to me. It has the kind of gorgeous madness in it which only a very sane imagination can produce."

I have knuckled down at last and unloosed everything that refused to come up before. I said to myself today, as I was shaving, "This is like the Clichy days!" Things are popping up into my head, ideas, feelings, plans, desires.

Anyway I am terribly excited about your arriving there and all it means. It's almost as though I had gone myself—better, because I can imagine more.

HENRY

[Villa Seurat]
Dec. 12th [1934]

Have to write this very fast to catch boat mail at gare. I am sending you this section of the Lawrence book on Proust, Joyce & L. after a long talk with Queneau who just left, who had read it closely and with great interest. A good talk in which we understood one another clearly. He was very much impressed and said that undoubtedly, when the work was finished, it would be accepted by a French editor. Nothing important on Lawrence has been written here yet. Said it was "déconcertant" for les Français, but énormement intéressant, provoking, un-French, etc., and therefore would be keenly enjoyed. Said the erudition taxed him. He liked all about Spengler (knows his Spengler well) and also, what I liked better, understood and appreciated the part about *China*. (This is not in section I send you, of course.)

Now then—he thinks it almost impossible to send it to a French review until translated—that is, sections of it. He thinks the *Cahiers du Sud* would certainly take portions of it once it has appeared in an English or American magazine—and then they would willingly translate it. He urged me to try to finish it, that it was important, etc. Bien entendu. But that I don't intend to do now.

However, with this in mind, and with the letter of Stuart Gilbert which I am enclosing as a piece of honest and valued criticism, would you see what could be done with this, as a section of the book. It's 50 pages, but it could be published in two or three installments. They have permission to make cuts, etc., if necessary. Tout va avec moi— but try to get a sign of hope, of interest.

Jesus, I realize I am giving you lots of things to do. And you're really overworked. Forgive me, will you? I've got it in my crop that this final section is good material and I must see what can be done. I sent you several large packets now of Mss.

Despite everything I am working. Faith—that's what I've got.

HENRY

[Villa Seurat]
Friday night, Dec. 14, 1934
TWO A.M.

ANAÏS,

Boat train leaves at 9:30 A.M. [Blaise] Cendrars came at three P.M. and I have just gotten away from him, had to run away. As a man I must have disappointed him. I was almost taciturn. And yet, what a day! What a night! I received the most magnificent homage I have yet received from another man—from a writer, that is. Fred was here. Fred is still with him. I ducked on the pretense of having work to do. It wasn't very chic on my part. I won't now give you the details of our meeting. It's too vast. It was epic. (All in French, by the way, because he refuses to speak English par principe.) I feel battered now.

And soaked with *fines* and liqueurs and good wines. I had thirty francs in my pocket. When it came time to eat he was still talking—and he is the greatest storyteller I have ever listened to! (A cross between Jack London and Knut Hamsun—he knew these two when they were fairly unknown.) Came dinnertime and I had a date at the Café de la Paix—someone who wanted to blow me to a dinner. Alors, seven o'clock we take a taxi to the Chambre des Députés, where Fred had some business to attend to, and then to Montmartre, the rue des Abbesses, Restaurant des Fleurs. What a place! The first time in my life I have seen so many beautiful Frenchwomen. He said we would eat cheaply and I thought we would go Dutch. Then he began ordering. Asked me did I like to eat. Why certainly! Alors, lobster, oysters, pigeons, desserts I never saw in my life, wines extraordinary, *fines,* Chartreuse, coffee etc. etc. I was embarrassed as all hell. 30 frs. Mortified. A friend blows in. Cendrars looks rough, like a sailor—he is one at bottom—and he speaks rather loudly, but very well. Has only one arm, the empty one, or half-arm slung affectionately around my neck while he tells the whole restaurant what a great guy I am, what the book is about, why it must be published in French, where I belong in the great Catholic tradition, etc. etc. etc. Perhaps the finest moment in my life, in one sense. But it went flat. I had nothing to say. I wondered how long it would continue. I was a perfect ass. And trying at intervals to break away. Finally we go out, four of us now, and we must have some more alcohol in the bars along the Boulevard in Montmartre. Whores hanging on to us, and Cendrars hugging them like a sailor, and urging me to take one, take two, take as many as you want. After two or three of these bars and more whores hanging on our necks I ducked—very unceremoniously too. An au revoir. I don't know what he must think of me.

In the afternoon he spoke at great length about what was to be done. If it weren't that he was leaving for Brazil in January he said he would have undertaken to translate the book himself. But, he will do this he says—that is, he said this earlier in the day, and again at the table. He would speak to the head man in Grasset, who is a friend. (It was through Cendrars that Dos Passos was translated.) He said he would try to sell them the idea by talking first about my Lawrence book—because Grasset wants a good book on Lawrence! Then he would wind them up about the *Tropic of Cancer*. He would try to select the translator. Said it required the most tactful translation. He repeated constantly that I was in the best tradition, stemmed from Rabelais, had guts, etc. (He said really marvelous things which it is too bad I haven't time to give you.) Said there would have to be severe cuts, and the spirit would have to be rendered by one capable of understanding me. Said it would probably not have a big audience, but the best in France. (What I liked principally in all he said was his realization that I knew the streets intimately. Said he had never read a book by an American, or any foreigner, that could compare with it in this respect.) No *chique*. Said he walks the streets from morning to night, hates to write, but quand même he is a big worker, a formidable one. He's a real man, I tell you. Perhaps he is that one man I wrote about recently, the man I expected to come forward and hail me.

Well, that's that. Enclosed is a letter from Pound, the latest. Kahane was elated to know that the famous T. S. Eliot might print Pound's review in his magazine. I'm not.

HENRY

[Villa Seurat]
Monday, 20th [April, 1936]

DEAR ANAÏS:
Your two letters, from Casablanca and Fez, just arrived. Began to think you had changed your itinerary, not hearing from you sooner. Posting this by avion and hope it reaches you in time.

When I read your wonderful descriptions I realize that nothing is happening here. The most amazing thing to me is how you can stand the smell! Apparently this is the first time your delicate nostrils don't rebel. Is it because the eyes are so delighted? You evoke the whole scene marvelously—here's where your diary practice reveals itself. You seem to have packed it all into one letter. I'm glad for one thing, that you aren't disappointed. Because Fez is supposed to be the greatest of all the old cities—the most intact, I mean. And what I detect, though you don't say so exactly, is that even where those handsome faces *are* bitten away by disease, what remains is still beautiful, like ancient fragments of the Parthenon, etc. Right? Here you could never stand the sight of a worm-eaten hag in the street—the market women, you called them. There you have what Spengler calls the "fellaheen," and despite the monstrosities they still retain their dignity, their blood and race. Yes, all this handicraft sounds good to me—the doing things patiently and laboriously and lovingly. And the silence goes with it, because the human hand moves silently. And that's what creates a deep inner peace and satisfaction. And the rich and poor can crowd together—when there is a religion to hold them together. It's splendid all that you reveal. I can wait. Someday I suppose my turn will come. Meanwhile you feed my imagination. Richly.

I say nothing's happened, and yet a few things have. For one thing Kahane has started the printing of *Black Spring*. I saw him twice and he seems full of pep, full of plans, ideas. At any rate, as far as finances go, we're all right. The 2,000 is wiped out by the earnings. As the account stood at the end of the year I owed him about 700-odd francs, mostly on account of the printing of *Aller Retour*.* But this too has been wiped out in the meantime, through sales of *Tropic* for the current year (he's sold close to a hundred so far this year). When June comes there will be a check for royalties.

So since your departure I just had time to reread the *Black Spring* again and make a few more changes—mostly deletions of sentimental items. It seems O.K. to me in the main. Have picked up the *Hamlet* ** and recommenced. Fraenkel was going to London today but has changed his mind again.

Marcel Duchamp is sending me some of his colored discs—had a nice note from him. Colette and Ed [Rogers] told me of their trip to Asia Minor—spoke glowingly of Constantinople—Istamboul now. No mail yet from N.Y. since we arrived. And, by the way, your book hasn't come from the printer yet.

(An order for *Aller Retour* came in from Baghdad.) Oh yes, and that Librairie d'Etrème Orient in Shanghai has made a contract with Kahane to act as his sole Oriental representative—taking so many books per year. Very good, this. I also have some photographs of skulls with beads and money which Thérèse le Prat gave me—I want to show them to Kahane for possible book jackets. They were done as cover

---

* In December, 1934, Henry Miller went to New York and returned in May, 1935. A limited edition of 150 copies of *Aller Retour New York* was published in October, 1935, by the Obelisk Press, Paris.

** Michael Fraenkel and Miller, in November, 1935, began a lengthy correspondence ostensibly about *Hamlet* which continued over the next three years. (See Biographical Notes.)

designs for Poe's *The Gold Bug*. They'd do for *Black Spring* just as well methinks. But I suppose Kahane won't want them.

And so, as I say, practically nothing has happened. I see you're marching quickly. You ought to be back before the end of this month at this rate.

HENRY

[Villa Seurat, April, 1936]
Thursday

ANAÏS—

The second letter from Morocco just arrived. Read with increasing astonishment. Quelle vie! Et la Fatima, quoi! Meanwhile, things have happened here. Fraenkel flew the coop—to London. He says he will be gone only a few weeks and then return for the summer.

The book hasn't come yet, sorry to say. I am waiting until your return before drawing up a circular.

The painter who lives just above Fraenkel took Fred and me to Corti, the librarian on the rue de Clichy (the Surrealist Shop). Fred is getting an estimate for the printing of his book [*Le Quatuor en Ré Majeur*] from Corti. He thinks he is going to raise the necessary expense by subscription. Corti has promised to put my book in the vitrine.

Have the latest Saroyan book—*Inhale and Exhale*. Looks interesting. Queneau also sent me his latest book—*Les Derniers Jours*.

From Fraenkel I inherited a bookcase full of his precious books. Including the beloved Funk & Wagnall's Dictionary.

As far as the Hamlet book goes I think it will be even better writing it at a distance this way. It saves a lot of useless discussion. What I think I'll do now is to tackle the June book again—and Hamlet on the side.

Had a note from Lowenfels saying that the "boys" were most enthusiastic about the "Tailor Shop." They want to publish some 20 pages of it—the most fantastic part (Celestial Burlesque, they call it).

Well, I am waiting for your next letter to know when you think you will be back. It's been cold and rainy here—but we have heat again.

HENRY

P. S. That was a wonderful Nin line—about the birds "gargarizing with tropical fervor." And the Arabs "shitting carefully, conscientiously." What a picture!

Villa Seurat, August 24, 1938 *

For me Cancer means the Crab, as it was known to the Chinese sages—the creature which could move in any direction. It is the sign in the Zodiac for the poet—the halfway station in the round of realization, which changes when one comes to the constellation Libra. Opposite Cancer in the Zodiac (extremes of the Equinox—turning points) is Capricorn, the house in which I am born, which is religious and represents renaissance in death. Cancer also means for me the disease of civilization, the extreme point of realization along the wrong path—hence the necessity to change one's course and begin all over again. Nietzsche's doctrine of eternal recurrence, also, in a more profound way, the essence of Buddhism: Cancer then is the apogee of death in life, as Capricorn is of life in death. The two symbols are found in geography as tropics (which is another word for hieroglyphs), Cancer lying above the Equator and Capricorn below. Myself, as I have said frequently in my books, am trying to walk the hairline which separates the two. The line is only imaginary—there is no boundary line to reality.

HENRY

---

* From 1936 to 1938, both Miller and Anaïs Nin were in Paris. Lawrence Durrell, who had started a correspondence with Miller in 1935 (published in 1963 by E. P. Dutton, New York, edited by George Wickes), visited Paris in September, 1937, and stayed until April, 1938. During this time, the "Villa Seurat" series of books by Miller, Anaïs Nin and Durrell was initiated, and Alfred Perlès, in July, 1937, became editor of *The Booster,* later renamed *Delta,* which for six issues was the "house organ" of the Miller circle in Paris.

[September, 1938]
Thursday, 3:00 P.M.
Hotel Majestic 2, rue de Condé
Bordeaux

ANAÏS—

Just arrived here from Perigueux. Sending you this by airmail. Will probably stay a few days here—you can write me here in any case. I'll write again from here saying what I plan to do.

Can't say I am enjoying myself. The trains, hotels, meals, porters, valises, occupy too much attention. Haven't seen anything startling. Perigueux was so quiet and dull it made me nervous. I didn't even bother to visit the caves—felt dubious.

Decided against Toulouse because everybody said it was uninteresting. Came to Bordeaux, which I never intended to see, because it's a city. It doesn't look so hot either, but I can always stick it out better in a city. The country and the dull peasant oafs drive me crazy. I have too much baggage too—it's annoying and costly.

If things don't improve I'll be back in Paris in a few days. It does me no good to travel about from place to place. I want to see something *different*—but everything is the same—frightfully dead and monotonous.

Anyway, you can write me here—make it airmail, if you will. I will notify you if I plan to go elsewhere or come back—perhaps by telegram.

I feel like a ghost being shoved around. Maybe tomorrow it will seem different.

I see that *Arcachon* is 50 kilometres away.*
More soon.

HENRY

---

* Anaïs Nin, as a child, had spent some time there vacationing with her father.

[Bordeaux, September, 1938]
Tuesday, A.M.

ANAÏS—

Got your letter and telegram and this morning the corn plasters! You think of everything. You say you don't want me to "get" neurotic. I laugh. I *am* neurotic—to the nth degree. I don't think of moving to some better place now—no place is any good if there's war. I stay here because the boats are here. If we're lucky we might get out by the sea. I don't think you should stay in Paris until the moment war is declared. You may never be able to get out. I would accept the war as a fact—reading this morning's paper, the latest speeches and communications show no improvement. Neither side wants to give ground—that's bad. They are preparing for war, not for reconciliations. Don't you see? If there is still time—you should get this tonight—move my things out of the Villa Seurat. *But only if you have time!* Maybe you could dump the whole business at Kahane's place—might be easier and it's just as practicable, I'm thinking, as at American Express. I give you Kahane's telephone numbers —at office and home. He might have a truckman to send to Villa Seurat, as I think he makes his deliveries that way.

I wrote him about money yesterday or day before—no answer yet.

I give you also address here in Bordeaux of American Consulate, in case things have already started and you don't find me at hotel. I would leave word there for you of where I am or what I am doing. It is *4 rue Esprit-des-Lois.*

If it starts October 1st, as predicted, and if there is no way of getting a boat immediately, perhaps I can move out of town, to some little place. I prefer getting out of France if possible. The confusion will be terrific, there will be difficulty getting money or it may be deflated to zero. Everything will be the worst imaginable. I can't see any bright side to it, really.

I sent Durrell a letter by airmail asking if he could send me money, should I call for it, also what he plans to do. If Italy sides with Germany, as it looks now, it would be impossible to get to Corfu.

I thought last night to send a confidential letter to the American Ambassador at Paris, urging him to get together the "Gueules

Cassées" * of the whole of Europe, ship them to Hitler in airplanes, as a demonstration of the last resort. To have them say to Hitler that they would not leave his presence until he made peace—and if he refused to place themselves in a huge body at the Czechoslovak frontier, where the Germans would invade, and notify the German people that they would have to walk over their dead bodies if they intended to march in. That would be dramatic and spectacular— equal to Hitler's own spectacular gestures. But I'm afraid nobody would listen to such a plan. In my opinion, it is worth trying anything and everything. If you think there is any merit in the idea notify the head of the "Gueules Cassées" in Paris, through some diplomatic chan- nel. The American Ambassador probably would not have the right to make such a suggestion. I thought of telling Kahane, but he is too phlegmatic. Also thought of [Conrad] Moricand **—you might speak to him about it—unless you think it's crazy. What gets me is the fatalistic air with which everyone accepts the war. Think what an effect it would have on the whole world if these horrible mutilated men went in a body to Hitler—or camped on the border and met his army!!

HENRY

[September, 1938]
Thursday 6:30 P.M.
Bordeaux

Just got your letter which you posted before leaving Paris. I am still here and will remain and wait for events. Kahane sent me 3,000 francs and that makes me feel O.K. I may hear from the cables too. It isn't so much that I want to jump about as that I wanted *to be able to!* Now I feel a bit free and can breathe easier. So I'll just stay here and bide my time. Soon as it looks *definitely* settled I'll probably return to Paris. I still haven't much confidence in the statesmen. It's that which undermines me more than anything. If there were real states- men it would never have come to such a pass. However, all that's an- other story. I'm glad you went to Le Havre, because I feel it is much

* Literally, "broken mugs"—a reference to the amputees and wounded vet- erans of World War I.
** See Biographical Notes.

safer for you. I am not so worried about losing my hide as you seem
to think. Sure, the neurosis. I know it myself. The doctor will now
have to cure himself. But in a way I'm cured of Europe. If they don't
settle things *magnanimously* it's no use living in this part of the world
any longer. People ought to be changed after an experience like this
—but my fear is, like after the last war, that they won't. I have less
and less confidence in human nature. It may take a few more foot
races around the seven planets before they reach the stage of wisdom
we have. I don't want my *Mars* to come forth—that would be the
ruin of me. Now I am using my head and my instincts. The others
will use all the Mars, don't worry. That's precisely the trouble.

How would I have settled the problem? Why, by ceding everything!
I'm a Chinaman at heart, not a European. When people resort to guns
etc. I duck. I am not ashamed of that. Well, let's hope anyway that
they will arrive at even a half-assed solution.

It's too late to send a telegram—that's why I send this by airmail.
If you telephone by any chance while I am out they will probably tell
you I am still here. I am not doing anything rash. Just walking around
and meditating.

HENRY

Bordeaux [September, 1938]
Friday night

ANAÏS—
    Leaving for Lourdes tomorrow noon. Feel I ought to see
something different before returning to Paris. This city is a nightmare
to me. I didn't break the silence until today when I had a discussion
at dinner table with an old Frenchman. That was one of the hardest
things of all about the situation—to keep my mouth shut and be in
a strange city—to do nothing but read newspapers and walk the
streets. If I had been at Villa Seurat it might have been different.

You spoke a lot of *neurosis*. I don't believe in the interpretation
that has been given that word—not any more. Anybody who was not
"neurotic" during this period must be abnormal. Your letters never
swerved me one bit in my decision to obey my instincts. Even if I
were out on the ocean now I would not regret it. That was the right

thing to do—and I should have done it in the beginning. One can always come back after the show is over. I don't believe in sticking it out till the last minute. What happened—what was *allowed* to happen to Europe—was criminal. For me it's just as though the war did take place. I feel just as the men must have who came back from the trenches. With this difference—that they were tired of it all and too disgusted to care any more what might happen. But I am full of rancor now and determined while I am still alive and have any strength left to do my utmost to bring about not only Hitler's downfall but the castration of the whole German people.

Naturally Hitler and his cohorts stood the strain well. They are consecrating their lives to this international gangsterism. They have nothing to lose by a fight, since they want no other life. I say that if we others are *really* intelligent, really have a sense of reality, then we ought to work now while there is a short respite ahead of us, to find ways and means to undermine this German machine. This is only a truce. The Germans won't stop here. They're going on. They're just like surgeons working on a weak body—a little operation today, a brief rest to recuperate, and then another amputation—and so on. It's no good going to war with them. I would have given ground right away—and trust to my head to find other ways of defeating them. There are more ways than one of killing a goose, is the old saying. To imagine that the Germans mean what they say is suicidal. We must consider them like mad dogs—the whole 73,000,000! When I say "we" I mean the whole world.

Well, Kahane sent me 3,000 francs. With that I can voyage a little easier. But when I get back to Paris I intend first of all to beg and borrow from all sides in order to have on me permanently the price of a *first-class* ticket to America. I wouldn't stay *five minutes* when the next threat comes. I mean this! I would rather live in the desert than in such an atmosphere as we survived. I feel like I was 100 years old. And those German bastards know this too—that's another thing they count on. They know that the moral shock is even greater than the victory on the battlefield. That's why I'm enraged. Now I don't mind letting the Mars come out—it may be effective now. A dead man with Mars inside him is of no use.

I'll never till my dying day forgive these German bastards. *I may even go to Germany*—to see for myself, and to better describe it and kill it. I don't think I'll finish the books I planned. I consider everything that happened before this and hoped and planned to do as wiped out! That we got out by the skin of our teeth means nothing to me. I consider it a defeat—we were killed off *morally*.

I don't know just what I'll write, but I'll devote myself henceforth to one end—and I'll use any and every means. No German will ever darken my door or sit at my table. They don't belong to human society, that's what I think.

Yesterday I still thought that we should be "magnanimous"—give more than they expect in order to remove their suspicion, their "psychosis," if you like. Today I don't think so. It's too long, too difficult, too dubious. I want peace *now*.

I go to Lourdes to find a calm and dignified atmosphere. If it is not already too cold, I'd like to see the Cirque de Gavarnie—they say it's splendid and awesome. But I'm afraid the season is already too far advanced—I have no warm coat. I may go back by way of Toulouse, which I understand *is* a good city and *does* have good music. And then for the war! With my own special weapons and in my own fashion. Even if I have to carry on from America—it makes no difference. I would carry on even from Tibet, I imagine.

That's how I feel! But don't talk to me again about neurosis. I want to be more and more neurotic. The statesmen were wrong—they didn't get us out of this. It was the weakness of the overcivilized Italian people! Perhaps we will see a revolution yet. I hope so. Well, more from Lourdes. Perhaps in a more cheerful vein. In a way I'm glad I was alone. It was an ordeal—but that's good for one too. The only way to realize things.

HENRY

P. S. I sent Fred and Moricand a 100 frs. each today and Pelorson * 200 frs. for September issue [of *Volontés*] but told him that after the next issue I was through. I'll hold out money for the rent too.
P. P. S. Better try to get letter from Poste Restante, Le Havre. May have said something seditious in it.

---

* See Biographical Notes.

Lourdes [September, 1938]
Sunday, A.M.

ANAÏS—

Getting out of here at noon, by first train—for Toulouse. Monstrous place. So vile, so ridiculous, so palpably fraudulent and commercial, that I laugh out loud in the street. Have been laughing hysterically ever since I arrived last night. The Basques must be a degenerate branch of the Semites. Lousy people—and hypocritical to boot. I can see that the country roundabout is beautiful, perhaps even grandiose, but I don't want it at this price. These people, this bloody Catholic farce, poisons the atmosphere *and* the landscape. The illuminated cross on the mountain top drives me mad. I hate the Spanish-Swiss architecture too, with the worst taste in colors—pink and brass, imagine that! At 7:30 A.M. I was at the gare to buy a ticket for Toulouse. The landlady, who reminds me of my Puritanical relatives, trying to persuade me to stay and see the sights. Told her it gave me the horrors. She nearly keeled over. If she had asked me then if I were a German I'd have said yes! Rather be a slave under Hitler than a free citizen of Lourdes.

HENRY

[Villa Seurat]
February 21, 1939, Paris

In the beginning was the word, but for the Word to come forth there had first to be a separation of some kind. To detach itself from the bosom of creation there had to be a need, a human need. The word is always the reminder of a more perfect state, of a union or unity which is ineffable and undescribable. Creation is always difficult because it is an attempt to recover what is lost. To regain we must first feel abandoned.

You know all the joys and terrors of creation. You have been playing God ever since you were able to talk. In that Neptunian atlas which you are consecrating to posterity you have recorded the protean metamorphoses of your unions and separations. It is the ark and the covenant of the lost. You began the construction of your vessel, like a true mariner, on the face of the waters. You consign it to the waters of oblivion. You carve your own image in the prow of the boat. You remain fixed there, cutting the waters endlessly. Whichever way the wind blows you point the way.

To me the Diary is like the moving needle of the compass. Though it is always pointing north, it moves nevertheless with the ship and with those who are sailing it and with the currents that direct the ship's course. If we imagine your ship to sail endlessly on, as it undoubtedly will, the destination will change as the stars themselves change their course. The direction will always be due north, but the voyage will be elliptical, changes of climate rather than changes of latitude and longitude. In your interminable log only the handwriting remains unalterable. The signature will always be your own, always swift, precise and legible. Most people's handwriting changes with age; everybody's signature changes with death. But in your case neither your handwriting nor your signature will ever be altered, because you are writing from a point beyond change. You are recording the constancy of change, the eternality of metamorphoses. You have chosen not to create but to record creation. You are feathering your oars in the flux of time. You have always been reluctant to recognize and accept the Pisces element in your being. But you yourself, in all your actions, are constantly revealing the symbolic nature of Pisces.

You are always striving to fill the empty vessel of life. At first literally, by giving things—the food and substance of life—later, realizing that it is a futile task, that you cannot possibly hope to cope with all the needs of those who come to you, transforming the loaves and fishes into the wine of life, giving from the endless fountain of wisdom which alone can give life.

And finally you will realize that even that is not sufficient, not effective enough. If the whole world is now slowly moving into this new sign, and if that means simply that life has got to be renewed, that we have exhausted the old forms, dried up the very source, perhaps your objection to the abstract character of Pisces will be removed. As the last of the air signs, Aquarius would simply mean the spiritualizing of the intellect. We cannot retrace our steps, cannot look to the past, to what we have already traversed by experience for aid. We must look ahead. We must take this intellectual life which we have on our hands and transmute it, as we have our experience in all the other mansions of the sky.

To pass from one realm of the Zodiac to another requires the same modulation as in music to pass from one key to another. Every realm is the right one for us, the best there could possibly be. The very fluidity of your Piscean soul was but a lesson in metamorphosis. At this critical juncture all our past experience is being transmuted to enable us to make the supreme step to another and richer mode of life. Your sense of security in your chameleon-like virtues will have to give way to a higher sense of security—the airy security of the bird which has left the waters behind. The ship which you sail in your dreams must take wing. Before the dove can fly from the Ark the waters must recede. There must be a spot of dry land, a mountain peak on which to rest for a while and gather fresh significance.

Even the earth does not veer steadily about her elliptic course. As she swings round she gradually turns on her heel, never actually foundering, but unloading her passengers as it were. The axis does not point due north eternally. The axis shifts, the climate changes, the north becomes south and east west. This is the earth's fourth-dimensional change, her spiritual evolution and involution.

They say that the solar system remains forever locked in the coils of the Dragon, but this is only a symbolic way of saying that the core of life is faith. The center is the solid heart which never questions what it knows. It is. All these journeys through the Zodiacal houses represent the sustained prolonged effort towards a total grasp of life. The Zodiac itself changes as we change. The day will come when the earth and all its inhabitants will enter a totally unknown realm. We will all pass into another phase of existence. The earth itself will no longer know itself—it will have ceased to be the earth. The earth, instead of being a satellite, can become a sun. More, it can become pure light. The very fact of writing this is the proof.

The astrologic is only the symbolic record of our trails. It holds as long as we see in aspects the proof of our doubts and fears. Interpretation will eventually cede to truth, which needs no demonstration.

If, as Balzac says, all creation is but transformation, then creation too will eventually give way to being.

The word was never meant to be engraved on tablets of stone nor imprisoned between the covers of a book. The word is light and the truth becomes flesh. It is incorruptible. The search for immortality through art is only the acknowledgment of the powers of death. Writing is life, but what is written is death. And it is death precisely because it seeks to preserve what cannot be preserved through form and substance. The most solid materials perish, as do the mightiest thoughts. And the greatest book ever written can convey only a tiny fragment of the artist's real emotion. No, we are only building tombs for posterity to admire with our words. We are trying to record the changing ego, but the Self will not be revealed thus. We are only throwing off sparks.

While one sits in the body of the whale recording the changing temperature, mapping and charting the inner dynamism, the great whale itself is plowing through the deep. We must drop the pen, the pencil, the brush and become the whale itself. The real experience lies yonder, in the deep waters through which the whale is swimming. You think you are nourishing the world—but you are only nourishing the whale.

The same difficulties that impede one in writing impede one in life. The reason why it is bad to use the will is the same as why one should not struggle in writing. The harmony which permits free action also gives a free flow in writing. It is a question of assimilation and integration. Better to stay on the lowest level and function smoothly than to struggle on a level for which one is still unfit. The "automatic" writing of Balzac is not just a Neptunian gift. It was a result of long concentration and deep meditation. Part of him had attained to another and higher level of being. He was incapable of sustaining this power because he had not been sufficiently chastened. What stood in the way continually was his own ego. He was continually prostituting his gifts for material ends. He wanted fame, recognition, power etc. He had learned the discipline of work but he had not learned to enjoy the fruits of his labor. He did not take the rest required for true development.

I see a great difference between real desire and mere wishing or the exercise of will and the driving whip of duty. I realize that growth comes only through desire and the recognition of the relation between truth and being.

When I say, as I often do, that my life since twenty-one up until recently was but a detour I mean that a large part of my efforts were wasted in an unacknowledged struggle to adapt myself to the world, the final adaptation masking itself as an effort to conquer or seduce the world through my creative powers as a writer. I should have been adapting myself to myself. I should have been trying to bring about that identification of the two vital centers, as in the example of the horse I told you about. Unconsciously I was, no doubt. With endless groping one finally becomes aware—the random shots in the dark are too striking to be ignored. Every deep realization of this sort is a real advance, a real consolidation in the hitherto blind grasp at truth. Suddenly you perceive that, if you listen properly, the truth is always speaking in you. And then you become terribly quiet and contained. You cease trying to do more than you can do. You also never do less than you are able to do. But you work and act from a new level which is like an inexhaustible reserve of strength and inspiration.

The conception of truth which was bound up with ideas of right and wrong, just and unjust, falls away. It is absorbed in a higher conception, allowing the right and the just deed an automatic expression. All the immoralists were so named because, in discovering a greater reality, they also discovered a larger, more inclusive truth.

By an unflinching regard for one's self one gradually becomes so in harmony with the world that he no longer has to think about his duty toward others. One ceases to think about causing the other pain or sorrow or disillusionment because one's acts and speech become so transparent that the heart's intention always registers. Fear vanishes when one is convinced that he can do no evil, when he does as he pleases because it is the only thing to do. We often think we may cause harm by our behavior but we think so only because we have not enough faith in the other's intelligence and sympathy. We imagine that those who admire or love us do so because of our good qualities only. But more often than not the other person is fully aware of our frailties and is more prepared for our misbehavior than we ourselves are. The sage, you will notice, does not lie or palliate matters. If he does not reveal the truth he maintains silence. If he must hurt the other he does so gently, not out of zeal for truth, but because he realizes that at certain moments pain is better than illusion. Truth he always endeavors to present to the other by putting him face to face with reality. And since reality is not an "aspect" of life, a view which has to be defended and safeguarded, he has no fear of the ultimate outcome.

Reality is not cruel or oppressive, but a balm, like the earth itself, in which, as you tell me, the natives of South America bury themselves to staunch their wounds. If it is from the earth we spring and to earth we return, why should it not be healing to our wounds. It is the same with reality. What englobes us cannot be the cause of pain. It is only the effort to conceal, to shut out the totality, which hurts and wounds, ourselves as well as the other.

HENRY

[Villa Seurat, April 1939]
Monday

ANAÏS—

By the time you get this we'll probably know whether there's to be war or not. It's difficult to think about anything else. Everybody is excited or depressed. Am waiting for Hitler's famous speech tonight. The whole world sits and waits to hear what one man says—it strikes me as thoroughly ridiculous.

The other night Moricand * and Fred were here—and we had a wonderful time of it. I haven't laughed so much in ages. To see Fred dancing around Moricand and *interrupting* him is quite a sight. They hit it off well, despite the tremendous contradiction between them. Anyway, Moricand had brought along a graph of the sky for Hitler these days. According to every sign Hitler should either die, be assassinated or fade out of the picture entirely now. We were comparing it with Balzac's graph—the day of his death—which, by the way, is tremendously convincing. Everything squared to everything else—except Neptune, which was unaspected—open for the celestial path beyond, so to speak.

[Hans] Reichel ** got out of the hospital—I met him on the street the very day—just said hello to him. He grew a moustache and looks "different"—younger and stranger somehow.

I am still going to the dentist—won't be fixed up until Friday maybe. Can't leave here—in any case—until I get a front tooth put in!

Read in morning paper that America will have gunboats off Eng-

---

* For a full account of Conrad Moricand (pen name Claude Valence) see Miller's *A Devil in Paradise,* New York, New American Library, 1956, incorporated in *Big Sur and the Oranges of Hieronymus Bosch,* New York, New Directions, 1957.

** See Biographical Notes.

land to take citizens back. Can't make up my mind at all to accept that. What bothers me more is the fact that Roosevelt has just announced that America does not sympathize with either side. That might make it unpleasant for us, if war is declared. We will be detested for a while.

Moricand made me a gift of a beautiful rattan cane with elaborate carvings—from somewhere in the Antipodes. It was as though he had given over to me the magic wand—Aaron's rod. As though the seer were handing over the insignia to his faithful disciple.

I had a couple of bad nightmares myself—but easily attribute them to the disquieting events and conversations. I have a strong feeling that something quite unexpected will happen—not a war, but a big breakup in Germany itself. It may be only a wish—but it's hard for me to believe that a whole people are going to voluntarily commit suicide. This may be the supreme test of all this will-to-power nonsense. The bomb may go off, in other words, in their own hands—before they can throw it. I have another strange hunch—that when the whole world is focusing attention on one man, as it is now, it is almost impossible for that man to escape the curses and maledictions that are being showered upon him. Few men—in recent times anyway—have created so much hatred. He will have to answer for it. It is possible he may go off his nut yet!

I am waiting for Lantelme * to appear. More later. But don't go into a panic! I feel very well protected.

HENRY

P. S. There is a letter for you from Durrell—should I send it to you?

[Villa Seurat, May 25, 1939]
Thursday

Still rushing about—thin as a rail. But everything executed. Just sold the lamp now—6:30 P.M.—after 8 visits to the electrician —150 frs. Such a running around—never did so much in my life. Glad to get out of Villa Seurat—what a swamp of details! I even enjoy the idea of being in a hotel for a few days here in Paris. I'm on

---

* A Frenchman from the Midi, who was secretary to Anaïs Nin's father, and taught French to Henry Miller.

the street—right at the Porte! A terrific din—an inferno—but pleasant. I wanted to say that the valise with my things has my initials on
it. I put the salad fork and spoon and the thimble and some ashtrays
in it—as a souvenir of Villa Seurat.

I'm getting so many letters these last few days and so many requests
to do this and that I'm bewildered.* I'll move out of hotel slowly,
Friday or Saturday—is today Thursday? I'm not sure. Anyway, one
day of calm here and a last visit to Ménilmontant. Then, as I wrote,
to Rocamadour—another place I've always dreamed about. This time
I don't think I will be disappointed.

I'm not even getting visa for Greece yet. Will do that in Marseille.
Why shouldn't I pass leisurely thru Italy? I'd like to see Florence,
Ravenna, Naples, Rome, Taormina. Corfu is always there. Last thing
I had to do was to mail the 3 blankets to the Durrells. Taking your
Ms. [*Winter of Artifice*] along with me.

Why should I hurry to go anywhere? I'm fed up with activity. It's
crazy.

HENRY

Rocamadour, Saturday 10th [June, 1939]
    Am off on an auto trip again to Padirac—where the "gouffre"
is. Yesterday was one of the most wonderful days I ever spent in
France for sightseeing. I discovered at last the *real* France—i.e. the
Dordogne!! The river is like out of the Rilke poems, the most still,
dark and magical river I ever saw. I found two places I must go back
to, if only for a few days. *Domme*—an old fortified city on the Dordogne overlooking the river—panorama splendid—like a dream! In-
quired pension rates—only get pension if you stay a week—is 40 frs.
a day per person, in a decent hotel. I told man I would come for a
week. But I may go to the other place first—*Sarlat,* not so far from
there. To me that is the most unique city in France—the first which
lives up to my expectations. But it is decrepit in a way you wouldn't
like. It is dead and dreary to the eye—like old Brooklyn pushed to
the extreme. But I was enchanted with it and met there a *libraire*
who promised to show me around. It looks like a typhoid town—but
I could write ecstatically about it and probably will.

---

* In February, the first edition of *Tropic of Capricorn* had been published by
the Obelisk Press, Paris, 367 pp., 60 frs.

Incidentally, there are fine people in this region. The Dordogne is God's own country. I could take a house here somewhere and live contentedly the rest of my life, I imagine. It is perfect country.

I feel that there is a big area round about which is just the country I always wanted to see. Full of natural wonders and historically interesting—Gallo-Roman, Medieval and troglodyte everywhere. Saw Les Eyzies—the Cro-Magnon caves—and had the most wonderful lunch there I ever had in my life, tout compris, for 20 frs.

By the way, just as I was leaving Paris, 5 minutes before cleaning out, I ran into Cendrars again. He seemed very cordial—gave me the name of a friend to look up in Toulouse. Said he had just received the Chinese review with my article in it about him.* Seemed really pleased, but as usual, too embarrassed to talk about it. Said I had "bombarded him from the sky." I am glad I ran into him. I'll write again saying where I will go from here. Seeing the Dordogne makes up for all the rottenness in France.

HVM

[Nice, June, 1939]
Thursday Eve.

ANAÏS—

Got your letter this evening after a big outdoor day. Must have walked 10 or 12 kilometres myself. Sat on beach but didn't take my shirt off—too cool. But this was a marvelous day. What a clear atmosphere! Never saw things so bright and clear in my life, I feel. I went to Cagnes s/mer this afternoon. Climbed to the top and had a high tea on the terrasse of Jimmy's Bar there. Was amazed to find it such a beautiful and immaculate town—and interesting too in construction. I understand better now why people go there—it's natural. Titus has a villa and an extra house to rent. Saw him watering his estate. If there were many days like today I'd feel fit for the rest of my life. After all the exertion I don't feel a bit tired. Like drinking champagne. You set so well aerated here you can't accumulate poisons. But today was exceptional—that steady still wind was mar-

---

* "Tribute to Blaise Cendrars," in *T'ien Hsia Monthly,* Shanghai, November, 1938, later included in *Wisdom of the Heart,* New Directions, 1941.

velous. And cool and hot at the same time. You hardly perspire. It's great.

The day before I was almost down with nervous prostration—tremendous fatigue. It was a stormy sort of day—heavy. Went to Monaco to do a water color but couldn't muster up the energy. No gambling. Don't even think of it.

Tried out the typewriter for a couple of hours. Strange. It lacks an exclamation mark—you can't make one, no matter what you do.

Had a nice note from Dr. Dausse, assuring me it was natural—recommending Paraffin oil and Biskana powders, if necessary. But I am O.K. now. Better than ever. The night porter still asks me if I'm staying or not—"*continuez,* etc." He's cuckoo.

Haven't found a good restaurant yet. Tried the old quarter yesterday, but no good. Too cheap. Found the Russian Church too—it's a miniature replica of the Moscow one, they say. Quite interesting—but not red, like the postcards.

No word from Kahane yet. Suppose he's saving his letter to send with the others—to save 90 centimes. But I'm sure your book [*Winter of Artifice*] will be out in a few days. There's no reason to delay it now. I'll worry him to death about it—and about the [second edition of] *Aller Retour* too, which is over a year late.

Saw a marvelous documentaire on the Malay jungle last night. Saw a tiger fight a cobra—a python. Neither won. The tiger was almost crushed to death. I thought he was gasping his last. Then suddenly he leapt up and wriggled himself free, but bruised and utterly exhausted. Saw several combats between strange animals—without issue. Very strange sight. One always thinks it's a fight to the death. But apparently it isn't. Every animal has its match, it seems. To see a crocodile and a python fight is weird. Well, I'm staying on, I guess. It's beginning to agree with me. You get burned very slowly here, I notice.

In America, after a day in the sun, you'd look like a lobster. Here it's gentle—*French* sun! Today I really got an idea of what the Mediterranean can look like. I was thunderstruck. At the horizon it was a pale lavender and violet. The islands near Cannes were purple—in midday! And blues and greens like opals gleaming. Cagnes from the sea was perfect. You could see every house clean and sharp—a kilometre away. No wonder Renoir had a house there. It's great for the painters. The clearest atmosphere imaginable. Like desert country almost.

It's the first time in my life I wasn't tired out from exercise. Can't get over it. But I think it's treacherous. I think you can suddenly drop dead from overexertion, before you are aware of fatigue. And the sun *is* powerful, even if it doesn't boil you right away. I realize that. I keep my hat on—and my shirt on. I can take a sun bath nude at my window very comfortably.

Well, I am now going to a movie—just in time to see the *third* one. Keep your spirits up.

HVM

P. S. Maybe tomorrow I'll feel depressed. But I don't think so.

[Nice, June, 1939]
Saturday

ANAÏS—

Moricand writes explicitly about the gambling. Advises period between 26th of June and 7th of July. Sextile étroite between Jupiter and Neptune. Gives me a "martingale" to try out. No matter what number turns up I should place a chip on each of the following at one coup—"until I get satisfaction."

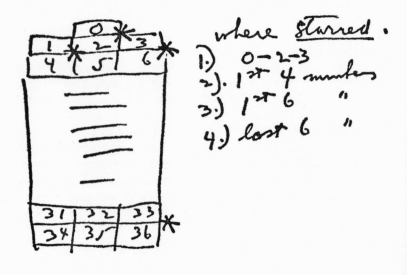

Last night I stood and watched 2 tables, without playing, to see how it goes theoretically. If I had played it immediately the first few times I'd have won several hundred frs. Afterward it fell off. On the other table I would at best have broken even. Watched about 1½ hours. M. gives certain dates even more favorable than others. Says I should also play any number that strikes my fancy—in addition to the "martingale."

I'll wait till the 26th and risk a hundred. No more. Yesterday I received the 377 frs. mandat from Paris. So I am quite all right. Have 8 or 9 hundred frs. at the moment. Holding on to it. Paid electricity bill and bought a new supply of my medicines. I have a regular laboratory.

Today a magnificent storm—best I have seen in years. But when the weather changes—when it's sultry and cloudy—I feel enervated. Get weak and nervous. Never noticed this before.

By the way, that fool of a girl sent all the books to New York—because I didn't write in time. There's a chance they may be returned, as they were not sent to the Gotham [Book Mart], but to another office. But if they're seized it will be bad. I'll have to make good somehow. However, I feel luck is with me. Not worrying about it.

The restaurant man is a Greek from Smyrna. Told me all about the Greek islands. Says the weather is very much like Nice. A good supportable heat. He's a very fine, tender sort of guy. I thought he was Hungarian or Rumanian.

Also—am reading Nostradamus! Makes my hair stand on end. I believe it thoroughly. You must read it. My intuitions are sound, all right. Paris will be destroyed—in the night, by air raid. The Germans will break thru the Maginot Line. Their defeat will occur at *Poitiers!!* Bad defeat. Then a King of France—at Avignon. France bigger than ever, and allied with Spain. The war will begin between Italy and Germany first. Italy will be wiped out. And England will lose all her power. Sounds right to me.

HVM

[Nice, June, 1939]
Monday night

ANAÏS—

Got your note this evening on my return from Grasse where I spent the afternoon. If it weren't that there are no buses at night I'd have stayed on. Am thinking of going back there tomorrow and stay overnight, probably leaving this place Wednesday. Grasse is better than all the places I've yet seen! You must go—after I leave. Explore it thoroughly. The old town lies on one side of the main street, in descending layers of labyrinthian coils. Superb decrepitude and very much alive. Hasn't such monuments as Sarlat, but more picturesque still. The site too is wonderful. I like the air too—very light—about 300 or 400 meters up. Better than Nice—I noticed that immediately. I would like to go back there for a stay in winter. It's just what I like—the old port which is quite big, or seems so, at first sight. I could kick myself for not having been here sooner. Why don't people talk about these places? If ever I write anything about my trip it will be about Sarlat, Domme, Grasse, etc. You must go there. The service is better from Cannes. After 7:15 P.M. no more buses to Nice—and no railway. If I go tomorrow night to stay over it will be without baggage. I would come back to the hotel and probably leave for Marseille in the afternoon. I'm sorry I didn't know about this place sooner. I've have spent a few days there. Infinitely more interesting to me than Nice, though the old Nice, which I've explored thoroughly, is quite good.

I still have the rheumatism in my shoulder, but am baking it out in the sun. Too cold yesterday and today for swimming. But the wind is fine. If that's the Mistral, I love it. When the wind blows steady and the sky is clear then I like it best. It agrees with me. Heat alone enervates me.

I'm mailing you the pamphlet on Eze. I read thru the pamphlet on Perigord too. There are still more interesting places to visit. I urge you, when I leave for Greece, to make a thorough exploration of the whole region—you won't regret it. Only eat à la carte! I wish I had seen the place where Montaigne lived. That sounds fine. The Dordogne, by the way, is supposed to be the best river in France for fishing. Try to stop at Domme where you get it at its best.

I enjoyed my second trip to Cagnes even better than the first.

Found the *real* Cagnes which is the other side from where Titus lives. Renoir had a house outside the town for many years. All these villages situated on hills are more or less alike—and to me the best sort of places to live in. The seashore is only good for a week—after that it gets monotonous. I like the medieval places—the gloomier and more sinister they are, the better. More soon.

HVM

[Marseille, July, 1939]
Monday A.M.

ANAÏS—

Got a second letter this morning but you forgot to put my name on the envelope! Just the hotel address. By the way, don't be confused by change of street name.

Half the street is called by the old name—Blvd. Dugoumier—and the other half by the new name—Blvd. d'Athènes, no. 25.

The noise is terrific here—haven't had a decent night's sleep since I arrived—but he's changing my room tonight.

I haven't had a letter from Kahane yet nor the money for the check I sent him over a week ago—and only two letters forwarded me. Think something is amiss. Maybe he went to the country and hasn't received my letter.

By the way, did Durrell say whether he would go to Athens to meet me? I haven't received word from him either yet. He was to recommend me a hotel in Athens, in case I have to stay there a couple of days.

You're entitled to (6) books, I believe. Good to hear about Gotham B.M. Miss Steloff * is a very generous person, I think. Really kind and helpful.

I won't dispatch any letters to arrive later than the 12th. Probably no more after this—unless a telegram.

If Kahane doesn't send me my money (he didn't even mail me the check for the 500 he owes me) I may need 200 frs. on the 12th. I'll see. I'll try to manage without—and probably will. These people here seem like peasants and being near the gare they don't trust anybody.

---

* See Biographical Notes.

I may give them a couple of hundred francs now in advance, to allay
suspicion. Can't bother to change hotels again—it's too complicated
and my mail will go astray, I fear.

It's frightfully hot here in Marseille. Torrid heat. Nice was infinitely
better.

HENRY

[July 18, 1939]
Aboard the *Théophile Gautier*

ANAÏS—

Only 9 A.M. and the heat is terrific! One wakes up sweating
—like in a Turkish bath. Found I was in a cabin with 3 others. 2nd
Class here is like 3rd Class on a big boat. Very slow and old boat
filled with Levantine peoples—mostly Turk, Syrian and Greek.
Everybody says Corfu is excellent—for cool climate. Athens is hot,
they say. Will let you know when I land. These last few days seems
to me it must be around 100° all the time. The boat stopped at
Naples for about 8 hours and I saw the city and went to Pompeii.
Nearly got sunstruck. Worst heat I ever experienced in my life. Incredible!!! Even the Sahara couldn't be worse. But I liked Naples
immensely—and the Italians particularly. Wonderful robust, gay,
simple, expansive people. A pleasure to see and talk to them. But
everything extremely expensive by comparison with France. Cost me
200 frs. to go ashore. But well worth it. Especially since I never expected to see Italy. I'm glad I saw Naples first and the Cathedral Sunday morning. Like a bourse! Everybody at home there. Wonderful
naturalness. Warmed me toward the Italians.

Pompeii was excellent, except for the overwhelming heat. Just
about as I had pictured it in my mind. But what bad taste they had!
The art is atrocious. Only the construction of the houses is interesting. Suited to the climate. But the frescoes are lousy. Cheap, vulgar—
almost like American art today.

The Orientals here on board with whom I talk are disappointing.
Thoroughly materialistic, pragmatic, nationalistic—trying desperately
to "evolve" (!) to European-American standards of life. All of them
born arguers. Worm-ridden with logic. I am looked upon as very

singular—"extravagant," "bizarre," "original," they say. They listen
to me as they would to a man coming from Mars. The Germans have
made a great impression on them all. They want to be modern, strong,
independent. That makes me laugh. They are like old children. All
very commercial-minded. Talk science and industry. But there is a
young Greek medical student with whom I have long and interesting
conversations. He is from the North—Byzantine Greece—and loves
the Nordic writers—for their mysticism. Especially Knut Hamsun
who is popular in Greece! He too deplores the ancient Greek "harmony" and the French equilibrium. He has given me a pretty good
idea of the Greek character and temperament. It seems that the
peasant is the real person in Greece. He has all the good qualities—
is genuinely superior to the others.

Well, I think once ashore the heat will be more supportable. Here
we are exposed to the sun. The boat moves so slowly it creates no
breeze hardly. Everywhere the ventilators are going. I have nothing
on but a pair of pants and an undershirt—and perspiring like a dog.
Even the Greeks feel hot!

From what I gather I must not leave Greece with more money than
I bring in. If I receive money while there it is made a record of. I
think however I'll need what you thought to send. There are 3 drachmas to the franc, but the standard of living, they say, is about 2
drachmas to a franc. A taxi from the port to Athens—8 kilometres—
costs about 100 to 120 drachmas, they say. And the hotel per day, at
Athens, for a room, between 60 and 80 drachmas. However, when I
see Larry I'll know better. Reserving space for my first impressions of
Athens. Expect to like it. Cinema begins at 10:30 P.M. Dinner at
9:30. Like Spain a bit.

Athens

19th Arrived this morning 8:00 A.M. in blistering heat. Climbed up
the Acropolis. No Durrell in sight, no telegram from him. Going to
take boat for Corfu tomorrow. Heat here would drive me crazy. It's
expensive here, it seems to me. You get a lot of drachmas in exchange, but they count in 50 and 100 at a time almost. Can't say
much now except that I must get out of here before being sunstruck.
More from Corfu. Worse than the Sahara, this heat. New York is
nothing compared to it.

HENRY

Corfu—Sunday
22 or 23 July, 1939

DEAR ANAÏS—

It's only 7:30 A.M. and I've already been in for a swim—up and about an hour ago. Arrived yesterday from Athens in sweltering heat and had to ride in open car for about an hour. Larry and his brother were there to meet me at the wharf. I tell you, Corfu really is marvelous. It's somewhere between Palestine, Arizona and Greece. Excellent distinguished port of entry—very sportslike. Then we go out into the sticks. They chose a lovely spot and the house is ever so much more wonderful than I had expected it to be. A sound, substantial Greek house on modern lines, which I think Nancy laid the plans for and supervised the building. They are still adding wings to it, but it is already ample and spacious. The heat is much more bearable here—it cools off in the evening and the early morning is fine too. Imagine—Albania is right in front of us, so near it seems that you can feel its presence. I see all sorts of countries and costumes here —can feel the near Orient, what with the olive trees, the goats, the craggy mountains, the volcanic rock, the physiognomies. Larry and Nancy are sort of distinguished here. Makes it very pleasant. In short, Corfu comes up to all expectations. Surpasses them. I can row about in the big rowboat and do all the things I longed to do. And then they've given me a fine room with a writing table etc.—very comfortable. The waves lap right under the window at night—so wonderful it keeps me awake. No more tired groggy feeling. Am wide awake —and wouldn't be surprised if I wrote a bit.

It's a world of intense light. The sun is magnified a few times, it seems. Even at 6:00 or 7:00 P.M. it is still powerful. Immediately I landed at Corfu Larry bought me a big straw hat. I swim with it on.

Another thing very important—the Greeks are very friendly to English and Americans. They really make you feel welcome—they have a genuine smile and they're well-meaning and simple and direct. I like them—especially the peasants. I am going to learn a little Greek at once—I don't think it's too difficult.

It's a new world entirely—light and rocks! Hoary with age—and ravished by cataclysms. Still volcanic in spots.

Luckily the boat from Athens took a roundabout course and so I passed many famous isles—all rising up in a mist of heat like dream

islands. Very impressive sight. All looking uninhabited and unin-
habitable. Athens too I liked and hope to go back for a short trip.
Quite the strangest city I ever saw. From the Acropolis a truly marvelous panorama—you feel it to be one of the sacred spots of the earth.
I'm quite O.K. financially too, for the time being. Believe everything
will work out all right no matter how money is sent. Anyway, I feel
like anchoring here for a good spell. It's just what I like.

In the hotels and restaurants the money flies. Though actually the
scale is about ½ or ⅓ of the American scale. But you are always paying
out big sums because the drachma is like a penny in America. That
frightens one at first.

I'll send letters by air mail usually—but its goes slowly. Larry never
got my letter until the day I landed in Athens. They could hardly
believe I had come. It's too bad I didn't try it before. The food, incidentally, is simple and substantial—it agrees with me. The most
impressive thing is *a glass of water!* It assumes a new value here—you
respect it and appreciate it. Larry and Nancy send their love and hope
you can manage to join us.

                                                            HVM

P. S. Soon I'll sign my name in Greek letters.

                                           [Corfu] July 27 [1939]

DEAR ANAÏS—
          No letter from you since arriving here. We are a good ways
from the town—over an hour by bus or boat—and these go only once
a day. We go in only rarely—mail is sent out sometimes by the boat.
The end of this week we go camping on an island some distance away
—for a week. Won't be in touch with the world at all during that
time. I am certainly at home here and almost gone native already.
Everything goes smoothly. Walking, drinking, swimming, sailing, eating all day long. No more medicaments. Am in excellent health. We
have already made some wonderful excursions. Saw a great part of
the island, which is tremendously interesting and variegated. It grows
on me more and more. It's all legendary, idyllic! I certainly won't
budge from here until the rains set in, unless something unexpected
happens. There are no guests here. The girl Larry analyzed was here

and left—*cured by the Sun,* I imagine. We are now awaiting a Greek
Oxford Professor who from the description should be a marvelous
man. But one needs nothing. Funny thing is I am not at all sluggish.
I am wide awake, no matter how hot it gets. Though Corfu is far
cooler than Athens. The Venetians were here for four centuries—and
the Turks too—all visible.

I swim at night sometimes—the water is always warmer than the
air—in fact, it's tepid—like Majorca, I imagine. No shock to go in.
I have a huge straw hat and espadrilles and am now getting a pair of
khaki shorts.

If you don't get an answer immediately to a wire or air letter you'll
know it's because we're on a trip. I've had no mail from Kahane since
coming, so don't know anything. I understand I can receive my money
and take out what I don't use. But I live as tho' shut off from the
world and thoroughly indifferent to what's going on. No thought of
newspapers, books, cinema, publishers, etc. And the day passes
quickly.

If you could manage to come I am sure you would love it here. You
can't imagine what it's like. Perhaps a little like Majorca.

We are exactly opposite Albania, the spot where the Italians landed
—can actually see the village from the top of the hill nearby. The
olive groves and the wells are fascinating. And the peasants too—
very close to the Spaniards in some ways, I imagine.

Anyway, it's all far better than I pictured. I wait to hear from you
and learn how you are getting on. Wonder if you are still at Saint
Tropez.

Larry wants to know if Eduardo is coming down. They both seem
to adore him. Going into town now with this—up at 5:30 A.M. One
sleeps less—you take short naps now and then. I think in a short time
I might even write here.

More soon.

HVM

P. S. Learning a little Greek.
P. P. S. Still waiting for the copies of your book.*

---

* Anaïs Nin's *Winter of Artifice* had just been published by the Obelisk
Press, Paris.

[Corfu, 1939]
Sunday—July 30th

DEAR ANAÏS—

Leaving tomorrow morning for the camping expedition and will be cut off from the world for a week, so that if I don't receive any mail from you in the morning when we go to town I won't see anything until our return. No letter from you thus far. Hope nothing amiss. As for myself I am improving by leaps and bounds every day. Just the right kind of activity for me. And getting brown as a berry. We have two or three little secret coves where we go bathing in the raw—and that's wonderful. It's like a tonic. I go about now in a pair of khaki shorts and barefooted. You'd be amazed to see the rough jagged cliffs I scramble over in bare feet. I'm toughening up. And the rowboat is splendid exercise. Here the fishermen stand up to row their huge boats and we imitate them. Their boats are beautiful. Like Van Gogh pictures. Curious weather here too. Every three days it seems to turn. There are four distinct kinds of wind. The most dangerous is the "maestro"—which is cold and furious and makes sailing dangerous. Sometimes blows the fishing boats over to Albania—and now and then the regular service boat which brings our provisions and mail, etc. The food is simple but excellent. Lots of olive oil, which agrees with me. In fact, I rub it all over me now every day. Fine feeling. I'm taking a notebook along and your unfinished book to the camping place. Perhaps I'll finish it there. We have to first construct a shelter for ourselves. And sleep on the ground. Can you imagine me doing these things and liking it? I've changed rapidly.

I'm also getting a better slant on the money situation. Things are cheap all right, except for articles which are not made here. A fairly good meal in town costs about 50 drachmas, for example. Postage is very high, for some mysterious reason, or a Turkish towel! The cigarettes (Greek) which I smoke cost only 6 drachmas a package. And so on.

I am letting my beard grow. Why shave? Use about 2 handkerchiefs and 1 shirt a week. Down to bedrock.

There are three little children here—quite beautiful and very well behaved. They are learning English. The English predominate here. Even the King speaks English preferably, I'm told. More and more I can see the resemblances to southern Spain, from your description.

Except that I don't see the overbearing pride in these people. They are soft and gentle. Move quietly and easily, gracefully too. The young peasant women are often great beauties, but fade quickly, and there are donkeys and ponies here, again like Spain. But the language is difficult—barely any connection with English or French. Even yes and no are thoroughly strange—Malista (Yes)—Ochi (No). Only the scientific, metaphysical and mythological terms resemble.

Will try to add a word or two to this in town. Dark now and the oil light is dim.

MONDAY MORNING—
No mail yet. We're off. If there's a village within walking distance, I'll drop you a line from the camp. Haven't received your books yet either. Hope you are all right.

HVM

[Corfu, 1939]
Sunday—August 6th

ANAÏS—
Just got back from the camping trip which I enjoyed immensely, except for minor discomfits such as sand in the food, ants, *flies,* etc. But feel great and am well burned now. Also have grown a beard, which is pepper and salt color. The peasants thought I was Larry's father! A bald head and a beard here is a sign of age. They guess me to be 60! But I feel like 30 now. Can do everything the others do and remain cheerful and not too fatigued. But I do hate flies! I don't think I'd have had so many if I had been alone. I would have camped under the olive trees instead of on the sand. Durrell keeps saying I look marvelous. He's surprised how quickly I adapted myself to the life. I think I was fit two days after arriving at Corfu.

Everybody is pleased with your book—inside and out. I haven't yet begun a serious examination of it, but will soon. Everything serious or literary gets put off till tomorrow. I can't even hold a continuous discussion. Why *discuss* anything? All I do is clown it, or go silent and sit and meditate peacefully. I can sit hours without moving or thinking. But if I must get up and climb a precipice I am ready

in an instant. One shifts gears here easily. Nothing disturbs me. I
could live on like a rock, I imagine. There is plenty to read here, if
I wish it. But even that is not important. I read part of Giono's book
at camp and reveled in it. *That,* strangely enough, seemed more real
to me than the life we were leading. Because, really, *this isn't life*
now. This is only illusory living—a relapse into the world of nature.
To live one needs artificiality, which thinking and all art is. But I accept this now gracefully, because I need it. But I don't fool myself
about it. It's a kind of pleasant death, or at least, arrest of life. Only
a highly civilized person can enjoy it. The peasants and the fishermen
don't enjoy it. *They live it.* And then it's something quite different—
much more difficult, complicated and sadder and grimmer. The life of
a natural man is really grim, hard, austere, sad, I think. Full of blows
and catastrophes and measly little things which we don't notice in the
city.

I am cured of the movies, however. Never the slightest desire to
see one. Now and then try to paint—but not with much success. I
am more interested in observing how my feet toughen up. They are
like leather already—the soles of my feet. All cut to ribbons at first
and baked by the burning sand, then toughened by the constant
drenching in the sea. Coming down to the camp from the mountain
top was a piece of sheer agony. We had to take off our sandals to run
across the sand. It was like an ordeal by fire. If it had lasted two
minutes more I'd have gone stark mad. To sit in the auto after it's
been standing in the sun is another trial. The leather burns right thru
your pants—terrific. And if you touch the metal parts by accident
with your bare arm it's like touching a red-hot poker. I tried to find
espadrilles here, but they don't make them. My fine, Tibetan sandals
look worn out already—I'm getting them fixed now. Yesterday I entered the restaurant in Corfu carrying my shoes in my hand—my feet
as dirty as any peasant's. I look like a beachcomber. Will try to get
a photo taken with the beard—see how you like it.

The money came thru all right. You needn't do it that way. Direct
to me, in any fashion. I can take out any amount if I show that I
received it from abroad. Naturally I give the Durrells part of it—to
defray expenses. But I am well fixed and there is no need to worry
or hurry about it ever—unless I send you a cable, which is hardly
likely. So if any money comes from America I will be able to receive
it here. I look forward to staying on down here thru September—to

visit Athens again, which is an interesting place, and Ithaca and
Crete. Especially Crete. All my life I've wanted to see the Palace of
Knossos (Palace of Entrails). It's extremely hot there now. Durrell
is expecting a good Greek friend here soon, named Theodore, who
is an Oxford graduate, and a highly interesting natural scientist.

I am making a bit of progress with the language. I listen in on the
English lessons he gives the little girl, and I write down all the idioms
I can. I think it would be easier for you than for any of us. The sound
of it is not at all like Spanish but I rather think the construction and
syntax is. The spirit here seems very Spanish, or Moorish to me. I'm
crazy about the olives, the olive oil for inside and out, the wonderful
homemade bread, the luscious fruits and vegetables. It's a good
healthy diet, I must say—for this kind of life even better than French
cooking would be.

So you see, I really like it. It doesn't pale a bit. And I did have
the right hunch after all. Everything in due season, I suppose.
Whether I shall ever write anything here or not, I don't know. I feel
I may. It's not improbable. But I am not trying to do anything. As I
say, I am more interested in the state of my feet, my agility, my sunburn, my rowing and swimming prowess, etc. Going naked is in itself
the greatest cure. I think 9/10 of all the world's neurotics could be
cured thus—and thus alone. Just by the sun and water playing on the
naked body. It's very chastening too. There's nothing sensual about it.
One becomes a rock or a tree.

Haven't heard anything from Kahane—I don't write him either.
Know nothing about the fate of *Capricorn* and care nothing.

Durrell is strumming the guitar. Both he and Nancy send their love.
They keep asking me what are your plans. They certainly have curious notions. Now they are talking of raising money to bring [George]
Barker, the poet, and his consumptive wife out here— and Desmond
Tester, the young movie actor, and God knows whom else. There
wouldn't be room for half of them. And it's so good here without
visitors. But they need people around them.

Fred is still in London apparently. [David] Edgar * I haven't heard
from at all. I imagine him to be still sitting at the Select where I last
saw him.

Well, I must take a swim now—lunch is almost ready and I'm
famished. My ears have not given me any trouble thus far. I manage

---

* See Biographical Notes.

to swim without getting much water in them. My eyes are decidedly improved. The salt water seems to strengthen them. I can go out into the glare of midday and bathe without feeling a great need for the glasses. That's wonderful. I seem to think I can even see better! More soon.

HVM

P. S. Despite my lack of Greek I notice that I make friends with the peasants easily—even more successfully than the Durrells. One old fellow at the camp to whom I talked a deaf and dumb language came back with 3 musicians to entertain me. Said he wanted to see "the nice man," not the Durrells.

Corfu, August 10th [1939]

ANAÏS:

Had quite a batch of mail from all quarters of the globe yesterday. Your name crops up continually, people asking about your work or promising to write about you, etc. Durrell too has had some fine new reviews, especially of his poetry. I got the *Phoenix* and the *Partisan Review,* with my things in them.* Paul Rosenfeld ** writes that he has written several reviews of *Max* [*Max and the White Phagocytes,* published September, 1938, Obelisk Press, Paris] and *Capricorn* in American magazines but they have not yet appeared. Says he hopes to write about you shortly—is waiting for space, that's all. Meston writes that some editor or poet in Sante Fe, New Mexico, was very much interested in your *House of Incest.* And Audrey Beecham says she is reading or just read *Winter of Artifice*—will probably write you direct—a little afraid of you; but enjoys the book immensely. Says she likes best the second part. The effect of it reminded her strangely of Rimbaud's Vierge Folle in *Saison en Enfer.* Says she is rereading it. (You see how this machine works. Can't get

---

* *The Phoenix,* Woodstock, N.Y., Spring 1939, carried the account of Miller's aborted trip to England, "Via Dieppe-Newhaven," and *Partisan Review* (Summer 1939) his answers to seven questions on "The Situation in American Writing."
** See Biographical Notes.

used to it—very slow reaction.) Says she never received your *House of Incest*.

Also a letter from the Baronne Leonie Ungern-Sternberg, Keyserling's sister, asking me to contribute something for a book which she will have printed as an homage to him in celebration of his 60th birthday next July. She is in Manchukuo, Siberia. She also said she would be glad to have something from Moricand if he would send something to her, so I have written him to that effect. He ought to jump at the chance.

Life goes on here blissfully and smoothly; yesterday dolphins were swimming outside the house. The big boats also pass here occasionally, on their way north. Strange sight from our window. We are thinking of going camping soon again—that is, the Durrells are. I could go on living here indefinitely—camping is all right, but why take on ants and flies, etc.? However, I'm getting used to these little inconveniences. Often my room is absolutely flyless—I am the only one who has screens. It certainly is a fine monastic room—with plenty of air and light. And worktables and books, etc. I am doing water colors now, and have already knocked out two or three really fine ones. No, I hear nothing much yet about the book, except through letters, all of which are very flattering. Have yet to see a solid review.

Will send you some snapshots soon which Larry took while we were in bathing. You will see the beard and perhaps the sunburn. I look like an American pioneer, Larry says. And I take more exercise than anyone. Am enormously hungry—can hardly wait for meals. Perhaps a trifle stouter, but not much. But a good tone. And a deep calm. Nothing disturbs me, not even ants and flies. Have seen quite a bit of the island too, which is splendid. Longing to see Crete and Ithaca and Lesbos. Have to wait a bit, because it is hotter in these spots than here. Must say the weather here is ideal. A heat which is supportable. And the water is just right—never a shock. I could stand it colder, to tell the truth. And I don't shiver when I get out. In fact, I have to duck in repeatedly to keep refreshed. The sun is powerful, but dry. I'm sorry I didn't buy espadrilles in France; they are unobtainable here. And they are the one essential thing for walking. Shoes are too slippery. And sandals are not practicable. As much as possible I go barefooted. But I haven't yet learned to walk over thistles in my bare feet. I see from the photo that you do look fine. I feel just the same way as you do—as though I had taken off twenty

years. Can't imagine now ever going back to the indoor life, to rain
and fog, to stuffy bistros, etc. But the good weather won't last forever.

Don't bother sending letters airmail. They are delayed here anyway. I never mail your letters myself. They are picked up by the boat
here, taken to Corfu, picked up by Spiro Americanus who can't read
or write and mailed by him in his own fashion. If someone is leaving
for Europe he probably gives them to him to mail. Everything is done
here in Greek fashion, hit and miss. No hurry about anything. Tomorrow, tomorrow. It's all very Spanish to me. I'm sure you'd agree.

Incidentally Nancy has hung a lot of Henry Moore reproductions
here—sculpture. Seems very good to me. Is this the man you met in
London?

It is a fight to get in any work at all—I mean such as reading or
writing letters or painting. If I don't begin the day properly nothing
gets done. After dinner we stay indoors because it is too difficult to
walk about in the dark—too perilous. The paths are only for goats
really. So I try now to do something in the morning. Afternoons it's
bathing and sunning and rowing or walking, with a light siesta in between. One can go a long time without sleep, I notice; it must be the
spiritual nourishment which is in the air. Fatigue here is totally different than in the city.

The olive tree is the best thing about Greece. I am crazy about the
old olive groves, which are here for almost a thousand years. And the
trees certainly look it. They are gnarled and grayed and full of black
holes in the gray bark and branch out like octopi everywhere, sometimes holding on only to a bare rock, it seems. Wonderful tree, and
the olives themselves are infinitely better here than abroad.

Well, I must stop now and try to think what to write about Keyserling for Madame la Baronne Leonie Ungern von Sternberg, née
Keyserling.

We talk a lot about you, but it is difficult for the Durrells to write.
They, or Larry, at least, is congenitally lazy. Swimming is work for
him—he says it makes you too warm. He's surprised at my physical
activity.

                                                                HVM

[Corfu] August 15, 1939

ANAÏS:

Your letter with the Nougat heading just arrived, but no Moricand letter with it. Yes, everything is much delayed, I imagine at the Control Office, where during the summer perhaps they have more letters to go through. My letters pass through so many hands before reaching the house here it's a wonder they ever arrive. Delay is the normal here. And no use sending them via avion. Incidentally, when I go back to Athens I am going to take the plane—it is just as cheap as the boat trip and takes two hours instead of two days. And from Athens to Crete I may do the same. We are so cut off here—haven't read a paper since landing—that nothing disturbs me.

I was certainly delighted, and so was Larry yesterday, to read of the first receptions of your book, especially by Rebecca West. At the same time came a letter from Fred saying that everybody in his circle liked your book immensely, especially Symons and [Hugh Gordon] Porteus. So we were all wrong about Porteus, after all. So much the better. I have a feeling that the American critics will be favorable too. That will be fine—it means that the Villa Seurat Series will have had a 100 percent success in time.* Not a word from Kahane ** since I came down here—I don't write him at all. If I want anything I write direct to Maurice,† who is very conscientious. We received all the books we expected now. At any rate, I predict, as I always have, that your book will be damned well received, may even cause a storm.

I enclose the first serious bit of writing I have done since my arrival—the Keyserling thing. Hold it for me, in case I should need the copy. It's overdone, of course, and a lot of it sounds as if I were writing my own obituary, I think. But that's the result of not writing for so long. I go to the machine now for a couple of hours every morning—naturally, instinctively. Am writing something for [Huntington]

---

* The so-called "Villa Seurat Series," published by the Obelisk Press, Paris, was conceived in 1938, during Durrell's visit to Paris, and included Durrell's *Black Book*, Miller's *Max and the White Phagocytes* and Anaïs Nin's *Winter of Artifice*.

** Jack Kahane, Miller's first publisher, died two weeks later, on the day World War II began.

† After the death of his father, Maurice Kahane, who was then eighteen, took over the management of the Obelisk Press. See also Biographical Notes, under Jack Kahane.

Cairns * now, at his request—about my aim in writing. I don't know
that I am yet prepared to begin another volume of *Capricorn,* but I
am flirting with the idea. Incidentally I just received the two-volume
work, *The Secret Doctrine,* of Madame Blavatsky. She is or was an
extraordinary woman. It's a gargantuan work, well written, enormous
in scope, and sounds authentic—also staggering in every way. She
must have been a female Colossus. Her first book, also grandiose,
was called *Isis Unveiled.* She is undoubtedly the Neptunian *and*
Uranian type combined. A great order to her work, despite the bewildering reaches into the blue which she makes. It excites one from
the very opening, which begins with a blank circle with a tiny dot in
it. There are plenty of good books here to read, if I wish to read. But
I only seem to find time for about a half hour's reading a day. At
night one can't read—the lamplight is too feeble. We go to bed soon
after dinner. That's the only thing I don't like very much. I miss my
perambulations. But I don't miss anything else about the city life.
There is no pull whatever. I am in a new world with a new rhythm
and I accept it absolutely. I am a real Chinaman.

It's funny what strange luck I always have with my books. On the
boat coming from Athens I met a Polish chap who was very fine. I
gave him the only copy of *Capricorn* I had with me. He was visiting
a Greek family here in Corfu. The other day the Greek family made
a long trip here to see me, bringing their lunch and some fine wine
and butter etc. from their own farm—expressly for me. They knew
Larry and Nancy, but had never visited them before. They had the
book and had devoured it; and now I suppose it will go the rounds in
Greece. We are all invited to visit them at their country home for a
weekend; we almost had a visit from the King, it seems. Not because
of me, however; but he had heard of this strange English family, and
is very curious to meet the Durrells. He sailed by the other day in his
yacht, as if flirting with the idea of making an impulsive landing. All
it needs is a little formal ceremonial.

One of the curious sights here is the policeman's thatched hut, just
a shelter off the ground, in which he has a bed and his few belongings;
it is right on the beach. He sleeps there day and night. There are
about 200 people in the village, it seems to me. At night, when there
is no moon, the fishermen are out with their nets, beating the bottom
of the boat to drive the fish into the net. They carry torches, and look

---

* See Biographical Notes.

weird hidden away in the rocks and caves at the shore. Sometimes they sing while they row, and they sing well. I have heard a lot of singing by the peasants—very beautiful, strange, melodious, and sad and fierce at the same time. A haunting repetitiousness, which is not quite Moorish, but which is certainly Asiatic, Byzantine at any rate. Like their physiognomies often. In Crete there is another distinct type, short, round-headed men, also fierce, but interesting. They are very old, racially. Everything started there in Crete, some 5,000 years or so ago. I mean everything Greek. What is obsessive is the volcanic rock everywhere. You are always reminded that this is a world left over from some terrible cataclysm. I understand that in ancient times the country, all the islands, were thickly wooded, and the climate was more temperate. There is a campaign now against the goat, because the goat eats everything, including the young tree shoots. They are taking the goats from the inhabitants in some parts, and replacing them with sheep. They say the whole country can become green and verdant again in about 40 years' time, if properly tended. And I believe it; you speak of rain, but we haven't seen a drop since I came. Nor do I miss it. I hate even to see a cloud pass over the face of the sun. I like it bright and hot perpetually. I am used to it now, and find it stimulating. Only if you take too long a sunbath do you get drowsy. But an hour or so at a time and you are energized for the whole day, it seems. I am in and out of the water, getting frequent sunbaths of short duration. Turning a reddish brown, copperish. And now we have a closed flat-topped canoe on which we stand, lie or sit, and paddle or roll over into the water. You can go at top speed and it makes no difference if you turn over because you can easily right it. Marvelous exercise for the stomach. And makes you an equilibrist too. Today we are going to hike to a neighboring village, where there are the remnants of a Roman palace which Nero once visited, and also Cleopatra and Mark Antony, and there we will see a dancing festival given by the peasants. Theodore [Stephanides], the scientist, is here, and very interesting; he knows all about the stars. I am learning the various constellations. Now in August the sky is full of falling stars; about thirty to forty every hour, all through the night. It's marvelous. I suppose you have noticed Jupiter and Mars every night— they stand out from the others noticeably, especially Mars, which is quite big and copperish-looking.

I haven't yet reread your book for the errors, if there are any. Nor have I added a line to the little book for you. But I found a photo of the houseboat, and am going to try to make a water color of it for the book. The day flies; we get up quite early and go to bed around eleven or twelve: how it goes I don't know, but it is fast. And I am famished an hour or two in advance every meal. Can't seem to eat often enough. Yet I am still thin. But I feel a strength which I didn't have in Paris. Am capable of performing any activity, regardless of what time of the day, or what heat. In fact, it's a real pleasure to drip with perspiration—and then plunge into the sea. This morning it was icy cold, for the first time. And what a pleasure. The tepid bath is not so good. It seems like a good idea, but it really isn't. One needs a shock.

Don't know anything about the political situation. Imagine it is about the same, or we should have heard something; I keep looking at Albania hungrily every day. Would love to go over there, but you can't now. It's a wonderful sight from here; for me it's like making a trip to Nevada. In the evening, just as the sun is setting, the colors are wonderful. And what a distance one can see. I was out sailing the other day in a flat-bottomed fishing boat with a lateen sail, in a strong maestro wind. We had to stay in the cove, racing back and forth at top speed: if we were to go out in the open sea we would be turned over. It is a Greek schoolmaster who takes us out. He is as strong as a bull—the strongest man I ever saw. And speaks French. If I hadn't such confidence in his strength I would never venture out in such wind. But he handles the sail, the oar, the rudder, all alone, and if the boat turned over I imagine he could right it again all by himself. But the force with which the wind hits the sail, in short quick gusts, is terrific. You feel as if you were being blown out of the boat. And that's right in the bay here, with hills all around us. Outside, the waves get very big and the fishing boats are driven home. And the passenger boat stops running, sometimes for two or three days at a time. Then another wind sets in—the sirocco, bringing hot, sticky weather, and flies; there are four different winds, and always one of them is blowing; very curious phenomenon. And makes the climate delightful.

Well, tell me of any more notices you get. I am just as keen as you to hear about the success of the book. Did you send one to the Chinese review [*T'ien Hsia Monthly,* Shanghai]—I think they would give you a good review.

Now that the nights are dark, no moon, the men go out with long spears, tridents, to hunt for octopus. I had some the other day, but the sight of it is too disgusting—couldn't eat it. Tastes like rubber too, and nothing but tentacles to eat. Disgusting. Must stop now. Regards to Eduardo when you see him. Don't worry about *Capricorn*. Everything will right itself with time. I haven't a speck or crumb of ambitiousness; nor vanity, nor egotism. No photos ready yet—maybe next mail.

HVM

Corfu, September 9, 1939

A week of war and here I am in the dead silence of a tiny Greek village—Kalami—writing you tonight. Strangest of all is that I feel absolutely tranquil, sure somehow that everything will turn out all right. I had such a good hunch about your book, about its reception. I think in general my hunches are good. Why I elected to come back here alone, when there were so many opportunities of one sort and another in Athens, I can scarcely say. I feel that something good awaits me here. And if nothing else comes of it I shall at least learn the meaning of solitude about which I have spoken so much. This may be a sort of training for a greater solitude later. At any rate, for the moment I feel rich. I feel as though it would require years of isolation to exhaust my present richness—and perhaps it will prove to be the reverse—that I shall grow still richer, in unsuspected ways. And as long as I can write to someone I don't feel cut off. And even when I don't write, when I just sit still and dream, I am communicating with everybody. I never feel really what you would call alone.

The good thing about your book, as it seems to affect people, is its humanness. Everyone finds it so—and discovers too that you are a great personality. That the women, especially, should think thus is a great tribute to you. They find it rich and varied—but above all, true, precise, definite, penetrating. And unique!

I am hoping that just as I was first translated into that strange tongue, Czech,* so you may soon be first translated into this language

---

* The first book of Henry Miller ever to be translated was *Tropic of Cancer*, published in Prague in 1938.

I am studying, Greek. And what a strange Greek it will make! That orchestra part, for instance. Can it be done? The Greeks themselves, so I am told, have been unable to express themselves freely. They have a language problem. There are those who would "clean up" the language, restore it to its ancient purity, and those who want another kind of purity, viz, the authentic language of the people, which is always more pure than that of literary folk. The great writers here are fighting for the "demotic" tongue, naturally. The government favors the ancient mode, naturally. Battles have actually been fought over the question. You can appreciate the situation. But notice here that what the real writers are fighting for is the maintenance of the root-tongue. They want to enrich it in every way possible, but not muddy the source. The one thing that impresses me continually, here in Greece, and the reason why I like it so, is the nudity and simplicity of the landscape. A simplicity which is by no means monotonous, on the contrary. Here, as they well say, everything has individuality, even the rocks and the trees. No rock is like another. No two olive trees resemble each other. No two men think alike here. Even the goats are "different." The whole country seems as if it had existed from eternity. One feels it will go on forever, always bare and always full of surprises. Often, amidst the most barren rocks, in the most inaccessible places, one sees a little monastery, shrine, or sanctuary. Larry says it is the country of the "desert fathers." Anyway, from time immemorial men have lived here in voluntary and blissful solitude, warmed and nourished by sea and sky. One can still do it. There are two categories, two types of men here—the islanders and the highlanders. Like Jung's division of extroverts and introverts. And then there must be another rarer type also, who knows how to look above and beyond, as well as within and without. These were the men, I feel, who gave Greece its form. Greece stands between the Arabian world and the European world, between the Occident and the Orient, in every way. That is why it so often makes me think of Spain, and why too I long more and more to see Spain. Especially Andalusia. This strange "d" (like a hard "th") alone forms a link. There are sounds I cannot yet make—but *you* can. To me the Greek language sounds yet like a loud whispering. And when they whisper to one another it is an interesting sight. It is a "physical" whispering, done quite elaborately. And when they say no! it is unlike anything you ever saw anywhere. It has to be seen to be appreciated. It is "reverse

English," to use a billiards expression. It is the opposite of emphatic.
It is like a quick and surprised verbal retreat. It is mid-Asiatic. It
expresses the Greek character eloquently. Because the Greeks are
above all a "Yes" saying people. They say yes first—and then no.
They have an aversion for saying no—or "I don't know." I like this.

In France "je ne sais pas" is typical. They say it instinctively, even
when there is no need for it. They are falsely modest. The Greeks do
not believe in work for its own sake either. They prefer not to work,
if possible, but if they must they do it manfully and ungrudgingly. I
approve of that too. And when they hold conversations they fabulate
—they use the famous "historic present." They believe in long details
and roundabouts. They like to make everything vivid and interesting.
There is nothing abstract about their thinking. On the contrary, they
are very concrete. They are true mythologists. A Greek lie is no
ordinary lie—it is a fabulation. The plain honest truth is too dull.
They prefer legends. Here again we are close to the Spanish character.
And far from France! As for me I am so far from France in heart
and soul, that it seems almost as if the ten years I spent there were
lived on another planet, in another incarnation. I seem to be through
with it for good. The war revives no tender feelings. I feel indifferent
toward the French. I know they will win out eventually. I wish them
no bad fortune—but I have no hunger to return, to resume life there.
They are sufficient unto themselves—and I am sufficient unto myself.
It is like an algebraic equation. We equal each other out. Stasis.
Q.E.D. (Have just stepped out to have a look at the sky before turning in. Jupiter gleams strongly—stronger than Mars tonight. A good
omen! I bank on Jupiter—always.) Incidentally, certain brilliant
stars, and specially planets like Mars and Jupiter, cast a strong beam
of light on the water when they are rising—almost like the moon. It
astonished me the first time I noticed it. I never knew the stars threw
beams of light.

And by a strange paradox, one evening, when we were studying
the stars attentively, from gazing at them so long, so steadfastly, so
earnestly, I suddenly realized that what we call light is really darkness, compared to that blaze which there must be when one gets off
the earth and well out in space. The occultists speak of the sun behind
the sun, the real sun. We see only the lens, as it were, of something
so blazingly brilliant that it would annihilate us if we could seee it.
But again, the real thing isn't see-able. To apprehend the real glow

of the sun one needs other senses. Anyway, standing on the rocks here, listening to the learned Theodore (who is really ignorant as a babe concerning the true things) I suddenly realized that the universe is nothing but light, light, light! I realized more—that actually there is no light and dark at all! In this great void—space—in which everything swims there is a nameless energy which is by turns light, heat, motion, etc., anything and everything we are capable of making or naming or using, once we comprehend. Whatever world we have represents the maximum of our penetration of this unceasing void—which again is not emptiness, but its very opposite. As though—and truly it is thus—the only reality is the one we create through understanding. Through desire, I might say. Desire is the primal thing—the breath that moves the waters of the deep. The whole architectonics of the universe is governed by desire which achieves its aim in realizing its containedness.

9 A.M. the 14th. [September]
On the rocks facing Albania

Sitting here nude with the fountain pen in hand and the sun blazing down with a sort of torrid heat. Wondering if I can add a few words on style and form here in this Adamic state. Just sitting still I am sweating profoundly. Everything is shrouded in a heat mist. The fountain pen itself is getting hot in my hands.

6:30 on the piazza

Now it is getting dark rapidly. The whole day is scheduled according to the sun's progress. Have just been for a stroll through the olive grove back of the house. Due to the rains the earth and the rocks have taken on new colors. When Emil used to tell me of such colors as raw and burnt umber years ago in Brooklyn it meant little to me. Here I see them vivid. And what is called "terre d'ombre." There is a great deal of pink in this volcanic rock, which one only notices gradually —after rain and in the twilight. The peasant women are sitting in a group in front of a house at the shore. They are spinning (eternally spinning) wool and gossiping. But very calmly and quietly. Sometimes one gets so calm here that one gets a bit afraid. You have to get used to it—like to everything else. What gives you a slightly uneasy feeling perhaps is the fear that you may hear something coming up inside you that you never heard before. Real life seems to be divided into two equal parts, like night and day. When you get very quiet and peaceful inside, you are like a razor's edge—you can either begin the most furious burst of activity or fall back still further, into a trance-like state. You become so intensely aware of this that, as I say, you get a bit queasy. The great question *why* to do anything comes up. It's not neurotic. Quite the contrary. It's the height of awareness and what crops up is *values.* You make *decisions,* instead of acting automatically thru habit or instinct or dull routine. And when you are in that fine state where you can really decide, elect what to do, doing itself becomes highly questionable. The only man, perhaps, who doesn't need to question what he does, or whether to do or not to do, is the man who is living close to the soil and who is wresting a living from it by hard and incessant labor. Here the automatic life is right and just. But the moment such a man is granted real leisure—not enforced idleness through weather conditions, etc.—the whole metaphysical panorama opens up. Too dark to continue . . . I look at the flickering light I am to eat supper by, the sun, and from outdoors it looks like a red speck, absolutely dull.

HVM

Dec. 11, '39, Athens
        Since the last entry I have seen a great deal of Greece. Much of it I have told you about in my letters—the rest I will give you verbally. Now I know I am to return to America, I am not dismayed or disheartened. I feel equal to it this time. Things have piled up there which I must liquidate sooner or later. I have to make my peace with these remainders of my old emotional problems. I never felt more poised, more serene, more ready to face my problems. It isn't Greece alone which has done this for me, but the cessation—the deliberate, sustained cessation—from work. In resting my brain I also rested my body. The Yoga philosophy is absolutely right. There is no separating the physical and the psychical. Whenever I have spoken about making life an art it was in this sense.

    It is not strange either that certain ideas or theories follow me about wherever I go. One attracts what belongs to one. Here in Athens I was handed three books on Yoga by a Greek painter—the man whose house I visited in Hydra. Everything I read seems to be a corroboration of our talks. But the principal thing one gets from such books is the necessity to get beyond talk, to begin to apply the theory of life, to practice it in earnest. The most remarkable aspect of the Yoga philosophy of action is the attitude toward the will, the idea of so concentrating upon a desire as to put space around it, isolate it, *insulate* it even. I interpret this in terms of "desire"—of pure desire, as opposed to the muddied plural *desires*. All this is fascinating for the writer. No one understands better than he the subtle connection between will and desire, or the flexibility of freedom within the rigid frame of necessity. Who knows better than the writer how futile is will alone or desire alone even, if the life one lives is a contradiction to the thing wished. One sees so clearly how each tree brings forth its own fruit. One knows that things must be done according to law. Nothing happens accidentally or whimsically. Whatever perfection one achieves is always the result of training. Few are the writers who have mastered their craft like the Yogi masters life. When it happens we get something imperishable.

At Corfu I put into practice my own words. I stopped. I put a vacuum around this seemingly ceaseless activity. And when one day I sat down to write about writing I found to my great pleasure that I could write exactly what I wanted to write. And I stopped again. I didn't allow myself to get wound up like a clock. This image—of the wound-up clock—is an apt one. That is the usual condition of the writer—he winds himself up and then he runs down. It wouldn't be so bad if, when he was running down, he realized it and stopped work. If he only worked cyclically, I mean, it would be distinctly better than the case usually is. But I am aware that there is a condition beyond this, or at least I think I am. And that is never to let oneself run down, to be always a dynamo, with this difference, that when one is not working, not expressing himself, one should shut off the motor. That's a different sort of arrest from the dead stop which comes from running down till there is not a drop of juice left. The Yogi, I read, does not sleep much. He doesn't need to sleep since he knows so well how to relax and how to replenish his energies. It should be the same with the artist. He should always keep his genius on tap, so to speak. He should not be a blinking idiot in the entr'actes, as so many of us are. Another thing—we all seem to be agreed that the practice of an art is a "compulsion," and that is true, as things go now with the artist. But it is a false basis and explains why so many artists crack up, or commit suicide, or degenerate into academicians in the prime of life. About the last thing an artist ever does is to ask himself why he is doing what he does. I don't just mean why the next book and next—but why am I writing at all? Is there a deep need to do it? Is there something to accomplish, something to be gained? Does it bring joy? Why think of it always as a travail? There is no more reason why the writing of a book should be a great and painful labor than why mothers should suffer so in giving birth. Healthy mothers don't suffer. Healthy artists don't suffer either, I am sure of it. We haven't had any healthy artists for centuries, I'm afraid, but that's no reason why we can't. I feel now as though it were better never to write another line than to write with pain and effort. To become a sick man in order to produce a great and healthy work seems to me now like a contradiction in essence. Facility is the important thing. The blind professor in Passy was right. Genius is the norm. The normal is the abnormal or subnormal. Perfection grows from the roots. If one does not begin at the beginning then sooner or later one has to return to the beginning and begin again. That's the law and there's no escape. If you try to slide through you get caught and mangled. The great simplicity and abstraction which Greek nature provides has the most salutary effect upon one. There is a condition of repose here in the very landscape which is not only therapeutic but instructive and inspiring. One feels the dynamic quality of life, though all is seemingly still and at rest. It is a "center" which is at rest. It is this which gives the great sense of equilibrium and of harmony. It is not an intellectual equilibrium, a willed harmony, as with the French, but something innate, ordained, something based on truth and therefore eternally viable. It is the outer demonstration of that which we all understand when we become truly silent and know ourselves. In all the great places I have visited I have had this strong feeling of a vital rhythm which came of coordination, which produced acts and not activity. The essence of the Greek spirit is drama, which expresses itself in myriad forms. And drama can only happen between bodies in equilibrium.

The drama is almost entirely absent from our literature today. There is analysis and criticism, dissection, proliferation.

HVM

Delphi, December 21, 1939

In all my journeying about Greece I have carried this letter with me. It has been in some extraordinary places—Epidauros, Mycenae, Knossus, Phaestos, and so on. And now I am at the ancient, or one of the ancient, centers of the world, the place where Apollo held sway for over a thousand years. Here for the first time I see a nature which is convulsive, restless, writhing, tormented. It is the supremely mystic spot of Greece. On the hillside opposite, the road is forked like lightning. We arrived toward four in the afternoon in a fast-gathering mist out of which the eagles fly as though driven from their crazy nests. The gulf of Corinth lies below invisible except for a fuzzy patch of light from a hidden sun. It is unearthly, supernal, a scene almost too grandiose, too awesome for mere men. The stadium where the great games were held is pitched on a small plateau almost at the top of the mountain. Here they held their chariot races—in the clouds, far above the Temple of Apollo and the spring whose waters brought the gift of prophecy. The mountains are formed of a rock which was upended by a great cataclysm. They are red and gray—the live bluish gray which excites the retina. The soil is brown, lavender, rosy, reddish, with bare trees that look silvery, frosty or wispy with heatherish brushstrokes. Everything is quickened, intensely alive, active, vibratory. When it was in its splendor, when it was swarming with temples and statues, it was still more electrical. Everything was in riotous colors—bronze, gold, silver; even the marble was polished so as to gleam more brilliantly. It must have been barbarous, luxurious and terrifying in its splendor. It was a great treasury of the gods. From all over the world the conquering nations sent their gifts to Apollo. Neptune played a part also—perhaps in the dim memory of Atlantean days. They say that the Minoans of Crete inaugurated the cult of Apollo. Perhaps it goes further back. There are open hemicyclical tombs in the rocks of prehistoric age. It is a pre-Adamic world. For me the great experience began before I ever reached Delphi, before Thebes even. Before you come to the land of the Boeotians is a narrow and frightening pass, you descend into a vortex of agonized rocks, a veritable deathtrap near which somewhere was situated the famous Sphinx whom Oedipus questioned. (Oedipus—swollen-footed.) Suddenly the scene changes. You come into the great smiling plain of Thebes. The earth is red, primordial red clay out of which man was made. Now begins a different sort of drama, the drama of unique monotony. The colors shift rapidly, the light changes, the ground rises like an ocean swell and heaves like a woman in labor. In the distance the most famous snow-capped mountains, those where Diana hunted, those where the Muses gathered. Everything changes rapidly in the midst of a silent, untenanted plain. Every plant, tree, shrub you look at takes on a meaning. A solitary sheep or goat becomes the symbol of all goats and sheep.

We enter Thebes, walk through the town and ride out into another plain. It is even more wonderful. It is so lovely, so intimate, so silent, so peaceful, so beautifully luminous that I wring my hands with desperate joy. I weep. It is the maximum of bliss. We ride on with a scene constantly augmenting in splendor and grandeur. We pass Mont Parnasse, the veritable one. We are coming nearer to Delphi. We move up into the clouds. The earth is rosy, lavender-colored, or else carpeted with skinlike greens and browns. Suddenly there is a bend in the road and it takes my breath away. The earth is bubbling like a great caldron of boiling water—only that this liquid mass is one endless patch of cultivated land—a sea of varied colors like great sails fastened down upon a swollen sea. I have no more words, no more emotion to expend. I am almost out of my mind. I am looking at the most civilized and yet the most savage, dynamic land imaginable. It is the quintessence of contradictions. This is Dionysian. And from this sprang the Apollonian—or else everything would have reverted to chaos and idiocy. What is contained in these few kilometres before Delphi expresses the inexpressible. It is the apotheosis of man vis-à-vis nature. Here he had to become godlike or perish. Nothing can possibly compare with it. From here on to Delphi the unifying conflict rises to a crescendo which lifts you completely out of the world and puts you in the clouds among the immortals. This trip is the summation of all the previous experiences. The oracles were here because here one comes to the end, the navel, the vital hub and center of all human experience. Here the human modulates into the godly. It is not God with a capital G any more—it is the god spirit, the god in man triumphing. One has to get beyond ecstasy. One has to conquer all human emotions—even of worship and adoration. One has to become that which one bows down before. One has to be lifted up —up to sheer madness—and either sink back into an endless abyss or sail onward, upward, like the solitary eagles which infest the summits here. This, I feel, is the secret of the Apollonian power and majesty—this rising above the conflict, above the drama, above one's very self, to incarnate a god, as a sublime and exalted spectator. In the theatre situated at the foot of the steep cliffs one does not have to raise his voice to be heard—no matter at what distance. Here the slightest whisper carries. Here silence speaks. It is awesomely impressive. The so-called personality collapses. The inner man comes forth or else is vanquished, silenced forever. There is no compromise possible. And this is the great virtue of Greece. It does not merely charm, seduce, or enslave. It demands the utmost of you. Greece attracts only those who are capable of responding to the highest appeal. To say it is beautiful is to belittle it. Greece is like the projection of your own consciousness. It reflects, it gives back in the measure that is given. It will respond to any demand made upon it. It is not a passive object to be taken in by the eye. It is the living mirror of the human spirit. It is nature breathing with a human rhythm, adapting itself to the changes of rhythm and reflecting the complete gamut from infancy to godhood. Before I visited Greece nature was to me something apart. Only here have I understood the meaning of nature. Perhaps because not until I saw Greece did I come to a full realization of what I am. Now I feel both less and more than I thought myself to be. Less in the sense of personality, more in the sense of manhood. Here all conflicts are resolved in a fusion between spirit and nature. It is the great truce one has to make in order to achieve individuation. I would urge no one to come to Greece unless he is prepared to meet himself face to face.

HVM

Aboard the *Exochorda*
Jan. 12, 1940

Two weeks at sea, and it seems as though a curtain had fallen over the recent past. Greece has fallen back into the well of experience. Something happened to me there, but what it was I can't formulate now. I am not on the high seas—I am in America already. America began at Piraeus, the moment I set foot on the boat. Greece is fading out rapidly, dying right before my eyes. The last thing to disappear is the light, the light over the hills, that light which I never saw before, which I could not possibly imagine if I had not seen it with my own eyes. The incredible light of Attica! If I retain no more than the memory of this it will do. That light represents for me the consummation of my own desires and experiences. I saw in it the flame of my own life consumed by the flame of the world. Everything seemed to burn to ash, and this ash itself was distilled and dispersed through the airs. I don't see what more any country, any landscape, could offer than this experience. Not only does one feel integrated, harmonious, at one with all life, but—*one is silenced*. That is perhaps the highest experience I know of. It is a death, but a death which puts life to shame. And now on the boat, in the midst of the American scene, I feel as though I am living with people who are not yet born, with monsters who escaped from the womb before their time. I am no longer in communication with anything. I am in a world of broken eggshells. Nothing is being hatched. Eggs are no longer in demand. It is like the after-death state which the Tibetans talk about. What is happening about me is just as real as if it were life, but it is not life. It is something somewhere between death and birth. We shall come to port like a cargo of well-nourished, well-preserved and exceedingly animated ghosts. Through the radio we are permitted to keep in touch with everything that is going on in the world, but the world seems always out of reach. It is the place where things have just happened or are about to happen. But for us nothing is happening. Dimly I seem to remember that but a short time ago I was alive, alive in full sunlight. There is another light which envelops me now. It is like the illumination from a cold mechanical reflector. The house is dark. Only the stage is lit up. The curtain is rising.

HENRY

Part Two : U. S. A.

Editor's Note

Henry Miller returned to the United States, aboard the American ship *Exochorda,* in January, 1940. "I was confident that for the first time in my life I would look upon New York and what lay beyond without a trace of loathing or disgust." But as the boat approached Boston, the first stop, his mood changed. "When I came up on deck to catch my first glimpse of the shore line," he later wrote in his Preface to *The Air-Conditioned Nightmare,* "I was immediately disappointed. Not only disappointed, I might say, but actually saddened. The American coast looked bleak and uninviting to me. It was a bad beginning. The sight of New York did nothing to eradicate my first impressions. To the image of stark, grim ugliness which Boston had created was added a familiar feeling of terror. No matter how many times I escape I am brought back, like a runaway slave, each time detesting it, loathing it, more and more."

After visiting his family in Brooklyn, and avoiding most of his friends in New York ("I don't want to relive the past with them because the past is full of wretched, sordid memories"), Miller moves for a brief stay into Caresse Crosby's home in Virginia. Back in New York, he finishes the memoirs of his Greek experience, *The Colossus of Maroussi,* and writes *The World of Sex.* Possessed by the idea "to get away from New York, to experience something genuinely American," Miller decides to make a trip through the United States, to visit some of the places he has thought about while in Europe. With his old friend, the painter Abraham Rattner, who now has a studio in New York, Miller conceives the idea for a lavishly illustrated book on America. But the publisher, who backs Miller's project with a five-hundred-dollar advance, considers the idea of illustrations too expensive. Rattner goes along anyway, at least for part of the trip, and early in October, 1940, they take to the road in a 1932 Buick. The trip is recorded in *The Air-Conditioned Nightmare,* a book that was rejected by the original publisher, as well as by several others, and eventually published in 1945.

Anaïs Nin, after the outbreak of World War II, had also returned to the United States. She had taken up residence in New York, on the periphery of Greenwich Village, and soon she is again a part of the artistic life of that city. Her home is always open to writers, artists, experimental film makers, avant-garde theatre people and musicians. Among her friends are Richard Wright, Truman Capote, Gore Vidal, Isamo Noguchi, Robert Duncan, George Barker, Edgar Varèse, Marguerite Young and many others. She continues her Diary, she embarks on new projects, and she remains the staunch champion of Henry Miller's work. Her own work, which meanwhile has drawn praise from many quarters—Rebecca West, William Carlos Williams, Paul Rosenfeld, Kay Boyle, Carl Van Vechten, Stuart Gilbert, to name a few—in the eyes of American publishers remains "uncommercial." So, she sets out to realize an idea she had discussed with Miller in Paris, in the early 1930's. She establishes her own press.

"After *Winter of Artifice* (already published in France by the Obelisk Press) toured the publishers in the early 1940s and was said to be 'uncommercial,' " she recalled later, "I decided that I would publish it myself. I found a friendly and generous bookshop, the Gotham Book Mart, and spoke to Frances Steloff who knew my earlier books. She advanced me a hundred dollars on copies of the book to be delivered to her later. I found a few friends willing to advance their subscription to the book. I had in all two hundred dollars. With this I rented a loft on McDougal Street. I bought a secondhand press for seventy-five dollars. I bought one hundred dollars' worth of type. The paper I had thirty days to pay, and the book binder could be paid thirty days later too. To begin with I had to learn how to print. I worked eight and nine hours a day. In two months the book was done. It was a beautiful book, with line engravings by Ian Hugo, which I printed directly from the copper plates according to an old forgotten technique invented by William Blake. I made an edition of five hundred copies. Today, they are a collector's item, selling sometimes for twenty-five or thirty dollars."

She does her own publicity and promotion for the book and produces a second book, a collection of her stories, *Under a Glass Bell,* in the same fashion. Edmund Wilson, who saw the book, praised it in a review in the *New Yorker*. "The next day, I received phone calls from three big publishers," and a contract arrived a few days later. But, she recalls, "I am probably the only writer who did not celebrate his first conventional contract with a big publisher."

Recognition of Henry Miller's work in the United States also proceeded slowly. James Laughlin, of New Directions, had published his first book, *The Cosmological Eye,* in 1939. In 1941, he published *The Wisdom of the Heart.* But while New Directions have a first call on Miller's work, they cannot absorb all of his production, and his books, thought "uncommercial" by the big New York publishers, appear in small editions, under unfamiliar imprints. Ben Abramson, a Chicago bookseller, publishes *The World of Sex.* William Roth, in San Francisco, brings out *The Colossus of Maroussi.* Bern Porter, in Berkeley, California, has some miscellaneous items printed. Little magazines here and there publish articles, essays, pieces from his books. But Miller's economic situation remains precarious. When he returns from his tour of the country to New York, in October, 1941, the prospects are dim. Friends in California have offered him living quarters in their home in Beverly Glen, on the periphery of Los Angeles. He takes up their offer in June, 1942, and stays for two years. His efforts to find work in Hollywood remain unsuccessful. At times, things look bleak indeed and he is forced to appeal to his friends and readers. But his reputation grows, editors ask him to review books, people buy his water colors, and by 1944, more than twenty of his books are available in French, English and American editions. But his "Paris books" are still banned in the United States and in England. Pirated editions appear in China, Japan, Mexico, Hungary, and copies are smuggled into this country. The struggle against censorship continues. In February, 1944, Miller visits his friend the painter Jean Varda, in Monterey, and two months later Keith Evans, who is called into the Army, offers him (thanks to the intervention of Lynda Sargent) his log cabin on Partington Ridge, near Big Sur, which eventually becomes Miller's "home" country.

With the end of World War II, Miller's fame has spread around the world, he is an international success, well-known, deluged, sought out. What began in 1931, when he hesitantly showed the first draft of *Tropic of Cancer* to Anaïs Nin, has finally born fruit.

G.S.

February 6, [1940]
Fredericksburg, Va.

ANAÏS—

Got your letter here. Returning to Orange tomorrow night for rest of week. Was very hospitably lodged and entertained at Orange, but found it rather boring—except for the country which is really beautiful. The house of Mrs. Gray, where I was invited for dinner one evening (where Emil [Schnellock] has been staying so many years) is a marvelous Southern home in the genuine old style—a miracle of good taste, spaciousness, simplicity, light, etc., something to warm the heart. But the people empty, the life dull. The people are extremely kind, generous, decent—and yet I feel I would go mad if I had to live with them. The snow has made everything more beautiful. The stars the other night were even more brilliant than I had seen them in Greece. It seems tragic that nothing should be born out of all this beauty. It saddens one profoundly.

I go back again because of a possible trip to Charlottesville (to see Monticello—Jefferson's old home *and* Richmond, the capital, where I sneaked out of a hotel before the cop called for me). I must say that the architecture all about is fine—great simple taste—early Revolutionary Colonial style—really adorable—like dolls' houses—and immaculate in and out. After this weekend I don't know what. I may be back or I may go elsewhere for a few days. I hear wonderful things about Key West, Fla., and New Orleans. Something will have to be extraordinary because otherwise I'll want to fly the country. I'm afraid of the monotony everywhere, the uniformity, the lackluster life or lifelessness. I begin to wonder if it's any use knocking about the land—though it may be unfair to judge the whole by the little I've seen. The *land* is all right—it's the people—the bleak absence of anything vital or meaningful. That eats into one quickly. One would have to be a Colossus to withstand it. It's like a tree trying to live in a sandy soil without heat or light.

Maybe it will have to be Mexico soon. We'll see. I imagine you must feel about the same as I do.

Until Sunday then you can write me c/o Mrs. L. B. Gray, Orange, Va. I'll write you then what I'll do. It seems as tho' I'm just marking time. Wasting myself. Emil is working very seriously. His colleges are wonderful *buildings*—but I don't know what good it does. Everything seems quite futile to me.

Well, hope you can stand up under it. More soon.

HENRY

P. S. The darkies are fine—the one redeeming feature. I envy them. *They* have a life—the best life possible under the circumstances. Just to get near them is heartening and vitalizing. The others are dying of "white heart rot."

[February, 1940]
Washington, D.C.
Wednesday

ANAÏS:

Got the two large envelopes of mail here this morning. Previous mail, directed to Richmond after leaving Orange, hasn't reached me yet. I left Richmond after 24 hours of most wonderful spring weather—thermometer over 70 degrees at midday. Couldn't stand the life there, though the city itself was quite beautiful—too sedate and prim, however—immaculate. Was quartered with a dentist, friend of the Grays in Orange. Went down with a load of dressed turkeys for the market. The Grays of Orange, incidentally, were fine people, all of them, and did everything to make me comfortable and happy. They lead a good life on their beautiful big estate, an enviable one. I am certainly in the midst of the real American life, and it's very uninteresting and dead, when not completely insane, I think. I begin to wonder will it change anywhere—will a change of scene do anything to alter the people. I hardly think it possible. On top of this I receive a letter from a girl in Mexico whom I wrote to inquiring about the life and the prices, etc., saying that she was quite disillusioned about Mexico City, at least, that it was thoroughly Americanized, touristic, etc. I don't know what I'll do next. I'm just getting acquainted with Washington now. There was a small blizzard yesterday; as a city it is superb—far more beautiful than any city I can think of. Staggeringly rich and luxurious, seemingly. I am bewildered by it all. Went to [Huntington] Cairns' office yesterday and met his chief and some other associates at lunch—all very kind, cordial, sympathetic and favorably disposed toward me. A marvelous building—sumptuous and Southern in style: Cairns' office is fit for the President of France almost.

I am going to the Library of Congress this afternoon. Will see if we are properly listed there. Wrote N.Y. library only yesterday.

I'll surely stay on here till Monday—Washington seems more interesting in every way than the other places. They will motor me about in the country, and over to Baltimore, though I shan't have a chance to meet [H. L.] Mencken now as he is off on a trip. Anyway, I'll write again and let you know what I plan to do. I may come back to N.Y. too. I need to settle somewhere soon and begin writing.

Had a fine letter from Keyserling's sister telling me my essay * was the best she had ever read about him. Asks me if I can come to Manchuria and visit her—that's crazy too. I haven't yet heard from Dorothy Norman ** about the essay. Probably in the next mail.

It's strange to hear you are not feeling well. I think it must be this artificial life. Physically I'm thriving—I've gained weight since I left N.Y. But morally and otherwise it's debilitating. I feel like a vegetable. I've heard nothing but drivel since I arrived in America. And yet everybody so good, so kind, so decent—that makes it worse, too. It makes you quite desperate. The best thing that has happened to me so far has been a visit to the Phillips Memorial Gallery here, where they once speculated about showing my water colors. They have a fine eclectic collection of European and American work—it was the first genuine contact with life I have had, imagine it.

More shortly. What about Caresse Crosby? Any real news? Love.

HENRY

---

* "The Philosopher Who Philosophizes," written in Corfu to commemorate Keyserling's sixtieth birthday (July, 1940), published in the collection *Wisdom of the Heart,* New Directions, N. Y., November, 1941.
** See Biographical Notes.

[October 28, 1940]
Monday P.M.
Between Lancaster & York, Pa.
(on the Lincoln Highway)

"On the highway" gives the true note. We're in a tourist cabin and the car is in our private garage right next to our cabin. Hothouse heat—soap and washrag and towel free. Excellent accommodations for $2.50 for the 2 of us. But a hotel is better—only because it's more real, like the train. This is part of the moving traffic belt which throws you off and leaves you betwixt and between. Everything gets more artificial and abstract. We take a long bus ride to eat somewhere.

The country, ever since 20 miles out of Newark, has really been wonderful, I must confess. Particularly today's trip—from New Hope, Pa. to here near the Susquehanna River. Big rolling hills, fat farmlands, canals, etc. We just left a religious region where the "Amish" people settled in 1710. Almost paradisical. Amazingly beautiful. The people themselves look terrible—in ancient costumes and bleak, frozen, fanatical, empty faces. It's already a strange and fantastic drugstore world—wholly unlike what you know. No reason to live. Complete imbecility. And nature so kind and generous to all!

I liked New Hope very much—almost Old World in its atmosphere. An old canal with quaint bridges and a sleepy Delaware River and houses from 1600 and 1700's—really quaint and interesting. Visited a half-dozen more or less prosperous artists whom [Abe] Rattner knew 20 years ago when at the Pennsylvania Academy.

The best bit was a sudden drive into a wilderness at night to see an old Czech building a home for the future with his 2 sons. An incredible stone fortress, as in Europe, built for the future—already 3 years at it—may take 5 more to finish—all the work done themselves. So un-American. The old man looked like Renoir himself.

We stopped at Valley Forge—or nearby—at places like King of Prussia and Paoli (!) to find an American sculptor whom Zadkine * had said was the best in America—but he was out. Went thru many back roads into real country—which I enjoy greatly. Am beginning to like the driving. Drove 3 or 4 hours today without strain or fatigue.

---

* The sculptor, Ossip Zadkine, born in Russia in 1890, was an exponent of cubism. Miller became acquainted with him in Paris, where Zadkine lived most of his life.

I drove out of N.Y. into Newark Saturday—that was really tough. The Holland Tunnel is a nightmare. Faster, faster—and God help you if there's a blowout! Something demonic, like an Hieronymus Bosch invention. And that skyway over the dirty meadows out of Jersey City—simply diabolical. Then suddenly, 20 miles out, traffic thins out, country begins. Like coming out of a great intestine.

Tomorrow we will stop awhile at Gettysburg to see the battlefield and then probably head for Frederick, *Md*. Next day Washington, I imagine.

You can address me there c/o Cairns, when you get this. It seems quite cold here nights—tho' not yet down to freezing. But penetrating. There was snow on the ground for 2 days at Valley Forge just last week. That place looks exactly as you imagine it from the calendars. I could see the Revolutionary Army freezing to death there—and the Delaware frozen tight. Glad we are heading south.

Rattner's friend—Bill Ney—at New Hope was a really fine man. Another gentle spirit—and a lost one. How a man can paint in such forlorn places I don't know. There seems to be no reason why anybody should be an artist in America. It's a bleak picture. Life centers in the drugstores which are lit up with fluorescent lights and crowded with a million useless objects. Surrealistic, if you can detach yourself. More soon. Tired. To bed now at 10:30 P.M.

HVM

[November 3, 1940]
Sunday night, Washington, D. C.

ANAÏS—

Only leaving here Tuesday morning for Fredericksburg where Emil teaches. Will probably drive there alone as Rattner is returning to N.Y. tomorrow afternoon for a day or two because of an urgent matter. Paul Rosenberg, the great French art dealer, is starting a gallery in N.Y. and wants to see him about handling his work (this is confidential). I'll wait for him at either Fredericksburg or Orange or Bowling Green, according to how long he is absent. Everything is going well so far. Rattner makes pen-and-ink notes as we ride along.

We rather rushed the first lap to Washington. We'll go slower from now on. It'll be more interesting from here too, I believe.

I met a man by accident who had copies of my books and yours —was looking for *Winter of Artifice*—a stranger. Invited us to his home and had people in to meet us. Quite a surprise. Am meeting some of the big guns of various depts. (particularly art)—that's why we prolonged our stay. Had quite a session in the Bureau of Indian Affairs—and came away with a beautiful map of the Reservations and lots of dope on the Indians. We'll come to the Cherokees first—after Asheville—in the Great Smoky Mts. of N.C. and Tennessee. We'll also see a great deal of Virginia which is a big and varied state. Sherwood Anderson wrote me from N.Y.—he won't be at his Va. home.

Went to Annapolis in the car today to see the Naval Academy. Rather dull. Comic opera setting. Nice little boys with their sweethearts and parents. Utmost air of respectability.

Had a taste of Sunday driving. Roads hereabouts (Maryland particularly) are wonderful in that they are all curves and hills. Good experience. I am fine on the road—but no good in Wash. Refuse to drive here. It's far more dangerous and difficult than N.Y. So I let Rattner drive—tho' I'm really better, I think. It's too nerve-racking. On the road I'm at ease. I could easily become a speed driver—but stifle the impulse. Hold her down to fifty or 45 an hour. Car holds up fine—but uses more gas than I originally thought. It's a powerful and heavy car too. Feels important.

It's amazing how little traffic we encounter on the open road. Very lucky for us. And we get off the big belt line often. The old macadam roads are the best! I can't say enough about the country itself—it's beautiful. So different from the impression you get in the train. But the life is nil.

Exception—first—was in walking thru Negro district here in Wash. First sign of life! Tried to enter a café and they wouldn't let us in. I like that too. That's what they ought to do in Harlem. Washington is a Nigger Heaven, they say.

I haven't written a line yet, but that's because of the newness of driving which made me dog-tired each day—as I do most of it—*willingly*. Nothing thrilling to report yet anyway. But I can well believe that when we hit the deep South there will be. Just being inundated by the darkies will be something.

Will probably be at Caresse's place Wednesday or Thursday—or

both days. I'll send you a telegram if I stay there at her place and you
can telephone me there maybe. It's expensive telephoning in daytime
—first call cost $1.45—must have been over 3 minutes. Expenses
running around $4 to $4.50 a day so far—including everything,
which is not so bad, I think.

Rather like Symme's * letters—not about myself—but his style.
Reminds me a bit of Durrell. By the way, do you see what the Greeks
are doing? The Finns of the South, what!

HVM

[November 9, 1940]
Richmond, Va.
Saturday Night

ANAÏS—

Arrived in Bowling Green last evening and stayed until noon
today. Tried telephoning you twice during morning but no answer.
We're leaving here tomorrow morning for Williamsburg, Jamestown
(Pocahontas) and Yorktown (Surrender of Cornwallis) and then return to Richmond to go west to the Blue Ridge Mts. and Shenandoah
Valley. Am down to 5 dollars now and will need money when I come
back into Richmond Tuesday or Wednesday. I think I did pretty well
considering the ground we covered and the number of places we
stopped at—including visit to dentist and getting car greased. Rates
should be less and less as we go along. I didn't stop at Censor's in
Washington nor with Emil at Fredericksburg and Orange. The tourist
places average a dollar to $1.50 per person. Meals vary. Often a fairly
good spread for 50 or 60 cents. Sometimes we get fooled. I don't
much like staying in people's homes—the tourist places. But must say
they are usually very clean—almost luxurious.

The country continues to be marvelous—Virginia is beautiful and
we are seeing so much more this way. But the contrast between the
earth and the people who inhabit it is tremendous. Nowhere else is it
so marked, I imagine, as in America. Is it because they (or it) have
no soul? It's a schizophrenic relationship.

We often spend the evening taking a long walk. That's the most
interesting thing to do. I might write, of course, but lack the place or

---

* Symme is the poet "Robert Duncan" who wrote to Anaïs Nin about Miller.

the inclination. Can absorb a lot before feeling a need to put anything down. Here space and emptiness are synonymous.

Just walked a little way into Negro section of Richmond. We had to stop as it was too sinister and terrifying. Complete blackout—houses and streets dark and silent as if everyone were dead. Now and then a lone figure standing in the darkness against a wall or fence. Or a burst of revelry—*drunken*—from a deserted house. And passing the Negroes they look at you menacingly or yell at you. *No whites at all* here. Can't even hop a bus. Walk thru a wilderness to get back to house. Could be murdered easily—saw one cop all night long. Complete contrast to picture we glimpsed in Summer riding home with Flo and Dudley. * Tonight a chill fog as from the grave—a Paris night, in many ways. Only thoroughly dead inside. When we return I may do the rounds with a newspaper reporter whom I missed tonight—a friend of [John] Slocum's.*

There is nothing really interesting so far. I think it will improve as we go into the black world, however. But I do like nature itself. I do almost all the driving. Like it now. Car still going fine. We just reached the 1200 miles since I bought it—700 since leaving N.Y.

Dali seems more vain and cuckoo than ever. Gala has gone to New Mexico. He never leaves the house—says it's the same at North Pole as here or anywhere. Never addressed a single word to me after salutation. We rode past him on way out without greeting. He was dressed in a dressing gown—Gala's—and looked like a fairy. A complete egocentric all right. And Caresse seeming very pleased with him and complaining of having no one to drink with! Shep and his family are the real people there. I visited them and felt fine talking to them. Several of the family were in the hospital—after an automobile accident.

I don't know where to say to write again—unless you can get word to me to Richmond by Wednesday. I'll probably telephone Tuesday or Thursday morning. Fine letters from Dudley. And from Greece. Time seems to fly. We pack, eat, drive, stop, walk, bed, off again. Emil said he was sending Minotaurs—hoped he'd get them back again. More soon.

Hope you're feeling well.

HVM

P. S. I'll be back soon at this rate. Kaleidoscopic impressions.

---

* See Biographical Notes.

Richmond, Va. Tuesday
[November 12, 1940]

Have been riding all day in mist and driving rain and got in too late to go to P.O. today. Hope there's something waiting for me there—need it badly now. Since we left here Sunday morning it seems as if we had been halfway around the U. S. We have been going steadily day after day since Washington and I'm beginning to feel groggy. We may rest up for a day or two in Charlottesville—our next stop. The trouble usually is that no place is inviting enough to stay very long—so far! So we keep moving. The country is splendid—the landscape, I mean. Today under a leaden sky it was rich—all the "local" color, as Abe puts it, comes out strongly. Between Norfolk and Petersburg the ground was a flaming burnt sienna with dark umbers and lush greens and then cold slate grays. To go from Hampton thru Norfolk and Portsmouth and not lose the route was a trial— especially in the rain. Last night we stayed at an inn right in the college grounds—Hampton Institute for Negroes—and it was good. We listened to a rehearsal of folk songs by the boys—wonderful voices and wonderful melodies. The first real warm human touch on our trip. Generally it's a blank every night. We walk around or thru the town, go back to the room, read a bit and fall asleep.

Williamsburg, the re-created Revolutionary town, is a very interesting place—as a piece of re-creation. A real plunge back into the past —except for the fact that the buildings look new and show no signs of age. But the layout, the space between, all that is excellent. I imagine it would be terrible to live there though—what with the steady stream of tourists.

The food problem is the worst. Thoroughly uninteresting everywhere. Have to beg for fruit. Begin to lose interest in eating. And these double rooms we get are just big enuf to hold 2 beds—never a table to write on. Now and then we'll have to stop at a hotel and get space and privacy to work a bit.

Today I had a difficult bit of driving, over a road being repaired. Had to go at a good clip on a narrow slippery strip with a line of cars behind me pushing me faster and faster. I gave up when we got to Petersburg and night coming on. Abe took it over and did well. You can't imagine how difficult it is to ride in the dark on an unfamiliar road and try to keep on the route. The intersections are badly marked.

The worst roads are the good roads—the moving belts, I call them. But often enough we get off them. The country roads are wonderful —let you see things and let you ride in peace.

It *could* be a marvelous country—if the people knew anything about living. The earth is so rich, the scenery so varied. But the towns are graveyards. However, I think it will improve as we get deeper into the country. All day today it was like going thru a battlefield—as tho' the Civil War had ended only a few weeks ago. One big stretch thru a place called "Dismal Swamp"—really dismal, all right.

Tomorrow we strike westward toward the mountains again. Maybe we'll get to Asheville before I come back to N.Y. I rather think so. Am wondering if there'll be enough money for me to take the train back. I haven't indulged myself at all. Not even a movie. We're as economical as possible and still it comes to around five a day—counting laundry, cigarettes and all the extras. I hope I've earned a little something. Nothing definite yet about the Greek book.* Still haven't written a line—haven't opened the typewriter. Seems we just pack and unpack every few hours. To find a place, a restaurant, get our bearings in a new town—all takes time. I realize now what the life of a traveling salesman must be! Yet the kaleidoscopic effect has its value—helps you to judge quickly what's interesting and what's not. If I had to *live* in any of these towns I think I'd go mad. *Now* I think constantly of Europe—of the great difference. Well, I'm going to sleep now. May add a postscript or send another letter when I go to P.O. in morning. Probably telephone you Thursday morning. Today we lived on Route 460.

HVM

P. S. At night in these tourist places you hear the whizz of cars rushing by all night. You get motorized. I can feel the engine chugging inside me.

---

* *Colossus of Maroussi,* written in 1940, before embarking on the American trip.

Boswell's Tavern, Va.

November 15th (Friday) [1940]

Still at same place I phoned you from—a good inn where we are resting up during the rain. Also having the radiator of car cleaned out as it was all clogged up and heating up the engine. I'm thinking to return on the 24th or 25th—the Wedding Anniversary [of Miller's parents] is the 26th. We may make Asheville before turning back. Will try to find out the railroad fare, one way, tomorrow when we go into Charlottesville. After I pay up here and pay for repairs to car I figure I'll have 30 or 31 dollars. That will carry me only to the 20th or 21st, if everything goes right. I'll try to let you know in my next letter how much I'll need to get back to N.Y.—hope you can raise it. Anyway I'll be telephoning again soon and you can let me know how things stand. We wouldn't save anything by driving back as the living expenses for 3 days would eat it up.

I needed a rest all right—felt pretty battered from the constant traveling. A nervous strain more than anything. And this is the first good eating place we've struck—but it costs us a dollar more a day than we usually spend. Most of the addresses given me are for farther South. And a few people we were to see were not home when we called. Visited [David] Edgar's old home near here—a very baronial place—but could learn nothing about him as his family had moved away some time ago. Very impressive place, I must say.

You ask why we didn't stay at Bowling Green. Well, the place is different now. We were really politely warned *not* to stay because Caresse was expecting some hunting folk from Warrenton. It was good to see Shep and his family—*they're real.*

Tomorrow we head for the Sky Line—Blue Ridge and Shenandoah Valley. The southwestern corner of Virginia is supposed to be the best in every way—especially as to scenery—all mountains. I repeat —the country itself is marvelous—far better than I ever expected. But the life is empty and dreary and monotonous. There is no connection apparently between the earth and the people who inhabit it. Do give my regards to Dudley and Lafayette [Young].* Is Dudley being drafted soon?

I think when I return I'll go direct to the Royalton—44 W. 44th

* See Biographical Notes.

St., N.Y. It's a little cheaper than Weissberger's and better service. Glad to hear you are in such good shape.

And regards too to Eduardo. There is a Cherokee Indian Reservation near Asheville. I have the list of all the Reservations and all the Federal Prisons and Penitentiaries—with letters of introduction.

HVM

Staunton, Va. Sunday Night
[November 17, 1940]

ANAÏS—

Just trying to figure out problem of returning to N.Y. (Haven't gone to P.O. yet for mail.) Found that it will take 2 days to get back by bus (the cheapest way) sleeping overnight somewhere and perhaps taking train from Washington as bus takes 9 hours against 4 on train from there to N.Y. Don't know yet from what place we'll take bus homeward but expect to turn back the 23rd and arrive before night on the 24th. Fare from Bristol, Va. (Tennessee border-line) is about $10.00. If we take train from Wash. might be a dollar or so more. We are two or three days away from there, as well as we can estimate. Might not go there either—it depends. Anyway, if nothing unusual occurs I can hold out until the 21st—then I'll be broke—unless there's some unexpected money in the mail from someone to-morrow morning. I know it's going to be difficult raising money before payday. As best I can make out I'll need about $30.00 on the 21st. And I'll have to telegraph you where to send it. Maybe I'll telephone you Tuesday morning. Expect this to reach you also maybe Tuesday A.M. If you can't raise that much I think [John] Slocum would lend you something for me meanwhile. Maybe when I get the mail (if I do) in the morning I'll have some good news. And if it comes to the worst I'll forego the trip. I thought of coming back by car but it would take us *days*. We're not capable yet of driving several hundred miles a day. We average a hundred to 125—and even at that feel rather worn. I wouldn't risk night driving at all! It's fantastic—we had a few tastes of it only for short stretches. You've got to be made of iron to do much of that.

Today I drove over the Sky Line Drive (Blue Ridge Park)—about 45 miles or so. Quite a feat—and yet the roads were excellent. But circling constantly around a mountain with no fence at the edge of the chasm is dizzying. I did it for the experience and it was good—certainly the most wonderful panorama. Going up the side of the mountain, a long steady steep pull, the car is weak—had to go in second at about 20 miles an hour—trucks and everything passing us. But on the level and for ordinary hills she's fine. She's just a bit old [1932 Buick] and shows it when it comes to a severe test. The thing is getting to be like an animal now—I know its moods and its potentialities. Can tell by the hum and feel of it.

Also I notice we look in good condition now. Getting a color. In this Shenandoah region the air is frosty and bracing—everybody looks the picture of health and poise—a red apple look. Our one great problem is food—where to get a decent meal. I eat fruit a good deal and take buttermilk often—just as medicine. We walk as much as possible too—you have to.

Today we visited the Caverns [Massanutten Caves] (sent you photo cards in mail). You would have enjoyed it. A world of fantasy and illusion. Marvelous when the man turned out all the lights and we stood in silence in pitch-blackness for several minutes—hearing only the drip of water. Water and rock—the only signs of life there. Living, growing rocks. I have a piece of a stalagmite for you. It's millions of years old.

I'll leave a space in case there's any news in mail.—

No—nothing of importance in mail!

Had letter from Greece from the wife of the Colossus [George Katsimbalis].

HVM

Asheville, N.C.
November 20 [1940]

ANAÏS—

Arrived here this afternoon about five o'clock after crossing a very high mountain chain—the Great Smoky Mts. Found no letter or telegram either at P.O. or Western Union. Presume you mailed

letter when I phoned and just missed the airmail. P.O. closed tomorrow—will look there on Friday the 22nd and again at W.U. Office
where I said to telegraph me funds. Maybe you didn't understand it—
or maybe you understood Knoxville, Tenn. Anyway, if nothing arrives the morning of the 22nd I'll telegraph you because I thought to
leave the 23rd—could of course leave the 24th and arrive the 25th—
trip takes 18 hours by train and costs around 15 to 17 dollars without
sleeper (can't get exact price as R.R. office closed at 9:30 this evening—incredible thing!). Fortunately, after telephoning you I telegraphed [Barnet] Ruder * for 20 bucks as I was down to a couple of
dollars—and last night as we went thru Johnson City, Tennessee, I
got it and that's what I'm using now. It was lucky too because we had
several repairs to make yesterday and today. Our brake lining is worn
out and we ought to get that fixed before doing any further driving.
Can't complain however—car has held out well for first 2300 miles.
We've gone 1800 miles since leaving N.Y. There are little repairs always because it's old—but she responds well. Only going up steep
hills no power—we crawl up. On the flat we can do up to 60 an hour,
but usually hold her to 45 to 55.

Yesterday I phoned you from Marion, Va. Sherwood Anderson's
place was 20 miles outside the town in a wonderful nook on a dirt
road. But coming away from there we tried to go thru a pass in the
mountains to join the big highway and there for 20 or 25 miles we had
a terrific test of our ability. Never saw such a narrow, rough, dangerous road. We just crawled along at 10 miles an hour in 2nd or 1st
speed. Passed one car only—at a safe spot—fortunately. Don't know
what we'd have done had we met it any other place in that wilderness.

Typical moonshine country with occasional mountaineer's cabins
of the crudest sort. I did the driving—for 6 solid hours on an empty
stomach. Had a bite at 4:00 in the afternoon. Then we arrived in dark
at Johnson City, Tenn.—a lugubrious railroad town, like a western
place—terrifying. Circled around and found a good lodging place. But
we were so groggy we could hardly walk straight. And yet we had
only traveled 160 miles. It was the most exciting day we had. Funny
thing is the great changes of climate from one stop to another. Some
places we freeze—like at Pulaski, Va. in the mountains—and again
it's balmy, like at Hampton, Va. Here it's spring—and we're over

---

* A collector who was interested in Miller's work.

3000 ft. up and surrounded by mountains. The one thing I learn from all the driving is to be careful. It's been a great experience. I still hate driving in towns of any size—especially when you don't know the place. It's quite confusing.

Last few days—since hitting the Shenandoah Valley—from Harrisonburg, Va. on down—has been marvelous. For a couple of hundred miles it resembled Greece a bit—the sky and the smoothly worn hills—these are very old mountains, you know. And we always meet a Greek restaurant owner and talk about Greece. But the food in these places is terrible. (The Greek places!)

This "Tourotel" is the very finest thing I've seen yet. $3.50 for the 2 of us a night. But what a place! They've thought of everything. The enclosed tells you a bit. You have privacy and comfort—carpeted floor too! Why there aren't more, I don't know. The ordinary tourist place is ugly really. A private home. Nothing but the 2 beds—the toilet and bath in the hall. People who run them all pretty much alike. Now and then a sympathetic soul—but very rarely. The day goes like lightning. Rattner is slow. I would be started 2 hours earlier each day were I alone. His reflexes are retarded. But he's very good otherwise. And he's rather dumfounded by it all—dazed, I should say. Has the same reaction as you would. In fact, I agree myself. If I hadn't to write a book I might never have gone thru with it. It's *worse,* in a way, than we thought. As to *life*—but as to country—far better than I remember it to be. In fact, amazingly beautiful. The mystery is that nothing has happened to the people living in the midst of such wonders. Or do we misjudge them?

Just telephoned Eduardo—will see him in morning. Going to bed now—10 o'clock. Sometimes I'm in bed before that. Either exhausted or disinterested. We come into a place and in a half hour we know it. Like dogs on the scent of game. Getting expert at picking places as we drive thru our stopping place. Drive clean thru the town, noting with eagle eye the likely spots. Double back on our trail and pick the best one. Unpack, wash, choose restaurant, walk a bit, to bed. Mornings wash, pack, eat, tank up and off.

No time to write. Couldn't. Trying now here to do something. And maybe in N.Y. So it goes.

I wish we could pack this Tourotel up and take it with us. The first real comfort we've had.

May be back the 24th. Will telegraph time of arrival on leaving—

and will go to the Royalton where you can phone me should it be too
late to call you—that is, after 6:00 P.M.

HVM

P. S. Dudley and Lafe [Young] would have enjoyed this if they had
been along. Virginia is a big and very interesting state—and the people in the west, in the great valley, are fine types—real warm friendly
genuine sort. The *common* people, I mean.

Asheville, N.C.
[December 4, 1940]
10:30 P.M. Wednesday

ANAÏS—

Just got here—traveling since 7:20 A.M.—from Lynchburg,
Va. Maddening slow train. Will stay till Sunday at this place.*

Incidentally I wired Slocum for $25.00 and got it. Forgot that I
would have to pay for repairs to the car. And a big laundry bill. The
stopover was costly too—taxis, tips, meals on train etc. When you're
low everything seems enormous.

Dead tired now. May add a line from P.O. tomorrow before mailing. Was bitter cold last night, but considerably milder here.

(Next Morning)

Will have lunch with Eduardo tomorrow, Friday. Weather is perfect here. Going to get the car now.

On leaving N.Y. had telephone calls from Slocum and Steloff. Saying they wanted to go ahead with the Emergency Fund idea—I am
to write the circular. They are calling another meeting to discuss
practical ways and means. No doubt you'll be asked to go and I
would, if you can, just to see. Dorothy Norman will also be asked, I
believe.

I have a number of good ideas about the scheme, in talking to
Rattner on the way down. Am sitting down to write it this afternoon.
It may not be so much a question of how much money can be raised

---

* Miller left the car in Asheville and briefly returned to New York for his
parents' wedding anniversary.

immediately as of stimulating and generating ideas among writers and others as to what they can do.

Met a pathetic fellow on train—the news and candy vendor. Had been 22 years in prison and just recently released. He still haunts me. How he felt when he was released—and what he fell into to earn a living—very moving. Rushing this off. Will give new address. Soon as I know.

HVM

[December 8, 1940]
Sunday—Asheville, N.C.

The time flies. We plan to leave here tomorrow morning, visit the Cherokee Indians at Cherokee about 70 miles away and arrive in Chattanooga, *Tenn.* by Tuesday evening. I'll probably wire you or Bettina [Rattner] to send money to Chattanooga—we'll stay thru Wednesday the 11th surely. After that Atlanta, *Ga.* where we'll be for Friday and Saturday surely and where you can send me mail if you like. Then we'll head for Charleston, *S.C.* and Savannah, *Ga.* and Florida.

We just came back from a visit to Black Mt. College where we heard a piano recital. The college itself very interesting—a sort of Tibetan landscape all about. Were received cordially and invited to dinner and could have stayed overnight. The students were crazy to get hold of my books—had a hard time saying good-bye. Gave me their home addresses, urging me to see their folks en route—California, Texas, etc.

Had an exciting time with an ex-convict (a recidivist) who had put in 22 years of his life on 3 sentences in jail—including the Georgia chain gang. He was all battered and scarred and told us the most gruesome, harrowing stories. The result was Abe gave him some money and I parted with my new briefcase—so that he could hock or sell it and get the money to go on his way. I'll probably write about him when I get down to the book on America.* It was a big earful— a pattern of temptation, vanity and disaster—just born for prison. His pet obsession was a sentimental solicitude about women and children

* See chapter "The Soul of Anaesthesia," in *The Air-Conditioned Nightmare.*

—they should be treated decently. His boast was that he never used a knife or a blackjack on a man—but he was always quite ready to use his fists. His description of a jail riot wherein 300 men were killed after failing to blow up the place was ghastly. The convicts were armed with meat cleavers. They cut the guards to pieces—the blood was inches deep in the gutters—arms and legs lying around and heads too. He had a pair of eyes that were really criminal. As tho' he looked at you from behind a cloudy veil. He said he often paralyzed a man just by looking at him. Endless stories—all in the same monotone—as if in a trance. To cap it all, we found out after he left that he was a dope peddler. (He was the Union News vendor on the train.) "News butch" they call them. We had to do some detective work to run him down.

The car goes beautifully since it was tuned up—it purrs. And now I notice how differently the brakes act. We hardly had any brakes before—the lining was completely worn down. I paid out $36.00 for the work done—Rattner gave me ten toward it. But I'll get to Chattanooga all right and if you send funds Wednesday why it will be O.K.

Trying to finish the circular for Steloff and others about the Writers' Emergency Fund. It's hard work. The days are too chopped up. But I guess I'll have it done by tomorrow. I think there's a good idea in what I propose—you'll see.

Anyway, I'm not rushing any more. I'll see what I can and not worry. I visit an old boyhood friend in Atlanta—now a colonel in the Army—haven't seen him for 30 years. Also the Federal Penitentiary there. The ex-convict says—"Be sure and see the dungeons below. Don't let them show you the nice places only." It's mild here— beautifully so—and yet we're 3000 ft. up. Curious climate.

How are *you* getting on now? I seem to be taking on weight—from riding, I guess.

If you see [Edgar] Varèse * give him my regards. I think of him warmly. He's a real human person. I never meet one in my travels. Tell him so.

More soon. Don't worry about me. I think everything will work out smoothly.

HVM

---

* Miller devoted a chapter, "With Edgar Varèse in the Gobi Desert," in *The Air-Conditioned Nightmare* to the French-born (1885) American composer, who lived in New York at the time.

[December, 1940]
Atlanta, Ga.
Friday the 13th

ANAÏS—

Just got your letters with enclosures of Slocum and [Kenneth] Patchen. Didn't know you had tackled Slocum for me—thought I told you I did. I returned half of the money in Chattanooga when I got yours. Want to keep straight with him because he *is* decent. Wondering if the ideas I suggested to the group will bear fruit. Keep thinking of the subject—of sanctuaries (like the birds have at gov't expense) for writers and other artists. Of teaching writers how to set up type by hand and by linotype—as part of their training. Here and there islets where not only food and lodging could be had but technical means to get out his precious Ms. if he wanted to do it himself —just the bare facilities. And so on.

In short, how to stop the mendicant business—how to give him status, like other workers. There are so many places which could easily be converted to such ends—and so many natural retreats where with a little will and cooperation, sanctuaries could be established and simply run—just bare asylums.

Writing this from bed—just resting up—too lazy to do anything— glad to do nothing. Weather bad, rainy, gloomy and Atlanta, tho' a big city, no more interesting than the others.

Your essay on Patchen is excellent *—I can't suggest any changes. I don't quite agree with your viewpoint, though. It may be true that as a person he isn't born yet, but as a writer, expressing himself about world conditions, I feel *he's* born all right but the world he should inhabit is not. He's giving the emotional picture of what the world at present looks like to a sensitive artist. In that I feel he's dead right.

Incidentally, Eduardo loaned me a book by Gerald Heard (*Pain, Time & Sex*) which I'll send you when I'm thru with it—to return to him. *He* has solutions to offer—*one,* really, and a daring one—the occult one, I should say. You'll see. Anyway, for a religious type, no one could speak more emphatically and unreservedly against the whole world order. But he has a positive and hopeful attitude (which Patchen, because of his youth, lacks). I feel very close to Heard in that after going thru the blackest despair I see issues—issues which

---

* Manuscript version in Anaïs Nin's Diary.

demand still more of the individual and do not look for collective improvement. You'll see what I mean when you read the book. What I mean is (anent Patchen) that the artist does well if he states *what is* —the solutions may come if people individually here and there *realize* what's what.

Anyway, I think you summed it up better than I could. Nobody that I can see (unless some mad young poet) is going to see the book clearly. Anyway, too, I don't worry now about him personally. I have only been trying to fight for his work—to get him a hearing. And that's what I think of mostly in trying to solve the whole artist problem. How to give every man a hearing. Fate decides what will live and who will live. But this basic stupidity and injustice could, I feel, be rectified—and must be done by writers themselves—not by charitable organizations. It doesn't affect me personally so much any more because, if I really had to, I could give up writing.

The thing that appeals to me now is a quiet spot—a sacred spot— such as I saw in Greece. There are none here—so far—the externals are there, superb sites, etc. but something in the atmosphere kills it off.

But this is going on everywhere in the world now. That's why something will have to be done soon. It's like a dead end. Either we sink or swim. I think we'll swim! I'm sure of it. Solutions come out of desperation.

I can easily get back to N.Y. now if that's the plan still. May spend Xmas in Charleston or Savannah. Think the fare from either place should be about the same as Asheville. But will tell no one I'm coming back to N.Y. I could then meet Rattner at Key West.

We've about finished the mountainous country, I believe. The scenery has been continuously marvelous—until now. Georgia thins out—desolate rather, so far. Atlanta is quite horrible. A sort of Southern New York—but a N.Y. of 50 years ago in architecture. Just hideous. I begin to doubt that *any* American city will appeal to me. I get more and more disgusted. And yet, each day, at the wheel, the eye is so satisfied that I forget until the car stops.

I'm also beginning to think that when I write the book it will be so distasteful to D.D. & Co. [Doubleday, Doran & Co.] that they will refuse to publish it. I don't need any ugly words to make the picture I now have. It will be unpalatable even in the finest language. If I were a Czar I'd wipe the whole population out—leaving just Indians and Negroes.

The Indian Reservation at Cherokee, N.C. (smaller than I thought) was a wonderful contrast to the white lands. Simply idyllic—and utterly silent and peaceful—no mechanical civilization noticeable. Struck up an acquaintance with first one I met—a long talk which resulted in quite a pact. Could go to his home in Oklahoma any time and stay as long as I like. I believe I'll have similar experiences in the West. The curious thing was he was talking almost at once of the soul, of God, etc. You could see the rift between the two races—how they split. Told me of a miracle by a Spanish priest who converted a Pueblo tribe—and how even to this day no white man knows how to get to the spot alone. (If an Indian takes you there it's in the night —thru caverns etc.—sometimes blindfolded.) The country, when you travel over it slowly, is impregnated with the Indian life. So many, many names of places, mountains, creeks, rivers—all Indian. It's as tho' we're here to stay a little while, mess it up, fail, die off, and then revert to its rightful owners. With all the fury and zeal of his labors the white man here is building nothing—everything strikes you as impermanent and insecure.

Well enuf! Write me now to Charleston, eh?

HVM

P. S. Father writes that he hasn't received cigarettes yet—Will you send them—or shall I? Just one carton of the long ones.

P. P. S. The bright Star and little Star about 2 feet apart, near the moon in early evening, are Jupiter and Saturn in conjunction. I have observed them for months without knowing what they were.

[December, 1940]
Charleston, S.C., Tuesday, the 17th

ANAÏS—

Just got your letter here this morning. Charleston is simply marvelous—can't quite believe it's true yet. The very first city I've found in all my travels in America. Like the old world—very distinctive, dignified, elegant, original—and the sordid Negro quarters, which we walked through last night, are great. Like walking around in Paris again. Could live here if I wanted to. Has all the atmosphere I crave

—and a fine climate, fine sky. Last night walking in the rain without an overcoat and hat off—about 72 degrees Fahrenheit!! Every house original in style and many of them—not just a little area. Some buildings of the 18th century remind me of Nîmes and Arles. One can be happy just walking about, not knowing a soul. It's musical. Will tell you about the other places later.

Yes, I got a letter from Patchen with yours today. Answered it but have nothing to suggest. Can only write an appeal for him, if he thinks it will do any good.* I doubt that any other publisher will take his book. Someone may arise to do it privately eventually—that's all I can see.

I wasn't surprised about the rejection of the Greek book. I'm not sure Slocum will find a publisher easily. The more I travel around the more I marvel that anything is read. There's no place for art in America—it's a sheer luxury. So don't work too much on it. Let Slocum worry—it's good experience for him. (I have no other copy incidentally.)

You say you had another bad attack. That sounds bad to me. Do you really know what causes them? Does the doctor, I mean? You're spending too much time at the doctor's. Too much treatment. If there's not something organically wrong then you've got to change your way of living, that's all.

I'll stay on here 4 or 5 or 6 days, I imagine. Am at the Timrod Hotel on Meeting Street South—an old and well-known place, in case you wish to telephone. In case you don't catch me in, leave word when you'll telephone again and I'll be waiting for your call. Rattner will go back to N.Y. for Xmas, I think. So we may leave here the 22nd or 23rd. It takes eleven or twelve hours from here—better train service than from Asheville.

Am trying to write the long piece for the Laughlin book.** Slocum says contract will go thru now in about ten days, he thinks. I must finish this by end of this month. Have done no writing yet—but feel capable here since I'm staying put a while. And in N.Y.—if nobody finds me out—I can finish it. I'm not telling anybody that I'm com-

---

* Kenneth Patchen was trying to find a publisher for his new book, *The Journal of Albion Moonlight,* and Miller subsequently made several public statements about the book.
** *Wisdom of the Heart,* published by New Directions in 1941. A collection of pieces, most of them previously published.

ing. I'll just leave them guessing as to my whereabouts for a while.

Glad you're meeting Luise Rainer. Expect you to make a real friend there—*more,* I expect her to do something for you, I have a strong hunch about it.

Glad too you sent the cigarettes. Father must have written me before you sent them off. He says he's gotten lots of literature from you. They're all fixed up for Xmas. I don't need to spend any money there. I'm doing my best to conserve. Just bare living expenses means a lot here. It's a crime, too, to spend the money for such a purpose. But maybe, when the book is published, we'll get it all back. My star is steadily rising, I know, despite any petty drawbacks. Nothing can stop the forward march. That's why I can mark time with confidence. I know Fate will do the necessary. More soon.

                                                                        HVM

                                                          [January 5, 1941]
                                              Timrod Hotel—Charleston, S.C.
                                                       (Meeting Street South)
                                                                      Sunday
ANAÏS—

        Got here yesterday afternoon after stopping overnight at Richmond. Arrived at 3:30 only to find that the Post Office had closed at two o'clock! Am only beginning to get over the indigestion or whatever it is. The druggist frightened me out of it, I guess, by asking me if I were sure it was indigestion. Said it could be my heart. The thought of that cured me. I took some Bi-sodol for the indigestion, went to bed, slept 14 hours, and awoke feeling almost fit. If the pain continues I'll go to the doctor—but I think it's going now. Anyway, Charleston looks beautiful. I arrived to find the weather balmy, the sky soft and delicately tinted, the houses bright, the people good-natured and leisurely. It looks even better to me now than at first blush—which is saying a good deal. The man at the garage didn't know what to charge me for storing the car—said it hadn't been in his way. I offered him a couple of dollars and he said, "I couldn't take that—give me half and call it square." That's phenomenal, what? I have a beautiful room with five windows thru which the sun streams all day long. I began rewriting and am improving it still more. Believe it will go well now—I have it under control.

Last night I read some of [Dane] Rudhyar's tracts. They are remarkably good—and about the artist and his role correspond exactly with my views. I was delighted to read him. (I notice tho' that like myself about America he goes off the track whenever he speaks of Europe! It teaches me to watch out—not to generalize too much.) In the main his view is not only sound but inspiring—and in accord with the very highest views everywhere. I'll point out later, when returning them, which to read carefully. He's no slouch! As my father says—it isn't all *lorry-forry*.

Do you know why I like this place so much? It reminds me vividly of Avignon (the roofs), of Monaco (the Italianated walls), of Orange (the Roman influence), of Nîmes (the queer little temples). It's very like southern France in parts. And it's immaculate, dreamy, serene.

Every step brings a surprise. Nothing is repeated. There is great pride here, but well founded. It must be the last stronghold of a cultural aristocracy. Timrod, after whom the hotel is named, was a poet. There is a statue to him in the park opposite. There are numerous statues and crazy ones too. It might almost be a foreign land for all the names mean to me. But the great thing is the sky—at sunset. Something exquisitely delicate, like a water color done on moist paper. And behind the delicate hues a light almost as sharp and translucent as in Greece. The result is that for an hour or two the buildings glow with an effulgent aura, as in Paris after a rain. White here doesn't glare and blind—it radiates a milky warmth which makes one city at least in America seem actually benign and blessed. That's a lot—coming from me!

I think I'll be here till Tuesday at least. Next stop Savannah, *Ga.* Will write again before leaving, however. Anyway, I feel calm as if enjoying a convalescence. Hope you keep thinking about the printing press.

HVM

[January 6, 1941]
Charleston, S. C.
Monday

ANAÏS:

Just got the mail but no checks and no contract or letter from Volkening.* Have just wired him to ask if he sent it or not. Had a letter from Fraenkel saying that he is printing another batch of the *Hamlet* letters in Mexico.** Mostly Christmas greetings, together with a letter from Patchen saying that Laughlin will publish the book if he can get [Edmund] Wilson of the *New Republic* to sponsor it! I've just written both of them, Patchen and Wilson. To Patchen a fine letter which should set him right for once and all. I'll probably leave here Wednesday morning for Savannah, Ga. Will go for mail Wednesday before leaving.

I enclose a letter from a Madame Jodjana, a Dutch woman married to a Javanese dancer. She writes me as a friend of a Mlle Germaine Berder who lived with her, a Frenchwoman whom I met in Paris through Fred and Mr. [W. T.] Symons. She is a "spiritual" sort of person and this letter from Jodjana comes as a result of obeying her request to write Jodjana a simple, short letter (which apparently she couldn't do from England for some reason or other) telling her that Mlle Berder was all right and wished her well, etc. Whereupon I get this extraordinary request! Before I answer it I want to honestly inquire if anything could be done for them—in the way of a tour. Obviously I don't know anybody who could help, but I thought of Joaquin,† his acquaintances in the musical world, etc. Perhaps you might send him the letter and ask if he knows anything about this Javanese dancer and whether I could send this appeal to some agency

---

* Russell & Volkening, New York literary agents, represented Miller's work at the time. See also biographical note on John Slocum, who worked for the agency.

** When the so-called "Hamlet" correspondence between Fraenkel and Miller (originally thought of as "The Merry Widow") came to an end in October, 1938, it added up to some thousand pages of letters. A first volume of the correspondence (incomplete) was published by Fraenkel in Puerto Rico in June, 1939. The second volume—465 pages—was printed in Mexico and published in June, 1941, under the imprint of Carrefour, N. Y. A second (complete) edition of Vol. 1 was printed in Mexico and published in July, 1943, under the imprint of Carrefour, N. Y.

† Joaquin Nin-Culmell, Anaïs Nin's brother. See Biographical Notes.

here in America? You may remember that it was this dancer who said he knew what was wrong with Nijinsky, that they had had similar cases of so-called insanity in Java, owing to a disturbance of the "chakra" dealing with the sense of space. As if, so to speak, the dancer, not knowing the danger he was inviting, had drawn upon some secret resources known only to initiates and, having made use of his powers blindly, had been unable to revert to a normal condition. Something of this sort. . . .

In any case, return the letter to me sometime so that I may answer it. Some of the nonsense about the household, the flowers, the damages to property etc. in her letter, are obviously intended for relay to Mlle Berder. Why they can't communicate directly I don't know. It's mysterious. Don't make it a problem. We have no responsibility. It's just possible, though, that her husband is the greatest living dancer, in which case it would be something to be of use, if one could.

I'm rushing with this to the P.O. to catch the airmail. Sorry there was nothing more encouraging. I feel better—the pain is almost entirely gone now. Have a feeling Rattner won't show up. Must again comment on Rudhyar—am still reading the pamphlets. He seems to have solved all problems—a gigantic undertaking.

Hope you haven't had a relapse. More tomorrow.

HENRY

[January 8, 1941]
Charleston, S.C., Wednesday, P.M.

ANAÏS—

Got a telegram from Rattner saying he was only *leaving* N.Y. today. Guess he won't show up till tomorrow—he didn't say when he'd *arrive*. But I will be in Savannah, *Ga.* by Saturday, whether with him or without, so unless you hear to the contrary, why, wire me funds there % Western Union, will you?

I feel considerably better today—and am now tackling those Liver-culture pills you gave me—hope they're not stale by now. The pain is all gone but there is still some feeling of indigestion. The worst I ever experienced. Being alone, however, I kept quiet, did my work, rested, etc. Today I took a drive for four hours, after doing my pages.

Went searching for a little town called *Secessionville*—just to show you how proud they are here of being rebels. It was near Ft. Johnson where the first shot was fired in the Civil War—the attack on Ft. Sumter. Anyway, it was nothing but some dead houses, a bit of livestock, some Negroes and a tablet (in the midst of a manure pile) to the dead. But getting off the road takes you to interesting country always. That's the first auto ride for pleasure I ever took—you can tell I must have been sick.

The contract from Laughlin turned up too! It was pigeonholed at P.O. owing to postage due. So I signed it and sent it off. He will pay the agents $100 to my a/c on receipt of it and another hundred when I send in this story I'm finishing. I asked Volkening to let me know how I stand. I discovered that the Greek book is now with Viking Press—not Doubleday. Don't know yet whether the latter rejected it or not. But if the astrological dope is correct I should soon find a publisher for it. I told you about Fraenkel, didn't I? About bringing out Volume 2 of the *Hamlet* from Mexico?

In the contract Laughlin gave releases on 5 books. He still holds an option on the Paris books—but that doesn't bother me. The second fragment of Greek book should appear in the *New Republic* in mid-January.* So there surely will be more money soon!

I'm drinking loads of orange juice—and I found a good digestive called Bi-sodol. Take it once a day. I notice another thing—my suit is too tight. I can't wear the vest any more. That cramped me. So I must have gained weight during this trip—strange.

If Rattner arrives tomorrow we'll leave Friday and be in Savannah Friday evening. It's only a little over a hundred miles. Then we'll speed to Key West, I hope. It's been cold here—tho' not disagreeable. They freeze quick here. For them 35 above is cold. No mail from you—but expect some in Savannah.

HVM

P. S. The drive today—which is typical of what's ahead—was beautiful. Under arched trees loaded with ghostly whiskers. Gives you an eerie feeling, even in broad daylight. At night it must be terrifying.

---

* The first fragment appeared in *Town and Country,* January, 1941, under the title "The Colossus of Maroussi." The *New Republic* published "Peroration to a Book on Greece" in the issue of April 21, 1941.

[January 13, 1941]
Jacksonville, Fla., Monday A.M.

ANAÏS—

I got everything in Savannah all right. P.O. closes there at noon—was too late to mail letter from there. Also got bad cold and felt lousy. Clearing up now though—mostly head cold.

We're changing our itinerary—won't go to Miami and Key West after all. Crowd in Florida looks terrible—the dregs from all over the country. It looks like Broadway and is cheap, vulgar, trashy. So we're heading for New Orleans. Will be in Mobile Thursday or Friday and thru the weekend. Next week in New Orleans where we'll stay a few days or a week. So mail things either place. Telephone Miss Steloff and tell her of the change, will you, as I mailed her a postcard yesterday saying to forward things to Key West. (May go to St. Augustine this afternoon and back again. Car is being overhauled—something wrong with the generator.)

I finished the thing for Laughlin and am mailing it out now, 52 pages. Think it's O.K. I changed it some. Cut some of the material. Volkening says I'll just be square when Laughlin pays in the $200. That leaves only the hope of *New Republic* fragment and the Greek book. But I'm thinking now there's good hope of winning the Guggenheim—middle of March. That's my most favorable moment astrologically. More soon. Rushing this. Have quite a few letters to get off. Think Rattner will quit me at New Orleans.

HVM

P. S. Excuse this haste. Writing from restaurant.

[January 13, 1941]
St. Augustine, Fla.
Monday Eve

ANAÏS—

Wrote you a hasty note at forenoon—thought we were leaving Jacksonville then, but had to wait till almost 6 o'clock before we could get the car. Again, no fault of the car's really—just used-up old parts. Paid $9.00 for the job. We started for the ocean drive, which is off the main route. Passed 2 cars in 40 miles! The most desolate, god-

forsaken stretch we have so far encountered. But St. Augustine itself
—at night—looks rather good. Will know better tomorrow. If you
look at map you will see we plan to cut due west across the state—
thru Tallahassee to Pensacola and Mobile. We will cross the Suwannee River too. Notice it has its source in the Okefenokee Swamp in
Georgia. We may see part of this—not sure.

Forgot to say we passed near St. Mary's on our way from Savannah Sunday—but I felt bad then—could hardly see out of my eyes
and sneezing and coughing continually. St. Mary's is right at the state
line. Funny, the moment we left Brunswick, Ga. we felt as though it
were Florida already. Climate had altered. It's only warm in the daytime however. The nights are really chill, damp, treacherous. N.Y.
weather is better somehow. I never did like *semitropical* places. I say
it's unhealthy. It's phony always. The palm trees always give me a bad
impression—they're faky.

The picture one gets at Jacksonville of the *potpourri humain* in
Florida is depressing. It's just like it was 15 years ago—only worse.
Something disgusting and unappetizing. The uprooted lost souls of
America milling around in a rabbit stew. I think we've done well to
head for the Gulf shore—the so-called Riviera of America—which
I believe is practically ignored.

I'll probably wire you again from Mobile Friday. May need a little
more money Saturday—have about $33.00 or so now.

Volkening sent me copies of [Paul] Rosenfeld's and [Edmund]
Wilson's statements about Greek Ms.—both highly flattering. Rosenfeld thought it a joyous book—miraculously so, for these times!

Going to bed now—9:30 P.M.! Pretty groggy still. Guess I'll be
immunized when the epidemic really gets unleashed.

By the way, the money at Savannah came thru the *Postal* Telegraph
Company. You know I inquire only at W.U. office. Lucky, I opened
the envelope containing notice of the draft. I was going to throw it
away without opening it—thinking it was an advertisement. But so
long as you send it c/o Gen'l Del'y it makes no difference which
office it is. Only remember that in the South here Post Offices are
closed at noon Saturdays usually. If I arrive after 12 noon I will have
to wait till Monday—unless you wire direct to W.U. office. They're
always open. Or if you tell me either one I'll look in both telegraph
offices. Maybe you're nearer the Postal Office in N.Y.?

HVM

P. S. Savannah wasn't interesting at all. Dirty, squalid, grimy, gloomy, somnolent. *Etc. Etc.*

[January 16, 1941]
Mobile, Ala., Thursday Night

ANAÏS—

We got here at noon today—a bit ahead of time. I think we'll move on to Biloxi, Miss. for tomorrow and be in New Orleans Saturday or Sunday. Mobile is not what I dreamed of in Paris—tho' it has some qualities. Particularly the climate and sky. We are on the Gulf of Mexico now—ever since we passed Panama City on our way to Pensacola yesterday. The water looked beautiful—an emerald green, despite the storm. We rode all day in a driving downpour—torrential —tropical—with thunder and lightning playing. It *is* a Riviera—but they haven't done anything with it.

Northern Florida is one huge desolate wilderness—forest tracts, swamps, etc. From Jacksonville to Pensacola is like some monomaniac's dream. Very balmy here, as in Pensacola last night. Temperature around 56—at night! In the afternoon the sun is a ball of fire—really threatening! And the sky here is dramatic—heavy green-blue, turquoise, with puffy storm clouds or else clear and soft as velvet. At night magnificent. We crossed the Suwannee River day before yesterday, I think. Got out to look at it. Quite dreamy and romantic—beautiful trees with Spanish moss, etc.

Anyway, making this trip right across the widest part of Florida we followed the old Spanish trail which began at St. Augustine. They must have had great courage and endurance. It was a formidable undertaking then—is even now. For forty and fifty miles at a stretch no house, no human being—not even a gas station. But the most velvety new road—a charcoal black with red borders—quite lovely. We try to drink orange juice en route—only have "canned" orange juice— some concoction of Dr. Phillips—doctored and denatured. Yet everywhere bags of a hundred oranges for 50 cents and less. In the restaurants no fresh fruit—sometimes not even preserved fruits. Lucky indeed if we can get stewed prunes. It's a crazy country.

The greatest danger has been to avoid hitting hogs and cows which are on the open range hereabouts and encumber the roads. Lots of dead ones lying on the roads. The young pigs look ghastly—as if they were struck down naked.

The Spanish and Indian names are beautiful—but nothing of their life lingers. Passed a town called Panacea—famous for its curative waters. Near another town called Sopchoppy! Not far from Old St. Joe. Sounds wonderful, eh? But you should see them!

Well, if New Orleans isn't a great improvement I'll get really disgusted. So far I'm still hoping, hoping. Never can quite believe my eyes. That's why we keep pushing on so fast. Always the rainbow ahead.

Rattner has one or two friends in or near New Orleans. I have some names also. We'll probably put in a week there. Will look up the records on your great-grandmother too.

I'm over the flu since yesterday. Now Rattner has it. It seems to be raging here in the South. But I feel immunized now. How are you?

A.M.
Standing at Post Office now. Going to Biloxi, Miss. now—tomorrow we should be in New Orleans.

Will you remember to send my father cigarettes? I think it must soon be time when you get this.

Just saw a cart drawn by a bullock. The deep South! Feeling bully today.

HVM

Monday—January 20th, 1941
New Orleans

ANAÏS—
Arrived here Saturday noon and met some friends of Rattner's. After the first two meals I felt sick—food too rich, too spicy —quite different from anywhere else. We are going to the country Wednesday—till the end of the week, I suppose—to stay at his friend's home in New Iberia—the place I once described to you. It sounds interesting. I'll let you know later in week where we go next. Rattner may drop out from here or he may go on to Memphis, Tenn. with me and leave me there. That means going thru the length of the

State of Mississippi, following the river largely, thru Baton Rouge, La., Natchez, Miss. and Vicksburg, Miss.

Have had no letter from you since the one on blue paper—at Jacksonville, I believe. Maybe you wrote me to Miami and Key West?

We're going to take a boat ride in one of the old steamboats on the Mississippi tomorrow. It was cold as the devil last 2 days—freezing. In Biloxi we almost froze to death. Now it's warming up. Must be bad in N.Y.

New Orleans is a very big city and quite lovely. The old French Quarter is far bigger and better than I thought it would be. Really picturesque. People very cordial and hospitable too. We go, then to Iberia, into the Evangeline country—where people still speak French —the old French. I am going to look up dope on your great-grandmother today perhaps. Don't feel very energetic yet. Resting up. Hope you are well—beginning to worry about you.

More when I get to the old house in New Iberia.

Sent you 2 little glass bottles from Biloxi—did you get them?

HVM

New Orleans, Jan. 29th [1941]

ANAÏS:

Just came back from a long trip in Dr. Souchon's * car which he loaned me to see some interesting places—his chauffeur driving me. I have eight telephone calls to make and one of them is to Mrs. Garcia, one of your distant relatives. It'll be fun to see what these people are like.

But about New Iberia . . . A theatrical place, haunted by a constant stream of tourists who pay to get in and visit the grounds. Weeks Hall, the last of his line, is a first-class neurotic who stopped drinking four years ago after smashing up his arm in an accident. So now he talks—a steady, unending flow, and sometimes interesting, sometimes not. I made lots of notes from his conversation—tales, anecdotes, traditions, names of flowers and trees, menus, etc. etc. He's no fool, but

---

* See "Dr. Souchon: Surgeon-Painter" in *The Air-Conditioned Nightmare*.

somewhat of a strain. He was a painter and knows his subject well, but doesn't paint any more.

Instead, he created Dr. Souchon, through whom he does his work. A very queer Frankenstein case. The doctor is thoroughly normal, un-inhibited, released, joyous, equilibrated—a man who started in at 60 and is already one of the best painters in the country, his canvases bold, colorful, joyous and of good value. The most efficient and dy-namic man I ever met—twice as young as any of us. Gets up at four every day, retires at eleven; does three or four men's work in a day. He's been very kind to me, though he's hard as nails in his Creole way. It seems to me that the Creoles are more French than the French. The Spanish I don't detect very much. They hated the Span-iards, you know, and the Spaniards were usually of a lower class—artisans, peasants, etc.—whereas the French were aristocrats. There is a public square here, where the Cabildo stands, which is almost like the Place des Vosges in Paris, flanked all around by "hotels" in the old sense of the word—the first apartment houses, they say, in the New World. The whole French quarter is more French in feeling, in architecture, than Paris itself. The buildings are far more interesting with their colors and balconies and variety of style. And however much you love it, you get a shock when you speak to the shopkeepers—they are cold and hard and mercenary, just as they were in France.

I have been in a number of fine homes, with beautiful gardens. These gardens, often in the heart of the city, are surrounded by high walls, and make you think of Louveciennes, though usually more for-mal. Weeks Hall's place was really ducal—with lovely statues hidden away in the foliage under big heavy dreamy trees and swamped with flowers, principally the camellia and the azalea. There were plenty of mosquitoes too—even now in winter. What it must be like in summer I dread to think. Sometimes the thermometer, while I was there, reg-istered over 80. The weather changes rapidly here—almost as in New York.

I give you the menu of one luncheon at Avery Island, where I found the statue of the Buddha. The hostess was the widow of the man who invented Tabasco Sauce—all the food here is highly sea-soned and spiced—too much so. Here's the menu:

Grapefruit, small diamond-backed terrapin with garlic sauce and tender chopped livers of the turtle together with wild rice from Min-nesota; broiled chicken with french fried potatoes and new cabbage, orange bread from Oklahoma, frozen grapes with salad, Charlotte russe and sponge cake, spanish coffee and Cointreau. The Charlotte russe was extraordinary—served in a big bowl, like a custard—a specialty of these parts. Sunday morning breakfasts, I was told, often consist of creamed sweetbreads and Charlotte russe! A favorite dish is called "la mediatrice" and is made of fried oysters smothered in rich sauce and hidden inside a loaf of bread which is heated in the oven. Frozen cream cheese takes the place of ice cream and is far more delicious. Lunch in the old plantation days was often like this: a slice of bread and butter spread with marmalade or guava jelly accompanied by a slab of jujube paste and washed down with lemonade or orange flower syrup or tamarind juice. (Later I'll give you a description of the old plantation balls and what they ate and how—incredibly beautiful.)

I heard wonderful stories, of course, some perhaps untrue. Here's one. About a man who was about to be married and sent to China for spiders; before the wedding he put the spiders in the garden and had them spin their webs across the bridal path; then he ordered the Negroes to sprinkle gold dust over them!

Another one, which is vouched for—that some owners used certain Negroes as studs—would send them around the country to fecundate the women—sometimes ten and twelve in a day—like a bull!

The names of the flora and fauna roundabouts are marvelous. They grow anything down here at the mouth of the Mississippi. Today I walked along the levee, thru swamps and forests, at once desolate, wild and hallucinatory—with cows trying to graze, cows looking like a mixture of cats, goats and ponies. Mangy-looking beasts with thick coats of fur, and dwindled. The Spanish moss is not a parasite, I find; it is an air plant, living on air entirely—and will grow just as well on telegraph wires, which it does sometimes.

Some names: the magnolia fuscata, the aspidistra, Barbadoes lily, Persian lilac, Louis Philippe Rose, Picayune Rose, wild jessamine, Michaelmas daisies, the sassafras, the cucumber tree, the Chinaball tree, the banana, the crepe myrtle, the osage orange, swamp myrtle, bamboo, etc. I went through a bamboo grove, the bamboo shooting up to about fifteen feet or so. Marvelous unreal sensation, of light and shadow, of rosy-cream earth, of jungle and spaciousness, of filtered, powdered light, of silence, of unworldly colors. Saw crocodiles sleeping like stone, their tails hanging immobile as rock in the still swamp

water which had turned green and gray like the bodies of the crocodiles—a frozen scum with frozen beasts of antediluvian times. Nearby
(this at Avery Island) flocks of birds from the southern regions that
come here to breed and fly away again. Perched on the topmost
branches of slender trees, looking like inflated white and pink blossoms. Wild geese flying overhead, fish of all kinds below, stud bulls
standing quietly grazing, exotic plants and grasses of all kinds, and
mosquitoes, mosquitoes . . . The flowers—camellias especially—like
nothing I've ever seen. Can understand the passion which people in
the Gulf region have for this beautiful flower. They talk a language,
about the camellia, which is pure Greek to any one else. They live
for their azaleas and camellias.

What this world was like in the old slave days you can well imagine.
A richesse and luxury unknown in Europe, except among royalty.
Near New Iberia is St. Martinville, the home of Evangeline whom
Longfellow wrote about. The Acadians were a sturdy peasant type of
French and they predominate still. You hear French everywhere—
shopkeepers must speak two languages. Some of the Negroes have
mixed with the Indians and produced a strange type, especially when
you hear them talk French—which, by the way, is not so difficult to
understand.

To come back to Weeks Hall. Everybody of any prominence has
visited his place. I saw the register he keeps—includes Paul Claudel.
He used to be drunk all the time and did wild things. He had his
guests sign their names on the door, for one thing. Once when drunk
he ordered the Negroes to clean the house—in 24 hours—which
meant hiring quite a crew. They did it and very thoroughly. The
names were washed away. When he sobered up he saw what had happened, so he unhinged the door, crated it, and sent it around the
country to all the people whom he could remember and asked them
to sign again. Now I see all the movie stars' names, and of course
writers, painters, etc. He is like a caretaker—says there is no way out
of it. Pretends to be sick of it, but secretly enjoys it. Telephones and
telegraphs his friends every few minutes of the day. Studies everything exhaustively—in order not to go crazy. Eduardo would love to
have his horoscope—I couldn't get his hour of birth. He's a Scorpio.
Anyhow, if Eduardo would write him he might get somewhere—
address him "The Shadows," New Iberia, La. The shadows! First
thing I did was to throw back the turkey red curtains and open all

the doors and windows I could. It was like a dungeon inside. He had even brought in the bones of some of his favorite ancestors—used to sleep in the iron coffins and spread the bones out on the floor and bed. Found the dog eating the bones one day, so he said. Another time they were thrown out with the garbage and he had the servants dive for them in the bayou outside his garden. At night, when it gets misty and the traffic lights turn a real ruby-emerald color in the heavy fog, it's wonderful to go to the summerhouse by the bayou and watch the boats going thru the drawbridge. They seem to be suspended in the air and you can't distinguish sky from water and it's all a thick blue haze, very very Chinese in effect. I tell you all this about his house because you escaped something when you gave up Louveciennes. One could write a good story about the sacrifice which this man is making to keep up a house and a tradition which is greater than himself. He understands it thoroughly, but confesses his helplessness. With it all he's extremely human, tender, likable—a beautiful failure, I would say.

Well, enough. I must go to eat. It's nearly nine o'clock.

HVM

P. S. Towns nearby like "Des Allemands," "Violet," "Paradis" etc. Nothing but French and Indian names everywhere.

[February 5, 1941]
Natchez Hotel, Mississippi
Wednesday

ANAÏS—

Here's a little note I just got from my father. I take it he must have received cigarettes *and* money from you just after writing this. When you send cigarettes again, why, send him *Julep* if you can, eh?

No mail from you on arriving here—but maybe tomorrow.

Had a wonderful day yesterday inspecting great old homes and gardens of antebellum days. Most of them are sadly in need of repair —the owners are poor but proud—or else cracked. (All except the Tourmaine Château which is owned by a doctor from Michigan who is restoring it.)

But at Rosedom, where the gardens are so marvelous, the 26-room house is like a junk shop. Three old spinster sisters live in it and they have not talked to each other in years. The one who showed us around wore the most poverty-stricken clothes—and dirty too. Real poverty—in the midst of ancient treasures from the ends of the earth —Egypt, India, France, Italy, Greece, etc. A sort of insanity. Rosenwald, the millionaire, offered them $150,000 for the place, to be taken over only after their death—but they wouldn't do it. *Afraid he would let Negroes in!!* Can you imagine that? They were educated abroad but now speak like servants—even worse—a sort of degenerate language which is indescribable.

This morning on the way to Natchez I stopped off to see a 2,000-year-old Indian mound of the Natchez tribe. There were illustrations everywhere showing their customs. One obviously dealt with the homosexual problem.

Told in circumlocutious fashion how certain men dressed as women and were allowed all privileges tho' obliged to do women's work. If they were caught out of bounds they were buggered by the other males. They could do as they pleased with the women. . . .

Natchez is an old old place—the beginning or end of the Wilderness Trail. When there were only 48 millionaires in America, 2/3 of them lived in or around Natchez.

Mississippi seems like a beautiful country—just as one imagines it. Lots of darkies here—the very deep South. Last two nights—Baton Rouge and St. Francisville—I nearly froze to death in the tourist cabins. We had a cold snap and these places are only heated by little gas stoves. When you turn the heat off it gets like the grave. Even outdoors it seemed worse than up North—tho' only down to freezing point. Something deceptive about the South—and treacherous. In Louisiana at night, walking along the deserted roads, you have a feeling of being thousands of miles from civilization.

I stopped at editorial office of the *Southern Review* located at Louisiana State University, Baton Rouge—a huge affair, amazing for the South (which incidentally seems to have marvelous universities everywhere). One of the editors knew me as soon as I mentioned my name. Had bought *Capricorn* in France *during the war*. Knew your work too. I was quite surprised. Because when you're down here it seems incredible that anyone should know you, much less read you. Shows how books travel, though.

I forgot to tell you that Weeks Hall's dog loves black coffee—goes crazy over it. And ice cream too. They have the coffee drinking habit strong in Louisiana—just as in France. And when it's pure it tastes like the good coffee in the good cafés.

I'm eager to hear how that data on your family impressed you.* You could learn more no doubt by writing the ones I mentioned. If Souchon comes to N.Y. you must meet him. I forgot to give him your address. You can do so if you like. He's really interesting—*and 100% alive* as few young men ever are or will be.

Well, this is all for now. Glad you got rid of the monkey.

I found out that there's a photo-printing process, which reproduces text exactly, and which is maybe half as cheap. In case you ever want to reproduce a book. (I have two addresses.)

It's warm here. Took a bath and lay on bed without covers—windows open. Strange climate from one place to another.

I should be in Memphis, *Tenn.* from Saturday or Sunday thru Monday.

Did you hear from Rattner? The Arrow Editions is a woman friend of Laughlin's—a Puritan. I heard of her when in Paris.

Notice how much closer Jupiter and Uranus are now. You will find them near the moon—one bright, the other small. They're far less brilliant too than a couple of months ago.

                                                        HVM

                                              [March 3, 1941]
                                              Cleveland, Ohio
                                              Monday

ANAÏS—

Just got here after spending the night in Pittsburgh—a hellhole.** Today I passed thru Warren, Ohio, where Patchen comes from. If you could see it you'd understand Patchen even more. The

---

* Anaïs Nin's great-grandmother was born in New Orleans, where the French part of the family (from Anjou) had settled. Dr. Souchon undertook some research into the family and discovered that a diary of her ancestors existed in New Orleans.

** While in Natchez, Miller received word that his father was dying. He flew back to New York immediately, but arrived two hours too late. His father had died on Monday, February 8th, at 7:10 A.M. Miller stayed in New York during the rest of the month and resumed his trip by train on March 2nd.

whole journey today thru Penn. and Ohio was like a ride thru an Inferno. I got such a kick out of it that I'm going to start the American book tonight from this point—the center of industrialism, the sink of democracy.* It's almost beyond words—so grim, so black, so terrible. Like the planet Vulcan, if there is one. (I think this is the one they're looking for!)

It was good I had the hunch to make this trip north—it gives me the impetus I needed. If I had come this way first I might have given up —in despair.

I finished the Ramakrishna book in the hotel last night and I'll mail it to you, soon. You must read it—he's a powerful figure. Skip the dry parts, if you like, about religious theories, but take a glance now and then at the footnotes. Some of them are marvelous. When you're through either mail it (*registered*) to the Swami or bring it to him. Swami Nikhilananda—c/o Ramakrishna-Vivekananda Center, 17 East 94th St., N. Y. City.

I just met Porter Welch of the Burrows Book Shop who used to write me in Paris. Had to autograph books etc. He asked about you and your Diary. But I couldn't talk to him about our scheme—it's not the shop for that.

I'm going to Detroit tomorrow.

HENRY

[March 5, 1941]
Detroit, Michigan
Wednesday Night

ANAÏS—

Leaving here tomorrow noon for Chicago. Won't bother to visit the Ford plant which is ten miles out. Can imagine it from the looks of this place. Detroit is terrifically new, dynamic, dazzling, ter-

---

* Miller had been commissioned by Doubleday, Doran and Co. in New York to write a book about his trip through the United States, and had received an advance of five hundred dollars, which he subsequently returned, when the manuscript of the book was turned down by Doubleday. A number of other publishers also rejected the book. *The Air-Conditioned Nightmare* was eventually published by New Directions in 1945. See also Miller's Preface to the book for a detailed account.

rifying—and a Mecca for salesmen. The most disgusting types too—
hotel is full of them. I feel like starting a fight. Air is electric, like a
cold needle bath. Everybody looks preternaturally healthy and energetic. It's a sort of Siberian machine center. Saw the *Mannerheim*
picture—not horrible, as I imagined, but a sort of unconscious metal-
lurgic drama on another planet. Doesn't arouse one's sympathies for
either side. Very stupid in a scientific, ruthless way.

Since I left N.Y. Sunday—seems ages ago!—I've been thru revolu-
tions. This trip thru the industrial regions gives the full impact of the
real spirit of America—which is barbarous to the nth degree. I have
the impression of being with weird insects who are masquerading for
some diabolic purpose as men. I can see only disaster ahead—there
is no way out of this! I feel more like Céline at the moment than like
Ramakrishna. (He was here, you know, and I think he worked in
the Ford plant.)

I've written about 15 pages—mostly vitriolic. Can't help it—getting
enraged now. It's a foul world—or else I'm foul! Never sensed anything so dehumanized as these last few cities.

Well, this will be the test. When Slocum gets these pages I have a
feeling Doubleday will not want the book. I'm not doing it purposely.
I just can't hold back any longer. By comparison the South is Paradise. A dull one, though.

You know, the more I see of it the more I think Patchen's book is
lucid and clean—like the fires of wrath. If I had been put thru this
as a youngster I'd be a raving lunatic.

There were lunatics in the cinema too tonight—cheering the Red
Army like epileptics. I wait like Stalin, but behind him, to see *all* the
armies and navies destroyed, and all forms of government and all reli-
gions. The world looks insane to me. Saying this, I realize I've come
to just the opposite conclusion of the great Ramakrishna. He saw
nothing but God everywhere. Maybe I'm simply impatient. But I can
see thousands of years of this nonsense and ignorance accumulating.

I had a tremendous inspiration in the train but burned up too fast.
What I'm writing is only dead fire. Jacobsohn's * prediction about
changing my view was completely wrong. He must be feeding me
Martian dynamite. I feel as tho' I had thunderbolts in both hands.
Feeling fine physically and urinating moderately. I'll write him a re-

---

* Doctor Jacobsohn, whom Miller had consulted in New York, had
prescribed some medication to alleviate digestive upsets and restore energy.

port shortly, as he asked me to. But the philosopher is becoming a fire-eater. I could throw bombs! Maybe I've got to make a new synthesis on the level of my new-found health and energy. I shout about Peace—but like a snorting bull. It's queer. It's as though I had been given an injection of blood from a war lord.

Will be in Chicago a few days surely. Will probably see [John] Dudley and Flo too. Hope you're feeling well now. Will look for mail in Chicago. Guess I've got my release now. Feel I could write and write and write!

HVM

[March 8, 1941]
Chicago—Saturday, A.M.

ANAÏS—

Am going to Dudley's place on Tuesday and will stay a few days there, writing and visiting Milwaukee. Will probably be back here in Chicago the next weekend—i.e. a week from this Saturday. If you want to send anything, send it to me c/o Dudley—in Kenosha, *Wisconsin*. [Ben] Abramson * is going to give me some money on the *Tropics*—how much, I don't know yet. He's quite all right—I rather like him! We are going out in his car tomorrow to cover the town thoroughly. Then I'll talk things over. To date no time—he is always interrupted. A very busy fellow—fine shop—free and easy manner—shrewd, clever, but agreeably so. I have hopes of doing something. He has a prejudice against your writing—*House of Incest*—but I think I'll break that down. Anyway, I have to feel my way. He's cordial and hearty—has the West in his blood. And a dynamo of energy.

I could have stayed at his home but he has a wife, kids, dogs, etc. and lives way out. I expect to meet [Somerset] Maugham at his shop tomorrow or Monday. Everybody comes to his place—it's famous. (He sold over 150 *Capricorns*—until Paris fell.) He knows everybody. He has ideas.

Chicago is very alive—very dynamic. The climate is electric—even

---

* See Biographical Notes.

more so than N.Y. You either prosper or die, I imagine. It's also enormous—like London.

Glad you put Slocum and Rattner together. Give Rattner my regards if you hear from him. I never saw him while in N.Y.

I'm really in fine shape—the bladder seems absolutely normal now. And I'm warm thru and thru. In fact I sweat. Had to go to the chiropodist to have my feet treated—I sweat too much.

Met a Swami here yesterday—friend of the other. A jovial medieval monk—a Bengali. Got along marvelously with him! Very affectionate. Going to see the great Bahai Temple now and maybe the slaughterhouse. Some writer here is taking me around, in his car. I find I'm well known here. Had to sign loads of books already. Will finish first installment of American book for Slocum at Dudley's. Feel rather optimistic about everything.

HVM

[Chicago, March 10, 1941]
Monday Noon

ANAÏS:

I got $25 on account from Abramson this morning and may get more on my return next Friday or Saturday. I have $50 in my pocket after paying hotel bill—so don't send me anything until I wire you for it. My expenses should be light for the next few days.

Had a long talk about business with Abramson. He's reading my thing on *World of Sex* to see whether to publish a limited edition (which would yield me 2 to 3 hundred dollars) or to sell in typescript only.* He goes to the hospital for ten days a week from Wednesday —to rest up and read Ms. He would be glad to read the condensed version of your diary. If he likes it he may get something done about publishing it. I don't want to spoil the chance of something bigger and better for you. I am progressing gently and cautiously with him. It's necessary to let him see that I am (and you too!) something more than he gathers from the books. I know he likes me and I feel he will extend himself in the future.

---

* Ben Abramson, at the Argus Book Shop, Chicago, published a limited edition of 250 copies, at $7.50.

Watch newspapers on 15th or 16th to see if I got the Guggenheim Prize! I may forget. Off now to Kenosha.

HVM

Des Moines, Ia., March 19th

ANAÏS—

Today Slocum writes that I have about $130 to my credit. *Atlantic Monthly* came across with a $250 advance—for magazine rights to American book. I am writing him to give you this money— all but ten dollars for Cairns—you might need it meanwhile.

Hope you weren't disappointed about the Ms. Have another slender hope here—after meeting Karl Weeks, a millionaire who built a replica of Salisbury Manor here and has a colossal library, including everything of Lawrence's by or about him—*including your book*. He didn't know about me. Lafe will tell him after I leave.

The trip thus far has been highly interesting—every day some new surprise. Loaded with material.

Lafe's [Lafayette Young's] home is the most beautiful home I've ever been in. His folks were very rich once—and his ancestors were powers in the community. He is all enthusiastic now to go to Mexico and begin publishing there. Wants to do one or two of my books, Dudley's letters, Durrell's etc. etc. I think he could too—without loss. I think he could do what Obelisk failed to do. (I'm always thinking of the Diary—maybe *there* we will eventually get it done.)

I am going to Kansas City, *Mo.,* tomorrow for the weekend. Will stay with Frederick Kann (the painter from Paris!) at his home. Then to St. Louis and Memphis en route to Natchez. I should be in Natchez, *Miss.* before the end of this month. I am returning various things now—it's going to be warm. Spring is here—in Des Moines, tho' we had a devil of a cold spell recently.

Just got word from Guggenheim that I *failed* to receive the award. But, as usual, if I fail here I gain there.* More from Kansas City (*Mo.*) Feel good—optimistic.

HVM

* See the "Addenda" at the end of *The Air-Conditioned Nightmare.*

P. S. Met Dudley's folks—fine people. Saw some of his early paintings too (at 15, 16, 17!)—astonishingly good—like an old master, really. Proves to me that he has the genius.*

[March 21, 1941]
Kansas City, Missouri
Friday night

ANAÏS—

Met [Frederick] Kann ** here, stayed overnight at his place and then looked for a hotel—too uncomfortable on his couch. Talked about Tibet, etc. He has some wonderful books and pictures. Saw photos of 2 "Masters" (who influenced Blavatsky)—incredibly beautiful faces! Too bad you are not in mood to read about Ramakrishna (*not* Krishnamurti, as you wrote!). But you will come to it later no doubt. A page of R's life is worth a library of other books, I assure you.

Sorry you feel let down about your Ms. Nothing can be done quickly, I realize. I feel—about my own activities (which I see are fruitful)—that it's slow, steady work. R——, for example, used to shout and beat his breast in loneliness, waiting for his disciples to come. I know that everyone I talk to about your work I leave indelibly impressed. One day something will come of it. I don't get weary of it—neither must you. And as for the money—I believe it's going to be easier and easier as I go along.

Don't let things drop—it takes time, you know.

I guess Little Rock was a bad idea. Maybe Texas then. Here in Kansas City I definitely feel the real West, for the first time. Tremendous largesse, abundance, vitality, health, expansiveness. About the most secure spot on this globe, at present. It's noticeable.

I could have put up in a beautiful house in Des Moines indefinitely —with a rich middle-aged widow. People are easy and free and generous out here. The faces are those you see in every country—the *tourists!* Their homes are loaded with treasures. And how they love the table!

I'll be mailing Slocum some pages now from here—the book's

---

* See "Letter to Lafayette," *op. cit.*

** Miller had first met Kann in Paris in 1930.

definitely under way. I see it clearly now—how to do it. One vast out-
pour without breaks. A great chaos, like the country itself.

I'll leave Monday and be in St. Louis till Wednesday noon probably. Then Memphis for a day or two. I may go by auto. There are
agencies which solicit business—help pay your way by riding with
others. Cuts fare considerably. Anyway, I'll see. It's quite a distance
from here to Natchez.

It's very warm here. A rush of spring. The other night in Des
Moines it was down to ten degrees!

More soon.

HVM

[March 27, 1941]
Memphis, Tennessee
Thursday—27th

ANAÏS—

Got your telegram this morning. Have about $25.00 in my
pocket now. Used up considerable since leaving Des Moines. The
distances are enormous! I rode yesterday from St. Louis to here 9½
hours in the train. (Didn't take auto from K.C. to St. Louis, as I
thought I would. Didn't like the types sitting around in the travel
bureau.)

Traveling is expensive, due to hotels, tips, taxis, porters, etc. From
here to Natchez is another long jump. I am breaking it by going first
to Jackson, Miss., the capital. Will be in Natchez Sunday and Monday, I expect.

I feel O.K.—not excessively energetic, but normal. The traveling
—fast traveling—is wearisome. Once I get out of Texas and send
Slocum 200 pages of the book I'll breathe easier. I've seen good country too, of course. If I only could stop longer it would be better. You
can't get much flying like an eagle. Tho' I have a good eye, I find, on
comparing notes with people. Especially for sizing up a city at a
glance.

I missed Maugham in Chicago and Louis Bromfield in St. Louis.
Also Leland Stowe, the newspaper correspondent.

This sounds hectic, like it is. In and out of hotels, trains, taxis, restaurants—walking strange streets, timetables, etc. etc. A grand farrago.

Rode with the Spanish teacher of Des Moines a ways. Talking of Paris and the Midi all the time. He knows ten languages—including Aramaic.

Haven't time really to explore Memphis. It doesn't seem worth it anyway. Nothing like Egypt! But Cairo, Ill. (which I passed in the train) looked interesting. All thru Illinois yesterday dilapidated Negro villages. The most god-awful shacks—worse than any African savages could ever live in! Savages live well, by comparison—that's my belief.

I'm almost sure I'll be in Little Rock, Ark. by next Wednesday or Thursday and will probably stay till end of week, as I can use it as a base to explore the country roundabout and also do some work. I'll probably stay at a hotel or tourist camp. But everyone tells me Arkansas is really fine country. Missouri looked good to me too—and the people were fine. St. Louis was like N.Y. in the 1880's. Same tempo, same architecture. Belonging neither to South, West, nor East. I begin to think I like best the people in the so-called "backward" states or regions. They're like the Grade B movies which are more human.

The South has a fine smell always—the green wood burning, I guess. And the sun is warmer. That lifts one up.

Kenosha looked like Siberia—the Great Lakes when frozen are overwhelmingly glacial. And it *is* cold there. Ice in the air winter or summer.

Going to eat now. Just passed thru the famous Beale Street (the Blues!). Looks rather dismal.

Sign in street says: "From today on begin to live!"

Looking forward to your letter at Natchez!

HVM

[March 31, 1941]
Monday, Natchez

ANAÏS—

Got here last night, feeling rotten—had cold. May leave for general direction of Little Rock tomorrow—ought to be there Thursday and stay thru weekend at least.

Have yet to test the car out. Wondering if all the parts are intact. It's pouring now—delta weather here. Place full of tourists for the spring festival. Paying $4.50 for a room. Must find another this afternoon.

Rattner's show sounds wonderful. I didn't say anything perhaps about *your* painting—I was certainly surprised. But why not? Why shouldn't you be able to paint too?

Had a letter from the Howards * saying the *New Yorker* refused to accept a "profile" on me. As a matter of fact I'm dizzy trying to write a few pages as I move rapidly from place to place. I can't get the feeling of being free and having time of my own. Always the pressure from behind. I do need a halting place soon somewhere. I don't like this fast pace at all.

Slocum seems to like the first pages on America that I sent him recently. I have another batch almost ready. Then I must do the 2 things for *Town and Country*. But if I don't keep moving the continent grows larger and larger. It's like an incubus. I've got a hell of a cough and can't shake it off. Sound like a consumptive.

I see and hear so much now—it's overwhelming. Like that Western Union experience a little bit. Anything but the life I want to lead. I asked for it and I got it! The book will be mad.

Had a letter from Patchen saying he's publishing his book himself by subscription.

Have a slew of mail to answer. Then a new hotel and to bed for a rest.

HVM

[April 3, 1941]
Little Rock, Ark.
Thursday, A.M.

ANAÏS—

Arrived here last night. I'm staying at a tourist court a couple of miles outside the city. Will stay till Monday, I think, in order to finish up some writing. I think now I'll change my itinerary. Will probably head due West from here—see map—thru Oklahoma City,

* A couple Miller met in Chicago, friends of Ben Abramson.

Amarillo, Texas, Albuquerque, New Mexico, to Santa Fe, where I hope it will be pleasant and picturesque. That means I won't go all thru Texas, as I thought, and not to Mexico either. I've got to begin to eliminate. Anyway, I'll let you know before I leave here.

I had some tire trouble on leaving Natchez. Got 2 flats in the middle of a dismal swamp in Louisiana. Waited several hours on the road in a broiling sun for a garageman to come and change tires. Then I decided to get some new inner tubes—and one shoe, as the old one was ripped to bits. The car is running fine otherwise—seems almost to get better and better.

Little Rock certainly looks different from other towns. I rather like the people here in Arkansas—poor and honest, extremely kind. The country is also poor-looking but has a certain charm. Will make some trips into the mountains from here, I expect.

There was no mail here this morning from you but maybe I was at P.O. too early—8:00 A.M.—after walking and riding streetcar for an hour. I wake up at all sorts of hours when I go to bed early.

Best remedy for a hacking cough I find is a 5¢ box of cough drops —*Luden's!* Had my first peaceful night's sleep last night in 4 nights.

HVM

[April 12, 1941]
Santa Fe, New Mexico, Saturday 2:30 P.M.

ANAÏS—

Have to rush this to catch airmail at 3:00 P.M. Arrived this morning with $5.00 in my pocket because after mailing your letter— at Santa Rosa—I had to buy 2 new shoes and come in with one bad one still on. Man told me I was in grave danger of blowout. I am waiting anxiously now for money. Nothing at Western Union yet. There's a 3-hour difference in time, you know. I expect you'll get this by Monday some time. I'll just about hold out, I guess.

Can't say yet what I think of Santa Fe. It's 7200 ft. high and makes you very nervous. I'm jumpy. The last 300 miles were quite grueling. More in next mail.

HVM

[April 12, 1941]
Saturday Midnight
Santa Fe

ANAÏS—

I can't say whether I like it or not here—am dubious. It may be that I'm worried—still no word at Western Union. Fortunately, I no more than arrived and at the W.U. office inquiring for message when I met a man from the newspaper here—a queer-looking fish, freakish, who asked me if I were a writer. Immediately began to interview me. In a few moments I was at his lodge and he was looking up his medical books to see what the doctor had given me—said it was nothing but a sedative. Talks of everybody and everything. Found me a room here at a lousy little hotel (like a cheap French hotel)— $1.25 a day and not worth 75¢. Spoke of Rudhyar and Alfred Morang. Meets everybody who passes thru here.

Anyway, if nothing comes for me by Monday morning I'll probably ask him to lend me the price of a telegram and feed me till something comes.

It's been snowing hard since sundown—imagine it. Strange place. Altitude is extreme. I've been gradually climbing since Oklahoma. But from Albuquerque this morning was the final climb—magnificent scenery. The car just gasped its way in—and by afternoon I was gasping too. It's supposed to be good for most all ailments here—the ultraviolet rays of sun are very powerful.

From a quick impression I don't like the city nor the people—and especially not the Indians and Mexicans. Taos, I am told, is very small and accommodations may be difficult—but I will run up there and see for myself. Hard to get acquainted with the Indians, everybody says. Those roaming the streets look vile, degenerate, faky, phony. But this is first impressions. I'll know better in a day or two. As soon as I hear from you I'll change my quarters. This is a dump.

I expected a picturesque town—it's not. It's touristic and cheap-looking. No character. I'll take a place by the day only and look around in my spare time. May find a more interesting isolated spot. A man I was going to look up in Las Vegas (whom I met in Paris) is down and out now, a wreck, and his wife in an asylum—from drink. Drinking is strong here. Mexicans plenty drunk and quarrelsome. Indians full of diseases, etc. Fine picture. And the country so marvelous!

Lots of poor starving artists here—for their health. Crazy bohemian parties with brilliant paralytics carried in by their lackeys and talking like brilliant statues. Men on six months' drunk, etc. etc. The Bohemia of the Wild West.

Civilized Indians seem sluggish and stupid. Naïf as hell—dull. Prefer the most ignorant Negro to them. (First glance—this is.)

Rich oil people from Texas pay $35.00 a day for a suite of rooms, give banquets, 50 people, etc. It all has a bad smell.

The natives are not cordial and hospitable as in Arkansas but surly, brusque, rather suspicious and without character. It seems to me this sort of thing always goes with the grand scenic and climatic places— Florida, California, etc.

Well, I'm starting in to write anyway. I'll get my bearings soon. The ride here from Arkansas was hard—it's tough even on a machine. Nature is all-powerful. Distance alone is overwhelming. And then the wind, dust, heat, lousy lousy food—the anxiety about the tires and the lack of money. I arrived quite done up, thanking my stars I got thru safely. Maybe all this accounts somewhat for the rather pessimistic picture I'm giving you. We'll see. I'll let you know from day to day. Hope everything is all right—

HVM

[April 17, 1941]
Albuquerque, New Mexico
Thursday—17th

ANAÏS—

A queer thing has happened. Today when I went to get my mail the man said he had been forwarding it to some place in Colorado. There's another Henry Miller traveling about—and I fear he's gotten some of my letters. The P.O. here telegraphed postmaster there to return mail "if not for their patron." But if the man's dishonest I'm in a fix. I was expecting some money orders from several sources. If his name is exactly the same he could cash them. When I pay for the repairs on my car (now in a garage) I will have about 8 dollars

left!! I sat down immediately on arriving here and wrote airmail letters begging for help and explaining the situation. Some of the people
may not yet have had time to answer—that's my one big hope. Also,
the other Henry Miller may be honest and return the money orders,
if he opened them. But it's a great temptation.

The car got thoroughly burned out going up the steep grades—I
saw the whole insides of the engine with my own eyes. The wonder
is that I got here safely. On its reputation, I guess.

I bought the last new tire needed—it was imperative—and paid
for little repairs and being towed to a garage after being stuck at the
bottom of a huge hill coming back from Taos, which I couldn't make.
I've had lots of anguish, I can tell you. Now I am at peace, working
fine—will probably have both articles done by Tuesday (for *Town
and Country*) and may stay another week to write another batch in
the American book.

Don't you worry unduly.

HVM

Albuquerque, N.M.
Thursday 22nd [April, 1941]

ANAÏS:

I'm doing fine. Have decided to stay here until the end of this
week surely. Almost finished with the second article for *Town and
Country* * and believe I will commence the narrative for Laughlin
immediately thereafter—here in Albuquerque. That would release another hundred dollars. It's a good spot to work in—nothing to distract
me. I almost hate to leave it. I figure I'll do another sit-down when I
get to the Grand Canyon. Am not sure yet which way to go from
here. Terrible miserable weather—dust storms for days, now heavy
rain, and cold as hell. In the mountains roundabout it's snowing. One
can't get up there—roads blocked with snow and ice. Imagine it!

Had another letter from Lafe today—seems he's definitely going to
Mexico—due there early in May. He'll start off with *Capricorn,* and
then do the others gradually. I think it's a splendid opportunity. Had

---

* An essay on Dr. Marion Souchon of New Orleans, which was not used by
the magazine but later became a chapter in *The Air-Conditioned Nightmare.*

a letter from Abramson, too, saying he has already given my stuff to the printer and that Howard has been reading proofs on it. That will mean a little income in another six weeks or so. So you see, things are not looking so bad.

Just think, had I wanted to, I could have gone to Mexico with a couple I know—they leave in two weeks from now. But I don't think I should—it's too distracting now. I must get on with the business in hand. But after this tour, Mexico surely. The more I hear about it the better it sounds. I got shaved by a Mexican barber yesterday who was just down there—it took him two hours to give me a haircut and shave—he talked so much. (He admits too that they hate us—the Anglos, they call us. Says we think we're superior, and they know we're not! Says we never bother to learn their language, etc. All too damned true.)

Today I visited the first Indian settlement—Isleta. It was raining hard and made things look dismal, but I was highly intrigued by it all. Very primitive pueblo—like the dawn of creation. Wonderful little Catholic church—gay and simple. Entered the home of an Indian woman 96 years old. She was like a mummy. Spoke Spanish. Most of the Indians know Spanish if not English. A little girl of six offered to take us to someone else's home and after she had driven us about to her heart's content she quietly admitted that she didn't know where she was leading us. She just wanted the ride. I liked that very much. I bought a string of corn, a necklace, made up of all kinds of Indian corn, untouched. The corn grows here in different colors. The weirdest of all is the blue corn. Real blue—just incredible to behold. Nothing else in the food line is blue that I know of. I can't get over it. They make a good breakfast food out of this corn. The ovens are out in the open—that looks good too. So natural. They're dirty, I hear, and live without much ventilation. People say they stink—I didn't notice it myself. But it was like going back 10,000 years.

Thirty years ago, Dr. Peters told me, there were no roads to speak of out here. Trips that take a day now took four days then—and one had to carry food and water always. If one were hungry one could go to a ranch and help oneself to whatever food he found—the owners often being away—but the law of the land required that you leave money on the table—*and wash the dishes*. By automobile one could make about forty miles a day, fording streams, going backwards uphill, etc. When you hear such things you realize what a vast change has come about. But only on the paved roads! I can see myself what a desolate wild country it is just looking to right and left. The Indians were given all the badlands of America. I have been studying the big Indian map the Indian Bureau gave me. It's a pretty story. Right now I am on the edge of a great square, which embraces part of four states, and which is the most arid, unpopulated—and even unexplored!—region in America. This is the heart of the Indian country.

I bought two more tires today, to replace the bad spares. I don't want to run any risk going through the deserted Navajo country in Arizona and Utah. Sometimes there is not a town or gasoline station for over a hundred miles. And I don't think the Navajos worry much if a white man's car breaks down in their territory. You can die of cold or heat or thirst in this region without anybody knowing of it. It's exciting.

This altitude and climate is fine for me. I have lots of energy and work well. As soon as things go smoothly I'm O.K. It's a moral lesson I'm learning. What a relief it will be when I am through with this trip, this book. I won't want to write again, or hear from publishers and agents, for a good long while. If I get to Mexico I'll just take it easy and do nothing—mañana, that suits me. What I'll do then is sit down and read all you've written these last few years. That will occupy me for a long while, I think.

HVM

Albuquerque, Thursday, 24th
[April, 1941]

ANAÏS,

Just got your letter—the mails are slow, I think. You seem worried about the American book. Don't let it disturb you—that's just the preamble. I will have seven months now in which to put it all down, and when I get through it will come out all right. I am now on the piece for Laughlin—I am making it the story about that "unhappy man" in New Orleans, the story I told you.* It belonged in the book for D.D. & Co., but I have lots of material and this ought to

---

* "The Alcoholic Veteran With the Washboard Cranium," published in *The Wisdom of the Heart*, New Directions, November 1941.

make a good narrative. Once I get that off I am free to think only of this present book—a great relief.

Volkening hasn't said anything to me about waiting for further material before giving the 60 pages to *Atlantic Monthly*. I won't have another batch for a couple of weeks.

I am getting wise now, as to how to proceed. Make a jump of a few hundred miles, to some good spot, and then stay a few days or a week and write. I can see my way clear now. I am in the heart of the West. And I know what I want to put in the book. Naturally most people are not going to like it. I expect that. But there are plenty who will. And in any case I don't care one way or the other. I am not staying in America to receive their praise or blame. This trip winds up my life in America, that's definite. All I look forward to is a good easy rhythm, to work on the future Capricorns in peace and quiet somewhere, in a foreign land. After that, and after the Lawrence book is finished, I have nothing more to write. I retire. So far as American opinion is concerned I am blithe and serene. I believe Lafe will print all the Paris books in due time—and if he fails, someone else will come along, it is inevitable. I met a publisher here who would like to do the Greek book, but I am holding him off until Volkening exhausts the "commercial" ones. Meanwhile I am giving him Durrell's poems —he likes to print poetry—and is not interested in making money.

I saw the N.R. [*New Republic*] review etc. Typical of the communist-minded youngsters. Pathetic, in the last analysis. Such a feeble groping, stabs in the dark. Paul Rosenfeld said wonderful things about the Greek book—I liked that more than any criticism I've ever received. He hit it on the head.

Also, you mustn't think because I tell you the truth about my reactions that I find the trip insupportable. I don't look forward to enjoy myself. Only to get done with it. I could tell that there would be nothing ten days after I started out. Only the scenery is compensating. Around here it is quite magnificent. The mountains are bare, rocky, scintillating—rising up to 12,000 feet and covered with snow. There are less than 500,000 people in the whole state. The best country is always where there are the least people. Only the Indians and Mexicans have the sense to live it out here, to take root, to find a life for themselves. It will all revert to them again, I am sure. This continent for the white people is doomed. I would like to write a prophecy and bury it in a vault for some one to dig up 500 years from now.

About help—no, I can't look for help from the regular ones—but I do know for certain I will always receive help from the abnormal ones like myself. I meet just enough of them as I go along to convince me that they exist. Our lives don't fit into general patterns. We have a little world and one that suits us. I wouldn't want it any different. Honestly, I don't care a rap any more even if I am totally ignored and forgotten.

I don't doubt that it would have been better to have learned to accept America, but I can't rise above my limitations. I urged you to read the life of Ramakrishna because he is the exact opposite of me, and I admire him no end. But I am not that great. You must read both books—the other, too, on Vivekananda, an heroic character. His journeys thru India are simply unbelievable. I actually wept with joy in the train on reading it. And I am going to write about it. I found in the book one passage about the 24 Buddhas who had preceded the great Gautama—that passage marks the high-water mark in the view of humanity. It's about the greatest men who are unknown. More of this later.

The whole point is, I suppose, that I am only here physically. My mind is on other things, on a wholly different life. This is like living thru a bad Karma, voluntarily. What I am getting out of the trip is not anything from America, but soliloquies with myself. Confirmations and affirmations. And then too you must remember that the book was intended to be purely subjective and personal. I am not trying to give a picture of America as it is—that has been done by others. I am just giving my own personal reaction to the scene. The average American knows more about America than I ever will.

The great lesson I've learned is to be careful hereafter about what I desire to do or have. All prayers are answered. One must think twice before asking.

HVM

Albuquerque
April 28th [1941], Monday

ANAÏS,

I'm leaving for the Grand Canyon, Arizona, tomorrow. There is a post office by that name there and I'll look for mail there for a

week or so to come. It'll take me two or three days to get there. I will
be crossing the Great Divide day after tomorrow. For me a big event!
Once over that crest the rivers flow the other way, toward the Pacific
Ocean. I'll be dropping down a bit in altitude too. My plan is to stay
a week there, writing and making little trips around the Canyon,
which I love—next to Tibet the greatest spot on earth—and then I
will work up toward Utah, into Zion Park and over east again into
Colorado, to Mesa Verde, where there are great abandoned cliff
dwellings, thousands of them. I can't get up that way now as the roads
are blocked with snow and ice. Nor can I do any exploring in the
Indian country here in New Mexico, because of the rains. To reach
their places you have to leave the paved roads—and I am warned by
everyone not to risk it as the clay soil has no bottom and there are
quicksands which just devour you car and all. This is a wild state.
The roads are like little threads of mercury. Off them it is savage.
The Indians are well protected. But I may swing around here again
in a month or two.

The car has been tuned up to perfection, as far as one can tell. All
the garage people say "it's a nice automobile," meaning it runs beautifully. I have a two-gallon tin full of water in case she heats up going
over the big ridges. Tested her out this morning—was up at six—thru
the Tijeras Pass or Canyon east of here. Beautiful drive for twenty
miles thru movie scenery. See little shepherd boys with goats and men
on horseback with ten-gallon hats, boots and spurs. Nothing but
huge wild desolation, drying rivers that look like condensed milk in
the red clay. Very much like parts of Greece on the whole—all except the towns and people. There is the rub!

Yes, I read about the Greek campaign. As the Germans neared
Athens it was all very familiar terrain to me. Mt. Kyteron, Thebes,
Corinth, Missilonghi, etc. I mentioned these places in the book. And
I remember too describing certain murderous passes which had undoubtedly been defended against the Medes and Parthians and Per-
sians. The worst thing about it is that England so obviously "used"
the Greeks—and the Australians. They never fight till the last man,
you notice. Always a safe withdrawal. Now Greece has to swallow the
bitter pill, while the English fight on elsewhere, defending their indefensible possessions.

Well, I finished the two articles and am deep in the Laughlin narrative now. I'll be all set to write the American book with ease and grace now. I feel immensely relieved.

I hope to be able to last till the 10th *without* calling on you for help.

Abramson never sent me any money, but I guess I can expect something once the *World of Sex* is out. He said I could earn between three and four hundred dollars on it.

More soon.

HVM

Cameron, Arizona

April 30th, 1941

ANAÏS—

Am only about 60 miles or so now from Grand Canyon. Arrived here toward sundown, having started out this morning at a quarter to six without breakfast, driving thru the Petrified Forest. The country gets wilder and grander—no more white man's land—pure Indian country. No wonder the French writers described it as "too grand." It's terrifying. It's just about as close to being on an extinct— or *almost* extinct—planet as you can imagine. I am up since yesterday well over 6000 ft. Sometimes climb higher and drop again. At 8:00 this morning—in cool weather—I had to wait to let the radiator cool down. Again this afternoon—when it was actually chilly—after the gauge had dropped *below* normal. Rose 40 degrees climbing long steep slopes. When I left Flagstaff, Ariz. at 5 o'clock and realized ten miles out of town what sort of country I was going into alone—with hardly a car passing me—I almost turned back. But it was worth the risk. Wine-colored mountains, mesas looking like sponges dipped in rat poison, chocolate frappé landscapes, a pea-green vegetation clinging desperately to volcanic soil. San Francisco Mt. looming up and dominating everything—snow-capped all year round—12,600 ft. high. Not a soul in sight—nor bird, nor animal. Horizon stretches away for hundred miles.

I came rolling in to Cameron on roller skates. Found it nothing but a trading post with tourist lodges and hotel. *No population whatever!* Just like Ducktown, Tenn.—only wilder. Indians living at side of road in their hogans—the most primitive round hut imaginable. Beautiful spotted mustangs coming out of nowhere. The Little Colorado River swirling under a high bridge—all red and swollen and moving between red volcanic rocks in a deep gorge. You look down the winding road for 40 miles—nothing in sight. Well, it's stupendous, awesome, devastating. It's like a preview of this Earth 50,000,000 years hence. This is really "bad land," as is nearly all the country for 5000 square miles or more. Last night at the edge of the Painted Desert— same impressions. Nothing out there in that tremendous wasteland of gorgeous colors but petrified trees, rattlesnakes etc. For the Indians to have survived is almost incredible. I can see them patiently awaiting our passing. All that is east of the Mississippi (and see how crowded it seems) is but a tiny vestibule to this. Two-thirds of America lies west of the Mississippi. And this 2/3 is the toughest land any one could ask for. It's heartbreaking. Of course there's verdant California—a strip of it—and the irrigated desert country etc. But New Mexico, Arizona, Montana, Idaho, Wyoming, South Dakota, etc.!!! Tomorrow the grandiose will reach its apotheosis at Grand Canyon. The river gorge here is about 300 ft. deep and looks impressive in its moonlike desolation. But at Grand Canyon it is *one mile* deep!!

There are some stretches I've ridden which I'll surely never forget. From Tucumcari to Albuquerque is one—first glimpse of the "enchanted land"—the fabulous land which drove the Spaniards mad. Today was another great event—from Winslow to Flagstaff, and again from Flagstaff to here. The vistas are so tremendous, the earth so weird-looking, the formations so topsy-turvy, that when I pulled in here I was actually dazed. The left side of my face looks like a raw steak. And doing it alone in a big car on lonely roads in lonely lands —well, it just does something indescribable to you. Sometimes I think of nothing but how I will sleep if I'm stuck between places. How I'll curl up in the back seat and wait for morning.

Just about 30 miles from here suddenly 3 cowboys on marvelous horses dashed across the road—off into space—like phantoms. Indians appear and disappear—all sudden and miraculous. They haunt the country like ghosts—living out of sight. And even so we are now snooping into their private life—their very souls. I feel ashamed even to approach one. They must loathe us.

HVM

Grand Canyon, Ariz.
May 1st [1941]

Got here about 10:30 this morning and found a good room at reasonable rates at the Bright Angel Lodge right on the rim of the Canyon.

First glimpses of canyon superb—no deception, no letdown. In fact I *trembled* looking into it and got to laughing. I took a room for a week. I may stretch it out to ten days, as that would give you the chance to send me something here, before I begin the next leg of my journey. I've got $55.00 in my pocket now.

It's 6800 feet up here. I feel it, but not as much as at Santa Fe which was 7200 feet.

I finished up all the pills. Am still using the drops. Will ease off gradually. More tomorrow.

HVM

Grand Canyon, Arizona
Saturday—May 3rd [1941]

ANAÏS—

Just got your letter—gets here quicker than the mail from across the canyon, ten miles distant. That takes 4 days, going thru 4 states!! No birds fly across it, no animals cross it either. Strange phenomenon. Well, it's one of the places on earth I dearly wanted to see. It's no letdown. The rocks are so cut as to resemble the façades of Hindu or Siamese temples. Some of the rocks which jut up alone and isolate are named after ancient temples. It is a tremendous drama of geology. I'll send you a little book on it soon—it's fascinating. Now it's pouring (we've had unusual weather in this country where it's so dry) and the canyon is steaming—like a huge caldron. At night, when you can see nothing, it is awesome. You *feel* this big hole—a mile deep. I haven't been down it yet—afraid to walk it because I might not get up—it's like climbing up five Empire State Buildings. To ride down on a mule costs six bucks. I'd like to live down at the bottom for a week or so. Only Indians could live in such a place.

Well, I'm just about through with the piece for Laughlin. Hoping and hoping I'll get money from him and *Town and Country* and Abramson and the Greek book. Hoping. Today a letter saying Random House had rejected Greek book—"too late"! It's maddening. First it was "too early."

I'll leave Wednesday—for Hollywood, a trip of two or three days, I imagine. When I reach San Francisco, if things look bad, I'll call the trip off, sell the car for whatever I can get and come back by bus in easy stages.

I'll write a good book nevertheless, I feel. Despite everything, it was important to see the country. To touch it and smell it. I suppose if you're an artist you're never satisfied until you do. That's the difference between the artist and the sage. I'm between the two now—I know it. I can't help it.

Of course I realize the change that is coming. I ask nothing better than to sit down and live simply. I hope in Mexico. I live simply now —it's only the traveling that makes it expensive. I know how to go without and not feel disoriented. I don't even miss the movies. And I never take a drink. My indulgences are cigarettes and stamps. In a way it's a great discipline. And being alone is another kind of discipline.

Moreover, with me nothing is lost or wasted. The trip will bear fruits, I'm positive of it.

HVM

Grand Canyon
Wednesday—May 7th, 1941

ANAÏS—

Am going to the telegraph office in a few minutes to see if there isn't a message from you. Beginning to wonder if you got my last letter—I posted it Saturday, I believe. Anyway, I'm merely waiting to hear from you before moving on. Have done a big lick of work here—am all cleaned up on back stuff (including even the "epitaph" on Sherwood Anderson for *Story* magazine *). Am into the next section of the American book and going strong. Will surely have a 3rd batch ready for R. & V. [Russell and Volkening] in the next few days.

---

* "Anderson the Story Teller," *Story*, New York, Sept.–Oct. 1941.

I wish I could leave tomorrow morning. I'm mentally set for the move. Have had all I want of this place. I didn't get down *in* the Canyon— just walked and drove around the rim, viewing it from all angles in all sorts of atmospheric conditions. It changes perpetually, like a chameleon. Haven't spoken to a soul since I left Albuquerque—until yesterday noon, when "a desert rat" seated himself at my table. That's a little chapter for the book.* The best talk I've had with anyone since leaving New York. All I told you of my intuitions about the Indians —the reconquest of America, etc.—he confirmed. He knows them— lived with them. Is a solitary prospector in the desert near Barstow, Cal. And a mystic and philosopher. Talked about the stars, the rocks, the earth history, the food in the air, the fossils (of camels, tigers, giant ferns, starfish, sponges, etc.) in the rocks of the highest mountains. A real communion. And at the end he apologized for "not being educated." I learned more from him than from all the professors.

Also, I gave up *all* medicines about 3 days ago—and, oddly enuf, I feel better and *urinate less*. Must be psychological too—the result of catching up with the work and feeling free to breathe a good easy deep breath again. The book will now advance by leaps and bounds. I've got a shark's hold on it now! And on myself too, I believe. I have some vitamin E tablets left—does anybody want them?

I sent you a [Henry de] Montherlant book—given me by Mrs. Knopf. I didn't read it—just glanced at it here and there. Ruder may like it—I don't—not now. Too machinatory. I'll be sending you a strange book on Mexico shortly, which Patchen gave me. When you're thru with it would you please send it to Alfred Perlès. You will get a different picture of Mexico in this book than I imagine you now have. I think he's a bit screwy—like Céline—and a queer, rabid English Catholic. But some of it must be true—the mosquitoes, the bad food, the stagnation, the violence, the treachery. That "treacherous smile and embrace"—sounds familiar to me. And the hysterical smile! What surprises me is that Mexico City itself is so badly painted.

I see you returned the two books to the Swami. (One I was to keep! But I've explained.) No comment from you on Ramakrishna. Perhaps you weren't in the right mood for it. Or else I recommended it too strongly.

---

* See the chapter "A Desert Rat," in *The Air-Conditioned Nightmare*.

I notice you say in a letter that you took out the "spit" etc. in my Ms. I was just rereading the 60 pages. Saw nothing wrong. Especially there—if it was at the Mecca Apts, Chicago. Very fitting, on the contrary. You can't imagine what it was like! Well, I'll have a chance to put it back in again in the book version—if you haven't convinced me by that time!

The symposium on Greece appeared—have you seen it? Maybe Miss Steloff has copies. *Greece 1821–1941,* it's called.* Paper-covered, like a review. I'm in *the* most respectable company this time. A surprise for you (therein) will be Klaus Mann's article—it's really superb. Far better than Thomas Mann's!

I'm off to Hollywood soon as I get your message. It's about a two-day run to Hollywood. I'll be glad to get down to sea level again. 7,000 feet is a bad altitude (Mexico City too!). I can stand 5,000 (Denver & Albuquerque) O.K. But not much above. Makes you gasp, bleed, blow your nose incessantly, gives headaches etc. How will I ever stand the Himalayas? They're 10 to 20,000 feet up! . . . Have a lot of people to look up in Hollywood. Ought to save on meals at least!

The sky now is perfect here—especially toward sunset. That electric blue I first noticed in Greece. And the stars at night like pinpricks on a cloth of unseizable velvet. The canyon itself is covered with green, a faded Byzantine green, of suede. Striking. I don't go into it in a letter because I want to write about it at length. I'm grateful to have seen it. One of the wonders of the universe. General Delivery, then, *Hollywood.*

HVM

P. S. It will be a long long while before an American *Army* ever lands on the Continent. But the war is getting closer every minute. Same old story.

---

* Published by the American Friends of Greece, in support of the Greek War Relief Organization, the pamphlet contains addresses and comments by politicians and writers, including Klaus Mann's "Homage to Greece," and an excerpt from Miller's *Colossus,* "The Spell of Peace," recalling his visit to Epidauros.

Hollywood, California
Monday, 12th, 7:00 P.M. [May, 1941]

ANAÏS—

Here's where I am for the time being—excellent $2.00 a day bright spanking vulgar Hollywood hotel. If I get invited to stay somewhere as a guest, I'll probably accept, in order to economize. Use this only in case of a telegram. Volkening is holding up my mail—not sure of this address. Please phone him, will you, to forward me everything c/o *General Delivery, Hollywood, Cal.* It'll save writing him.

Arrived on the outskirts of town about 7:00 P.M. last night, with only one lamp burning, so stopped in suburb of Burbank. Had been going from 4:30 A.M.—from Needles, Cal. (below sea level). Had left Grand Canyon at 9:30 A.M. soon as I got your telegraphic dispatch. I dropped from *over 8,000 ft.* to below sea level in a long hard ride thru great changes—fantasmagorical!! I will describe it all in a long letter—it was epic. The next day particularly—Sunday. Awoke at 3:30 A.M. Temperature had fallen in night, after midnight, from over 100° to about 80°—felt cool. At about 6:00 A.M. it was around 95°, I should say. After that it was just an inferno—150 miles of desert—unforgettable! The car so hot that I not only had to stop (in the roaring blinding heat) and let it simmer down a bit, but the heat causes a vacuum and gas doesn't work properly—result, I had to crawl along for about 75 miles at *25 miles* an hour. The last 2 hours of the ride marvelous. Rose to nearly 5,000 feet amidst snow-covered pasteboard Sierra Nevadas—staggering and grandiose—like all California coming at you with a rush. Raced along on broad, curving, long sweeps —in a millrace of Sunday traffic—heat sweltering, everybody out for air—mountains almost invisible in heat at times—just pink snow floating in heaven etc. etc. Too tired now to give it all. Just had a 3-hour nap.

I tell you, to go from Arkansas to the coast on Highway 66 is to do a Homeric voyage. Reminded me of that caravan trip in *Grapes of Wrath*. Because with an old car it's utterly different than in a new one. You taste the trip fully. Glad I did it this way. I know every inch of the road. I was so tired and exalted last 2 days that I couldn't eat— only drink, drink, drink. My coat was loose—normally I can't button it. Must have lost 8 to 10 pounds. The anxiety of getting stuck in any of these places from Grand Canyon on was terrific. To be hauled in these spots can cost from $50.00 to $100.00!! I just drove like mad, not caring if the bottom fell out so long as I reached my destination. Saturday night, within 2 hours of destination—*Needles!*—I suddenly was faced with the worst mountain pass on the whole trip. I waited till sun was setting and started over. Wonderful—I'm still thrilled. Dangerous, sharp, steep curves in the midst of a crazy world. Cars already blazing with headlights. Over the top a fierce descent—like some Coney Island invention. Night falling quick—and instead of coolth a greater heat—dropping to below sea level. In the dark for an hour like swimming thru warm horse piss—and then overpowering fragrance of desert blooms. Arrived quite giddy—more of it and one could go plumb daffy. I must write it out in detail and maybe use it for book.* Tho' I suppose others take it breezily.

This place is just as one imagines—maybe better. Terribly new, self-conscious, efficient etc. See so many faces I *think* I know—probably do!

Going to try to eat solid food now. May go to a cinema—like taking coals to Newcastle. Tell Volkening I believe I got everything so far. More pages for him from here.

HVM

P. S. As for my old trouble it's gone—gone with the real sweat and anxiety. To cure neurosis put patient into great danger—that cures everything.

Hollywood, Cal.
May 16th [1941]
(Friday)

ANAÏS—

No word from you since the first day I arrived—hope nothing is wrong. The mail goes to the central P.O. in Los Angeles, ten miles away—but it's all right to address it c/o General Delivery, Hollywood—all my mail comes addressed that way.

No time yet to write you the long letter about my trip. Just re-

---

* See chapter "From Grand Canyon to Burbank" in *The Air-Conditioned Nightmare*.

wrote the Anderson article for Rosenfeld—quite a job. And have added more pages to the American book. It will be 50 or 60 pages easily, this next batch.

Have met just a few people—may see Miriam Hopkins this afternoon at a cocktail hour chez a Bernadine Fritz, a woman from China (on *The China Critic*) who knew Emily Hahn (of *T'ien Hsia*) well— ten years there. She has a wonderful Chinese home here—deluxe!

I met [Dane] Rudhyar and his wife too. Seeing them again Sunday for lunch. Very much like his books. Speaks with a strong and peculiar French accent—almost Germanic. We got on well. He asked all about you.

Best event was seeing the movie called *Citizen Kane* by Orson Welles—*you must see it!* It's remarkable—and different.

I may be seeing Hiler tonight. He's still here. Met Jake Zeitlin, who has a fine rare books shop here. Immediately phoned Aldous Huxley to have me meet him. I go Tuesday with Zeitlin—to Santa Monica where Huxley lives. Z. says that Huxley is a very great admirer of my style—*he* isn't. But just the same, before I left, he was on the verge of taking the Greek book. Says it's *too long* for him.

I had a letter from Caresse—from "The Shadows," New Iberia. Staying with Weeks Hall. Said [Harry] Bull [of *Town and Country* magazine] had sent her and his wife to see the place. I hope that means he is taking my article. Haven't received my mail from R. & V. yet. They sent it ordinary mail—which takes about five days.

Patchen sent me five dollars—out of a clear sky. Said a rich woman had put up $500.00 and Slocum the other $500.00. And practically all the deluxe copies subscribed to already. Rather good. You see what might happen once you decide to do the Diary yourself. I think it was my blurb which really helped to put his book over. I can do it for you too. Don't lose heart.

Rushing with this to P.O. now. More very soon. I do hope there's nothing wrong. I'm getting anxious about you.

HVM

P. S. I think you'd like Hollywood. It's terribly new and full of dazzling shops. And cheap to live in, eat in, etc. Surprisingly so. I've had excellent meals for 50 & 60 cents. Glass legs with ferns and goldfish in them—to advertise Nylon Stockings. And signs everywhere saying —"Personal guide to conduct you thru the homes of the stars!" (Sic)

[May 19, 1941]
Monday, Hollywood

ANAÏS,

Still no time for the big letter. Rushed with appointments. This morning went through the R.K.O. Studios and saw five different sets in operation. Exactly as one imagines it—a terrible grind, repeatedly doing the thing over, like automatons. The cameramen are everything —the actors nothing. It's anything but glamorous. You feel sorry for them—they're like performing mice.

Find I'm well known by all the scriptwriters, directors, etc. and even by many of the actors. Received all sorts of compliments, auto-graphed a lot of copies—and of a pirated *Capricorn*(!) too—don't know who brought it out or where. Joseph von Sternberg, the director, has an erotica collection worth $100,000.00. Erotica goes here. I think I may have the bookshop man for you—I'm mulling it over, how to present the idea to him.

Volkening writes that Bull is sending a check for the Weeks Hall story, which he likes.* I'll get about a hundred dollars out of it, after deductions. Told V. to wire it to me soon as he gets it. I think too I'll get the $25.00 from *Story* before I leave here. And maybe a hundred from Laughlin. I'm to see him tonight here—he wrote and asked to see me—wants to "bury the hatchet," he says. But if all these fail momentarily to come through, why then you'll have to send me something on the 25th. But if I get Bull's alone I'll wire you "everything fine" or something like that, meaning *not* to send anything, with new address, and move on. Guess it will be San Francisco next, though I'm not sure. May stop off in between at Big Sur about which Robinson Jeffers wrote—the wildest part of the Pacific Coast.

Saw Rudhyar again yesterday for lunch, and his wife too. He's leaving this week for Texas. Seems very fond of me and trying to get me to promise to meet him in Santa Fe for the Indian festivals this August or September.

Had an offer of a job doing script work here, but promptly refused. Terrible world here—the movies, I mean. Hollow as sawdust. The real men are the technicians—they are really geniuses. It's all technique. The human element is just nil.

---

* "The Shadows," published in *Town & Country*, March 1942.

Haven't met any of the stars yet. No answers. Guess I won't see any of them. Saw Ginger Rogers rehearsing a scene this morning—her voice sounds utterly different from the movies.

Well, I see Huxley tomorrow and perhaps Isherwood and perhaps Gerald Heard too. Hiler is in Frisco at the moment. His father is there—and beckoning him as usual.

HVM

[San Francisco, June 8, 1941]
Sunday

ANAÏS—

Arrived yesterday morning from near Carmel—in Saturday traffic—terrific. City of tremendous steep hills—magnificent location —a sort of Naples. Lucky I didn't see Jeffers—just got your telegram at Carmel and dashed off. Didn't like the looks of the place—so arty.

This morning I got all my mail. Wm. Roth of Colt Press writes he wants the Greek book *—he had traveled very much as I did thru Greece—but on bicycle. I just wrote him to look you up—regarding your own work—he is in N. Y. now.

Hollywood was an oasis—because there one touches Europe again —thru all the émigrés.

But from L.A. to here passed thru marvelous country again—all golden hills—a Spanish country, I should say. It belongs to the Mexicans. And when you come upon one of the old missions you know it still belongs to them. Around Carmel it's marvelous too. *That* I can't deny.

I am more detached than you think. After all, I don't think of staying in America. But every experience, when you see it thru, yields something. The little people I've met were the best. One could make something of them—they are unspoiled. And they really belong in

---

* The manuscript of *The Colossus of Maroussi,* which Miller completed before he started his trip, had been making the rounds of commercial publishers unsuccessfully. William Roth, a small and independent publisher in San Francisco, had read the manuscript during a visit to New York and offered to publish the book.

the same world as the interesting people—it's in between where all is rotten and dead. Out here the rich are horrible—worse than any place I've seen. Predatory and medieval—loutish, brutal, drunken imbeciles. But I'm just a witness to it all.

Lafe is in Mexico—suffering from altitude—but likes it. Met Fraenkel and disliked him. Says he has "no faith." Lafe writes very good letters. I like him.

O'Neill lives near here. May be seeing him. Saroyan is the whole show, apparently. This city is like N.Y. in atmosphere. Electrical. And quite cosmopolitan. Big too. I'll be here ten days surely, I think, so if you want to mail Ms. why O.K. I'm getting the carbon retyped.

You know, I don't agree with you about *Citizen Kane.* "Rosebud" was only a device to hang the thing on. But "Rosebud" (on that Cocteau sleigh) stood, as I see it, for the love he was denied as a child and hence could never give. I thought the girl wonderful—that cracked childlike voice, making the emptiness still emptier. Orson Welles knows it. I met the actor, incidentally, who asked for the cigar. Well, we won't go into that now. I'm rereading Duhamel on America —the book you never liked. But he is terribly accurate in his diagnosis! [*Scènes de la Vie Future,* 1930.]

Am going to write some more pages here. You don't need to read them—better not. Read them years later in some other country. I feel very well equilibrated now about it. I crossed the Great Divide somewhere and am on a plateau now. Here it's cool—have to wear an overcoat at night. Different climate from Southern California. It's wonderful to be in sunshine continually, as down there. When you leave San Diego for Mexico you enter another world. Reminded me of Greece, Spain, Sicily—forbidding grandeur—empty—exciting. Something evil about it and mysterious. Mexico must be all the things everyone tell you about it—but above all violent, treacherous, deadly, malevolent. The women in Tijuana at the bars—hard and soft at same time. Whores of course. But violent ones. And the men like desperadoes, thugs, bandits. Gives you a shivery feeling.

And sure enuf, after eating a salad I got the diarrhea—still have it, but passing. I thought I would disregard the American warnings. But the poison is there. Yet I did enjoy that meal—like a cheap French restaurant.

HVM

P. S. The theatricality of the film was again a device to keep you conscious—to kill the "drugged spell" of the movies, as I see it. You participate and collaborate.

[June 9, 1941]
Monday, San Francisco

ANAÏS—

Just got your letter and extra carbon which I'm shipping off to have retyped.

Haven't yet received the pages sent by express, but suppose that travels more slowly.

Hope you meet Wm. Roth of the Colt Press. He's shy and slow, I understand. But honest and loyal—and, I think, intelligent.

Don't know what my plans are yet. A little bewildered by the enormity and strangeness of this city. Gets you winded to walk about—nothing but huge steep hills.

You say Dorothy Norman is taking a fragment of the Greek book [for *Twice A Year*]. Funny, V. [Volkening] wrote she wasn't. Let me know if it's true. I may be short of cash by the 25th of this month. Just laid out ten dollars for new glasses—lost a pair at a tourist court coming up here. First object I've lost so far.

I was going to send you a postcard from Gonzales, Cal. which I passed the other day, but it was too early in the morning—all the stores were closed. When I travel now I'm often up at 5 o'clock. I love the countryside. Hollywood was ideally located—from every standpoint.

More soon. Still answering mail.

HVM

June 24th [1941]
Pismo Beach, Cal.

ANAÏS—

Stopped here last night on my way back to Hollywood. Have had a wonderful long weekend, met some highly interesting people—

poets and musicians chiefly—and one saintly fellow of great charm, a biologist who is the friend of John Steinbeck.* Steinbeck himself I am not so sure I like—a bit like Cendrars—touchy, etc. A huge bulk of a fellow, looking like a deep sea fisherman and trying his best to make things pleasant for us.

We went thru the most superb country of all varieties of landscape. Took the famous ocean route from Monterey to San Luis Obispo, along the wild ocean front and passing Hearst's big château which looks or reminds one vividly of the shot in Orson Welles' picture.** I can't speak highly enuf of the scenery and climate. The coast is full of soldiers now—army trucks everywhere. You would think we were at war already. Reminds me of pictures of Germany (in Paris) when she was getting ready.

I suppose there will be a lot of mail waiting for me when I get back to town.

I keep thinking what a pity it is to be obliged to live in the East. This country has the climate and landscape you would love. About the people, that's another thing. In general bad—but you *can* meet the exceptional one here.

I will write again soon as I get your mail. I didn't go to see [Robinson] Jeffers—thought it better not to, but he knows I'm out here and was looking forward to my visit, I was told. Found a bookshop in Fresno which handled pirated editions of *Capricorn* and *Black Spring* published in China—sailors bring them in!

HVM

Hollywood, Calif. 6/26/41

ANAÏS,
    Got your batch of letters all at once.

I'll stay on here another week, I guess, and then strike out for the East—with the car, I imagine. Or I may sell it and come by train. I'm undecided. Haven't heard anything from Roth or Volkening yet about contract and advance on Greek book. *Town and Country* rejected the Ms. on Dr. Souchon. *Hamlet* Vol. II is out, looks good, and is selling

---

* E. F. Ricketts.
** *Citizen Kane.*

quite well already. I'm glad I wrote that book—everyone was dubious of it, but I find it good.

The thought of New York seems horrible after the splendid country I see out here. This last trip was marvelous. I almost got the feeling I had in Greece—except that here nothing is *sacred*.

The Bunuel program sounds interesting. Hope he can get revived. You think you'll like Provincetown? I always heard it *was* very arty. Dos Passos lives there.

I met a disciple of [Edgar] Varèse's—John Cage of San Francisco —very fine young man. Was interested in Bunuel, oddly enough. Steinbeck's friend (Ed Ricketts) also interested me greatly.

The West gave me a temporary hopeful feeling—may be delusory. At bottom America kills everything—but between the East and West there is a great difference. I have a feeling D.D. & Co. won't take my book—a hunch. That gives me an uneasy feeling. And Decatur Street again! Every time I break away I feel completely divorced from that past—and then it comes back at me again, like a trap.* I was in hopes of bigger, better things, that's all.

HENRY

1835 Camino Palermo
Hollywood
c/o David Commons
July 15th [1941]

ANAÏS—

Just moved to the new address above—a private place, two rooms and bath, over a garage—seven dollars a week. Wonderful place to work in and a beautiful part of Hollywood, on a street lined with fat, gigantic palms. The above chap is a scriptwriter—had been a dress manufacturer—from N.Y. If any mail comes to the hotel meanwhile it will be forwarded.

I feel a lot better in this joint. Have to walk a mile or so to the

---

* In 1901, when Miller was ten, his family had moved from 662 Driggs Avenue, in Brooklyn's 14th Ward, to 1063 Decatur Street, in the Bushwick section of Brooklyn, which Miller referred to later as "the street of early sorrows," since it marked a radical change from his earlier childhood.

restaurant three times a day—just what I want. I also have an open invitation to use a fellow's bungalow at the beach—Santa Monica— about 15 miles away. Hope now to go swimming in the mornings regularly. Incidentally, this fellow at the beach runs a radio program for the Beverly Hills Library. Asked me to give a talk on censorship —but I refused. I heard my own voice for the first time in 25 years the other day and was pleasantly surprised. Made a record, two sides, at Man Ray's house. What surprised me was the guttural quality—like a big bear humming to himself. One side I read off from Breton's *Nadja,* in English—the other was impromptu and much better. I can hear now how I have aged—like a wine cask.

I got the money for the Greek book—about 88 dollars. Am O.K. then. Also got a little "token" payment from Ben Abramson. I think he'll do a second book soon. Seems to me both *Hamlet* and *W. of S.* * are doing well. John Barrymore told one of the bookshops that the *Hamlet* was marvelous—that everybody should read it. I was quite surprised. I thought, being a ham actor, he'd resent what I said about Shakespeare.

From the hills—and I am on rising ground now—Hollywood looks quite different at night than any other big city I know. Or rather Los Angeles. The lights are more fairylike, as on the bridges over the Seine. By day the mountains are enveloped in a deep haze—you can barely see them, though they are very close. Must be the heat and the ocean nearby.

Well, I'm waiting to get a letter from you. Tell me more about Provincetown. Must be somewhat like [John] Marin's water colors, no? A bare rocky coast? And how is the town itself—isn't it full of Portuguese fishermen? Out here the foreign element is Mexican. The young girls, under twenty, are very beautiful—make the silly American girls look sick. But the Mexicans are treated like dirt. Lafe is at Chapala now and enjoying it. Is writing a book to me—*Letters from Chapala*—says he has already written 10,000 words. Wasn't it in Chapala that Lawrence wrote *The Plumed Serpent?*

Yesterday was exactly two years ago that I left France—at Marseille, you remember? Fluchère writes me now and then; evidently things are not so bad there. Did I tell you that the Swami here is a most wonderful man? In five minutes with him I got more than I

---

* *Hamlet,* Vol. 2, published June, 1941, Carrefour, New York; *World of Sex,* published by Ben Abramson, Argus Book Shop, Chicago, 1941.

could get from another man in years. I go once in a while to the little
temple he built beside his house—and meditate. More soon.

HVM

P. S. Gilbert Neiman * said you must be the most "aware" person
imaginable—got it all from the *House of Incest*. Said amazing things
about it. Spoke of your "mask"—your "dualities," etc.

[July 21, 1941]
Hollywood, Monday

ANAÏS—
        Nothing much new, except for the enclosed letter from Larry
[Lawrence Durrell] which just came—dated May 21st! I wonder
where they are now. I am going to write a note to him at this address,
but doubt if he will still be there. You notice he says Katsimbalis is a
prisoner.**

I just had two telegrams from Miriam Hopkins who suddenly discovered my address. Says she tried to reach me some time ago but the
hotel left no address, etc. Anyway I am to see her in a few days.
Sounded English over the telephone—very bright and breezy—alert-
minded, as in the pictures.

Glad you are making the most of it at the beach. But this is the
climate that would have appealed to you. It is continuously warm,
sunny, southern—in fact, if it keeps up, the bright monotony will
drive you nuts. I will appreciate a rainstorm when it happens. Recently in the eastern part of the state there was a cloudburst, creating
a wall of water 10 feet high and 100 feet wide which drowned men,
cars, horses, houses, everything.

Last night at a Hawaiian eating place I met a Reichel—a Czech
married to a crazy-looking Spanish woman—he is in the movies—was
a great character actor like Lon Chaney. Because I mentioned the
word "documentary" (films) he came back after driving home to talk

---

* See Biographical Notes.
** George Katsimbalis, the Greek poet, served as the model for *The Colossus
of Maroussi*.

to me alone. Told me of a great Chinese documentaire now showing here. The woman looked like the crazy red queen in *Alice in Wonderland*—white hair, crazy hat, big rings, astrological and psychic. The most incongruous pair I ever met. Later the owner came up and asked me if I had written *Tropic of C.*— He had read it. Another conversation.

HVM

P. S. Did you ever read about the life of the Marquis de Sade? Sounds interesting. But the books, no! Perversion is dull, I think.

[July 28, 1941]
Hollywood, Monday

ANAÏS—

　　Para ir a Mexico lo primero que necesito es apprender el Español.

Had my second lesson only yesterday. Typical Spanish behavior. "I will come every day, Henry, at 6:00 o'clock." And then no sign of him for four days. Thought he was ill. But he's a fine chap, Señor Rivas, and if we go to Mexico I will have some good addresses. This time I am serious about learning Spanish. I feel I will like it. I like that expression—*"no tengo ganas"*—so much better than the English equivalent.

The Spaniards, I feel, must be something like the Russians—in their clinging, getting into your hair, etc. Get intimate with you immediately. And forget about you the moment they turn their back. No?

No word from you these last few days. Are you there? Roth writes that he is making a hundred deluxe copies of the Greek book which I am to sign. I am very eager to see this book out—the others I don't care much about. But I would like people to like this book.

I'd like to quit writing altogether. I don't seem to care any more. Maybe I have nothing more to say.

Last night I lay awake thinking of the piano and the *clarinet* (sic!). Wondering if I could ever learn to improvise, to write my own compositions. I feel the need of music greatly. If I could play some instrument—*any* instrument—I would feel a thousand times better. Writing breeds loneliness. You write in a padded cell. And it gives no ultimate joy.

I was thinking of Joaquin and how in his restricted way he must really enjoy his work.

The other day I went to an expensive ear specialist for an examination. He frightened the life out of me—with the usual blunt American diagnosis. Said my good ear was going the same as my bad one. Something wrong with the Eustachian tube. "Not much to be done about it," he said. (Take vitamins B & Q, he adds, as an after thought. Such damned nonsense!) Pretends that I have the remnant of a tonsil in my throat—and that it is causing an infection. Sounds incredible to me. Anyway, when I get back to N.Y. I am going to look up a good doctor—perhaps Jacobsohn can recommend one.

I had an ear test—for hearing—and it was quite normal. Could even hear with the bad ear. He said I would never be stone deaf—that my inner ear and the bones were good. I don't know what to make of it. What bothers me is a feeling of pressure on the drum—as when you change altitude quickly.

Well, nothing new. Waiting to hear from you. The writing is going poorly. Get inspirations and then they die out quickly. Fortunately I have a few months yet in which to finish the book. But I have no heart for it.

Will go on a trip over the weekend with Jake Zeitlin (bookseller) and his wife—up toward Big Sur. Back Monday.

Give my regards to Dorothy Norman if you see her again. I haven't written her in ages.

HVM

Hollywood
Friday, Aug. 1st [1941]

ANAÏS—

Am leaving this evening on the weekend trip with the Zeitlins. He is going to introduce me to Jeffers—can't seem to avoid it.

My friend Rivas comes now and then—mostly then. When he does I make headway quickly. I must know already a good hundred words, including that phrase—"no me da la gana"! I like words like "andarin" (walker) and "alma" for soul, and again "no tengo ganas . . ." In any case "estoy encantado"! And the word for nothing is wonderful— Nada! Like Russian, no? In any case, mañana ire al campo, yes?

But the first thing you learn about Spaniards is that they, like the Russians, never keep appointments. It's wonderful. Rivas reminds me so much of your father—scrupulous, meticulous, scholarly, clean to a fault, buy a cloth at the five and ten to wipe your glasses! pride in poverty, morality, bad dramatist, classicist, etc. etc. Even looks a bit like your father. But very warm—immediately the friend. He is going to take me to Filipino restaurants in L.A., where they have good Spanish cooking, he says. And then there is his friend Navarro who married a rich woman and ran thru all her money in a year. He plays the guitar. And then, like a Russian, he says over and over—"tengo muchos dolores de cabeza." Which is a little different from just having a *jaqueca*. We must go on with it when I get back. What a pity I waited this long!

The other day I met a man at a soda fountain who talked for two solid hours about Russia—had just come back recently. An elderly American. Gave me a marvelous picture. And for the writer it sounds like a paradise. He says they can mobilize *30,000,000* men if they need to! And that the women are just as capable as the men. Sounds like a ray of hope for Europe. I hope it's all true.

HVM

[August 4, 1941]
Hollywood, Monday

ANAÏS—

No luck yet selling the car! And now, when I want to get rid of it she runs beautifully—haven't had any trouble with it for a long time. Like a woman. I don't know where the next remittance is coming from, but I have a hunch there will be something coming soon. It certainly is a pity you can't come out here. Anyway, as soon as I get the money to leave I'll write or wire you and then I suggest you send me a telegram as from New York signing it Lauretta and saying that mother is very ill come home at once. That will make it easier for me here, as the fellow I rent the place from has been very kind and rather expecting me to stay on.

Just had a long letter from Fred saying he has signed a contract with Allen & Unwin, English publishers, for five books! The first to be delivered the end of this year. He's still in the army and thinks the war will be over, with the defeat of Germany, next spring. He's optimistic. He sends a photo which makes him look quite English—like that fellow in the movies, Howard Lawson? (*Intermezzo*)

Went to a lecture yesterday morning by Manly P. Hall, who is the leading light out here. Does a wonderful business. Sells innumerable books and pamphlets and draws big crowds. Writes about all the things Moricand loves. It's always impressed me as singular that the two kinds of books which have a steady, permanent sale are the occult and the pornographic. Have you ever noticed?

I'm going to hear Gerald Heard before I leave. Have just written Huxley for information about his lectures. Some say he's magnificent. Dane Rudhyar writes again saying he will be in New Mexico end of this month—he may come to N.Y. this winter.

You say Dos Passos is not very human. Did you meet him? I had quite the opposite impression—found him very warm and likable. Don't judge from his books. I have a wonderful book on marine life of the Pacific Coast from my friend Ricketts at Pacific Grove. You'll enjoy it, even though it's scientific.

Tomorrow I visit a Jewish Buddhist monk at the Buddhist Temple in L.A. A Julius Goldwater! The cults certainly flourish out here. Even the old hags on the benches talk occultism and astrology. I hear ever so many conversations in the car about astrology. Especially about Aquarius, the new sign. My friend Rivas hasn't been here for several days now—I'm forgetting what I learned. Writes me a letter excusing himself, makes a new date, and fails to keep it. Sometimes I see him sitting on a bench resting himself. He's hungry most of the time—has a family in Frisco and two children—and trying to get a crippled war veteran, his brother, out of Spain. A typical Don Quixote. Always thinking of how to raise a big sum of money. Always looking overdressed, immaculate, businesslike, with a portfolio of plays and Mss. under his arm. Says the Portuguese are caricatures of the Spaniards—but that they have a fine literature behind them! Lafe writes he just came out of the hospital—had dysentery very badly. Yesterday I had some Mexican dish in L.A.—a thick soup with tripe and barley—stunk like horse piss and tasted vile. That's Mexican cooking! They're always drunk and stabbing one another. But they look interesting.

HVM

[August 6, 1941]
Hollywood, Wednesday

ANAÏS—

Have just received a letter from Bill Roth saying the proofs for the Greek book will be arriving very soon—to wait if possible because he hopes to get the book out around the first of September. Asks me also to send him the Emil letters—is interested.

(I made a mistake about Fred's contract—it was for 3 books, not 5.)

Fraenkel writes now not to look for royalties on *Hamlet* 2. Will have to bring out a larger edition if book is to pay costs. Just like him!

It's sizzling hot here now—all of a sudden. I'm sitting in an undershirt and the sweat rolling off me.

You asked about swimming. No, I don't go to the beach very often —water is full of oil from the oil wells—and usually at the beach it's cold and misty. I go to pools here in Hollywood occasionally. But since the ear trouble I stopped again.

Anyway, the delay I mention is not serious. I ought to get away before the month is over.

More soon.

HVM

P. S. Peggy Guggenheim (wealthy sister of Mabel McKinley) just arrived. Wants to see me, I'm told. She brought over Kay Boyle, her old husband, L. Vail, and a prospective one. Marcel Duchamp is expected soon also. I saw his early works—at Arensberg's. They are really wonderful.

[August 7, 1941]
Hollywood, Thursday

ANAÏS—

Just got the wire—fine. Am expecting the proofs any day now. Did I tell you of the documentary film on China? I think I did. Don't miss it and tell me what *you* think of Carmen Amaya—I'm puzzled. Are gypsies neurotic too?

Last night I went to a vernissage and met a lot of people. Had a long talk with Charles Henri Ford's sister who is in the movies here. Funny thing out here is that the husbands are usually more attractive than the wives. I never saw so many handsome men anywhere—but dull, of course.

I also wanted to tell you about those pictures (photos) of Tibet— how the woman who gave them to me (a Czech) seemed utterly oblivious of the mysterious element there. She liked it like a peasant likes the land. Yet when I see the movie (*Kuhan*) and catch just a glimpse of Tibet I feel everything. Even the colors of the priests' robes excite me.

Last night I ran into René Lefebvre-Foinet—the art dealer in Paris. Had been wounded in the war and got out thru Marseille. He's going to have lunch and tell me what happened to everybody. It must seem very strange now to those escaping from Europe—to arrive here in the land of ease and luxury and indifference. The interest in the war seems to me to be dwindling steadily.

Haven't seen Miriam Hopkins yet—more telegrams and phone calls. What a crazy life they must lead. They *earn* their money. More soon.

HVM

P. S. The Spaniard has dropped out of sight. In L.A. there are several theatres showing Mexican and Spanish films—open all night too.

[August 13, 1941]
Hollywood, Wednesday

ANAÏS—

Just read proofs on Greek book. Now Laughlin writes he is
sending proofs on *The Wisdom of the Heart*. So I will wait for that,
while I'm at it. May have to run up to Frisco to sign the hundred deluxe copies [of *Colossus*]. But then I'm definitely free and ready to
return. I think with what I get for the car I may be able to reach
Chicago and there I could make Abramson pay my fare to N.Y.

Are you going back to W. 13th St. after Labor Day? Tell me where
to write you next.

Saw another horrible accident on the road to Malibu Beach the
other night. Almost paralyzed me. Two men lying in middle of road
screaming with pain—oh help me! Help me! And cars whizzing by.
It's harrowing. This is about the sixth one I've seen.

Volkening writes that *Atlantic Monthly* is not enthusiastic about
the American book. Neither will D.D. & Co. be, I expect.

Soon it will be treason to say anything against America. I notice
however that there is less and less interest in the war.

Did you see *Kuhan* yet? Watch for the shot about Kum Bum near
Tibet—the lamasery there. It's beautiful. I saw it again. And Carmen
Amaya too—but I'm sure now I don't like her dancing. She seems
like a neurotic to me. Can that be the Spanish gypsy? I don't believe it.

My Spaniard has completely evaporated. They're volatile.

How do the stars look this month? I see nothing but work cut out
for me.

Was at Orson Welles' studio in Culver City yesterday. Fantastic
place. Especially from behind. They only put up a façade, you know,
when they make a set. You should see it—it's like America itself—
all front and no insides, no rear.

HVM

[August 25, 1941]
Hollywood, Monday

ANAÏS—

Got your long letter Saturday and this morning a check from
Ruder. Had just written him to send it as I was down to my last two

dollars. Still haven't been able to sell the car. A fellow is taking it out today to the airplane factories to see if he can find a buyer among the workers. It's like taking coals to Newcastle to sell a car here—they're as plentiful as bedbugs.

Anyway, I'll be returning soon. Would rather make it by train, I think. If you should still be in Provincetown when I get back maybe I could run up there.

The whole thing in the back of my head has been the thought, the hope, of living cheaply and sanely, amidst *natural* surroundings. Harlem doesn't tempt me at all now. I like the lonely life—doing simple things with my hands, solitude, wild surroundings, etc. I don't think city life can charm me any more. It's necessary once in a while—to get supplies chiefly. We'll never find another city like Paris. Nor a country like Greece. But if you have the books you like, and music, and a desire to work, the country—most anywhere—is good. At least so I feel now.

I'm glad you're over your emotional storms. God, what an omnivorous reader you are! It takes me ages to finish a book. I can't seem to get sufficiently interested. As for *Seraphita*—funny, just as you wrote about it Abramson sent me a copy gratis—because I had talked about it so much. I expect small checks from him pretty regularly.

Today the Library of Congress ordered a copy of *The World of Sex* at the full price. I was quite surprised.

When I get a large envelope I'm going to send you the photos of Tibet (Shangri-la) which were given me. Maybe you'll paste them in your diary.

I've done some few good water colors recently. Very curious to see *your* painting.

More soon.

HVM

[September 5, 1941]
Friday Night

ANAÏS—

I sent you a night letter to Provincetown—which crossed yours, I guess. Wondering if they mailed the notice on to you. If I don't hear by Monday I'll probably wire again. I said I would leave

Monday but may not be able to until Tuesday or Wednesday. I'm trying to dispose of a notebook (which I invented from my original notebook *) and some other books—and the car. It breaks my heart to let the car go for $35.00—but if I get 50 or 60 why I'll let it go.

I find that for about ten dollars extra I can return to N.Y. via the Northern route—Portland, Seattle, Butte, Minneapolis—which I'd like to do as I would then really have made the full swing around the country. I have to break the trip anyway. Sleepers are very expensive —and I'd rather get off the train and stay in a hotel and see a city— stretch my legs.

As I ordered my meal tonight in a Chinese restaurant I found a little slip of paper in front of me reading—"A great fortune is ordained for you. Be patient!"

I'm about ⅔ thru the book—will have ample time to finish when I get to N.Y. More before leaving. Anyway, I'm off!

HVM

[Hollywood, September 9, 1941]
Tuesday A.M.

ANAÏS—

I'm selling the car this morning—for $75.00—and will be off for Frisco and points N. & N.W. tonight or tomorrow morning. I think I'll be in Frisco till Saturday surely—% Colt Press—and will give them forwarding address when I leave—guess it will be Portland, Oregon, next stop—but am never sure which direction I'll take. I'm buying my railroad ticket jump by jump because it's just possible I'll meet someone with a car going my way. Don't expect to stay more than a day or two in each place. I have quite enough on me now for the whole trip. Sold some autographed books, old Mss. and got a $38.00 check for back royalties unexpectedly from Laughlin. I've expressed 2 valises back to R. & V. to hold for me.

---

* In Europe, as well as after his return to the United States, Miller kept a series of notebooks for jotting down ideas, drawings, water colors etc. Some of these notebooks Miller sold to collectors to raise funds. His *Red Notebook,* which covers the period of his trip through the States, was published in a facsimile edition (Highlands, N.C., J. Williams, 1958, 86 pp., Illustrated).

It's good it's turning out this way—the northern train route—clears my conscience about covering the whole country.

As I was taking a last spin in the car yesterday to Santa Monica I thought of Rank and how he liked California. That's a beautiful drive to the ocean from here. At times it looks Tibetan. Wonderful mountains and curved roads. I certainly learned to drive well—never grazed another car. But am relieved to be rid of it too. A perpetual nervous strain. Never once did I sit at the wheel but I thought of all the possible accidents. If I were rich I'd hire a chauffeur to drive me around. But I prefer walking. I'm an *andarin*. I guess I've forgotten all my Spanish by this time. But I'd like to take it up again when I get back to N.Y.

I never got to see Miriam Hopkins either. I finally decided it was silly going to see another movie star. Better to see them in the pictures —like authors in their books.

Yesterday a Greek girl, cashier in an Italian restaurant, asked me if I were a movie actor—because of my voice! That's the first time any one mistook me for an actor.

Ben Abramson is now talking about possibility of bringing out Fred and my *Aller Retour* in one volume—and perhaps the 3 stories also [excerpts from *Tropic of Capricorn*]. And Larry Powell, the librarian at University here, would like to do the chapter from *Black Spring* on the water colors. I think the Greek book will definitely make an impression. It's 350 pages in book form—and I thought it was a short book. It's been a good year for publishing at least.

More from Frisco. I hear Caresse Crosby and Dali are out here somewhere.

HVM

Reno, Nevada
Sunday P.M. [Sept. 14, 1941]

ANAÏS—
Just got in here this evening at sundown—with the Buick. Waited around for the fellow to take it in Hollywood—but he never showed up. Result, I only got to Frisco Friday evening—and left early this morning. Tried again in S.F. to sell it but was offered ridiculous

sums. Will keep trying as I go along. If no luck then I ought to arrive
in Chicago about 8 to 10 days from now. That means without spending any days to see places—just straight going by the quickest over-
land route. May send a nite letter in day or so giving an in-between
point in case you need to wire me about anything. Am not sure yet
of exact itinerary—i.e. which route is quickest. Have just got about
enough to reach Chicago. If I'm stuck Roth of Colt Press promised to
send me something. He put me up at his home in S.F. His parents are
wealthy—I was in a veritable palace. But they give him nothing for
his publishing—he saved that up from gifts they made him. Have had
a grueling drive today from S.F. to Reno. Reno as you approach it is
spectacular—the natural surroundings. Nevada is *terrific*.

More tomorrow—am heading toward Salt Lake City—ought to be
there day after tomorrow. Am groggy and dizzy from long mountain
driving.

HVM

[September 17, 1941]
Rawlins, Wyoming
Wednesday, 17th

ANAÏS—

Every day I am up at 6 o'clock and on the road riding till dark.
Have come straight thru and this is all the further I am. Will be lucky
to make Chicago by Sunday night. I've passed thru the most desolate,
godforsaken country since leaving Reno, Nevada. You can't imagine
what it's like till you go thru it with a car at 45 to 50 miles an hour.
An unending desert filled with sagebrush. And mountains to climb.
All Nevada, Utah, Wyoming is of an altitude over 5000 feet, even
when it's flat. Just crossed the Continental Divide today, at an altitude
of 7100 feet. That means I left the *"Far"* West behind. But it is still
a long way to the Mississippi River. Since leaving Los Angeles I have
done about 1700 miles. Guess I have another 1200 or more to go—
to Chicago.

It is very Wild West here—real cowboy land. Two wild horses ran
across my path today. Seems incredible. Distances between towns
sometimes 100 and more miles. And the towns are only 250 to 750

inhabitants. It will be this way for another two or three centuries, I feel. A huge wasteland. Most of America is of this caliber. It's awesome. My handwriting is poor because I'm still trembling from holding the wheel.

Went thru Salt Lake City—stopped there last night. God-awful place. Crossing the great salt flats—a stretch of about a hundred miles —was grueling. Like riding thru snow. Blinding light. Puts you to sleep. But I saw mountains upside down in the salt beds. Mirages. Today I was up in the clouds all day. Fantastic.

However, I'm getting along and so far the car is doing nobly. Hope to sell it in Chicago and take the train back. Will stay a few days there probably to rest up. I feel like a locomotive engineer.

Nights, in bed, I read a few pages of Céline's *Death on the Installment Plan*. Am fast asleep by 9:30 P.M. usually.

Tomorrow I go thru Cheyenne, and Oshkosh and Ogallala!! (the two latter in Nebraska).

Well—I'm dropping off with sleep already. More later. Will mail this from Cheyenne tomorrow sometime. Told Roth to transmit any telegrams during my absence to Cheyenne. Can't give you any place to communicate en route because I never know how far I'll get each day.

HVM

[September 28, 1941]
Chicago, Ill., Sunday

ANAÏS—

Expect to leave tomorrow or Tuesday morning. Am waiting for some money from Roth of San Francisco. Ben gave me $25 but it is not enough to get me to New York. I found on checking the account with him that I am in debt to him for almost $200. However, I am giving him the notebook to sell and there is the typescript of the *World of Sex* he is selling too—which would cancel out my debt. He's very decent and reliable and honest, I must say. And certainly puts himself out to sell my books.

It will take me a good four days to make the trip back. I ought to arrive toward the end of the week. Will go to the Royalton as usual—

for time being. Think I ought to find a cheaper place—maybe the hotel Lafe and Dudley stayed at.

Had plenty of rain since arriving here. So relaxed I sleep all the time—a great difference in climate. I certainly miss that wonderful California sunshine.

More en route.

HVM

[New York, Winter, 1941 *]
Friday

ANAÏS—

Forgot to tell you the most important thing! Harrison Smith said you were an extraordinary woman—remarkably beautiful etc. Wanted me to talk about you—what had you done, etc. I told him you had done most everything and *could* do anything—that you were an artist in life. He said—oh yes, yes! that you can see immediately.

He gave me no opportunity to expand, so I felt it wiser to be discreet and reserved. Didn't open up any whisky bottle or any cordial gesture. To him I'm just another guy who wrote an extraordinary book.

As I shook hands to go he was already reading another Ms.

HENRY

P. S. So you're beautiful!!!!—as though I didn't know it.

[Beverly Glen, L.A., June 18, 1942 **]
Thursday

I got here yesterday in Hollywood but it seems like several days ago. Am staying at the [Gilbert] Neimans' new home—a beautiful

---

* Miller had returned to New York on October 9, and he stayed there during the winter and spring of 1942.

** Miller went to California for the second time to follow an invitation by the Neimans who had offered him free quarters, and in the hope that he would find work in Hollywood.

little cottage which they rent at $25.00 a month, with a big front yard and a piece of a mountain in back covered with trees and flowers. Next door is a friend of theirs, with a bigger house, and I can stay with them if I like. Everybody very hospitable and affable—a different spirit here. The car and the telephone seem indispensable.

Tomorrow I will see my agent here and probably Budd Schulberg also. The journey from Denver was fatiguing—2 nights in a sleeping chair—bad meals, etc. The last night we were in the car with all the mothers and their babies. They have special cars reserved for them now. (Everything for the mothers!)

I must say it seems good out here—the sun is powerful, the air smells good. Everything seems brand-new. I always think of Rank when I come here—I understand why he liked it so much.

I left several things of mine in Chicago from which I expect some results. Haven't begun to show your book [*Winter of Artifice*] around yet. Now I am some distance from Hollywood and will go to town only when someone is driving in. You could write me here direct, if you like—1212 N. Beverly Glen Blvd., *West* Los Angeles—% Neiman.

I'm still a bit dazed from the traveling and the change of climate.

HVM

[Beverly Glen, July, 1942]
Wednesday—15th

ANAÏS—

Got your two letters today. I'm well taken care of here. The only thing I lack is space and privacy. I have been going out—swimming, riding, etc. Am getting tan already and feel wonderful. Tho' I stopped the vitamins for a while I notice no difference and my eyes are much stronger than last year when I was out here.

I stopped in to the Agents today. Place looks like a high-class funeral parlor. My man is away. Trying to get Marlene Dietrich's address from man in Pickwick Book Shop who knows her. But he's out every time I call. It's a bit maddening that way here—distances enormous. If you miss someone you lose half a day. Everybody urges me to take it easy and not be too eager—to wait for the other fellow to call on you. Hollywood strategy.

Glad to hear of your good luck with the press.* The write-up in paper was a bit lurid, no? But your photo came out beautifully.

I haven't begun to show your book around yet. I have to wait until someone is driving in to town—it's a bit hectic.

I'm also still waiting for new about my Mss. from Chicago.** If anything is sold I may rent a room of my own somewhere.

I have the *Julius Le Vallon* book of Blackwood and also [Jakob Wassermann's novel] *Dr. Kerkhoven*—picked them up secondhand here. The Blackwood seems disappointing. Not at all as good as [Blackwood's] *The Bright Messenger*. I'll send it to you later.

More soon.

HVM

[Beverly Glen, July 31, 1942]

Friday

Just got your letter—about Caresse, Goldberg † etc. You *are* doing fine! (By the way, is Goldberg going to let the *Black Book* be done?) If Caresse lets you do a few books it ought to be very successful.

I'm still marking time. The agent gets back from his vacation Monday, so I suppose next week I'll begin interviewing people.

Had another fine letter from [Claude] Houghton—exciting. And a couple from Fred—including a long obituary he wrote for Jacques and Roger Klein's deaths. (According to the story, Roger committed suicide a few days after Jacques was killed. Did you know that?††)

I am now deep in *Doctor Kerkhoven*—wonderful book—all you said it was.

Wassermann *formed* Thomas Mann, it seems. Sure, he is the greater of the two. Mann is full of upholstery.

---

* Anaïs Nin had followed through on the idea she had discussed with Miller ten years earlier in Paris, and set up her own press in a loft on MacDougal Street in New York, since none of the commercial publishers wanted to bring out her books.

** Miller tried to sell some of his manuscripts to collectors.

† Samuel Goldberg, lawyer for the Gotham Book Mart.

†† Jacques, the playwright, and his brother had been friends of Alfred Perlès in Paris.

It's a kind of scattered life I'm leading for the time being, due to living with others. I can't get down to anything serious—owing to lack of space and privacy. But I know I will soon have something and am not at all disturbed.

Everybody remarks that I have such integrity! Apparently they all capitulate the moment they get out here.

Donald Friede * is a frequent visitor next door—but I haven't met him yet. I'm going to Hiler's this evening for dinner. He has a magnificent house built a/c to his own ideas—but a bit of a prison, it seems to me. He always asks after you warmly. Has a great respect for you.

When I go in now I'll probably find a batch of mail. Am looking for news from Chicago—about the Mss. and notebook I left there.

Am trying not to bother you about the money—you need a vacation. Nobody will let me go without things here. If it gets too embarrassing I'll ask you. Going in now—car waiting for me.

HVM

[Beverly Glen, August 2, 1942]
Sunday

Here's a letter from Durrell which Fred just forwarded me. Saw Marlene Dietrich's secretary (Violla Rubber) today. She was crazy about my books. Never even mentioned the Dietrich woman— but I suppose that's to be expected. Anyway, she very warmly invited me to dinner Tuesday—to meet Erich Remarque. I suppose I'll get there after running the gauntlet.

The Wassermann book is splendid. Kerkhoven somehow vaguely reminds me of myself—I don't know why yet.

Met DeMille's son last night but I doubt if he'll ever introduce me to his father.

It's late—I'm just clearing up an accumulation of letters. [Jean] Gabin sails by in his car frequently—he seems to have white hair— and he is short.

HVM

---

* See Biographical Notes.

[Beverly Glen, August, 1942]
Sunday—9th

ANAÏS—

Suppose you are wondering what happened to me. I had a touch of sunstroke the other day at Warner Bros. Studio. Went with a director to see the permanent artificial streets they erected for future sets—formula streets—of N.Y., Chicago, Fez, Dijon, etc. Not a soul on the streets. And everything super-realistic. Had quite a pleasant shock strolling about—a new kind of dead city, in which fountains and parks and statues are moved around overnight. Would be interesting to live and write in such a crazy re-created atmosphere.

The other night I was given quite a royal banquet in a hotel in Pasadena—by a Greek woman who was crazy about the *Colossus*. She reminded me of you a little. For the first time I was able to see in you your Greek blood. Anyway, she was leaving for N.Y. the next day. I told her to look you up—and I think she will. Her first name is Melpomene! She's a cross between you and Luise Rainer.

I just finished collaborating with a foreigner on a synopsis for a film—a pure speculation. Haven't heard or seen the agent yet. This time I seem further away from the cinema than last year. But I think Violla Rubber (Dietrich's secretary) will prove my savior. I'm to see her and the daughter tomorrow. (The daughter lives with her, not the mother.) She has 3 addresses and all sorts of telephone numbers —Miss Rubber, I mean.

Last night I was rereading that book on Blake I once mentioned: *William Blake and the Circle of Destiny*—by Percival. You must get it and read it—it has things about man and woman, duality, etc.—but staggeringly profound. Makes Rank's wordy, windy theses look sick.

Hiler called me and invited me over. I arrive and find him asleep. The father lives really like an artist—very serene and productive. His paintings are adorable. I wish I could do as well myself.

Had a letter from Emil White telling me of the fine window display you had in Abramson's shop. Seems he stuck one of my books in the window too. We are always being mentioned together, you notice.

Dr. Friedman writes that he is coming out here before the month is up.

It's raining here today—4 months ahead of time. Seems queer, unreal.

Do you see Allemany now? Give him my regards. How is it there this time?

Yes—I got Eduardo's book.* But I really like it. The reproductions were very interesting. It's strange that he should be the first one to give his books away! Anyway, it was a good printing job again.

And your book? How is it going now? I'm trying to launch it in the good shops here. Anyhow—all the women who have read it here are quite bowled over by it.

More very soon.

HVM

[Beverly Glen, August 10, 1942]
Monday

ANAÏS—

Got your letter this morning and felt bad that you should feel bad—about my failure to get somewhere here. It's not that I've met a firm No! It's that I'm surrounded by veils of miasma. Everything can be very vague, draggy and ineffectual when they are disinterested. Maybe part of it is my fault too—lack of aggressivity. Only I see so much of that among those who are in that I instinctively lean the other way. But I am not discouraged nor have I given up.

The terrible thing to witness here is the disgust which everyone has for the work he is doing. It's so completely a money-mad world— and nothing more. (And yet you mustn't say that that's all you care about. You are supposed to pretend great interest. And I'm very poor at that.)

Faulkner is out here, I'm told, working for Warner Bros. He has to do it from time to time, as his books do not bring in much money.

There's another thing works against me—the fact that everybody regards me as "pure." Everybody expresses terrific disappointment that I should compromise. Nobody seems really convinced that I am willing to do as the others.

This is also my fault. Bad acting, no doubt. But you know, when I see the fawning, lying, cheating, conniving, etc. I get absolutely disgusted. I can't switch over into that role very easily.

---

* *The Round,* published under the pseudonym Eduardo Santiago.

Well, all this because I'm truly sorry to read of your disappointment. I wish you wouldn't worry about me. I am so sick and disgusted with being a burden. It doesn't matter what happens, really. I can put up with anything.

Please don't be disappointed—you make me sad. I can only fail in the world of moneymaking. And for that I'm willing to suffer the consequences—*I want to!* I don't want you to bear all the responsibility. All the old fears and terrors about starvation, etc. are gone. That's putting it negatively—later it may become something positive. Does this mean anything?

I'm working on "The Sleeping Sleeper Asleep" again. Hope to finish it soon and offer it as a book. It's going good.

Perhaps the real true difficulty is that, no matter what I say, what I wish or ought to do (and I admit this sounds terrible), I can only do what I want to do. For that one has to pay a price. And, as I said, I am ready now to pay the price. Otherwise I'll be perpetually guilty.

Today I see all the errors of my life clearly. Maybe the next step is clarity—action in truth. The very worst thing about myself which I realize in these moments is that, though never wishing to do harm to anyone, I bring pain and suffering to all about me. That really disturbs me profoundly—makes me think there must be some cruel self-deception going on.

Well, try to forgive me, even for the "disappointment." I'm giving myself the *curette*.

HVM

[Beverly Glen, August 16, 1942]
Sunday

Anaïs—

I got the birthday greeting from Eduardo—rather complicated —as the W.U. asked for my birth date and it didn't correspond. I said it was a joke.

I have some photos which Abramson sent me of your window display. Can't find an envelope hereabouts to fit them, but will when I go to town. I understand it attracted considerable attention.

The booksellers here are very cool to the book *—mostly because of the price, I feel. Satyr [Book Shop] is about the only one who is willing to try. Things are getting more and more prosaic in the book world, because of the war. Technical books seem to be most in demand. Art is out—for the duration. So many of the promising ones— the young enthusiasts—are now in the army. I suppose one has to wait again until the war is over.

I was just reading that part in *Kerkhoven* last night where he speaks of the benefits of war—to the physician. Sounds horrible and grotesque. I read it very slowly because I don't want to come to the end too quickly.

Once again—look up the Blake book! If you can't get it, let me know, and I'll have Abramson send you a copy.

Nothing of any account has happened since I last wrote. For the moment I'm stagnating.

Haven't been swimming either for ten days—because I am a bit leery of the sun now. It's amazingly strong and treacherous here. And when you're in the shade it's as though the refrigerator were open. Typical desert climate, I imagine. All extremes.

People are frightfully preoccupied these days about the war—even if they're not in it. I follow the news scarcely at all. I woudn't know there was a war if I didn't see the newspapers when I go to town. I'm completely disinterested.

John Cage writes again, urging me to write him something which can be used on the radio—with his music. Says someone is interested. So I am going to try. The only thing is I don't know what on earth to write! I feel as though I were in a vacuum.

How are you getting on there?

HVM

[Beverly Glen, August 17, 1942]
Monday

ANAÏS—

Just got your letter with the citation from Alyse Gregory's letter. I seem to remember her name from the *Dial*. It was good. Inci-

---

* A limited edition of *Winter of Artifice*, printed by Anaïs Nin in New York.

dentally, I am always getting most flattering comments about the book from women who have read it. Just the other day a girl from Majorca (Salt's ex-wife) told me about it. Now Miss Rubber is reading it. Yesterday was a big day at the astrologer's new home. What an affair! All his monstrous, horrendous rich clients from Pasadena were there, sprinkled with fairies and show girls—the most grotesque, incredible collection of human beings I have ever seen assembled. I am going to write about it. * Maria Montez, the dancer, was there—another victim, but a superb one! Ravishingly beautiful, but vain and pretentious as a peacock—insufferable. But following the astrologer's advice like a child, for every move she makes. Most of them were rich invalids, with limousines and chauffeurs, some noblewomen with buck teeth and crazy hats, as in Houghton's novels, the conversation absolutely asinine, so much so that I began singling the old women out and insulting them openly.

Then, a few nights ago, I met Stravinski at dinner—with his charming Russian wife—like somebody we know whose name I forget. He was very congenial, cordial, sympathetic, modest. Talked a lot about Cingria and Cendrars whom he knew well. I was not particularly fired by him—too smooth and suave and decidedly polite. Talked about little things, as Europeans do.

Another day, at the public library, I almost swore my father had come alive. There he was standing at a file case reading a book. He looked distinguished, like a savant. I never saw such a close resemblance. Almost went up to the man to ask his name.

There is a beautiful Russian wolfhound here where I sleep—I sleep and work next door at the Jordans'. I have become quite fond of the dog and take it for long walks. People stop their cars and ask me about the beast. Mornings it comes to my bed and licks my face to wake me up. Reminds me of that big dog in Louveciennes.

In a day or two Dr. Friedman will be here—I don't know whether to stay or go on vacation.

I'm doing the radio script now for John Cage. Must hurry it up, he says. Frankly these scripts bore the life out of me. I can't work up any interest. It makes me restless to get back to the *Capricorn*. One thing stands out like lightning. Everybody who comes out here comes to sell his soul! It's terrible. Young and old, native and foreign. No-

---

* See "Astrological Fricassee," in *Remember to Remember,* New Directions, New York, 1947.

body thinks of resisting. Just get the dough, that's all. Their stories are pathetic. I can only hope for one thing—that the Japs will blast the cinema industry off the map forever!

Gilbert may have to run up to San Francisco to see about a war job. I may go with him for the trip. But if so only for two or three days.

The L.A. public library intrigues me. One of the best in the country. Very bright, gay, cheerful, helpful, with all the books accessible and separate big light rooms to read in. There was an even better one in Santa Fe—done in Indian style—probably the best I ever saw.

Margaret hears from Frieda Lawrence from time to time. Frieda is like an old peasant woman, pottering around, making little things to sell, so that she can earn a few pence and keep the roof over her head. I begin to like her more and more—revising completely the impression I had of her from Lawrence's books.

The Wassermann book still fascinates me. I was dumfounded and delighted to come to Etzel Andergast, to read that swift recapitulation of the Maurizius Case which he gives in the middle of the book. What a stunt! And then the analysis of Etzel—the confession! God, I wish I could do that! It's a marvelous, torrential style, like a cataract pouring over your head. And full of abrupt halts, irrelevancies, queries, cosmic problems, insinuations, ambushes. He seems to do just as he pleases.

I got a book out of the library which Dane Rudhyar had highly recommended—called *Om* by Talbot Mundy—about India. Haven't begun it yet. But am very curious. Here in the L.A. library there is an open shelf marked "Occult" literature! Three copies of *Julius Le Vallon* on the shelf. (I must remember to mail you the copy I have.)

Funny impression, as of last year! It's the young men out here who are good-looking. Not the women. And they get hitched up with the most awful specimens. As in Greece, when the old rich peasant women married themselves to young men.

Enfin—I read Gilbert's novel on Mexico over and helped him with it.* He's not finished yet. But it was magnificent. I think I discovered a real writer. And it's all so Spanish—in a queer way. He has one character, a sort of grandee, who reminds me enormously of your father.

---

* *There is a Tyrant in Every Country,* published by Harcourt, Brace, New York, 1947.

Well, I'm going in to town now to do some errands. The car is waiting.

HVM

[Beverly Glen, August 23, 1942]
Sunday

ANAÏS—

Got the message from Eduardo—all fine. It's been almost cold here the last week. Like fall.

I'll get Abramson to send you a copy of that Blake book. You must own a copy. It will be a Bible to you.

Miss Rubber couldn't come the other night. Sent lovely flowers instead. All tied up now with Dietrich and the girl's father.

The other night I had a strong intuition something was amiss—in the heavens. Felt as tho' a catastrophe were imminent (an earthquake, especially). Called the astrologer to inquire and learned that there was an eclipse of the moon—and a quake registered out in the Pacific. He added that on September 10th there would be an eclipse of the sun—followed by famine, pestilence, etc. (sounded like Moricand!).

I'm now reading a fascinating book recommended by Dane Rudhyar—Om by Talbot Mundy. A fictional work on India and Tibet. Exciting.

William Faulkner is out here, working for Warner Brothers at $300 a week. I'm going to try to meet him. A quiet, modest little man, they say.

I have a feeling that when you get back to New York you'll be besieged by all the women I am recommending to you. I think the Greek woman (Melpo Niarchos) and Carson McCullers should prove interesting.

I haven't met anyone this trip whom I found absorbing or exciting. The astrologer predicts "great activity" soon. Am wondering what that means. I have a hunch I'll be back before very long. I have another hunch—that the Japanese are going to bomb and invade this whole coast.

I go to see a Pole now who has had some amazing psychic experiences. More soon.

HVM

[August, 1942]
Hollywood, Tuesday

ANAÏS—

Here's a letter from Durrell which came a few days ago. I was surprised to see that your book was known in Cairo. Maybe thru the war it will be carried to remote places. I met some young men from the Navy who told me my books were circulating strongly among the crews of the fleet.

Yesterday I was near [Robert] Swasey's place in Altadena. A marvelous location, at the foot of a great rugged mountain range. A rich colony, it seemed to me. We spent the whole day riding around to various kennels to find a suitable mate for the Russian wolfhound. (Here's an ironic note: the owner puts 5 gallons of gas away in case the dog gets in heat and they have to mate her quickly!) I saw lots of wonderful dogs—all well kept—better kept, of course, than human beings. One kennel I could have lived in myself—roomy, cool, immaculate. I told the owner so. I almost envied the dog!

With the gas rationing out here, transportation has become a problem. Five gallons a week isn't enough even for doing the errands. I walk a great deal—sometimes ten and twelve miles a day. I can outwalk the dog now.

Well, there's nothing much new. Met Donald Friede for just a few minutes the other day. He moves in today. Rather suave and pleasant on first sight. Completely egocentric too. I'm almost curious now.

More soon.

HVM

[Beverly Glen, August 30, 1942]
Sunday

ANAÏS—

Just a word to say nothing new has developed yet. Things haven't begun in earnest yet—but I'm meeting lots of people. Julian Johnson at Fox Films wants to see me. I met Vincent Korda—nice guy—looks like Zadkine a bit. Things go slowly and leisurely here, it seems.

Just began to do a bit of writing today—for Dr. Friedman, The Zweig book. A couple of French Jewish refugees from the cinema are after me to collaborate—I don't know yet if I will. I met a lot of actors, directors, scriptwriters, agents, promoters—socially. All terrible. All like leeches. So glitteringly eager for money. Vultures. I stand aside and watch it like some strange spectacle.

What I'm really enjoying is the layoff from work. I feel almost like I did in Greece. If I had a little shack of my own in the hills here I think I would become a hermit.

Margaret is feeding me a/c to the Hay diet—and it agrees with me marvelously. Man Ray is here with his Julie, waiting for us to come next door to eat. There's a sort of communal life in progress all the time. On the surface life seems so easy here. But in the studios they really work. Everybody who is in the game seems worn out, harried, disgusted.

Last night I saw *La Bête Humaine*—I thought it quite marvelous. Like an old lithograph. So tenderly French in all the details.

I also saw Orson Welles' new picture—*The Magnificent Ambersons*. Again I am bowled over by it. Wonder how you will take it?

Well, I must stop. Dinner is ready. Feel sober and inwardly calm, content. Quite different from N.Y.

HVM

[Beverly Glen, September, 1942]
Hollywood—Wednesday

ANAÏS—

Since writing you yesterday I saw Dr. Friedman and had a good piece of news about *The Maurizius Case*. He has the final papers from Switzerland, from the attorney of Wassermann's estate, authorizing him to sell the movie rights for this book and nine others.

I am now doing a synopsis of the book, together with an argument or brief for it, to appeal to a producer. Am tackling it with vim and vigor, as I have permission to do it in my own way. It does not necessarily follow that if the book is accepted I will be given the job of adaptation—but I may obtain the right to collaborate. Friedman promises he will do everything in his power, and I believe he will. I had thought that, to sell it, all he needed to do was to show that he is the exclusive agent. I thought Wassermann so well known that it needed no brief, but it appears not. Even Wassermann has to be "sold" to the movies! And yet, ever since his death, they have been trying to obtain the right to produce his work.

Rereading the book now, with an eye to bringing out the salient features of it, I am amazed at the multiplicity of threads and how skillfully it is all handled. What I overlooked before now assumes vital import—that his interest in the Maurizius Case (Etzel's) began, or was *mysteriously* linked with the letter from Geneva (from his mother). Wassermann stresses somewhere that for Etzel the key word was "mystery." The unconscious knowledge that his mother had been done an injustice by his father becomes a conscious fact in the case of the condemned man. There is a letter which he writes to his mother, and never posts, which I had forgotten about. I feel as though I were plunged into a whirlwind.

There is a Greek here in the canyon—Honest John's coffee shop— with whom I have interesting talks about Greece. He came from Sparta. He says, "I want you to come in often . . . I like to hear you talk. You don't talk like the people around here." Found him reading *The Lost Horizon* today. . . . Well, more soon.

HVM

[Beverly Glen, September 8, 1942]
Tuesday

ANAÏS—

Yes, everything is clear and understood. I'm in a much better frame of mind about everything. Have been on the Hay diet for over a week—marvelous experience. Didn't have a bite of bread for about four days—felt purified. *And*—began to lose my *false* hunger. Could eat heartily when I sat down—but no pangs, as formerly, when I *thought* I needed nourishment.

Then too, plunged deep in the *Maurizius Case,* I found great pleasure in making clear the meaning—which goes very deep, incidentally. I'll send you a copy (soon as Friedman types it off) of the prefatory pages, explaining Wassermann's dilemma vis-à-vis Etzel *or*—vis-à-vis the question of justice—and guilt and punishment. (His answer to everything—in all the books—seems the same—i.e. that "love" is the only solution (very much as in *Seraphita!*). The last book of his (where he writes another *Aaron's Rod*)—fuses the writer and the sage —is wonderful and terribly revelatory. His women characters I like better than in any other author, I think. All his own personal problems (as man and writer) strike deep.

I'm doing this one job (*Maurizius*) with a vengeance—a last desperate fling. I have a hunch it will be sold. But the theme is not particularly palatable now—it is against all we stand for. However, if it is accepted it will be turned into some foolish propaganda—I know that. No matter what the significance may be, the episodes are dramatic, the characters tremendous.

Friedman is going into partnership with some man—to establish an agency of some kind. I may have *part-time work*—which would pay my living expenses. Will know definitely in next 10 days.

Saw Miss Rubber last night—first time since I mentioned her name last. All very nice—but no definite progress. These people lead the most amazing "forgetful" sort of lives. You have no idea how many invitations I've answered—in the hope of getting a foothold—only to receive silence. Everything is diffuse, dispersed here—because *they* are so themselves.

The latest is that I'm to meet Erich Remarque (author of *All Quiet on the Western Front*). He is supposed to admire my work greatly. He is wealthy—and generous. Perhaps he will help me.

As for Argus, Fraenkel, etc. I do go after them. No results. I think myself that it is in my destiny (that means "my character," I guess) not to earn money. *Or*—it will come one day, all in a rush, by some fluke. (When I give up all hope, I suppose.) This is the one tormenting problem for me. That's why I always come back to the same idea —that if I can live on the lowest level, put the idea of earning money out of my mind, proceed quietly with my work, the thing will solve itself. But that I can't even earn that minimum is what licks me. The fault must be mine.

Yes, of course, I'll try to get orders for the press. Incidentally, Miss Rubber thought very highly of your book. I believe she's buying a copy. Anyway, "the world is in a state of chassos." (I met the Irishman who played "the Paycock" not long ago. Fine chap.) Also saw Noel Coward's play last night at [Max] Reinhardt Workshop—*The*

Astonished Heart" (about an analyst who makes a mess of his life). Very good, it was.

Friedman told me that the Dr. Kerkhoven book had been plagiarized recently—by the movies.

Yes, Ganna! I laugh my head off reading about her [Mrs. Wassermann]. Can't feel sorry for Wassermann here—it's so obvious that he was at fault himself. But from this experience he was able to explain Maurizius' failing vis-à-vis his wife and Anna Jahn. Tremendous pages here. I've tracked him down like a sleuth. In the light of all, Etzel's crusading appears fantastically futile. He is only the hater of injustice—he is that because his affective nature was amputated—thru deprivation of mother. Such people (and Hitler and Trotsky are examples of it) turn the world upside down, trying to right things—looking *outside* for the malady, instead of within.

Had a letter from Houghton again. Showed it to Donald Friede (who, to my surprise, *likes* H.). There is a possibility he will get one of the books before a producer. H. has already received overtures from Hollywood. I have no *real* traffic with Friede—just a polite, austere exchange. He's like a feeble Cagliostro, a bit. No slouch, though.

The weather is marvelous now. Like going back to spring. Strong smell of jasmine at night—overwhelming. Beautiful Chinese mists too. I explore all the bypaths of the canyon. What marvelous homes here! I am almost envious. I expect, though, that the Japs will take it over—the whole coast—before very long.

HVM

[Beverly Glen, September 29, 1942]
Tuesday

ANAÏS—

Friede says No to everything! The war again. Not even the possibility of finding me a job—now they must have only experienced movie writers. Also says nobody is interested in *The Maurizius Case.* Says it has been peddled around for years. That can hardly be true as nobody had the right to offer it for sale previously. He answered

me by letter. As for the Rosenfeld article [about *Winter of Artifice*] *
—I rather like it, to tell you the truth. It's very warm and apprecia-
tive, and even if it's a bit fuzzy around the edges and a bit off center
now and then, it's the kind of criticism that will do you good, not
harm. I don't think he realized that you were trying to keep it a secret
about your father. Few people will. None of these secrets can be kept
anyway—you'll see. The last paragraph is interesting, too.

Got the telegram this morning. Fine. By the way, Man Ray praised
your book highly—the form and workmanship. Said he was hoping
he could give you something of his own to print. Said it was the first
beautiful book he had seen in America. He liked the choice of type
very much. Said it was derived from the old Roman or Greek inscrip-
tions on gravestones and that it was chosen because it looked less like
the stereotyped lettering. The vowels are very large and the conso-
nants squeezed together. Very distinctive and appealing to the eye—
especially in the big print. He spoke very discerningly, as always.

I don't doubt you can get plenty of work to do—but what about
your eyes? Is it worth ruining your eyes? I don't suppose you've
found anyone to help you.

Incidentally, I have a book on the eyes—*Sight Without Glasses*—
which is quite a revelation to me. You should look it up—it's by Dr.
Peppard. (The originator of this theory is Bates—see his work if you
can.) Anyway, I wanted to tell you this. The way you read—taking
in a lot at one time—is supposed to be most injurious. For weak eyes
one should read slowly, *one word at a time!* I tried it out—not wearing
the glasses. It works! There are 3 or 4 simple exercises recommended.
Blink (like a cat), *shift,* and focus. That's the core of it. As to why
one loses sight—that's most illuminating! (A bit like the deafness
theory.) Everything is referred back to tension—anxiety. If, as in your
case, it is bodily fatigue, anemia, etc. then above all glasses are *not*
needed. One must go to the roots. The first thing to learn is to *not* try
to see! Don't strain. One sees with the brain. The eye is only a camera
made of muscles. The image is there always. We see what we want to
see—etc. etc. It's quite true—painfully true. And no doubt your
anemia has some simple explanation too. I mean, if Jacobsohn cured
it once, it must be that you live in such a way as to negate his efforts.
I don't believe at all that it has to do with *not* eating sufficiently. You

* *New Republic,* Sept. 26, 1942.

eat more heartily than I do, I've noticed. I don't think you know how to *rest*. You give the illusion of resting—but all the while you consume yourself.

These vitamins and injections are like all other forms of crutches. Doctors will get nowhere with us—it's all experimenting, just as with guinea pigs—until we have the desire to be healthy and stay healthy. Fundamentally man wants to be sick. It's the same as regards war and peace. There is yet no *real* desire for peace, for health, for joy, etc. We only fight against negatives.

I was reading a critique of Céline in *Accent* (Winter 1942 issue), where there is a good essay on *"Hamlet* (2.)" by Dudley Fitts. Céline, it was pointed out, realized deeply and bitterly this incurable malady of mankind. (The article is an attack, by the way.) He saw the unwillingness, the perversity in humans—and that discouraged and embittered him. He was poisoned by it. (Reminds me of the speech of Klakusch in *M. Case*—where he says he saw too much, knew too much, about human beings.) I'm writing a wonderful explanation of Wassermann vs. the world—I see him very very clearly now. He was going to give us a final book on *Illusion and Delusion*. How significant!

To get back to your remarks on the war and my attitude. Sure, I know all you say—how everything affects us. But you might just as well speak of tornadoes and earthquakes. I still am not interested. We have to reckon with them. Just as we reckon with disease and accident. It doesn't make much difference what brings about a man's death. He doesn't live by the knowledge of those things. All the fighting against things seems to me virtually futile. One has to remove oneself. The relatedness you talk of seems to me superficial. I am not related to those things. One is only related to what one is passionate about. Because we must have food and shelter, get sick, die, etc. is about the least interesting thing about life. That's all biological—as true for animals and plants, as for us. One gets nowhere thinking about those matters. A bit of goodwill and tolerance would take care of most of those fundamental problems. By the way, yesterday in Westwood Village, I saw walking down the street the man who played the monk in *The Lost Horizon*. Went up to him and shook his hand. All these actors from the screen look amazingly like their screen selves in life. One can never get over it. One always feels he knows the person intimately. It's uncanny to see them walking about. They're like live ghosts.

Well, more soon. Gilbert just got his radio and phono from Denver —with an amazing collection of good records. We have quite a feast now nights. Am also doing some fine water colors in my spare time. Wish I could help you with the press.

HVM

[Beverly Glen, October, 1942]
Saturday

Just got your letter and am terribly sorry to hear about your failures with the press.* All the more reason why you should do only your own work—I'm rather glad, to tell you the truth. I think it's terrible that you should become a *printer*. Undoubtedly a great factor is the war. Everybody admires the book tremendously. Normally you would have reaped a legitimate reward. It isn't your fault!

Well, I have a bit of encouraging news from Friedman. He's got some backing and is opening a sort of agency—with some other men. He promises me a hundred dollars—"down payment"—for my work on the Maurizius book thus far. If it is sold I will get a percentage. Others will have to tackle it after I'm through—for the final work. (These scripts go thru a regular mangler! You have no idea what they do to them—it's incredible.) Anyway, there is a likelihood of more work—or some sort of steady, part-time job, as adviser and collaborator in the initiatory stages of the script. I won't get the "hundred" until two weeks from now—but it seems sure.

Also, I discovered in the office where he works a girl I knew in Paris—she's chief reader there. She was just reading one of my scripts when I walked in! Didn't believe it was my work. I have hopes that she may do something for me. I hope that advertising fellow takes something of mine! If so, I'll have the fare back to N.Y. If only I could find someone in N.Y. who would offer me a room! Here I get

---

* Anaïs Nin started out with a secondhand press which was operated by foot like a bicycle and had to be inked by hand. It took her a whole month to print the first four pages of a book. She eventually set and printed two pages a day, later even four, but at this pace it became impossible for her to take on any outside work.

all sorts of offers—even Hiler wants to put me up—and Friedman too. With all the people going to war now there ought to be some chance. I believe the only thing for me to do is to live cheaply—earn what little I can—and continue with my own work. All other notions are wasteful. I've got to accept a restricted life—that's the price of writing as one pleases. So keep your eyes open—for a place to live.

And don't be discouraged. This "sense of reality" which others talk about is nonsense. That's the thing that leads the world into war—because all is based on compromise and eventually the naked reality gets the upper hand. Corruption starts from the bottom and poisons all levels. The work of the world is based on deception and falsehood.

I am not bitter about things. On the contrary, I think we're lucky. Lucky not to be involved—emotionally or physically—in the general catastrophe. The world will wake up—when it has had its fill of suffering. (We've done our suffering. And we've paid. The others don't want to face suffering—they consider it "somebody's fault.")

I think things will improve a bit for me now. I have a hunch that it said in my horoscope for the year that I would be unable to do anything these last few months. Do you remember? Anyway, this crackpot astrologer out here assures me I am now in for "a period of great activity." I feel it too. I've rounded some sort of bend. And with me, it always happens that at the lowest point there comes a gleam of light. I believe still in my good fortune. Now I'll have to console you! Don't abandon the press. Let's see if we can't do what we meant to do originally—*your own work*. Fight for that!

HVM

[Beverly Glen, October, 1942]
Thursday

Just got your letter and postal order too! Am trying to find my Clichy stories—have mislaid them. About that long letter for Glen Jocelyn—I wonder. I'd like to see it again myself before sending it to him. I had thought of two other alternatives for him—1.) the preface to Tyler's book on Hollywood; 2.) the little book I gave Emil Schnellock—on water colors—handwritten. (I could also give him the long piece—"Reunion in Brooklyn"—if I can locate a copy.) In breaking up I gave things to be kept safely. I must rack my brains.

It's possible that for Goldberg I could also offer, as substitutes, either a fragment from "The Rosy Crucifixion" or "The Sleeping Sleeper Asleep." I'm going to finish that up now.*

Just got thru with my abstract of *The Maurizius Case*—over a hundred pages. May have to do a shorter one now. But I think there's a good chance of placing it. If it is sold, my time here won't have been in vain.**

I'm going to see now if anything can be done about the Houghton books. The agency where Friedman has his offices is a good one and that girl I met the other day has a good position. Something may yet come of all this.

Funny about your horoscope! I too was thinking that way about you the other day. Maybe we're all due for a radical change.

I'll try to find the book you recommended at the library.

Meanwhile, I'm going to try my hand once again at an original movie script—a last chance. Once I return to New York I'm going to stick to my book—strictly. I've got new ideas for it, new urges. The Wassermann books did a lot for me.

I'll wind up things now.

                                                            HVM

[Beverly Glen, October 1942]
                                                         Monday
        Haven't written for days—because I'm busy retyping Gilbert's novel! He had to go to Sacramento, to take a job working with Mexican farm laborers. Viking begging for book—he is on the last chapter. So I buckled down to work—am nearly thru now. I also lent

---

* Glen Jocelyn was a New York editor interested in Miller's work. Samuel Goldberg, the lawyer, worked with Miss Steloff of the Gotham Book Mart, which occasionally issued its own publications.

** No film based on Miller's material was ever made but the Colt Press, San Francisco, published a 77-page book, illustrated with drawings and water colors by Miller, *Maurizius Forever,* in 1946, which summarizes Miller's ideas about the Wassermann novel.

him some of the money I got from Friedman—because the gov't won't pay him till the end of the month.

Meanwhile I've been telegraphing (3 times!) to Abramson to return the stories I want to send Goldberg! I forgot he had them. I thought maybe he would bite—take them, pay me ($350.00) I asked —and then send Goldberg other stuff.

Now there's a possibility of my doing an adaptation of a Graham Greene novel (*Brighton Rock*)—thru the girl I met at the agency. Not certain yet, though. If I do, I'll get a substantial sum—cash.

I've also had a letter from Houghton's Hollywood agents to see them. There's just a chance. I may do something for him—and for myself.

Did you see or talk to Glen Jocelyn? or do you want me to write him? I wrote him twice, when I first arrived—but no answer. I do hope he is serious. And Goldberg too. That would be a lifesaver!

About apartments—what I meant was "free" places!

I don't think it's necessary to pay rent any more—with conditions as they are. Out here I get all kinds of free rent, invitations. Must find somebody who's being drafted and can spare a room or a wing!

No, don't send any money yet. I have a hunch I won't need any for quite a while.

With the card you sent from Fred came a letter and more cards. Also a letter from Dudley. Seems he and Lafe want to come out here. I will try to advise them not to—it's another dream.

Had a receiver's notice from Colt Press—now it's public knowledge.* Maybe Mrs. Palmer will change her mind.

Your N.Y. life sounds glittering. Mine here is quite the opposite. I'm in very good spirits. Nobody will believe how simple this life can be—in the midst of bargaining and corruption. The days are lovely. And time flies.

Hiler is joining the Coast Guard. Otherwise he would be drafted. It's "cliches o chicharrones" now. (Tits or cracklings!) Gilbert's book is full of Spanish phrases, and Spanish food and music. I enjoy working on it. Do you suppose Goldberg will pay me—or Steloff? And how much? I wonder. It ought to fetch (the two stories) from 250 to

---

* The Colt Press in San Francisco, which had published Millers' Greek book, *The Colossus of Maroussi*, was temporarily in financial difficulties but continued its operation.

350 dollars, I think. By the way, I now have a long short story I could send to Jocelyn, if he likes: "Reunion in Brooklyn."

More soon as I finish typing.

HVM

[Beverly Glen, November 5, 1942]
Thursday

ANAÏS:

If the manuscript doesn't come from Abramson today I'll send you the carbons, which I now have from Herbert West.* Abramson said in a letter that he had sent them, by express, I suppose. Admitted he was dilatory and remiss, said if they were ever printed he would want to buy a quantity. So I'll express the manuscript to you, for Goldberg—as I can see he would be frightened even to receive them.

Incidentally, I send you two stories; if they [the Gotham Book Mart] only wish to print one, then it should be "Quiet Days in Clichy." If they print the two, the title for the volume remains the same.

And now I will write Jocelyn immediately. I must find out what kind of thing he wants. That's why I didn't send anything yet. But in his case, I do expect cash on the acceptance of manuscript, no?

Yesterday I got a check from Herb West for $15.00. Gilbert doesn't get paid until the first of next month! That's government red tape. Both he and Margaret are awfully honest and generous; they were wonderful to me, especially about money matters. When Gilbert left they were down to almost nothing. It was the least I could do to lend them the money. He likes his work with the Mexican laborers, but says that we are treating them like dirt. Some of them get their fingers chopped off the first day, not knowing how to handle our farm machinery. They want to work for him, Gilbert—can't understand why not. It's pathetic.

If you know where [Parker] Tyler is, would you ask him (I've written him twice and just now sent a telegram from [Wolfgang] Paalen *) if he will give me permission to use that Preface I wrote for

---

* See Biographical Notes.

his book. Paalen wants to publish it, and is going to press now.* I
fear he has moved.

No, you never showed me the *Seven Gothic Tales*. Better hold it
now until I return.

The Russian woman sounds interesting. And I was tickled to hear
that the public library is circulating your book! Did you send one to
the Library of Congress?

Living alone and cooking for myself I find I can live very cheaply.
If I find a place rent free, with cooking facilities, there'll be absolutely nothing to worry about.

The Swami is sending me a copy of that voluminous book by
Ramakrishna's devoted disciple and Boswell.** I'm delighted. We'll get
the Blake book when I get back—or if I can pick up one secondhand
here I'll send it to you.

From his letters, Paalen sounds like a very fine chap. Something
warm and generous about him. Lafe Young wrote me that he's like a
saint.

One of the strange things about Huxley's book on the eyes [*The
Art of Seeing*] is about "memory and imagination." He says, for example, that when you can remember a thing it is easier to see—not
just that thing, but anything. He gives exercises for bed, with eyes
closed, where you imagine yourself holding a rubber ball and squeezing it, or writing your name with an imaginary pencil attached to
your nose. Try it—it's amazing how you feel the muscles working.
Also, it's all nonsense that small type is injurious, if you read properly. This business of reading slowly, word by word, or even letter
for letter at times, is interesting and efficacious. I always read the
book upside down for a while, to begin with. Now I am keeping the
glasses off indoors quite a bit. And mornings, when I go to the
grocer's, I leave them off. I've had a spot in front of my eye, which
comes and goes during the day, ever since a week or so before I left
N.Y. I also juggle with tennis balls a bit—for the astigmatism. When
I sat up in earnest, was when I read that the eye is exactly like a

---

* "Preface to Parker Tyler's *America's Hallucination*," *Dyn*, Mexico, Fall
1942.

** Mahendra Nath Gupta (1855–1932) (who used the pseudonym "M."),
The Gospel of Sri Ramakrishna, translated into English from the Bengali, with
an introduction by Swami Nikhilananda, New York, Ramakrishna-Vivekananda
Center, 1942.

camera, that it has a hole in it through which everything is imaged, whether you look or don't look. To see you must stop trying to see— that is the basic principle. He talks of "dynamic relaxation." Sounds like Lao-tse. Anyway, it's against the idea of struggle. Even to see black, when you close your eyes, you must not think of black. You think of pleasant things . . . you forget . . . you wander. Then things grow black. Again he talks about having confidence, but with indifference as to the result. Very Oriental that. Right out of the Bhagavad-Gita. Because if you have only confidence you are apt to be disappointed when you do not get the proper results, and that undermines, vitiates all your confidence. Sounds highly sensible to me. I've often tried to think that way about my work, and when I am myself, I do. Wassermann reiterated this, when Etzel interviews Ghisels, his favorite writer. It was a wonderful passage.

I'm dying to get back to Céline and finish that book [*Death on the Installment Plan.*] He gives me a greater kick, as writer, than anyone. For style and freedom of expression. I don't mind his ranting at all —it just makes me laugh. Doesn't depress me.

One night, before Gilbert left, I had a great talk with him about Rimbaud, some of whose poems Gilbert translated marvelously (as he did with Valéry and Baudelaire). Gilbert, I may have said, reminds me somewhat of Osborn. But he has something—he *is* a writer. And has a wide reading acquaintance in three languages. I know his Spanish is excellent—and he prefers Spanish to anything and Spaniards (or Mexicans, rather) to other peoples. The Spaniard down there is called a "gachupin," pejorative term—I don't know what it means. Anyway, about Rimbaud. I was in bed. I got excited, and then I came out with this—which I mean—that I place Rimbaud, as writer, above any writer I can think of. Meaning for what he attempted, for his purity and fidelity. I added that in some way I had gone off the track myself. That I wanted—that would be my ultimate aim—to get back to that quality which Rimbaud had and which distinguishes him, for me, from all other writers.* (This leaves out significance and content.) It gets back to what I have said and written about "play." (Now you come with that word "jeu.") But the French word connotes something lesser than what I mean. In play, which I am asso-

---

* See also Miller's essay on Rimbaud which was first published in two parts in the New Directions *Annuals* 9 (1947) and 11 (1949) and later under the title *The Time of the Assassins,* Norfolk, Conn., James Laughlin, 1956.

ciating, or identifying, with the very essence of creation, one can't go wrong! That's what I mean. As soon as other things enter, there is adulteration. (Moreover, I do not mean that play and surrealism are one and the same; surrealism makes use, in part, of this thing, but is again defective, or poisoned, by ulterior motives.)

Gilbert has the faculty of catching the most subtle and often unexpressed thoughts. He has a flair. The same with people. I'll never forget how he described you walking—the multitude of details he summoned. And he was certain it was you—though he had only seen photos of you. But he seemed to catch your very spirit.

The burden of all this is that, just when you are about finished, you begin to perceive what it is all about. So much of our writing is purely compulsive. Just as one does not begin to live until one follows some high discipline—it needn't be Yoga, necessarily—so one doesn't begin to write until one is purified of the dross. Here art and life join hands. In most of the great books there are only flashes of this—the rest is stuffing, no matter how deep or purposeful the whole may seem. One should not struggle with the medium—one should be master of it and use it like a god. Small as he was, Rimbaud seems to me to have had more of the god in him than others—that's what I am getting at. Do you agree with me? You don't, I know. You wonder about Dostoevski and Wassermann, no? Maybe I'm a little too categorical. But there's a point in it. And everything I touch or think about, ties up with this little point. That's what I meant a while back about questioning everything, from the bottom up. I'm getting on to new ground. I feel like disowning more and more everything I've done, said or stood for. I don't want to just go on. . . .

H

[Beverly Glen, November 9, 1942]
Monday

ANAÏS:

I'm bringing all your Mss.,* together with my two for Goldberg, to the Satyr [Book Shop] this afternoon, to have them send you

* Anaïs Nin had sent Miller some manuscripts of work in progress.

by express. Had to send the carbon of my things, as I haven't yet
received originals from Abramson. I think they're legible, however—a
few pages I recopied altogether. If it goes to print, I would like it
understood that I see the final proofs and O.K. them, to avoid possible
errors.

I received $25.00 from Margaret and Gilbert Saturday. They are
both staying up there indefinitely, but holding this place, because the
job is not secure. So I'm alone and resuming work on my own things
until it's time to leave. I wrote Jocelyn a good letter the other day—
sorry to hear he's ill. I have had backaches too lately, and so has the
fellow next door. But it's gone now. I feel marvelously fit. Finally got
Parker's O.K. to give the preface to Paalen. If the London publishers
say they want the American book I may redo it, using only the good
parts and elaborating on them.

The radio is full of blasts about the invasion of North Africa.
Sounds wonderful. The first brilliant stroke on the part of the Allies.
I expect Italy will collapse now soon, and France will spring up in
revolt.

I was just loaned a copy of Prokosch's *Seven Who Fled,* which
opens marvelously—with a poetic description of Central Asia, even
better than in the *Asiatics.* And I've got the Ramakrishna volume—
over a thousand pages. The weather continues beautiful here—warm
in the daytime and cold at night. Had an invasion of rats—chewed up
some of Gilbert's and Margaret's clothes—I got off scot free, just a
pocket nibbled at a bit. They drive me nuts at night, scampering under
the roof over my head. Sound like monkeys. Now and then a gopher
pops up from some underground tunnel. Sometimes deer come down
from the hills and walk around in the yard. That's a wonderful sight.

Well, more soon. Going to town now. This going and coming
knocks out about three or four hours. I often walk, until I get a hitch.
I've never seen another person walking along the highway. It's amazing. In a few days, however, things will change. Four gallons a week
isn't enough for the people out here. Well, more soon.

HVM

[Beverly Glen, December 7, 1942]
Monday P.M.

ANAÏS,

As I was going down the road yesterday to visit the astrologer, Pierce Harwell, I found him coming to see me—with the enclosed note. I think you will see from this, as regards the "work" problem, that I had come to the proper conclusion myself. It's very curious, though, about this Saturn-Neptune "unhousing" of one another! No wonder you felt that you were cracking. Myself I don't feel any of this, however. I felt it more a few months back, when I wrote those long letters. Since then I have been wrestling with the problem, and am ready for it.

Today, going the rounds for a job, I was really elated. I hear of more and more jobs. One recommends me to another. Today, interviewing a man in the War Information Bureau, he refers me to the very man Russell & Volkening sent me out to see at the movie agency! I'll see him tomorrow—curious coincidence.

Was making application at a Probation Office for ex-convicts. Felt like those old W.U. days. But they said I needed a college degree. So tomorrow I am seeing the Juvenile branch—12-to-18-year-old cases. Also, have two introductions to leading personnel men in aircraft factories.

I feel as though I were interviewing them, not they me. It seems like I'm in a kindergarten. Naturally, these men are usually younger and inferior. I feel jovial when I see them. Sitting in the probation office, while the ex-convicts were coming to report and pay installments on their fines, I was intensely interested. I like the convicts—not the probation officers. The convicts too are just children who have gone wrong. What a flood of them. One man handling seven hundred and fifty cases! I felt sorry for him. And I noticed that he was utterly without sympathy for them. He said—"They have no personality problems." (Sic) One fairy, who was paying off a large fine (an embezzler), pulled out a roll of bills that was incredible. Very lofty too. Most of them were airy, breezy, nonchalant, good-natured, dressed in shabby working clothes—real guys. I warmed up to them. They had qualities. I was genuinely sorry to lose this chance. One Mexican boy, about twenty-two, the typical dandy-gangster of L.A. (there's a horde of them here, raising hell now), was the picture of insouciance, bravado, scorn and contempt. Incorrigible. You could see how much he despised the parole officers, who are just clerks at heart, really. I was sorely tempted to speak to them, go out and have a drink with them, see their homes, hear their stories. It reminded me of those days in the W.U., when I wrote my first book—*Twelve Messengers*. How much more I could tell now, about such experiences! I was raw and callow then. I didn't know what gold nuggets I was handling.

No, on the way home in the bus I felt in excellent spirits, despite the lack of results. It was like an excursion into the petty, everyday world, a reconnection with life in the raw, which I really don't need, but which, when I enter into it now, acts like a tonic just the same. I feel like a messenger from another planet. Naturally, my passport is not quite in order. But, I can see from the casual contacts, that I am going to meet the right man and then there will be another curious job, strange experiences, etc. I can almost summon the man out of the blue, that's how I feel.

A cable came from England (via Huntington Cairns) asking me to contact an editor (of *Tomorrow*) in England. Today a telegram from a visitor (another friend of Cairns), asking me to meet him tomorrow. Since I made the decision to plunge, the gods are helping. God helps him who helps himself.

This morning, at breakfast, a great talk over the radio by some homespun philosopher, about helping people to help themselves. As though expressly for my benefit. I laugh. When you have a problem and you decide to tackle it in earnest, you seem surrounded by solvers of that problem. Everything converges on you to ram it home.

By the way, the young astrologer's letter may not sound so hot— he's not a writer—but his talk is wonderful. He's far beyond Moricand. He knows. We understand each other perfectly. There was one image which he gave me, of my two bad squares—square of Neptune and Jupiter, and square of Saturn and Venus—which was excellent. As though I were held rigidly between two solid walls, forced straight on, and forced to s'approfondir (deepen myself). The bad period I am in will last another two years or a little over—it doesn't scare me in the least. Incidentally, I passed through a similar one when I was between 22 and 24—I've often depicted it to you—when I was with that "widow." This time I am immunized, at least to some degree. That sculptress in Paris (Wilson) once warned me of it. No, by God, Neptune isn't going to be sunk. The freedom of the soul—why, that's perfect. And that's what you struggled so desperately to give me. You couldn't insure me against the money thing—I see that plainly—nobody could, not even God Almighty. But I got something better, by way of security. I issue forth now, armed with the trident. Yes, I'll think of the shower of gold—in its most rarefied aspects.

Well, I'm wondering how you're feeling now. No letter today. I expect to hear though that you've taken a radical turn for the better. I don't think I'll have to be a riveter. I think something much more interesting will develop. I expect miracles, and I'll do my best to make them happen.

Must close—getting up very early in the morning. I'm on the track of the Isak Dinesen book—know where it is. That's a pseudonym, I hear, for a Danish woman. Just read what Trotsky wrote on Céline in 1935. Not so hot.

HVM

[Beverly Glen, December 14, 1942]
Monday, A.M.

ANAÏS,

I'm glad to hear you've taken a turn. Got your two more cheerful, hopeful letters. All right, I'm keeping the Postal check, but don't send any more, eh? I'm sure everything will come through fine. I'm enveloped in prospective offers. Two are very interesting. Remember the man I said I expected miracles through? Well, thru him, I went to Myron Selznick Agency—the best out here—where Friede was (he's now in the service)—and there I met a man who seems genuinely interested. He thinks he may find something for me with David Selznick, the film corporation. Also, Gilbert just wrote, to ask if I would take a job with him, similar work, working with the Mexican immigrant laborers. Says he spoke to his boss, and they think they might be able to use me, because of my personnel experience. I have to pretend a little Spanish, to begin with, and they will coach me once I get on the job. It may mean moving to another California locale for a while—not Sacramento. The Probation Office may also ask for me anyway—despite lack of college degree! For temporary work, till war is over. So you see, things are humming. The library work paid too poorly—35 cents an hour, 30 hours a week only. Now there's another library, near Pasadena, a rich one, where I might have translation work to do (French)—better pay, better surroundings.

I have again a full day ahead of me. Can't write much. I got a copy of the *Gothic Tales* and read that story.* Am going to write you more about it later—only this now—it's the nearest and best description of you I could ever hope to see! There is something baffling about it too —which I will thrash out when I reread it. My days are very full.

Had a letter from Politis, the Greek, urging me to write the *National Herald* ** about publishing *Colossus* in Greek. Thinks there is a chance—thinks I might be able to get $500 cash for the rights. My L.A. publisher won't say yet about the Letters. But I know he's eager to print me. Says he knows "I could make him"! (Kahane's words.†)

The signs are very favorable, despite the transit of Saturn. I suppose God helps those who help themselves! Which is what you've been trying to make me understand, no doubt. That's what Stalin discovered, didn't he? Yes, do take it easy! Rest! I feel marvelous. More soon.

                                                          HVM

                                      [Beverly Glen, December 19, 1942]
                                                          Saturday

ANAÏS—

Haven't had word from you for several days now. Hope you're not worse! Had a disappointing meeting this morning with two men at Myron Selznick's. They had sent me a telegram to call—I thought I was getting a job. But no, nothing doing. A complete contradiction of my previous talk with them. Asked me finally if I couldn't write just plain shit wrapped in cellophane (their words), with a little sacrifice in it, because they like sacrifice!

However, there are other things still open. I expect word from the

---

* Isak Dinesen's "The Dreamers."

** A Greco-American newspaper in New York, which later published an article by Miller ("Today, Yesterday and Tomorrow," February 28, 1943).

† Miller actually had no publisher in Los Angeles but there had been discussion of publishing some of his writings through the Satyr Book Shop.

Probation office any day—they have let down the bars, as I told you. Meanwhile I am writing a number of people to see if I can get book review work. Had a letter from the magazine *Tomorrow* (N.Y.C.) saying they would probably send me some books to review soon. And if I could do an article for them, to do so. They pay ten dollars for a review. I would only need a few of them each month to get along. So I am writing everybody connected with the literary world.

Politis sends me a good review of the Greek book from the London *Times;* is showing it to the prospective publisher. I have a hunch I will succeed here. I am now trying to persuade my L.A. publisher to reprint the book, since Colt has gone under.

Looking thru my address book I came across the name Norman V. Dagg, who was once editor of the *Modern Mystic,* London, that published two things of mine.* He's the man then who sent Cairns the cable the other day. I'm expecting him to commission me to do something.

Gilbert writes that they may put him in charge of an office hiring the Mexican laborers. If so, I'll be well taken care of. But things are still in a muddle. He hasn't even received his pay for the last half of November.

I got another check the other day. Don't know any more what to do or say. But there's one thing I do know—I am not disgruntled or discouraged or despairing about anything. I am doing my utmost and expect results. Every day brings some kind of good news. The other day a letter from Budd Schulberg, saying he was returning from Mexico and would look me up. Wants to talk to me about work with the movies in Mexico. He's the man I had expected to see when I came out here. Saroyan's agent, Stanley Ross, also visited me the other day. He wants to do something for me too. It does seem as though Fate were trying to help me. But I'm not depending on Fate any more.

Well, this will reach you just about Christmas time, I suppose. I'm sending you a water color for your Xmas. I see Arensberg tomorrow and get them all back from him. He said some of them were "positively fascinating." I hope he buys one!

HVM

---

* *The Modern Mystic* published two short pieces by Miller in 1939: "The Wisdom of the Heart" (April) and "Seraphita" (May).

P. S. I go to the planetarium tonight with the astrologer—to see *Saturn!*

                        [Beverly Glen, December 30, 1942]
                                          Wednesday

ANAÏS—

Writing this from book shop in Hollywood—caught postman on the wing.

Have lots of good news. [Cyril] Connolly sent me a check for 20 lbs. (80 dollars) for the first installment of American book in November *Horizon.** Says it's causing a sensation in London. Terence Holliday (N.Y. bookshop) is asking [Stephen Vincent] Benét to get me money from a Writers' Fund. Asked me to wire him collect if I wanted help—I did. So I expect something there.

I'm also getting promises of book reviews—from N.Y. *Tribune, New Republic,* etc. Getting 3 of my books as a gift (Shanghai editions) from a poet in Selma, Cal.

Also more offers to put up at people's homes. One says—free rent, food, cigarettes, stamps, etc.—"for the duration." A flood of wonderful letters from all over—fine ones! Like a change of tide.

I've worked for it, of course. These past 2 months I've written *hundreds* of letters! Really! Now the returns are coming in. I wore the typewriter and fountain pen out—both being repaired.**

Also getting a few small $5.00 commissions for water colors.

No time for more now. Tomorrow! Hope it changes for you now. Heard that the English edition of *Colossus* sold out in 30 days. Ought to be getting money from them soon. The Greek is sending me loads of letters, connections, little gifts—Politis. Am to meet Venizelos' son in a few days. *Hurrah!*

                                          HVM

---

* "Good News! God Is Love!", London, November, 1942.

** When Miller's efforts to get a job in Hollywood failed and his economic situation became critical he launched an appeal for support in an "Open Letter to All and Sundry," and asked numerous editors for work (book reviewing etc.). Fragments from this letter and other appeals were published in 1943 and 1944.

[Beverly Glen, January 3, 1943]
Sunday

ANAÏS—

Here is something from Pierce regarding your horoscope. Hope it means something to you. Strange that he confirms what I wrote you recently—about your extraordinary recuperative powers. I'm sending the Collins' book tomorrow.

I've been snowed under with letters. Every mail now seems to bring more good news. I had a check from Dorothy Norman for $25 and a promise to help in other ways. Two unknown friends in Chicago offer me food and shelter "for the duration." Book reviews are promised. The New Year began well. Holliday, the bookshop man, writes again —that he's asked Benét to help me—and says he'll do anything he can for me (Holliday)—to let him know.

I'll be getting the [Denys C. W.] Harding book [*The Impulse to Dominate*]. My friend [Lawrence Clark] Powell,* librarian at U.C.L.A., said as he was ordering it a few days ago he thought of me —thought I'd like it.

Margaret's back for a while. Is turning the house upside down, putting it in order. Gilbert is at Santa Maria—hopes to get a still bigger job—maybe in Mexico.

HVM

P. S. Still looking for Dr. Chew's famous Chinese herbs for you. Have you tried ginger—and honey? Anyway, you're not going to fade away, as you imagined. You have the nine lives of a cat—and look, now that I don't need any more help, will you be starting soon to print the Diary?

---

* Powell had been an American student at the Lycée Carnot in Dijon when Miller taught there. They met again when Miller moved in with the Neimans in Los Angeles, since Powell also lived in Beverly Glen.

1212 N. Beverly Glen Blvd.
West Lost Angeles, Cal.
Jan. 11th, 1943

ANAÏS,

Just came back to the house after taking Margaret to the bus station—she's gone to join Gilbert at Santa Maria, as he just got word from Covici that his book is accepted and now must send them some corrected pages—found my typewriter repaired, cleaned and oiled, and my fountain pen restored to its pristine elegance—and a batch of mail in the box. The first letter I opened contained a check for $200.00, a loan from the National Institute of Arts and Letters— thanks to Mr. Holliday! They ask if I will accept the loan and add: "You will at no time be asked for the return of this money, but should you ever be in a position to do so, it will be put back into our revolving fund and used again to help some other artist or writer in need." What could be more fair—this was our original idea months ago, remember? Seems rather just that I should get this now—since I tried so hard to get that loan fund started—sort of divine compensation, don't you think?

I'm trembling—it's so unexpected. Almost every letter I pick up brings more good news, more promises, more invitations—and more books. I wrote my last "business" letter last night. I have been at it steadily—like a monomaniac. I feel now as if I can go back to my book and write—with a free conscience. And if the review work comes in, as I most definitely know it will, I am definitely out of the morass. I hope this good news will give you a new lease on life. What with the marvelous words Pierce sends you on your natal chart you ought to be cured in no time!

I'm putting the money in the bank meanwhile. Imagine having money in the bank—I can scarcely believe it. God, I feel like a capitalist. And there are royalties soon due—from England, Laughlin and Colt Press. The latter are not out of business, nor in the hands of receivers—just suspending new publications for a while. They have 500 copies of the *Colossus* left—out of 2,000, and if they resume, as they hope, they think they will put out a second edition. Now I have to find a translator for the Greek book—Vlavianos will publish it, in Greek, if I can find a suitable one.

Well, I must stop. I feel almost as emotional this day as when the *Tropic of Cancer* came out.

HVM

[Beverly Glen, 1943]
Jan. 20th—Wednesday early A.M.

Just finished up a mass of letters. You asked if I have begun on *Capricorn*. * I did—one day—then I get inundated. Not only letters to and fro, but appointments; everything is descending on me at once, like a shower of sparks. As though, in addition to the outward appeal there was a response, well synchronized to the inner, silent appeal. It's never been like this before. Well, I just finished a last letter to a list of art colonies and prize foundations, to see where I stand with them. When I get the reports I'll let you know—for others who may stand in need.

Awfully glad you got Pierce's analysis. If you write him he will undoubtedly tell you more. And better direct that way. Yes, do send him a copy of your book—I am sure he would love it. I showed him it one night. How many have you left, by the way? Not many, I hope. Just today a soldier was asking the price of it at the Satyr bookshop, while I was there. He didn't have quite enough money on him at the moment. But he had your *House of Incest*—bought it at a fine shop in New Haven. Do you know that Satyr has under "Fine Books" on the most prominent shelf—hits your eye when you walk in—the following titles: Your book, mine, Fraenkel's, the Blake book [Milton O. Percival, *William Blake's Circle of Destiny,* Columbia University Press, 1938], Patchen's *Albion Moonlight* and several very fine works —the titles now escape me, just as I wish to give them to you. A most excellent collection, though.

I haven't seen *Dyn* yet.** I thought they were going to use the preface on the cinema. Maybe next time. You know, that fragment from the American book which [Cyril] Connolly used [in *Horizon,* London]

---

* Miller used the term loosely when speaking of the continuation of his "saga," which later became *The Rosy Crucifixion.*
** *Dyn,* a magazine published in Coyoacán, Mexico, printed Henry Miller's "The Ghetto," in the Fall 1942 issue.

is creating repercussions. Or perhaps I'm only getting responses from what the *New Masses* calls my "Trotskyite intelligentsia" audience. I had to laugh when I saw their dig. I have about as much use for Trotsky as for Stalin. His piece on Céline was sophomoric and conventional to an extreme. Like an old lady writing. Now I am scurrying through Arthur Koestler's *Scum of the Earth.* It is nowhere near as good as *Darkness at Noon,* which I once recommended to you. I wonder what you would make of this latter—it's a challenge for you. I don't know enough about these matters to say whether it rings true or not. Only—I like it, am inclined to believe him.

I don't quite know what you mean when you say "the voyage" itself in the [Bette] Davis film [*Now, Voyager*] gave you such a kick. The part I thought superb was the moment when, feeling weak, she returns to the asylum and, while waiting for the doctor, sees her former self in the person of that little girl—and then the illumination. But how they fumbled with that romance between her and the married man with the halter around his neck! The original story must have been different. The Hayes office created this dilemma, I'm sure. In *Random Harvest* the final use of "the key" will give you a thrill. Also, may I say, that "look of recognition" between the two at the end of *Random Harvest.* There was a world of significance in that. Ninety-nine percent of humanity is still split, from this standpoint. The story would have been still better if, instead of a shock produced by a bomb, it had been a shock from an inner struggle. What always gets me, however, in these themes, is the frantic desperation which seizes the character—to discover what had happened to him during his amnesia. Develop that little aspect and you have truly the drama of reincarnation. We have all lost "the memory of God" as it were. And memory is the clue to the soul-thread, so to speak. When memory goes it's time to be alarmed. I used to rebel against the insistence on developing the memory. I've discovered for myself since why it's important.

Pierce said tremendous things to me the other night. Words come from his lips, in talk, which are oracular and awesomely accurate. I imagine he writes poorly. But he has some special gift—he's pure, in a way, and sees flashingly when the power comes over him. The things he told me about myself gave me the creeps—so penetrating. Reminded me of the séance with the Armenian in Athens. Among other things he said I was the sanest person he knew—too sane. And I know what he meant. I know everything he means without bothering to translate it. He granted me that gift too. Said I could read a character better than the astrologer. His diagnosis of Gilbert was uncannily accurate too—in the subtleties. He realized at once that Gilbert was a sort of super-saint. And then of you, apropos of something, he remarked, "Her only weakness is her perfection." He gave a queer smile. Then after a few more words, a change of subject, he said: "Well, if that's how you feel, if you really mean that, why you're in Nirvana now. You're there—but you don't know it." And then suddenly I had that momentary feeling which I had with the Armenian, when he said "You will never die," and I understood but refused to face it, buried it instantly, very deep. The neurotic, if he will become neurotic enough, go to the bitter end, has a marvelous road before him. In the integrating process the part that the "adapters" would glue together really gets sloughed off and is put back, if at all, only as wings. The neurosis dies, like the afterbirth in women, and the child lives on. The mother part shouldn't be worried about at all—it's the child that matters. The mother is a constant, goes on forever; the child is a promise, a heaven-stormer. Well, enough. . . .

HM

[Beverly Glen, January 1943]
Sunday night, 1/30

ANAÏS—

It's been a hectic ten days—more like ten weeks—and I don't think I have written you. Lots of unexpected visitors, winding up with the Gilberts returning for a few days again. Was ill for a few days but recovered quickly. And all the time more and more good news—I can't keep up with the recording of it all.

Hope you received the Blake book meanwhile. Pierce said he got yours and wrote you a big letter. He found all sorts of marvelous things in your book. Indeed, he seems only to look for the marvelous. He's a wizard—more like Rimbaud than anyone I can think of—to have him around is like having a comet in the house. But I never met any one who can offer—and at lightning speed—more amazing interpretations. Burns like a geyser. Knows no fatigue. Has no hangovers. He's free, if ever a person was, but it's not an enviable freedom. All of which in no wise lessens the power of his words.

For some strange reason I picked up your book this evening and was reading the last 30 or so pages. I understood more than I ever had before. But again, toward the end of the experience with the Voice, I felt a mystifying element. I can see so far and then I am utterly baffled. The only clue I can give you is this, that whenever in speech or in writing you stress the word "human," the secret becomes palpable, though never fully revealed. It's almost as though the more frank and revelatory you become the more you succeed in remaining inscrutable. Which reminds me of Moricand's definition of *"reveler"*— do you remember? One of the strangest words in the human language.

It's like spring here now. We went from fall to spring without a winter!

HVM

P. S. I'm getting reviews now to do and *Town and Country* is taking a fragment of the burlesque on the Hollywood astrologer.*

Rudhyar is here in Hollywood and wants to send me a copy of his book. Do look up Arthur Koestler's books—*Dialogue with Death, Scum of the Earth* and *Darkness at Noon.*

[Beverly Glen]
2/9/43

ANAÏS—

Haven't heard from you in days! You're not ill, I hope. I just sent Pierce some clippings from 1942 numbers of *American Astrology,* which I'll send you soon as I get them back. They all seem to deal with Neptune—fascinating too! Neptune has entered *Libra* for next 16 years—since last October—and fantastic things are predicted therefrom. If you've already read them, tell me. Your ascendant is Libra and you're all Neptune—so you will be more involved than most people.

---

* "Hello June 26th! Yoohoo!", published June, 1943.

I just received my first book to review—a life of Kierkegaard.*
Opened it up to chapter called "Metamorphosis" and sat spellbound.
This concerns *me*. I'll send it to you soon as I'm through.

Letters still pouring in—more and more good tidings. I seem to be
swimming in a plenum—as though the "others" had at last found me
and were bathing me.

Do write and let me know if you're well.

HVM

Address now: Big Sur, California
April 21st [1944]

DEAR ANAÏS,

I had already seen the [Edmund] Wilson review **—several
people sent me the clippings. It was well-intentioned but inept and
inadequate, wasn't it? I was furious, myself. So that did the trick! It's
all so bloody spurious, what makes success here. The other night,
after reading proofs on my new book with Laughlin (*Sunday After
the War* [New Directions, published August 1944]), because I had
included in this book more pages about you, the Diary, etc. (things
you know), I went back to the essay "Un Être Étoilique" † and reread it. I had tears in my eyes. It is perhaps the best bit of writing I
ever did. Even if no person can possibly put in words all that may be
said about the Diary, I feel that I made a very wonderful attempt,
elliptically. (And how strange that George Orwell, the English writer,
should have used my phrase "inside the whale" for his left-handed
attack upon me! †† I am thinking all the time only about how to get
the Diary launched. I have suggested it whenever and whereever possible. I never let up. Recently a man named Kurt Wolff, saying he
knew you, wrote to ask if he could publish something of mine. I re-

---

* The review, which appeared under the title, "Prince of Denmark," in the
New Republic of May 10, 1943, was the first review Miller was ever paid for.

** A review of *Under a Glass Bell,* a collection of stories by Anaïs Nin. *The
New Yorker,* April 1, 1944.

† First published in *The Criterion,* London, October, 1937.

†† In 1940, Orwell published the first lengthy essay-evaluation of *Tropic of
Cancer* and *Black Spring* under the title "Inside the Whale" in an essay collection, Gollancz, London.

minded him that his first task should be to bring out the early volumes of your Diary. He has never answered me.

Now I come to Bern Porter. . . . I will tell you all I can. He came to me at Beverly Glen one day a few months ago. Said he wanted to print something of mine, anything available. He was young, rather alert, I thought, and at first I made no effort to help him. When he returned to Berkeley (he is a young scientist, I understand, and now does work for the government) he wrote me. Somehow then I woke up. And since then I have had much to do with him, by correspondence. He is a most ardent disciple of mine, I suppose I should say. He seems to be almost as much interested in the painting as in the writing. He has sent to press three little things, which he advertises on this letterhead I am using.* (It is his design—intended as a gift form.) He is using his own little savings to do this for me. He doesn't want to make money but to put money in my pocket. I find him a conscientious worker, faithful, loyal and generous. What more can I say?

Oh yes, unwittingly he took upon himself a bigger job than he bargained for when he proposed to do a bibliography for me, one that would include not only the books but everything printed in magazines, and reviews about me etc. etc. Being obliged to travel around the country for the government he has made stopovers at various places to look at letters, paintings, and whatever of mine he thought of value —all for his bibliography. Then I discovered the other day that he had written many of my friends to ask if they would contribute to a book about me—and he pays them for their contributions! This was intended to be a surprise for me, but unfortunately I found out about it. Perhaps that tells you a little more about him.**

I must tell you that I am trying to raise a good sum of money—to live quietly for a year and finish what work I have on hand. I have had to waste a good deal of time these past two years to keep going. It doesn't bother or hurt me—but it's sheer waste—I am already receiving promises and half-promises of substantial aid.

---

* "Semblance of a Devoted Past" (*Letters to Emil Schnellock,* 61 pages, illustrations), "The Plight of the Creative Artist in the United States of America," and "What Are You Going to Do About Alf?" The latter being a reprint of a 19-page broadside first published in Paris in 1935, soliciting funds to send Alfred Perlès to the Balearic Islands to enable him to finish his novel. With a new introduction by Henry Miller, 1944.

** The book, *The Happy Rock,* was published by Bern Porter in Berkeley, California, in 1945.

The other day, my [London] agent, Patience Ross, of Heath & Co., in ackowledging the fragment about you for the new book, expressed vivid interest in your work and said she hoped to be able to do something for you. She asked for a copy of the new book (of yours) and I sent her one. I urge you strongly not to neglect any proposals from the English. They have done a lot for me—much more than here. I get numerous letters from over there inquiring about you and your work, which I always answer faithfully and fully.

I still feel it is too bad that, with your enormous and truly "legendary" reputation, only glimpses of your great gift are seen. I urge you with all my heart to concentrate on the Diary. The world will be bowled over when the real manifestation of your spirit begins, believe me. As I said before, rereading my own words about you I was so stirred that I was beside myself. It must be maddening to you. It is to me.

All signs indicate that my own star is rising. There is nothing I want out of this so-called "success" but to force the world to move quicker, accept more readily, realize what is there waiting for them.

Money is slow in coming still. But it is there, and I ought to simply be patient. I have no real worries, none whatever. You ask do I enjoy my retreat. Yes and no. Yes, because I am living with nature more and more, and this Big Sur country (where I have been now for two months) is truly tremendous. There are only about 25 people on this mail route. Back from the coast, over the mountains, there is an absolute emptiness. It is almost as forbidding as Tibet, and it fascinates me. I should like to go back in there and live for a time quite alone. But I would need a horse and an ax and a few other things I have never used. I am a little terrified of it.

The other day I was offered a little house on a mountain—quite isolated—difficult to get to on foot (and I have only my feet to use) but I am taking it. I move in next week. My address remains the same. I shall have a taste of real solitude. Certainly I miss everything else—terribly. But I consider myself fortunate. And I am more and more at peace with myself. I don't know if you realize it, but this is the country Robinson Jeffers writes about. He lives in Carmel, but I gather he has walked and ridden all over this mysterious region. I met him one day. A very strange person—almost like a wounded animal—or a victim of shell shock.

About Caresse—I understand the pictures have been sent to her.

I expect nothing from the show [in Washington, D. C.]. Am just waiting for it to be over soon. I did so many when in Beverly Glen. Then everything comes too late. I gave away more than half, including my best ones. But I have made progress in this realm, and that's all I care about. I itch to get back to painting.

Will it surprise you if I say that the only writer I care to rival, or surpass if possible, is Rimbaud? I am working feverishly to wind up all my autobiographical work, so that I may embark on a totally new adventure in writing. The water colors helped me a lot, gave me courage. It's a strange story, too long to relate here.

Oh yes, I must tell you that there is a writer named Wallace Fowlie who would like to get in touch with you. He is a Catholic writer, a friend of Maritain and others like him. He is a professor at Yale and writes equally well in French and English—appears in two languages. He admires your work very much.

Also had a letter from Larry Durrell the other day, from Cairo (or Alexandria), saying that he and Nancy had parted. He asked me to send you his love. He seemed depressed—mostly about the war, I gather.

I wrote a prophetic piece, which will appear in the new book, and which nobody likes, apparently—called "Of Art and the Future." * I would like to know what *you* think of it, when you see it. It is not a very bright picture, I must say. People do seem to insist on making the future bright, and yet anyone with half an eye can see the makings of the future right now. They expect miracles, but refuse to recognize the real miracles which take place.

Well, this has been an outburst, but it seemed the right moment. There was so much I had been wanting to tell you.

HENRY

---

* First published in *Life and Letters Today,* London, March 1944.

[Spring, 1944]
Big Sur, California
Tuesday—25th

ANAÏS—

Just got your note. I prefer to buy and I can afford it! If Steloff has chalked it up against my account instead of sending me a bill, that is her fault. I have written several times asking her for a bill. I never hear from her. But if putting it on my a/c means that you do not get *cash* for these copies,* let me know, and I'll pay you direct. Tell me how much. I forget what I ordered of her—they're all gone out now. I ordered from several places—*and I do pay!* If I couldn't pay for *your* books I'd indeed be ashamed of myself. Do please stop telling me "I can't afford it." I know my finances are of a quixotic character, but I can keep things straight too. You mustn't expect me to keep my affairs in order like a banker or broker. The important thing, as I see it, is to distribute money where it is needed and does the most good.

Will the 2nd edition be the same price as the first? I'll let you know later what I can take of them. Don't *give* me them. It pleases me to earn them.

I'm surprised that you wish to write something for Porter's book. I don't ask it of you. But if you really wish to do it, fine! I'm sure you will say true things. (It was not my idea at all to put out such a book. In fact it embarrasses me.)

I just learned about the unsigned telegram in French. Had letter from this still-anonymous person yesterday. Seems he saw my "form letter" ** at Gotham and wishes to give me the money I asked for. Am to wait a few days for definite news. Meanwhile Cairns may also have a patron for me. And the millionaire in Iowa wants to do something. I guess something definite and tangible will materialize.

[Jean] Varda † finds your preface *mystifying*. But he is crazy about the book. He says he can't understand why *thousands* of people are not reading you. Doesn't want you "to abdicate"—as the "princess." ‡

---

* Anaïs Nin had published her collection of stories, *Under A Glass Bell,* under her own imprint of The Gemor Press.

** One of Miller's appeals for aid.

† See Biographical Notes.

‡ Among her friends, Anaïs Nin was occasionally referred to as "the princess."

Someday maybe you could let him illustrate a book for you. (*My idea*) But— I hope you will meet soon. I am sure the meeting is fraught with great things for both of you.

You *will* get a copy of the "Angel" book,* I learn. Though they have stopped further work on it, the gift copies will be made. I am glad. I think it will be a fine memento for you.

I shall have the new house rent free. Some one else stepped in and insisted on paying it. Really, every day I discover how many unknown friends I have. I *am* protected, it seems. We all are, I believe, if we would only acknowledge it.

HENRY

P. S. Pantheon Press has put out a book called *Life After Death* by Fechner who influenced the author of *The Bright Messenger*. It's short and marvelous. I think *you* will enjoy it.

[Big Sur, Cal.]
June 8th [1944]

DEAR ANAÏS,

I sent you a check the other day. Do please cash it. I'm afraid if you don't there may not be money in the bank. I should think you ought to use what you need for the binding of the other book [*Winter of Artifice*] out of this; you will undoubtedly recoup quickly from the sale of the second edition. I think too you will be hearing favorably from England—for an English edition; Patience Ross seems to be an admirer of yours. I said on a postcard that I had made some revisions in the text which appeared in *Circle* ["Letter to Anaïs Nin," Berkeley, Calif., April, 1944]—for the book due out soon: *Sunday After the War.*** In the book the section about you is called: "More about Anaïs Nin." It is in two parts, the first being the letter to Bradley about your Diary, which I thought a classic and which will now be most opportune—you will see. The second part is what was printed in *Circle,* and is quite improved, I think.

---

* A limited, numbered and autographed edition, with illustrations, of Miller's essay on doing a water color in Paris, "The Angel Is My Watermark," which first appeared in *Black Spring,* (1938). Fullerton, Calif., Holve-Barrows. $50.
** A collection of pieces published by New Directions, August, 1944.

I have an idea that Bern Porter may try to do the Diary for you; he knows about it and I suggested that, if he needed extra help, and if you were willing, he could or might make use of this. This is up to you, of course. He's pretty well exhausted his funds at present, getting out my things. But I think, when he wants to do something badly, he will find the way. He's quite an executive sort of fellow, a physicist, I think, and this is his hobby and excitement. His friend George Leite, who puts out *Circle,* is a very fine fellow—Portuguese descent—very sensitive and keen and earnest. All these young people are naturally a bit exaggerative, overenthusiastic, reckless, careless, and what not— mistakes or virtues of youth, which I don't mind myself, since I was that way too. They also make some terrible blunders at times, or leave things in midair, as youngsters will. And sometimes are tactless and seemingly insensitive. But they mean well. I know they are making quite a cult of me—I can't help that—it's the writing that causes it. That is part of my harvest, I suppose.

So many young people are that way; they begin by imitating their models. (Didn't you once imagine yourself a Joan of Arc?) This is the thing to remember, however, that they have chosen people like you and me, instead of others. They are all earnestly striving, and they are searching for someone to deliver them from the confusion in which they're drowning. The one person I did want to have see you is Wallace Fowlie, whom I know only by correspondence. But he's almost too shy, said he didn't know how to go about it. Though he's an ardent Catholic, I have a great admiration for him, as writer and as person. He has written about Rimbaud with a penetration no one else has shown.

To come back to the printing and publishing. . . . So many things of mine are coming out this year. I feel I must get some money in now or never.

I have a sort of Paradise here, as to scenery, but the work involved is almost too much. I live up a steep road, over a mile long, away from the highway. Three times a week the food and mail arrives, and I drag it up with the last ounce of energy in me. Coming down to get it I feel elated. Always think I am in the Andes, the view so magnificent. Often the ocean is hidden by thick layers of clouds or soapy mist or fog. But when I get back I have to go to the forest to look for dead limbs, haul it back, drag it, chop it, saw it, make a wood fire each meal—the chores are endless. I have about two hours for work—and

then I am not any too fresh. But it's a healthy life and I hope in time
to get adjusted. It's just that I'm not used to heavy work, especially
hauling and lifting.

Emil White is up here now, in a cabin six miles away. He wants to
get a burro for me—or he may buy a car. He comes sometimes and
spends most of the day chopping wood for me. I'm soon going to have
a kerosene stove, however. And screen doors. The flies wake me at
six in the morning! There are always poisoned apples in every Paradise! Emil told me how wonderfully you wrote him in Alaska. He is
a good person. I seem to be surrounded by helpers.

Well, in the last Open Letter which appears in "The Plight of the
Creative Artist in the United States of America" I try to tell how
finally I woke up to the fact that all over the world people are trying
to help me. I grow more conscious of this every day. I also remember
Moricand's last words about my horoscope. This is just the period he
described accurately to me: rewards and gains, the reaping of good
Karma. It will be very strange to see the discordances and discrepan-
cies in the contributions about me in that book Porter is getting up.*
He will change the title, yes! The show [of H. M. Water colors] in
Washington was a compete flop, as I expected. When you get ready to
send out announcements about the Diary remind me to give you a
new list of names—a huge good one, most of whom know about your
work. We will all work out a campaign for you when the time comes.
It will be an event!

I was just thinking today, learning of the invasion (which agitated
me tremendously, especially for the French! of whom I expect great
great things, fire, vengeance, blood as never seen before!) how strange
it is that it is now, at this great moment, just 30 years ago that you
began the Diary—and now we are on the eve of seeing it printed.
Thirty years! Could you ever have dreamed how it would end and
come to light and at what a moment in history?

I want to add that, if I were in your place, i.e., if you have it
printed yourself, I would not bother to send copies to the critics (they
are worthless, all of them), but I would put little inexpensive ads in
a number of magazines and literary sections of big newspapers; Emil
tells me he gets wonderful results this way, selling any old kind of
books. But ignore the critics completely. They will come to you finally,

---

* *The Happy Rock*, 1945.

and beg for copies to read. You don't need them. If a Wilson or a Rosenfeld asks to write about it, that's another matter, of course.

Well, I must stop. I just got back from my second haul, after dinner. It's now 10:30.

One more thought . . . Do not overlook the fact that in Switzerland they are putting out translations of books in several languages and distributing them abroad. Claude Houghton told me he had five of his novels done this way—Spain also took them. Imagine that—Spain in this bad period doing that!

HENRY

[Big Sur, Cal.]
June 21st [1944]

DEAR ANAÏS:
Returning the letters herewith.

I don't seem to know any of the names you mention. My memory for names is growing worse.

I am amazed when you write that $200 pays for 200 linotyped pages. What does this mean exactly? Not the final printed page? Just for the setting up of type, I suppose? I mean this—if a thousand dollars pays for a thousand pages, how much more, above that, does one need, for the final job? A dollar a page seems awfully cheap—cheaper than a stenographer's price. Mystifies me. But sounds wonderful. I hope everything will continue. Have hopes of finding one or two more patrons—I need them. I would like eventually to buy back, after an edition is exhausted, the plates for one of my own books, reprint it in my own name, so that I can have a small dependable income. My royalties never amount to anything—eaten up in advance by gift copies. Laughlin now gives me fifty *free* of each book, quite a help. [J. M.] Tambimuttu [editor of *Poetry, London*] writes his directors are thinking about giving me a small monthly stipend. The English, as publishers, are so much better than the French or Americans—in financial matters.

The invasion? I think only of one thing: how horrible it is to be liberated by vandals! What will be left of France after we liberate her? She will be a heap of smouldering ruins. Nothing is being accomplished, for good, by the war, that I can see. I am getting out soon a pamphlet of about a hundred pages called "Murder the Murderer"! * So far I have been right in all my predictions. The biggest one is the terrible revolution soon to come—starting in France. Russia will be the worst enemy of freedom, I predict. With England and America abetting her, to be sure. One of the allies will make up with Japan, you'll see, and provide more worries. China will be left helpless and in chaos. All the problems making for the next war are already evident. There may be a brief interregnum, but it will start up again—and worse. It has to be finished thoroughly—and this war won't do it. The whole edifice is still rotten. The new Peace Plans are not even as good as after the last war. It's a farce and a shambles. And the big powers will be still bigger, cockier, more warlike, more prepared, more devastating to all concerned. I am excited about the invasion, yes, but I know we will be hated like poison.

The design of the new letterhead is fine—looks like a linoleum cut. Looks Chinese and matches your name. The copy of Angel book I am sending you tomorrow registered mail. Hope you like it.

Did you meet Chagall? Wonder what he's like. Would love to know him.

HVM

May 25, 1945
Big Sur, California

DEAR ANAÏS—

You ask if I read the first section of your book [*Ladders to Fire*]. I don't believe so—unless it was that Arabian fragment which George is printing next issue. Is it that? I mentioned this in my last letter. I was rather baffled by it—i.e. as to what you intended to have the reader feel about the woman. I thought I saw things—and then I became puzzled and confused. Tell me which it is—has George got it? I keep shying away from reading things—not yours, but all the stuff that is poured in on me. I feel like a wet nurse. I'm rebelling. I never asked people to advise me in these matters. These young people are sick—no self-confidence.

---

* First published at $1.25 (Big Sur, 1944, 70 pp.) and later included in *Remember to Remember*, New Directions, Norfolk, Conn., 1947.

My only satisfaction, in reading, are the French books I get. I just finished Saint-Exupéry's *Pilote de Guerre*—found it magnificent.

Just had a letter from [Maurice] Girodias,* via Germany—as that's faster—i.e. thru an American soldier there. Mails from France take three to six months. He wants to reprint all the Obelisk books, in English and in French. Talks of doing 10,000 copies each in the English. The soldiers have bought up everything already. Talks of asking 120 frs. a copy and offers me 5% royalties. I advised him to make the price 350 or 500 frs. instead. I tell you these things only to give you an idea how things are there. (Fred sent a card from Paris saying it "was just the same, lovely as ever, and gay.") Others say differently. Queneau (at N.R.F.) writes that I won't recognize Europe. I suppose both views are true. Certainly Germany must be unrecognizable!

If people ask how to get my books say to write me. Most of them can now be had from England—all but the banned books.** The English are treating me royally. You ought to see Patience Ross if you pass thru London. She sounds intelligent.

I don't say what I'm doing because I doubt if you'd be interested. I've done odd things—a long study of *Maurizius,* for example. Now on a deep study of *Season in Hell.*

HENRY

June 15, 1945
Big Sur, California

DEAR ANAÏS—

Your circular [for the revised edition of *Winter of Artifice*] is beautiful. Put me down for a copy! I'll send you a money order a little later. Also, if you can, send me more circulars—I'll use them very judiciously, I promise you. Forty copies is very little. Won't there be any at a cheaper figure?

---

* Son of Jack Kahane and proprietor of Olympia (formerly Obelisk) Press. See Biographical Notes under Jack Kahane.

** *Tropic of Cancer* and *Tropic of Capricorn* were not published in the United States until 1961, and *Black Spring* in 1963. They were subsequently also published in England.

Delighted you asked Eduardo to write me about Rimbaud. Just heard from Rudhyar on him—he sends you his greetings. Got divorced recently and is happier now—living temporarily in Nevada.

I don't understand what you say about the Romantics but I said just about what you do in connection with Maturity (le roi soleil d'adolescence—poised on the peak of adolescence and rotting there in the cocoon). It's something to place beside the Balzac, Maurizius and A. N. pieces, this one. I also learned a lot about myself in doing it. (Does everyone find great affinities with him, I wonder?) I've drawn up sheets of analogies and correspondences!

I know *Kenyon Review* but loathe it, as I do *Partisan*. Seems utterly arid and scholastic to me. They represent the driest American critics. So I think, at least.

(I just notice that your circular is for the colored wood block prints! My mistake. What will be the price of the book—and how many are you printing?)

Thank you for sending George the "Mummy" photos—didn't know if you still had them. Also thanks for the Chinese photos by Lt. Dark. Some of them are quite wonderful.

Yes—the boxes at Louveciennes! Porter has even included Marius Battedou's name in the Bibliography! I often wonder what was in those boxes.

Did I tell you of young Kahane's projects for reprinting and for French editions? Quite ambitious. But 120 frs. a volume (for the English editions) seems too small to me. I should think 350 or 500 frs. would be nearer the mark.

Thru a soldier I had word from Tschann, the librarian on Blvd. Montparnasse. He was in a labor camp in Germany until recently.

I feel about the Arabian woman that it was just a preface to what you wanted to say. Where is the rest of it? But that isn't the mystery. Sometime I'll explain more in detail.

HENRY

P. S. Albert Cossery is sending me copies of the French (original) version of his book—*Men God Forgot*. Would you like one? It's very close to your way of writing about Fez, etc.*

---

* See also Miller's article on Cossery in *Stand Still Like the Hummingbird*, New Directions, 1961.

Anderson Creek, Big Sur
5/17/46

DEAR ANAÏS:

Yes, writing that script I knew finally it would not be necessary to send it out. But I had to write it out before I could see it clearly. When you surrender, the problem ceases to exist. Try to solve it, or conquer it, and you only set up more resistance. I am very certain now, that as I said therein, if I truly become what I wish to be, the burden will fall away. The most difficult thing to admit, and to realize with one's whole being, is that you alone control nothing. To be able to put yourself in tune or rhythm with the forces beyond which are the truly operative ones, that is the task—and the solution, if we can speak of "solutions." The guilt feeling is, as we both agree, based on the *real* knowledge that one is not giving himself completely. I say it one way, you another.

One thing I don't worry about, however, is what people think, how they misinterpret things. There's nothing you can do about that. It was so curious to read your words about "only initiates understanding what was meant." There I think you are only half right. What amazes me more and more is how much people do understand when you give them the full dose, when you hold back nothing. Especially the young —the others are beyond all hope. But that faint glimmer which you can detect in them sometimes, that eventually bears fruit. I can look back with an ever clearer eye now and see just what it was, how, when, where—the tiniest drop or morsel—which truly affected me. I can see that these little iotas were never lost, that they slowly built up an organism, you might say, which expropriated the false one.

I seem to see one other thing—that one has to permit people to become desperate, to become wholly lost, that only then are they ready for the right word, only then can they avail themselves of the truth. To withhold it then is a crime. But to nurse them along is a worse crime. And there is where much of the conflict centers, about that point. The *human* instinct to spare the other person his agony (which is his means of salvation, in any sense of the word) is a fallacious instinct. Here the subtle temptations, the vicious and insidious ones, because so confused and entangled, enter in. On this so-called "human" plane it is the ego which commands—often in the most amazing disguises. The temptation to be good, to do good, gets us all some time or other. It's the last ruse, I feel, of the ego.

You are the only one I ever knew who used silence effectively. It was really devastating sometimes—but I don't think you were aware of it. But people got more answers, and effective ones, from you than they ever did from me, with all my shouting and ranting, or cajoling and persuading. You threw them back on themselves. To do that consciously is another thing. I was never sure you did do it thus: Did you?

But this clamor and agitation which I seem to create all about me, even from a distance, proceeds from *me*. I know it.

I told you I am getting a piece of property—a home. It came about strangely. It *is* almost impossible to get land or house here. There was a neighbor on the hill where I lived, a Mrs. Wharton, who seems to understand me—without reading the books. She is supposed to be a Christian Scientist—but she's outgrown that. She's the only person I know who uses the word Reality as I do. That's our meeting ground. What happened is that she is virtually offering me her place. She's done everything to make it easy for me—the price is ridiculous. She even gets out of her house and will build another as soon as she can get material. That's the only reason we are not up there now. She has an absolute faith—and it's not in *me*, I feel, but in all humanity. She works magic around her.

Add to this that the spot itself is the very one I crave, the site which deeply satisfies me, and which I thought unobtainable. Sometimes I think, in offering me my dream, she is only teaching me another lesson. She says, for instance, in explaining her willingness to relinquish it, that it is now inside her, can't be lost. This doesn't fail to impress me, you can well believe. Have I not become more and more aware latterly that the things I deeply desire come without struggle? (I haven't spoken enough to you of the increasing magic going on in my life—of desires being almost instantaneously answered. It would amaze you.) All the struggle, then, is phantom play. The fighting with shadows. *This I know*.

So maybe, to answer a question you put me recently, what I am about to learn is simply the meaning of "home," the one thing I have never known. And when that finally becomes a part of me it won't matter where or how I live. That home in Brooklyn, which I always see when the word home is mentioned, is the insane asylum! That was never my home. And from that I suppose I extended the notness until I had almost eliminated the idea.

I go in tomorrow to see Varda's new daughter, just two weeks old. Lepska * is there helping Virginia who had a bad time of it—because she feared birth. I miss our baby. She's six months old now. Can't bear to be away from her for a day. She's overintelligent, I fear, but very joyous. Gives no trouble whatever, not from the day she was born.

As for Camus—he may be on his way out here already. Harry Bull wrote he was coming to see me. I know only his one book— L'Étranger. Am open about him. Sartre, on the other hand, I feel deeply attracted to. Everything of his I read strikes the right note for me. That piece of his in *Portfolio 3* echoed my sentiments to a T. Did you read it? And "Les Mouches"—superb, I thought. Not only in execution but in the philosophy behind it. I can't see him yet as in the "traditional" groove. But you have deeper insights about the French—you see their weaknesses. I like only to find their strength. If I could do that about America I would be getting somewhere, I guess.

The *Maurizius* book is out.** Will send you a copy soon as I get some. Will be very curious to know what you think of the Rimbaud (Part 1) which is in the New Directions Annual 9—just out. I am thru with Part 2 now and will do more on it. It grips me. You'll see why. Do be sure to come out here this fall! I am dying to see you.

HENRY

P. S. Must be a P. S. to this! The best news is that I am really approaching "The Rosy Crucifixion." Another two weeks' work and I should be free to resume it. And then I really believe I will write only that, just everything into one vessel, even if it requires six more volumes. I begin to see daylight again. What a struggle!

---

* On December 18, 1944, Miller had married his third wife, Janina M. Lepska, who was in her early twenties. She bore him a daughter, Valentine, on November 19, 1945. A son, Tony, was born in 1948. Miller separated from Lepska in 1951 and they were divorced in 1952.

** *Maurizius Forever*, The Colt Press, San Francisco, 1946.

[Big Sur, July, 1946]
Monday
DEAR ANAÏS—

I'm enclosing a review just sent me by Denoël of *Tropic of Cancer*. I thought you would enjoy reading it. For me it was like the apotheosis of all critiques. We've waited a long time to see an appreciation like this, haven't we? I receive almost as flattering ones on *Printemps Noir*. It means an awful lot to me. I began to think, that with all the changes going on, perhaps my work would be judged harshly.

Well, return it when convenient. I also just received two copies of *Cancer,* French version, bound in cloth. Looks very handsome.

I wondered since writing you last if your friend Dolly Chareau might pick up some money from Girodias on her way back—what do you think?

Wrote Gore Vidal on receipt of his book, tho' I haven't read it yet.

HENRY

Big Sur—July 19th [1946]
DEAR ANAÏS,

Here is the review I meant to send you—the best I ever received—by a young critic on a Communist paper! Please return it when you're through with it. Even the attacks from the Fascist critics are mild compared to the lambasting I get from American reviewers. The latest news, from a friend in Bordeaux, is that the Minister of State and some other ministers are thinking to take action against the books. (But I doubt if they'll succeed! The interest grows, the reviews mount, the discussion is becoming furious.)

I think it's well you gave up the Press here. By all means print in France, yes! No trouble these days getting a publisher—in Europe!

I had wonderful letters from Arnoldo Mondadori, the Italian publisher who has taken me up. Something quite beautiful and touching about his letters—so civilized, gentle, considerate and understanding. He is the best in Italy, 40 years in the game, and has published nearly every big foreign author. In answering him the other day I spoke passionately about your Diary and urged him to get in touch with you. He was in Switzerland during the war, exiled by Mussolini. Evidently a man of the Old World and a lover of freedom, in every realm. There are Swedish, Danish and Norwegian publishers too.

Don't bother to fight for my books—I don't believe any of these commercial American publishers have the guts or the power to do this. I can bide my time. I am being published in so many other countries, why worry about poor America? I can do without America's help. The French alone will keep me in pocket money, more than that.

Now you really can get the Diary printed, I'm sure of it. And it's high time. And I'm happy that you are going to start from the very beginning. Those first volumes in French will touch people's hearts, I'm certain of it. As for the English parts, I suppose you'll hand each of us a different copy to read. I don't expect to ever read the last word—unless from Heaven.

It's too bad you won't be coming out here after all. I looked forward so much to seeing you. Emil Schnellock is here on a visit—came by car, took him a month. He's intoxicated with the scene. And you would be too. I didn't choose this spot at random. It satisfies me as nothing else in America does. It has majesty and dignity. And the site of the new home is simply magnificent. I will be able to go there soon—by fall, I think. Every one is helping to get things in shape for us. That Christian Science woman, who sold me the land (and with it her own house) is remarkable. One of the very very few people I've met who lives what she believes. I do have luck, after all.

So you're really leaving in September? I wonder. I'm trying to persuade some editor or publisher to give me a roaming commission, so that I would have the means to travel, to make a trip of two or three months and see a good bit of Europe. I'd like to see Ireland first. But now, should I hit Copenhagen, Stockholm, London, Rome or Paris—what a different reception I would get! Strangely, now I would like to travel entirely by air—the quicker the better. The thought of being able to reach China in 24 hours excites me. And the rates are not too high. Well, more very soon.

HENRY

Some Biographical Notes

ABRAMSON, BEN—Owner of the Argus Book Shop in Chicago, who met Miller in 1941, on his first trip through the United States, and tried to help him sell his books and manuscripts. Abramson backed the publication of a limited edition of Miller's *The World of Sex* (250 copies, 88 pp., $7.50), 1941.

ALLENDY, DR. RENÉ FELIX—French psychoanalyst, born 1889, founder of the Société Française de Psychoanalyse and lecturer at the Sorbonne. Wrote his thesis on "Les Theories Alchimique dans l'Histoire de la Médecine," in 1912. Among his major works are *La Psychoanalyse* (Paris, Denoël & Steele, 1931), *Capitalisme et Sexualité* (Paris, Denoël & Steele, 1932). His *Aristote, ou le complex de trahison,* published after his death in 1942, was published in English as *The Treason Complex* (New York, Social Science Publ. Co., 1949). During the 1920's and 1930's he was closely associated with the Surrealist movement, particularly with Antonin Artaud, who was a friend of Anaïs Nin, and Miss Nin worked for Dr. Allendy in 1933.

BALD, WAMBLY—American newspaperman who, after graduating from the University of Chicago, worked for the Paris edition of the Chicago *Tribune.* In a weekly column, *La Vie Bohème,* he chronicled the gossip of expatriate life in Montparnasse and, according to Samuel Putnam, went about "seeing nothing, hearing nothing and telling all." He met Henry Miller and on October 14, 1931, devoted a column to him which was the first personal publicity Miller ever received. He left Paris after the paper was closed down in 1934.

BRADLEY, WILLIAM ASPENWALL—American literary agent in Paris who, in 1932, introduced Miller to his future publisher, Jack Kahane. Born in 1878, Bradley was educated in the United States and after publishing a volume of poetry (*Amicitia amorque,* 100 copies privately printed, 1901) established himself as an expert on etchings (*The Etching of Figures,* 250 copies privately printed; *French Etchings of the Second*

[341]

Empire, Boston, Houghton Mifflin, 1916; *Dutch Landscape Etchings of the 17th Century*, New Haven, Yale, 1918). After settling in Paris he married a Frenchwoman who became the center of a fashionable "salon" on the Île Saint-Louis and carried on the agency after his death in 1939. He also translated from the French (Paul Valéry, Wanda Landowska) and tried to establish the writer Louis Hémon (1880–1913) in the United States, whose *My Fair Lady* Macmillan published in 1923, in Bradley's translation.

BRASSAI (HALASZ)—Hungarian photographer, who had photographed June and Anaïs Nin, and whose work Miller admired. He paid tribute to Brassai in "The Eye of Paris," an essay which appeared in abridged form in the *Globe* (St. Paul, Minn.) with photographs by Brassai, in November, 1937, and was later included in *The Wisdom of the Heart*, 1941. Some of Brassai's photographs of Paris appeared in *Quiet Days in Clichy* (Paris, Olympia Press, 1956).

CAIRNS, HUNTINGTON—American lawyer, born 1904, who served from 1933 until 1937 as special legal adviser and from 1937 to 1943 as assistant general counsel to the U. S. Treasury Department, which ruled on the importation of "obscene" books. During 1940 and 1941 he served as chairman of the CBS radio program, *Invitation to Learning*. In 1943, he became secretary treasurer and manager of the National Gallery of Art in Washington, D. C., and edited several books on the great paintings in the National Gallery. An admirer of Henry Miller's water colors, he tried to arrange a show for him in the late 1930's.

CENDRARS, BLAISE—French writer (1887–1961) who, after the publication of *Tropic of Cancer*, went to visit Miller at Villa Seurat in 1934 to pay homage to him. Miller became fascinated with Cendrars' work (*Moravigne, Une Nuit dans la Forêt, L'Or, Les Confessions de Dan Yack*, etc.), which he devoured in French with the help of a dictionary, as well as with his life of adventure (Cendrars ran away from home at the age of fifteen, joined the Foreign Legion, lost his right arm in World War I, traveled in the Balkans, India, China, studied medicine, raised bees in France, worked as a juggler in a London variety theatre, became a friend of Caruso and Charlie Chaplin, etc.). "With the exception of John Cowper Powys," wrote Miller, "I have never met another writer who has given me more than he [Cendrars]. He is the Chinese rock-bottom man of my imagination, the man that D. H. Lawrence would like to have been." Miller's "Tribute to Blaise Cendrars" appeared in 1938 in the Shanghai Monthly *T'ien Hsia* (November, Vol. 7) and was later included in *The Wisdom of the Heart*.

COVICI, PASCAL—American bookseller and publisher whose bookshop in Chicago (Covici-McGee) was one of the centers of the "Prairie Renaissance" (Ben Hecht, Maxwell Bodenheim) in 1923–24. He later established the firm of Covici-Friede in New York and was responsible for sending Samuel Putnam to Paris. He died in 1964.

CROSBY, CARESSE—Widow of Harry Grew Crosby (1897–1929), who befriended many writers and artists in Europe and the United States. She published a number of volumes of poetry between 1920 and 1931 in Paris and New York (*Crosses of Gold, Painted Shores, Graven Images, Impossible Melodies, Poems for Harry Crosby*). Her voluminous correspondence was recently acquired by Southern Illinois University and her reminiscences, *The Passionate Years,* were published in 1953 (New York, The Dial Press). Miller first came in contact with her in Paris in 1932 and in 1940 he spent some time at her house in Bowling Green, Virginia. In 1944, she established a gallery in Washington, D. C., and arranged for a showing of Miller's water colors.

DUDLEY, JOHN—Young American painter from Kenosha, Wisconsin, who met Miller in New York in 1940 and, with his wife Flo, stayed at Caresse Crosby's house in Virginia during the summer of that year, when Miller also was a guest. A year later, Miller visited the Dudleys' in Kenosha and wrote the chapter "Letter to Lafayette," in *The Air-Conditioned Nightmare,* about their encounter.

EDGAR, DAVID—Young American expatriate who, in the early 1930's, introduced Miller to E. Graham Howe, Rudolf Steiner and Zen Buddhism while sitting at various café tables in Paris, and whom Miller called "a beloved member of the inner circle."

FRAENKEL, MICHAEL—American writer, book dealer, born in 1896, of Russian parents, who met Miller in Paris in the early 1930's. He owned the house, 18 Villa Seurat, where Miller stayed briefly as a guest in Fraenkel's apartment and later—from September, 1934, until May, 1939—as a tenant. Having made a modest fortune in the book trade and on the stock market, Fraenkel established the "Carrefour" imprint, which used the facilities of the St. Catherine Press in Bruges, Belgium, to publish books of his friends as well as his own (*Werther's Younger Brother,* 1931—400 copies; *Death in a Room,* poems written between 1927 and 1930, 1936—200 copies; *Bastard Death,* with an Introduction by Henry Miller, 1936—400 copies). In November, 1935, he embarked on a lengthy correspondence with Miller under the title of *Hamlet,* which continued for three years, while Fraenkel traveled in Europe and North America, and which he published eventually, in two volumes, under the Carrefour imprint, in Puerto Rico and Mexico, where he took up residence in 1940. Excerpts from his Mexican Journal (1940–1944) were published by Oscar Baradinsky, of the Alicat Book Shop in Yonkers, N. Y., under the title, *Land of the Quetzal* (1946). Fraenkel wrote a long essay on "The Genesis of *Tropic of Cancer,*" and when the first French edition of *Tropic of Cancer* (Paris,

Denoël, 1946) came under attack by French authorities he wrote *Défense du Tropique* (Paris, Variété, 1947). Miller's "Essay on Michael Fraenkel" was published in *We Moderns,* 1940, and in June, 1948, the French magazine *Arts et Lettres* published a "Lettre d'Henry Miller et Réponse de Michael Fraenkel."

FREEMAN, WALTER—Young American lawyer who worked with Richard Osborn in the Paris branch of the National City Bank in the early 1930's.

FRIEDE, DONALD—American editor and publisher, born 1901, who was a partner, with Pascal Covici, in the publishing house Covici-Friede, and, during the early 1940's an agent in Hollywood. Friede's autobiography, covering his adventures in the 1920's, was published in 1948 (*The Mechanical Angel,* New York, Alfred Knopf).

HILER, HILAIRE—American painter, born 1898, son of Meyer Hiler, whose extensive costume library was acquired by the Queen's Public Library, N. Y., in 1930. Lived in Paris during the 1930's and in California during the 1940's. His fourteen-page pamphlet, "Hilaire Hiler et la Vision Panoramique," was published in Paris in 1932. He invented the "Hiler color chart," first published in 1937 and included in *Color, Harmony and Pigments* (New York–Chicago, 1942). Served as a contributing editor on Samuel Putnam's *New Review.* Collaborated with Miller and William Saroyan in a book, *Why Abstract?* (New York, James Laughlin, 1945), and wrote "The Modern Painter's Dilemma" (Dallas, *Southwest Review,* Vol. 31, 1945) and *Why Expressionism?* (Los Angeles, 1946). In his book on America, Miller devotes a chapter to "Hiler and His Murals," in the Aquatic Park Building in San Francisco.

JOAQUIN NIN-CULMELL—Pianist and composer, brother of Anaïs Nin, who lived with her and her mother at Louveciennes. Left France for the United States in the mid-thirties, taught at Williams College and settled in California in 1948.

JOLAS, EUGENE—Editor of the magazine *Transition,* which was published in Paris from 1927 until the summer of 1938, with a brief suspension during the winter 1930–31, and published many of the important writers of the day. Elliot Paul and later James Johnson Sweeney were co-editors of the magazine for brief periods. Miller's essay on Hans Reichel appeared in the April–May issue, 1938.

JUNE EDITH SMITH—Miller's second wife, she also used the name "June Mansfield," who appears under different fictitious names in the body of Miller's work, and to whom *Tropic of Capricorn* is dedicated ("To Her"). They met in New York in 1923 and were married in 1924. In 1928, June and Henry Miller made their first trip to Europe, which lasted almost a year, and took them to various parts of France,

Austria, Hungary, Roumania, Poland, Czechoslovakia and Germany. When Miller went back to Paris in 1930, June remained in the United States, but made two visits to Paris in the fall of 1931 and during the winter of 1932. The marriage ended in divorce in 1934.

KAHANE, JACK—Miller's first publisher in Paris. Born in 1887 in Manchester, England, Kahane came to France in the early 1920's, after working in the cotton industry, and began to write novels (*Laugh and Grow Rich*, Brentano's, 1923; *Love's Wild Geese*, London, G. Richards, 1924). Eventually, he started his own publishing firm, the Obelisk Press, in Paris, whose first big success was Frank Harris, *My Life and Loves*. Under the pseudonym Cecil Barr he wrote a number of slightly risqué novels for his own press (*Suzy Falls Off*, New York, Boni, 1929) and, after the publication of *Tropic of Cancer*, which Anaïs Nin had financed, in 1934, he added Cyril Connolly's *The Rock Pool* (1935) and Lawrence Durrell's *The Black Book* (1938) to the titles which established the reputation of the press. In 1938, he wrote his autobiography, *Memoirs of a Booklegger* (London, Michael Joseph) which was published in 1939, six months before his death. His son Maurice, who changed his name to Girodias, eventually changed the name of the firm to Éditions du Chêne and later to Olympia Press, and continued his father's work.

LOWENFELS, WALTER—American writer, born in 1897, who lived in Paris during the early 1930's. His first book of sixteen pages, *Apollinaire, an Elegy*, was set by hand and printed privately (150 copies) on a handpress (Paris, Hours Press, 1930), with covers designed by Yves Tanguy. His friend Michael Fraenkel, under the Carrefour imprint, published 150 copies of his *Elegy in the Manner of a Requiem in Memory of D. H. Lawrence* (1932) and 110 copies of *The Suicide* (1934) which was part of an unfinished work, *Some Deaths*. Lowenfels eventually returned to the United States and published a few volumes of poetry (*Steel*, Atlantic City, Unity Publishers, 1938; *American Voices, the People Ask for Peace*, Philadelphia, Whittier Press, 1953) and edited an anthology of Walt Whitman's writings on the Civil War (New York, Knopf, 1960). A few excerpts from Miller's correspondence with Lowenfels in the early 1930's appeared in *The Outsider*, No. 1, New Orleans, Fall 1961.

MORAND, PAUL—French writer, lecturer, author of numerous books of fiction and nonfiction on his travels in the United States, Europe, and the Near East. Friend of Jean Giraudoux and Marcel Proust, who wrote a preface to Morand's *Tendre Stocks*, 1921.

MORICAND, CONRAD—French astrologer, occultist, born in 1887, pseudonym Claude Valence, who published *Miroir d'Astrologie* (Paris, Au Sans Pareil) in 1928. Was introduced to Miller in 1936 in Paris and became his guest in California in 1947. In his book, *A Devil in Paradise,* Miller gives a full account of their relationship. He describes him as "an incurable dandy living the life of a beggar." Moricand died penniless in Paris in 1954.

NEIMAN, GILBERT, HOWARD—American writer and translator, who invited Miller to be his, and his wife, Margaret's, guest in Beverly Glen, Los Angeles, in 1942. An expert in Spanish and French literature, Neiman shared Miller's admiration for Rimbaud, and had also translated some of García Lorca's works (*Blood Wedding,* Norfolk, Conn., New Directions, 1939). Neiman used his thorough acquaintance with Mexico as the background for his novel, *There Is a Tyrant in Every Country,* which was published in 1947 (New York, Harcourt, Brace). He devoted his doctoral thesis to a study of Miller's works ("Henry Miller: A Semi-Critical Approach," University of New Mexico, 1958–59). Miller dedicated his book, *The Air-Conditioned Nightmare,* to "Margaret and Gilbert Neiman, originally of Bunker Hill (Los Angeles), now somewhere above and beyond the Garden of the Gods (Colorado). In my memory and affection they are even a little higher than that, above and beyond the gods themselves, because so utterly and perfectly human."

NORMAN, DOROTHY—American writer, associate of photographer and art expert Alfred Stieglitz, who met Miller in the spring of 1941. Co-editor, with Waldo Frank, Lewis Mumford, Paul Rosenfeld and Harold Russ, of *America and Alfred Stieglitz* (New York, Doubleday, Doran & Co., 1934). Published studies of John Marin and Alfred Stieglitz and, in 1938, became editor of *Twice a Year* which published Miller's "Balzac and His Double" (No. 5–6, New York, 1940–41), and "Stieglitz and Marin" (No. 8–9, New York, 1942).

OSBORN, RICHARD GALEN—Young American lawyer from Bridgeport, Conn., who worked for the Paris branch of the National City Bank, from 1930 to 1932. He helped Miller after his arrival in Paris and harbored him in his apartment, 2 rue Auguste Bartholdi, during the winter of 1930. Miller dedicated *The Wisdom of the Heart* to Osborn, "who rescued me from starvation in Paris and set my feet in the right direction. May Heaven protect him and guide him safely to port." It was Osborn who, while doing some legal work for Anaïs Nin, introduced Miller to her, in the fall of 1931.

PAALEN, WOLFGANG—Writer, art critic, born in Germany in 1910, who published *Dyn, The Review of Modern Art,* in Coyoacán, Mexico, during the early 1940's, which printed several articles by Miller. A collection of Paalen's essays from the magazine was published in 1945 (*Form and Sense,* New York, Wittenborn). The German writer Gustav Regler published a book about Wolfgang Paalen.

PELORSON, GEORGES—French writer, poet, translator, editor of the magazine *Volontés,* which published, in French translation, a number of contributions by Henry Miller ("Open Letter to Surrealists Everywhere," February 1938; "Seraphita," translated by Pelorson, April, May, 1939—issues No. 16 and 17). Among the contributors to the magazine were Dr. Allendy, Eugene Jolas, Conrad Moricand, Raymond Queneau, C. F. Ramuz, Leopold S. Senghor. After some lapses in regular publication for lack of funds, and after the outbreak of World War II, the editors announced (April 1940, No. 21) that the magazine would resume "normal monthly publication" with the May 1940 issue, operating out of Maurice J. Kahane's office (16 Place Vendôme). But the German occupation spelled the end of the magazine. Pelorson (who later changed his name to Belmont), in 1933, published a translation of *Poems* by Emily Brontë and contributed poetry and articles to various magazines ("Connaissance—Le Soir," *Mesure,* October 1935; "Prologue to *Jules César, Volontés,* No. 17; etc.).

PERLÈS, ALFRED—Austrian journalist, novelist, resident in Paris since the 1920's, who went to England in 1939, joined the British Army during World War II and became a British citizen. Met Miller first in 1928 and became his friend when Miller returned to Paris in 1930. "It was by accident," recalls Miller in 1935, in a circular written to raise funds for Perlès ("What Are You Going to Do About Alf?"), "that I ran across Alf one day. The ass was out of my breeches and my tongue was hanging out. Fred, as I used to call him then, brought me up to his room [at the Hôtel Central, 1 bis rue du Maine]. He hid me there for several weeks. He brought me food and cigarettes. He left money for me on the mantelpiece. He found me a job [on the Chicago *Tribune*]. He sang and danced for me when my spirits lagged. He taught me French—the little I know. In brief, he put me on my feet again." At the end of March, 1932, Perlès and Miller moved into a two-bedroom flat in Clichy, at 4 Avenue Anatole France, which they shared, with some interruptions, until 1934. Miller's job as assistant finance editor on the Paris edition of the Chicago *Tribune* only lasted a few months but Perlès stayed until the paper closed down in 1934. During Perlès' employment at the *Tribune,* Miller wrote a few pieces under Perlès' by-line ("Paris in ut Mineur," March 3, 1931; "Rue Lourmel in Fog," April, 1932). In 1937, Perlès became editor of *The Booster,* which, after three issues, was renamed *Delta* and closed down, also after three issues, in 1939. Miller and Lawrence Durrell (who stayed in Paris from September, 1937, to April, 1938) worked with him on the magazine. Perlès recalls these years in his book, *My Friend Henry Miller* (London, Spearman, 1955; New York, John Day, 1956), which is not always a reliable biographical source, however. While in Paris, Perlès wrote fiction in French (*Sentiments Limitrophes,* later *Le Quatuor en Ré Majeur*). In 1943, Allen & Unwin in London published his book, *The Renegade,* with an introduction by Henry Miller, and, in 1944, *Alien Corn.* After World War II, Perlès visited Miller in California and wrote *Reunion in Big Sur* (Northwood, Middlesex, England, Scorpion Press, 1959). His correspondence with Lawrence Durrell regarding Miller's work and censorship was published under the title *Art and Outrage* (London, Putnam, 1959; New York, E. P. Dutton, 1961).

PUTNAM, SAMUEL—American writer, editor, translator, born 1892, who went to Paris in the late 1920's at the suggestion of the publisher Pascal Covici. He became an associate editor of Edward Titus' magazine, *This Quarter.* After a disagreement with Titus in the fall of 1930, Putnam started his own magazine, the *New Review,* a quarterly with a list of 73 subscribers which ceased publication with Volume 2, No. 5, in April 1932. Hilaire Hiler, the painter, was one of his contributing editors. The second issue (May–June–July, 1931) contained Miller's essay about the film "L'Âge d'Or," ("Bunuel or Thus Cometh to an End Everywhere the Golden Age") which was his first publication in a magazine in Paris. The third issue (August–September–October, 1931) carried Miller's story "Mademoiselle Claude," which since has been reprinted many times. Late in 1931, when Putnam made a brief trip to New York, he turned the editorship of Issue 4 over to Alfred Perlès and Henry Miller who wrote a spoofy "manifesto" about something called the "New Instinctivism," which was killed at the last minute by a cable from Putnam before the issue came out and, apparently, has been lost. In 1929, Putnam's *François Rabelais, Man of the Renaissance, a Spiritual Biography* appeared (New York, J. Cape & H. Smith). Among the many authors translated into English by Putnam is Joseph Delteil, a friend of Miller's. Putnam published his memoirs in 1948 (*Paris Was Our Mistress,* New York, The Viking Press) and died in 1950.

RANK, DR. OTTO—Austrian psychoanalyst, born 1884 (real name Otto Rosenfeld), who became a pupil of Sigmund Freud in 1905 and worked closely with him for twenty years. Chairman of the Psychoanalytical Society in Vienna. He came to Paris in 1926, after breaking with Freud, and established the Psychological Center, which he directed until 1934, when he left for the United States. Among his books are *The Trauma of Birth* (1924), *Technik der Psychoanalise* (1926) and *Art and Artist* (New York, Knopf). Anaïs Nin studied with him in Paris. He died in 1939.

RATTNER, ABRAHAM—American artist, who met Miller during his early days in Paris and designed the frontispiece for *Scenario,* Miller's adaptation of Anaïs Nin's *House of Incest,* which was first published in a limited edition of 200 copies (Paris, Obelisk Press, 1937). He accompanied Miller on the first part of his trip through the United States in the winter of 1940 (recorded in the *Air-Conditioned Nightmare,* for which Rattner designed the cover, although the publisher who commissioned the book had ruled out the inclusion of art as originally planned). Miller wrote about "The Rattner Portfolio" in the *College Art Journal* (New York, Spring 1957). See also Miller's long essay on Rattner, "A Bodhisattva Artist," in *Remember to Remember.*

REICHEL, HANS—German painter, who belonged to the inner circle of the Villa Seurat from 1934 to 1939. Miller first wrote about him in *The Booster* ("A Boost for Hans Reichel," Paris, September 1937) and subsequently in his essay "The Cosmological Eye" (*Transition,* Neuilly, France, April–May 1938), which gave the title to Miller's first book published in the United States (Norfolk, Conn., James Laughlin, 1939). Also included in *Wisdom of the Heart* (1941). "There never will be anybody like him," Miller said after Reichel's death in 1958. "He was not made for this world."

ROSENFELD, PAUL—American critic, born in Germany, in 1890, who became an early admirer both of Henry Miller's and Anaïs Nin's work. Rosenfeld published a number of books of essays on music, literature, painting, sculpture and dance. *Men Seen* (containing an essay on Wassermann), New York, Dial, 1925; *By Way of Art* (a collection of criticism), New York, Coward-McCann, 1928; *An Hour with American Music* (with sections on Dane Rudhyar and Edgar Varèse), Philadelphia, Lippincott, 1929; and *Discoveries of a Music Critic,* New York, Harcourt, Brace, 1936. After his death in 1946, Jerome Mellquist and Lucie Wiese edited a volume of selections from his writings under the title *Voyager in the Arts* (New York, Creative Age Press, 1948).

SCHNELLOCK, EMIL—American artist, teacher, one of Miller's oldest friends, who went with him to P.S. 85 in Brooklyn and with whom he had carried on a steady correspondence. Some of Miller's letters to Schnellock were published by Bern Porter under the title *Semblance of a Devoted Past* (Berkeley, California, 1944), and others in various little magazines. For many years, Schnellock directed the art program of Mary Washington College of the University of Virginia, in Fredericksburg, Va. He died in 1960.

SLOCUM, JOHN—American literary agent (Russell & Volkening, New York), who represented Miller during the early 1940's after his return to the United States.

STELOFF, FRANCES—Owner and operator of the Gotham Book Mart in New York City, which for more than a half century has been a haven for writers, artists and "little magazines" and the meeting ground of the James Joyce Society.

TITUS, EDWARD W.—Publisher, bookseller and editor, husband of Helena Rubinstein, who operated a bookstore on the rue Delambre in Paris and the Black Manikin Press, during the 1920's and 1930's. After the death of Ernest Walsh, he took over the magazine *This Quarter*. He published Djuna Barnes' first book as well as D. H. Lawrence's *Lady Chatterley's Lover*, which French authorities tried to suppress until Louis Aragon interceded. Publisher of Anaïs Nin's first book, *D. H. Lawrence, An Unprofessional Study* (1932).

VARDA, JEAN (JANKO)—American painter of Greek origin, who became a close friend of Miller's when he went to California. Miller stayed with Varda and his wife Virginia in their red barn in New Monterey, in the spring of 1944, and it was Varda who introduced Miller to Big Sur, where Miller eventually made his home. Miller's essay, "Varda, The Master Builder," appeared in *Circle* (Berkeley, Calif.) in December, 1944, and was later included in *Remember to Remember*. Varda also became a friend of Anaïs Nin's and several of his collages were used for her book jackets (an idea Miller had originally suggested to Anaïs Nin). Varda later moved to Sausalito, Calif., where he lives on a houseboat.

WEST, HERBERT FAULKNER—American critic and teacher of literature, born in 1898, who became a friend of Miller's and admirer of his work. In his book, *The Mind on the Wing* (New York, Coward-McCann, 1947), West devoted a chapter to "The Strange Case of Henry Miller." In 1945, Miller visited West at Dartmouth College, where he was a professor of literature, and made a trip with him through New Hampshire and Vermont. "Herb West," wrote Miller in his Preface to *Remember to Remember*, "also the son of a tailor, I discovered, was like a brother to me. Of all the professors I have met, in America or elsewhere, he is beyond a doubt the most human."

YOUNG, LAFAYETTE—Young American intellectual from Des Moines, Iowa, friend of John and Flo Dudley, who met Miller in 1940 and later tried to publish some of Miller's work in Mexico. He now operates a book store in San Diego.

Index of Names